The central question for both the victors and the vanquished of World War II was just how widely the stain of guilt would spread over Germany. Political leaders and intellectuals on *both* sides of the conflict debated whether support for National Socialism tainted Germany's entire population and thus discredited the nation's history and culture. The tremendous challenge that Allied officials and German thinkers faced as the war closed, then, was how to limn a postwar German identity that accounted for National Socialism without irrevocably damning the idea and character of Germany as a whole.

In the House of the Hangman chronicles this delicate process, exploring key debates about the Nazi past and German future during the latter years of World War II and in its aftermath. What did British and American leaders think had given rise to National Socialism, and how did these beliefs shape their intentions for occupation? What rhetorical and symbolic tools did Germans develop for handling the insidious legacies of Nazism? Considering these and other questions, Jeffrey K. Olick explores the processes of accommodation and rejection that Allied plans for a new German state inspired among the German intelligentsia. He also examines heated struggles over the value of Germany's institutional and political heritage. Along the way, he demonstrates how the moral and political vocabulary for coming to terms with National Socialism in Germany has been of enduring significance—as a crucible not only of German identity but also of contemporary thinking about memory and social justice more generally.

Given the current war in Iraq, the issues contested during Germany's abjection and reinvention—how to treat a defeated enemy, how to place episodes within wider historical trajectories, how to distinguish claims of victimhood—are as urgent today as they were sixty years ago, and *In the House of the Hangman* offers readers an invaluable historical perspective on these critical questions.

IN THE HOUSE OF THE HANGMAN

In the House

of the Hangman

The Agonies of German Defeat, 1943–1949

JEFFREY K. OLICK

THE UNIVERSITY OF CHICAGO PRESS   Chicago and London

Jeffrey K. Olick is associate professor of sociology at the University of Virginia.

The University of Chicago Press, Chicago 60637
The University of Chicago Press, Ltd., London
© 2005 by The University of Chicago
All rights reserved. Published 2005
Printed in the United States of America

14 13 12 11 10 09 08 07 06 05   1 2 3 4 5

ISBN: 0-226-62638-5 (cloth)

Library of Congress Cataloging-in-Publication Data

Olick, Jeffrey K., 1964–
    In the house of the hangman : the agonies of German defeat,
1943–1949 / Jeffrey K. Olick.
        p. cm.
    Includes bibliographical references and index.
    ISBN 0-226-62638-5 (cloth)
    1. Public history—Germany—Psychological aspects.
2. Nationalism—Germany—Psychological aspects. 3. Germany—
History—1939–1945—Historiography. 4. Germany—History—
1945–1955—Historiography. 5. Memory—Social aspects. I. Title.
DD256.48.O55 2005
943.087′4′019—dc22

                                2004027421

In the house of the hanged one should not mention the rope.
MIGUEL DE CERVANTES

*In the house of the hangman one should not speak of the noose,
otherwise one might seem to harbor resentment.*
THEODOR ADORNO

Contents

Photographs follow page 160

Preface

This book was first drafted in the year or so after September 11, 2001. In the period before then, a new U.S. administration had used the term "nation-building" as an emblem for misguided foreign policy, a synonym for long entanglements without clearly defined interests. Whatever else it did, September 11 changed at least this aspect of American foreign policy. With the destruction of the Taliban regime in Afghanistan and the toppling of Saddam Hussein in Iraq, American and other leaders have been facing the problem of nation-building in a way they have not since the end of World War II. Indeed, in many discussions, memory of postwar Germany has figured prominently. Much more than programs in Central America in the 1970s and 1980s and in South East Asia in the decade before then—which were more matters of regime-than nation-building—the German case has appeared to many commentators to provide the most apt comparison for contemporary challenges. Given the twin goals of preventing both a resurgence of German militarism and Soviet domination of Europe, the German story seems like an unqualified nation-building success, and thus a model for policy.

As we face contemporary challenges of nation-building and related tasks, however, we should remember that the supposed triumph of American policy after World War II was inevitably a more complex affair than memory has it. At the time and for many years afterward, many Germans—from across the political spectrum—reacted to U.S. policies with bitterness. There was also a strong sentiment in some corners that the German success was despite, not because of, Allied occupation policies, particularly efforts aimed at "re-educating" Germans for democracy, which were perceived as high-handed. There were others, particularly in the 1960s, who argued that the reconstruction of Germany after the war was more restorative than transformative, allowing the problems that had caused fascism to persist, and was thus no success story at all. Moreover, some have charged, the fact that the West's strategy for Germany helped win the Cold War should not distract from the ways in which that strategy contributed to bringing it about in the first place.

The story I tell in the following pages focuses mainly on debates about the Nazi past and the German future during and in the immediate aftermath of World War II. It is a fascinating story in and of itself, from the perspective of German history, and in particular as a case study of political culture and collective memory. I raise contemporary issues here, however, to point out the obvious relevance today of looking back at the complex story of the German transition to democracy. Evaluating the degree to which the triumphs and failures of the German case provide lessons for present and future nation-building endeavors requires close attention to the historical details. In the end, it may be that contemporary commentators have made too much of the analogy: Iraq is not Germany, and this is not 1945. But it is surely an interesting time to be looking back, and Germany is necessarily the first place to look, as much public commentary in the early days of the Iraq War showed.

This book is something of an accident. As a sociologist of collective memory, I first became interested in Germany because of the so-called historians' dispute (*Historikerstreit*) in the mid-1980s. Forty years after the end of the war, leading German intellectuals publicly debated how to remember the National Socialist past. On one side, conservatives argued that endless memory of National Socialism and of the Holocaust as a unique horror was historically and politically inappropriate; on the other side, liberals argued that these complaints about the persistence of memory from newly dominant conservatives were part of an attempt to rework the foundations of West German political culture by removing the obstacle to national pride: the centrality of German crimes. I wanted to examine whether critics on the Left were correct that there had been a profound change in the foundations of German political culture in the early 1980s. But in order to do so, I quickly realized, I could not focus just on the 1980s. To determine what had changed, I would have to compare what came before in at least as much detail. Unfortunately, I found that the literature on the history of German memory was not very strong empirically (this was the late 1980s). I therefore sought to look rigorously and systematically at the empirical record of memory throughout the history of the Federal Republic. I focused in particular on "official memory" of the West German state: what did the state's leaders say about the Nazi past in their official capacities? Which terms did they use for what reasons, and how did their representations change over time? My particular concern was for the role of memory in the state, and vice versa. This work will be published as another book, *The Sins of the Fathers: Governing Memory in the Federal Republic of Germany, 1949–1995*.

As my work on the history of memory in the Federal Republic progressed, however, I began to feel that I had become overly dependent on the methodological convenience of starting at the founding of the state in 1949, even if this was born of my substantive interest in the role of memory in the state. Certainly, like many other scholars working on the history of the Federal Republic of Germany, I intended to include a brief prologue on the period before 1949. But the more I explored the period before the state, the more important this period appeared to me, both in its own right and for understanding official memory in the Federal Republic after 1949. Contrary to much of the literature on German memory, I came to believe that the immediate postwar period, before the founding of the West German state, was no mere interregnum, no liminal period that, because of the unusual circumstances, had little in common with what came later. In order to understand how the German state came to terms with the past, I became convinced, one has to understand where those terms came from, and that means paying greater attention to the postwar period. My reading of the history of official memory in the Federal Republic has thus led me steadily backward, and the following hundreds of pages develop what I started out to handle in a dozen or two!

As I explored these questions of German history and memory, however, I sought to keep in mind issues of transitional justice and collective responsibility more generally, which are as pressing today as they were in 1945. Postwar Germany is a (dare I say *the*?) most interesting case for doing this, in part because it serves as an exemplar (positive or negative), and in part because some of the views articulated and terms originated in that context—in many cases by some of the last century's leading intellectual and political figures—have continued to resonate in contemporary contexts far beyond central Europe at midcentury. The confrontation with German guilt has raised issues that, in many ways, have defined an age.

*   *   *

The following people have contributed substantively to this work, provided advice directly related to it or on other important matters as I was writing, and/or supported me by loyally enduring what people endure when they have friends who write books: Karen Barkey, Peter Bearman, Aaron Beim, Courtney Bender, Fred Block, Lili Cole, Brenda Coughlin, Chares Demetriou, Kai Erikson, Simonetta Falasca-Zamponi, Priscilla Ferguson, Gary Fine, Judy Gerson, Eileen Gilooly, Carol Gluck, Mark Jacobs, Jens Lachmund, Danny Levy, Robert Moeller, Kelly Moore, Dirk Moses, Jan-Werner Müller, Jon Rieder, Joyce Robbins, Barry Schwartz, Allan Silver, Noa Steimatsky and Paolo Barlera, Adam Summers, John Torpey, Vered Vinitzky-Seroussi, Robin Wagner-Pacifici, and Diane Wolf.

Like so many others, I have benefited incalculably over many years from the advice of Doug Mitchell at the University of Chicago Press, though putting it this way should not be taken to imply there is anything standard about this—anything but. I thank Tim McGovern as well for his attentive stewardship of the manuscript. And I am grateful to David Bemelmans for his expert but gentle copyediting (readers should be grateful to him too!).

I would also like to take this opportunity to thank my colleagues in the Department of Sociology at the University of Virginia for their confidence in me and in this project.

As little adequate as a few lines such as these are to the task of thanking friends and colleagues, they are even less so when it comes to family. My parents and siblings have certainly lived through the ups and downs of this endeavor, as they have all the others, with courage and indulgence. My in-laws, *Familie* Winckler, not only provided me with a second home, but have been more open with me about difficult matters than anyone could reasonably expect, and have in the process contributed much to my thinking about the book's topic; I am particularly grateful to my father-in-law, Dr. Heino Winckler, for extensive conversations over many years. What I have to say to my wife, Bettina Winckler, does not belong in print, though her name does, given her substantive contributions to this book as to everything else in my life, professional and personal. This book is for our children, Hannah and Benjamin, who are too young to understand what I was doing all this time but sustained me nonetheless, perhaps even more.

Abbreviations

AMG	American Military Government
CDU	*Christlich-Demokratische Union* (Christian Democratic Union)
DP	Displaced Person
EAC	European Advisory Commission
ECEFP	Executive Committee on Economic Foreign Policy
EKD	*Evangelische Kirche in Deutschland* (Evangelical Church of Germany)
FDP	*Freie Demokratische Partei* (Free Democratic/Liberal Party)
HICOG	High Commission for Germany
HUAC	House Un-American Activities Committee
IMT	International Military Tribunal (Nuremberg)
JCS	Joint Chiefs of Staff
KZ	*Konzentrationslager* (Concentration Camp)
NSDAP	*Nationalsozialistische Deutsche Arbeiterpartei* (National Socialist German Workers Party)
OMGUS	Office of Military Government in Germany–United States
SCAEF	Supreme Commander, Allied Expeditionary Forces
SED	*Sozialistische Einheitspartei Deutschlands* (Socialist Union Party)
SHAEF	Supreme Headquarters, Allied Expeditionary Forces
SPD	*Sozialdemokratische Partei Deutschlands* (Social Democratic Party)
UNWCC	United Nations War Crimes Commission
WPA	Work Projects Administration

CHAPTER I

Introduction

Despite the fervent wish of many Germans for a "normal" national identity, one whose credit is not forever mortgaged to the memory of Auschwitz, a history of the Federal Republic of Germany could plausibly be written as a series of struggles over the meaning of the National Socialist past. For instance:

- at the Republic's very moment of birth in 1949, national leaders were preoccupied with a violent clash in Munich between Jewish protesters and police in reaction to the publication of an anti-Semitic letter in Munich's leading newspaper, an event that challenged the claim that such attitudes were no longer potent or that they were entirely suppressed;[1]
- in the 1950s, public discussion of reparations to Israel was followed by debate about Hans Globke, a former Nazi government official and legal commentator on the 1935 Nuremberg Racial Laws, whom Chancellor Konrad Adenauer had nevertheless appointed as his chief of staff;[2]
- in 1959–60, a wave of anti-Semitic vandalism created an international public relations morass for the West German government;[3]
- in 1961, the nation's and world's attention was captivated by the Jerusalem trial of Adolf Eichmann; later in the 1960s, *The Diary of Anne*

1. For a detailed account of the events, see Bergmann, *Antisemitismus in öffentlichen Konflikten,* 71–86.
2. For an analysis of the Globke affair, see especially Herz and Boumann, "Der 'Fall Globke,'" in Herz and Schwabb-Trapp, *Umkämpfte Vergangenheit,* 57–107.
3. See Bergmann, *Antisemitismus in öffentlichen Konflikten,* 235–77; Stahl, *The Politics of Postwar Germany,* 305–38.

Frank, the Frankfurt Auschwitz Trials, and a stage play charging the Catholic Church with complicity in the Nazi regime brought the past before the German public with renewed vigor;[4]

- in the 1970s, Chancellor Willy Brandt's famous kneeling at the Warsaw Ghetto Memorial represented a supposedly new posture toward memory, though it was followed by Chancellor Helmut Schmidt's vituperative exchanges with Israeli prime minister Menachim Begin, who sought to discredit Schmidt personally for his service in the *Wehrmacht* after Schmidt arranged the sale of West German tanks to Saudi Arabia;[5]
- in the 1980s, public outcry over U.S. president Ronald Reagan's visit to a military cemetery in Bitburg, and a so-called "historians' dispute" of 1985–86, demonstrated once again that the German past would not pass away, as one conservative lament put it;[6]
- and in the 1990s, the questions of a German contribution to the Gulf War coalition and of how to respond to anti-immigrant violence reanimated discussions about the concrete imperatives of German memory.[7]

This list, moreover, barely scratches the surface. Even so, it lends *prima facie* plausibility to the idea that German national identity since World War II has necessarily been tied to how it has processed the legacies of

---

4. The literature on the Eichmann trial is enormous. Most famous is Hannah Arendt's *Eichmann in Jerusalem: A Report on the Banality of Evil*. For immediate analysis and public opinion data, see Schmidt and Becker, *Reaktionen auf politische Vorgänge*, 107–41. The stage portrayal of the Frankfurt Auschwitz Trials, based entirely on trial transcripts, was *The Investigation [Die Ermittlung]* by Peter Weiss. Accusation of the Catholic Church's complicity was the main theme of *The Deputy [Der Stellvertreter]* by Rolf Hochhuth. Less controversial but equally (or even more) powerful in its impact was the publication, and subsequent stage adaptation, of *The Diary of Anne Frank*.

5. For an analysis of Brandt's gesture, see Krzeminski, "Der Kniefall," in Francois and Schulze, *Deutsche Erinnerungsorte*, vol. 1, 638–53, as well as Brandt's memoir, *My Life in Politics*, 196–209. For an account of Schmidt's conflict with Begin, see Deutschkron, *Israel und die Deutschen*, 404–24.

6. On the Bitburg affair, see Hartmann, *Bitburg in Moral and Political Perspective*; Levkov, *Bitburg and Beyond*. The literature of, and on, the historians' dispute is enormous. Original documents can be found in *Forever in the Shadow of Hitler*; other interesting materials are in Baldwin, *Reworking the Past*; excellent intellectual-historical accounts in English include Evans, *In Hitler's Shadow*; Maier, *The Unmasterable Past*.

7. On the politics of German memory since 1989, see Olick, "What Does It Mean to Normalize the Past?"

National Socialism—in other words, to Germany's collective memory of its difficult past.[8]

There are, obviously, important differences in the contexts and meanings of these various events and their representations of the past. Collective memory, we know from an extensive scholarly literature, is not fixed once and for all, but changes as the cultural and political profile of the present changes; within limits, we continuously make and remake our images of the past in the present from contemporary perspectives and for contemporary purposes.[9] So we should expect the dominant images of National Socialism to differ at different times and places, to change over time. These transformations, however, do not take place discontinuously, one image of the past replacing the previous one willy-nilly. Rather, images of the past form a dialogue over time. Later versions of the past, either implicitly or explicitly, are always responses to earlier ones.[10] The above list is thus no mere chronology.

In the German case, this means that struggles over the meaning of National Socialism were not just about the Nazi past itself, but about the adequacy of earlier collective memory. In the 1960s, for instance, a central feature of New Left rhetoric was the charge that collective memory of the Nazi period in the 1950s was deficient, repressing difficult legacies and thereby allowing unacceptable residues of fascism to persist in West Germany: a supposed "silence" about the Nazi past in the 1950s, critics

---

8. See Rabinbach, "The Jewish Question in the German Question." Rabinbach argues that every expansion in West German sovereignty was linked to the question of responsibility for the German past. Solidification of Western integration followed reparations to Israel, the Grand Coalition of 1966–69 and the beginnings of the new policy toward the East (*Ostpolitik*) followed the wave of public anti-Semitism in 1959–60, and the expanded sense of claim to national identity in the mid-1980s followed the attempted "normalization" of the past embodied in the Bitburg ceremony of 1985. It is possible to draw other specific connections or to highlight other moments, but the claim that images of the past are associated with the status of German sovereignty is strong no matter how that connection is illustrated. See also Olick, "What Does It Mean to Normalize the Past?"; "Hättich, "Geschichtsbild und Demokratieverständnis."

9. For reviews of this literature, see Olick, "Social Memory Studies"; Klein, "On the Emergence of Memory in Historical Discourse"; Wertsch, *Voices of Collective Remembering*; Zelizer, "Reading the Past against the Grain"; Brockmeier, "Remembering and Forgetting"; Prager, "The Psychology of Collective Memory"; Schwartz, *Abraham Lincoln and the Forge of American Memory*; Zerubavel, *Recovered Roots*; Connerton, *How Societies Remember*; Irwin-Zarecka, *Frames of Remembrance*; Kansteiner, "Finding Meaning in Memory."

10. On the dialogical qualities of commemoration, see Olick, "Genre Memories and Memory Genres"; Wertsch, *Voices of Collective Remembering*.

argued, constituted a "second guilt."[11] In the 1980s, a neoconservative reaction in turn charged the New Left of the previous decades with failing to recognize that "too much" memory in the 1950s would have caused the new democracy to fail.[12] The historical obsessions in the 1960s, in this view, were a form of national "self-flagellation" that denied the Hobson's choice West Germany's early leaders supposedly faced—and answered correctly—between "justice" and "legitimacy."

Clearly, memory of the Nazi past has always involved not just memory of the Nazi period filtered through the political and cultural demands of the present, but memory of earlier memory: in the 1960s, one looked back to the supposedly inadequate memory propagated in the previous decade; in the 1970s and 1980s, one sought to overcome the indictment of basic institutions this earlier critique implied. By the 1990s, many were proposing that the earlier debates—no matter where one stood in them—were no longer relevant, that there had been not too much attention to the past, but too much attention to debate about the past. Indeed, since the late 1990s, prominent intellectuals on both the Right and the Left have asserted a "new normalcy," in which older orthodoxies are seen as no longer operative.[13] Nevertheless, even the claim to be free of older orthodoxies is itself a reaction to them.

* * *

Such arguments about the proper way to remember the Nazi past—perhaps understandably—have proceeded largely through anecdote and polemic: emotions run high because much—including identity, legitimacy, and power—is at stake.[14] In recent years, however, a new wave of mostly younger scholars has sought to avoid the more egregious exaggerations

11. "Second Guilt" is a Talmudic principle that failure to atone for a crime is the same as perpetrating another crime. *The Second Guilt [Die zweite Schuld]* was the title of a widely read polemic by the German-Jewish journalist Ralf Giordano, first published in 1987. The most famous statement about the persistence of fascism within democractic society is Adorno, "Was bedeutet: Aufarbeitung der Vergangenheit."

12. The key reference here is to Herman Lübbe's controversial article, "Der Nationalsozialismus im deutschen Nachkriegsbewusstsein." See also Herf, *Divided Memory.* For a response, see Schwann, *Politics and Guilt.*

13. For an intellectual history of the "normalcy" theme in German discourse since the 1980s, see especially Müller, *Another Country.* See also Bleek and Maull, *Ein ganz normaler Staat?*

14. Just one example of such polemic from the Left is Haug, *Vom hilflosen Antifaschismus zur Gnade der späten Geburt* [From Helpless Antifascism to the Grace of Late Birth]. From the Right, see Mohler, *Der Nasenring* [The Nosering].

and distortions of this politicized "dialogue" by grounding the evaluative "memory of memory" in a more rigorously empirical "history of memory."[15] Was there, for instance, really a pervasive silence about the past in the 1950s? Before venturing this kind of claim, these scholars argue, one must examine in fine detail exactly who said what, where, when, and why.

It turns out that, technically speaking, there was in fact no "silence" about the Nazi past in the 1950s, during which time West Germany's political leaders were significantly preoccupied with the residues of National Socialism and, in particular, with the purgative measures imposed by the occupation authorities in the immediate aftermath of the war. The discourse—as well as policymaking—regarding National Socialism was enormous in these years. Of course, just as silence can speak volumes, speaking volumes can be a silence of sorts, so the matter is complex indeed. But the new historiography, in some contrast to a long line of polemic, has sought to ground such interpretative complexities in unimpeachable, systematic empirical research. And it is surprising how much of this history had never been examined in detail or woven into coherent narratives. In the last ten years or so, our knowledge particularly of the 1950s has grown enormously, leading to more subtle interpretations and to the refinement of older clichés.[16]

The present book shares many concerns with the new historians of German memory, though it focuses on a period that has not yet received quite as much attention from them as the 1950s have: the years, that is, before the founding of the Federal Republic of Germany in 1949. It is not exactly that there is no historiography of the occupation years, for there is

---

15. This new literature has grown enormously in recent years. The most general accounts (there have been many more narrowly focused studies) include Bergmann, *Antisemitismus in öffentlichen Konflikten*; Brochhagen, *Nach Nürnberg*; Dubiel, *Niemand ist frei von der Geschichte*; Frei, *Adenauer's Germany and the Nazi Past*; Fulbrook, *German National Identity after the Holocaust*; Herf, *Divided Memory*; Koshar, *Germany's Transient Past*; Marcuse, *Legacies of Dachau*; Moeller, *War Stories*; Reichel, *Vergangenheitsbewältigung in Deutschland*; Steinle, *Nationales Selbstverständnis nach dem Nationalsozialismus*; Stern, *The Whitewashing of the Yellow Badge*; Wiesen, *West German Industry and the Challenge of the Nazi Past*; Wolfrum, *Geschichtspolitik in der Bundesrepublik Deutschland*; Wolgast, *Die Wahrnehmung des Dritten Reiches in der unmittelbaren Nachkriegszeit*. A more polemical contribution to this literature from the Right is Kittel, *Die Legende von der "Zweiten Schuld."*

16. While the ages of the authors producing this literature vary widely, the discourse as a whole has the flavor of being very much post-1968, beyond, that is, the polemical cast of the New Left's critique of the early Federal Republic, and beyond even the neoconservative reaction to that discourse in the 1970s and early 1980s. This is the sense in which I refer to younger scholars and a new scholarship.

indeed an extensive literature.[17] Nevertheless, much of this work is concerned mainly with locating the origins of the Cold War and narrating the emergence of the West German state.[18] From these perspectives, the "Nuremberg Interregnum"—as one common trope describes the first two postwar years—is often seen as either an episode outside of history or a mere prelude to what came later.

Inspired by, but going beyond, the new historiography of memory, my approach to the postwar years is motivated by an interest in the origins and trajectories of memory of the Nazi period (which, as we will see, includes memory of the occupation period as well). However, this entails not only a *history* of German memory in these formative years, but a dynamic *sociology* of memory, an analysis of the ways in which earlier memories shaped the trajectories of, and formed objects for, later ones. Because images of the past, as my sociology of German memory will show, are always parts of ongoing dialogues, the occupation period is no mere episode from the perspective of the sociology of memory. By the same token, because the occupation years were a moment not only in the history of German memory, but have been a central a subject in, and filter for, the memory of German memory, the occupation period was also no mere prelude.

Starting Points

There are no absolute beginnings and endings in social life. But I begin from the premise that earlier moments of memory are profoundly important for subsequent trajectories because collective memory—like many other social processes—is "path-dependent."[19] Order, and particularly starting points, matter a great deal (though they are not the only factors that matter) for subsequent trajectories. In the pages that follow I demon-

---

17. For an especially insightful account, including extensive bibliographical references, see Robert G. Moeller, "Introduction: Writing the History of West Germany," in Moeller, *West Germany under Construction*.

18. Significant emergentist works include Benz, *Von der Besatzungsherrschaft zur Bundesrepublik*; Eschenburg, *Jahre der Besatzung*; Gaddis, *The United States and the Origins of the Cold War*; Gimbel, *The American Occupation of Germany*; Herz, *From Dictatorship to Democracy*; Kleßmann, *Die doppelte Staatsgründung*; Milward, *The Reconstruction of Western Europe*; Zink, *The United States in Germany*.

19. On the path dependence of collective memory, see Olick, "Genre Memories and Memory Genres"; Schudson, "The Past in the Present and the Present in the Past." For a review of the sociological literature on path dependence, see Mahoney, "Path Dependence in Historical Sociology."

strate that the occupation period—in which so many questions were open—was a constitutive moment both for the *history of German memory*—shaping how the Nazi period has been remembered since then—and, at least in regard to the supposedly punitive policies of the occupiers, for the *memory of German memory*—providing a contrast model for later German commentators of how not to remember the Nazi past. In the process, memory of the occupation years, I show, served as a powerful filter for memory of National Socialism itself.

* * *

From one perspective, of course, it makes sense for scholars interested in the history of memory in West Germany to start at the beginning of the state rather than focusing on the occupation period. There is indeed something special about speaking for a people in the way an official of the state does that is different from even the same person speaking before the state came into existence or before he or she represented it. Speaking *for* the state is different from speaking *before* the state or for oneself or one's partial constituency once the state exists. Since there was no official organ of German identity comparable to the Federal State between 1945 and 1949, there was no official memory, and thus no history of official memory to tell.

However, when historians of German memory begin their accounts in 1949, as many do, or include the period before the state in such accounts for mere contrast, they risk reproducing the basic periodizing mythologies established by the Federal Republic's first leaders. In one such mythology, 1949 represented a clean slate, or "zero hour" as the common trope had it, even if that zero hour required complex legislation and rhetorical work to establish.[20] Some public rhetoric, of course, and some historical accounts as well, have proposed different periodizations for other purposes. These include 1943 (beginning with the defeat at Stalingrad) to 1948 (the currency reform) on the existential foundation of German suffering, as well as 1945 (unconditional surrender) to 1955 (the end of the occupation) on the political foundation of German sovereignty.[21] Others see the "interruption" of German history beginning in 1933 and not ending until 1989.

20. The "zero hour" trope is as imprecise as it was widespread. The year 1945 was a zero hour in terms of the absolute destruction and unconditional surrender. But so was 1949 a zero-hour starting point.

21. For a discussion of periodization in German history, see the essays in Broszat, *Zäsuren nach 1945*.

Periodization, obviously, is a rather tricky business, and scholars must remain keenly aware of how they construct temporal boundaries and treat the continuities and discontinuities across them. Perhaps the best way to do this is to be aware of how political and other actors construct those boundaries and represent those continuities and discontinuities, and to remember that there are crucial differences between the reasons *analysts* have for highlighting particular boundaries and the reasons *political actors* involved in the relevant events have for doing so. For the memory of the Nazi period, for instance, West Germany's early leaders—despite their great trepidation about founding a partial state[22]—largely asserted 1949 as the relevant break. One purpose for doing so was to discredit the occupation years as an extension of wartime suffering. By the same token, some argued for a distinction between a formative epoch from 1945 to 1955 and a more "normal" life of the state thereafter. This allowed treating the open questions of Germany's formative period—the so-called "postwar"—as settled.

Even if only for methodological convenience, however, many historians of German memory have indeed shared these conventional marks with political actors, treating the history of official memory in West Germany as fairly distinct from the history of collective memory in the prestate years (let us call this the "episodic" theory), or seeing 1945–55 as a distinct period that laid the foundation for what came later (let us call this the "emergentist" approach). But sharing the assertions of the Federal Republic's early leaders—whether out of convenience or principle—often means overplaying the differences between a revolutionary period and a "normal" one or underplaying the extent to which the rhetorical and evaluative frameworks of West German memory formed during and in the immediate aftermath of the war, and in turn became contested objects for subsequent memory. Treating the occupation period as discontinuous, as a mnemonic landscape unto itself, thus risks missing powerful interpretive frames that unified perceptions both before and after 1949. By the same token, identifying 1945–55 as a period of emergence—often aimed at explaining the origins of the West German state or of the Cold War—distracts attention from the origins and continuities of memory.

---

22. The "temporary" status of West Germany was established in its founding document, which was for this reason called a "basic law" rather than a constitution, and which provided for its own dissolution by final peace treaty. The Federal Republic's first president, Theodor Heuss, who was also the president of the constitutional convention in 1948–49, famously referred to the new state as a "transitorium," playing on the more widespread term "provisorium."

My sociology of German memory thus seeks to avoid treating the occupation period as either an episode or a mere prelude: again, the occupation period was neither a mnemonic landscape apart nor a mere crucible of the Cold War and the West German state. Instead, I approach this fascinating period as a prologue in the literal sense of the preparation for a dialogue, whether the subsequent dialogue went in different directions or not. A motivating principle for the account that follows is thus my interest in avoiding the sterile opposition between episodic and emergentist accounts in order to grasp the constantly revised memory of memory as the fluid dialogical process that it was, in which continuities and discontinuities were themselves the objects of discursive struggle. Approaching this history in this manner, moreover, demonstrates that the occupation period was both a formative moment for how Germans and others remember National Socialism as well as a contested moment for the memory of memory itself.

*   *   *

A particularly important example of how a problematic assertion of discontinuity (the episodic approach) has sometimes tempted scholars into polemic is in discussions of the past-oriented policies of the early West German government. For instance, as already mentioned, the Left has long criticized Chancellor Konrad Adenauer's approach, which included an end to denazification, broad amnesties for those already punished and for those not yet convicted, demands for early release of condemned war criminals, and reintegration of discredited civil servants, among other measures.[23] Critics have often characterized these efforts as a repression of the past, an attempt to purchase short-term stability by allowing tainted elements to persist. Adenauer was well aware that "too much memory" would jeopardize his position by undermining support from discredited segments of the population and their sympathizers who did not want to be blamed; his choices, from this perspective, were thus especially cynical.[24] In contrast, many on the Right have defended Adenauer's policies by arguing that they resulted from his clear recognition of the trade-offs between "justice" and "legitimacy." Anything else, they say, would have been

23. Scholarship on these issues includes Frei's *Adenauer's Germany and the Nazi Past;* Hughes, *Shouldering the Burdens of Defeat;* Diehl, *The Thanks of the Fatherland;* Lockenour, *Soldiers as Citizens.*

24. According to Adenauer's long-time advisor and justice minister in the 1950s Herbert Blankenhorn, "If Mr. Adenauer had said in 1949 what we had done in the past, then the German people would have been against him." Quoted in Herf, *Divided Memory,* 226.

irresponsible of him, risking long-term instability; Adenauer did what had to be done to secure legitimacy for what has turned out to be a solid democracy. The proof is in the pudding.

While the Left thus disparages Adenauer's choice for legitimacy over justice and the Right praises it, however, they both seem to share the view that the choice inhered in the novel initial condition of the Federal Republic as a state. As a result, both underplay the degree to which early government policies were matters of conviction and perception as much as of strategy. In contrast, the analysis of the years before 1949 I present here implies a different view, namely that Adenauer and his cohort—with widespread support across the political spectrum—attempted to draw a line under the past because that is how they understood their responsibility to memory, not, or at least not only, because they felt compelled to do so by the threat of political failure. Adenauer and his colleagues were being neither cynical (as leftist critics often charge) nor particularly prescient (as conservatives counter) when they remained silent about German guilt at the individual or collective level except to deny it. The mnemonic frames of the early Federal Republic, my analysis makes clear, were thus not solely, or even largely, matters of *Realpolitik*, but followed directly on understandings of National Socialism articulated in the immediate aftermath of the Nazi collapse. Too much emphasis on the imperatives of state from both right and left and too great an assertion of discontinuity between the mnemonic problems of the occupation period and those of the new government in this way distract from the role of cultural frameworks of memory, which were defined clearly in a series of very public contexts before the founding of the Federal Republic. The reflexive and dynamic character of these cultural frameworks—both before and after 1945—are the topic of this book.

By the same token, when historians *have* looked closely at memory in the immediate postwar period, they have often focused either on the imposed mnemonic policies of the occupation authorities—primarily on the Nuremberg tribunals or on denazification—or on the personal, local, or regional contexts of German memory.[25] Again, the former have been

25. Important analyses of occupation policy and its impact on memory include Bloxham, *Genocide on Trial*; Bower, *Blind Eye to Murder*; Barnouw, *Germany 1945*; Brink, *Ikonen der Vernichtung*; Brochhagen, *Nach Nürnberg*; Douglas, *The Memory of Judgment*; FitzGibbon, *Denazification*; Goedde, *GIs and Germans*; Heineman, *Umerziehung und Wiederaufbau*; Henke, *Die amerikanische Besetzung Deutschlands*; Lange-Quassowski, *Neuordnung oder Restauration*; Merritt, *Democracy Imposed*; Peterson, *The American Occupation of Germany*; Tent, *Mission on the Rhine*; Würmeling, *Die weisse Liste*. For comparison to Soviet Policy, see Pike, *The Politics of Culture in Soviet-Occupied Germany*; Herf, *Divided Memory*; Naimark, *The Russians in Germany*.

viewed largely from the perspective of needing to explain the origins of the Cold War and the emergence of the West German state; from this perspective, the story of occupation-imposed memory—which went under the general rubric of "re-education"—is one of how early goals were modified and ultimately abandoned as geopolitical imperatives changed. The sense of prelude or emergence is thus reinforced.[26] The latter—personal, local, or regional contexts of memory—have been investigated in part as a way to portray Germans as subjects and not just objects of reconstruction.[27] This subjectivity, however, has usually been considered possible only in more narrow contexts, which corresponds to the Allied policy of controlling national-level discourse. On this view, continuities appear as rather subterranean, again reinforcing the sense that the imperatives of state *after* 1949 were primary in shaping the trajectories of German memory.

This analytical division between German action on the local level and occupation action on the national level, however, reinforces a number of other basic myths about German history as well. First, many critics, particularly on the Left, have argued that indigenous German efforts to purge Nazi residues were quashed by the Western Allies during and after the war. According to this argument, the Allies did not cooperate with German opposition circles, partly so as not to undermine the demand for "unconditional surrender" and potentially produce a new "stab in the back" legend.[28] At the end of the war, the Western Allies were concerned that the numerous German antifascist groups (known as *Antifa*) that had begun to form were too radical and would eventually play into Soviet hands. From this perspective, the failures of German memory were the fault of the Allies, who destroyed the foundations for German self-inquiry and then abandoned their own misguided efforts as soon as they ceased to be expedient. Without the Western Allies' arrogation of mnemonic framing to

26. Works emphasizing the inconsistent or transitory nature of Allied policies include Annan, *Changing Enemies*; Boehling, *A Question of Priorities*; Eisenberg, *Drawing the Line*; Goedde, *GIs and Germans*; Heinemann, *Umerziehung und Wiederaufbau*; Herz, "The Fiasco of Denazification in Germany"; Hurwitz, *Die Stunde Null der deutschen Presse*; Würmeling, *Die weisse Liste.*

27. The most important body of work here is that stemming from Lutz Niethammer and associates. See especially Niethammer, *Lebensgeschichte und Sozialstruktur im Ruhrgebiet 1930 bis 1960*. On this point, see also Flanagan, *A Study of German Political-Cultural Periodicals*, chap. 1; Goedde, *GIs and Germans*.

28. A prominent trope in Nazi rhetoric (though not only Nazi rhetoric) was that the German military had surrendered prematurely in World War I, thus stabbing the nation in the back. Moreover, at least part of the motivation for the "unconditional surrender" demand, as we will see in the following chapter, was the desire to prevent any premature separate peace.

themselves, some have therefore argued, Germany might have come to terms with the past more appropriately.[29]

Second, while many on the Left argued that it was the Allies who prevented deeper self-inquiry, others argued that no such inquiry was appropriate at all, whether imposed or self-generated. On the one hand, many Germans could not understand why the Western Allies did not immediately join with Germany to fight the Soviet Union. On the other hand, many (among the Atlantic Allies as well) argued that a policy based on guilt and memory was not likely to produce peace.[30] "The past," Nietzsche had put it in an earlier era, "must be forgotten if it is not to become the gravedigger of the present." In this argument, one could even—and some did—draw on no less an authority than Abraham Lincoln to discredit Allied strategies for a harsh occupation.[31] In his Second Inaugural Address, after all, Lincoln famously had called not for vengeance of the North on the South, but for Americans to "bind up the wounds" of the nation so that they may better heal. Of course, World War II was no civil war of brother against brother, though, as we will see, many German commentators portrayed National Socialism as a disease of Western civilization more generally, and World War II as merely the latest installment in a centuries-long "European Civil War." More pragmatically, as we have already seen, many argued that there was a clear choice for the new state (and the occupiers who supposedly wanted it to succeed) between justice and legitimacy; any German leader who sought more punishment would surely fail to consolidate the support of the people, and any Western authority that demanded such measures was working self-defeatingly against the success of the new democracy. Punishment, these critics argued, was simply too dangerous in this case, as it usually is.

Third, much German rhetoric began by pointing out that the first victims of National Socialism were, *after all*, Germans. The leaders were to be held accountable (though not the military leaders, who were worthy soldiers who had done their duty), but ordinary Germans had certainly suffered enough. Whatever debts Germany owed for its military aggression had surely been paid with German blood in the bombing nights and during

---

29. See especially Niethammer, *Die Mitläuferfabrik*, and *Deutschland Danach*.

30. A particularly controversial formulation of this argument was that of Swiss philosopher Hermann Lübbe, "Der Nationalsozialismus im deutschen Nachkriegsbewusstsein." See also Herf, *Divided Memory*.

31. As we will see, the Reconstruction following the U.S. Civil War was a common referent for American planners. For a comparison of Germany and the post–Civil War United States, see Finzsch and Martschukat, *Different Restorations*.

the expulsions agreed on by the "Big Three" at Potsdam. Indeed, at the time, many Germans charged that allegedly harsh re-education measures imposed by the Allies would be responsible for the *return* of National Socialist sentiments among the population.[32] This critique of the Allies was associated with the charge that for the occupation authorities to punish Germany for its misdeeds during the war without looking at their own misdeeds (the fire-bombing of Dresden was a favorite example) was hypocritical. We will see that the myth of German suffering—a "myth" because of its organizing capacity, not because it was false, though it was indeed one-sided—was one of the most important cultural frames through which many Germans evaluated the occupation as well as the war.[33] The banner of this German suffering after the war was the concept of "collective guilt," with which many Germans felt illegitimately charged. As we will see, however, collective guilt was rejected by Germans much more vigorously than it was ever posited by their occupiers. It was thus not just the harshness of re-education many Germans rejected: *Vae Victus* ("woe to the vanquished") most could understand; that Americans in particular were serious about re-education they often could not. Many Germans simply (and not so simply) parsed the question of responsibility differently.

Taken together, these arguments—that the Allies had no right to condemn Germans, especially given the inconsistencies of Allied policy and their failure to support indigenous German opposition, that harsh occupation was unwise for both the possibility of German democracy and the ability of the West to confront the Soviet Union, and that German suffering was *sui generis* and inappropriately exacerbated by the occupation—led many to repudiate re-education as well as the need for an inner transformation. Whether re-education was labeled arrogant, illiberal, misguided, or incompetently administered, many Germans at the time, we will see, spent energies that could have been used for self-inquiry instead for rejecting Allied policy and chimerical accusations of collective guilt. The following pages will show, however, that the claim that, left to their own devices, Germans might have come to terms with their past differently is at best a dubious counterfactual. In contrast, the failures of initial Western programs, I will argue, were not solely the result of Allied incompetence or vengefulness, as many believed; Germans played a significant role in these failures. Not understanding Allied motives and culture and why the Allies did not seem to understand them, many Germans saw Western policy as even more muddled than it was.

32. See the discussion of Eugen Kogon in chapter 5.
33. On the German sense of victimhood, see especially Moeller, *War Stories.*

We will see this all in great detail in the pages to come, but the reason to mention these problems here is to point out the difficulties that arise from the fact that many analysts agree with these German assessments of Allied policy. Re-education was in fact often conceptually fuzzy, arrogant, and inconsistently applied. There was indeed occasional hypocrisy. But, because scholarship largely agrees with the German critiques, we need to take extra care not to miss that the critiques could have been right for the wrong reasons and that they might have served other functions. In other words, just as with periodization, we need to separate our own historical reasons for assessing re-education negatively from the reasons Germans at the time had for rejecting it. Transformations in Allied policy proved to many Germans the occupation's injustice. But validating their (often sound) critiques can lead one to miss the ways in which this perhaps accurate charge against the Allies was also a blocking maneuver, whether intentional or unintentional.

*   *   *

It is worth mentioning one further risk of seeing national level prestate memory as the work of the Allies and indigenous memory as local: Is it really true—as those most interested in the origins of the Cold War and the emergence of the West German state often imply—that the most consequential interpretations of National Socialism in the occupation period were the work of the Allies and that German subjectivity is only truly visible in private or local settings (perhaps best captured through oral histories, survey analysis, and such methods rather than by intellectual or political history)?[34] It is indeed true, as I have already pointed out, that Allied policies absorbed much attention of German commentators. It is also true that whatever German public discourse there was to be was either sponsored, licensed, and/or reviewed by the occupation authorities. Clearly, there were privately held ideas that one would have been unwise to express in public. But to take these conditions as evidence that national-level German public discourse was merely *reactive* and that "true" German sentiments are best seen at the local level or in terms of private opinion rather than public debate is to miss a fascinating and important story. This story, moreover, despite being shaped by the Allies, was structured primarily by *German* traditions, experiences, and perspectives. Certainly this public discourse was a selective representation of German cultural legacies,

34. See, for example, the methodological argument in Welzer, Moller, and Tschuggnall, *"Opa war kein Nazi."* See also Pollock, *Gruppenexperiment,* which I discuss in the book's conclusion.

though it was less selective than one might suppose. One of the reasons for this book is my belief that this discourse has not received the attention it deserves, or at least not the right kind of attention.

There has indeed been some productive examination of the genuinely German public discourse in the occupation period, but—in part for the reasons discussed in the foregoing pages—not nearly as much as one might expect.[35] There have certainly also been numerous "cultural histories" of the occupation period, many of them excellent and informative.[36] And there have also been numerous studies of particular individuals, which cover, among other things, the parts of their careers in which they addressed National Socialism. But for the purposes of the present analysis these wider cultural histories of the period as well as case studies of individuals are helpful but ultimately unsatisfactory.

First, we have already seen the dangers of an emergentist account of postwar discourse, which privileges Allied frameworks and discounts the legacies of those frameworks as well as of German discourse in this period for later German memory. Second, while general cultural histories of Germany in this period do describe how intellectuals and artists responded to the Nazi past and to the occupation, the contributions of these cultural figures to *collective memory* of the Nazi past is often approached in such a way that treats culture and politics as more distinct than they were. The importance—even primacy—of *intellectual* work for *political* culture is thus less clear than it might otherwise be. Indeed, more than in later periods, the immediate postwar years were an open landscape in which boundaries among discursive fields were weak and the impact of seemingly esoteric debates—such as that over the return of the writer Thomas Mann to Germany—were hard to circumscribe.[37] While intellectual and cultural debates have always played a greater role in German politics than in some other places, the fact, among other conditions, that there was no German state in the immediate postwar years leant even more weight to the role of intellectual, cultural, religious, and other public figures as custodians of national identity than later. Broad cultural histories provide important

---

35. Exceptions include Eberan, *Die Debatte um die Schuldfrage;* Flanagan, *A Study of German Political-Cultural Periodicals;* Foschepoth, *Im Schatten der Vergangenheit;* Moeller, *War Stories;* Steinle, *Nationales Selbstverständnis nach dem Nationalsozialismus;* Stern, *The Whitewashing of the Yellow Badge;* Wolgast, *Die Wahrnehmung des Dritten Reiches in der unmittelbaren Nachkriegszeit.*

36. Perhaps the two most influential have been Glaser, *The Rubble Years;* and Hermand, *Kultur im Wiederaufbau.* See also Schivelbusch, *In a Cold Crater.*

37. On the fluid boundaries among cultural fields, see Bourdieu, *The Field of Cultural Production.*

background and context for my analysis, but my specific concern is with the ways in which that culture shaped how Germans dealt with the problems of transition, reconstruction, and memory—problems that concern me from a more general perspective than that of German culture alone.

Third, in studies of particular individuals, their contributions to postwar debates about memory are often treated as mere episodes in their lives' work, and often minor ones at that. The problem here is that this can distract from the autonomous structures of the memory debates themselves, which are not reducible to the personalities and life trajectories of the individuals who participated in them. Sweeping up explicit debates on collective memory in wider cultural histories of this unique period or treating the participation of famous intellectuals in public debates about the Nazi past in terms of their individual *oeuvres* is thus to risk missing a fascinating story, one that, moreover, is profoundly important for understanding the longer-term history of German memory as well as subsequent historical moments elsewhere.

A Profligate Stain?

The central question for both victors and vanquished in the wake of unimaginable destruction and atrocity was how widely the stain of guilt spread over Germany. Many German commentators feared that the stain of National Socialism would be profligate, sweeping up all Germans in a sea of collective guilt and discrediting all German history and culture.[38] Their challenge, then, was to limn a postwar German identity that would allow Germany to move beyond the unprecedented ruin of life, infrastructure, order, and pride perpetrated in their name without damning Germany forever. For a short time and in some respects, at least some of their fears of total condemnation were justified. At least as often they were not. Nevertheless, across a series of contexts and issues leading up to and immediately following the end of the war, many of the great names of German culture participated in the endeavor to reconstitute German identity. And despite the variety of speakers, contexts, and themes, there were some remarkable consistencies. It is in this sense that we can speak of a discourse of memory before 1949. To articulate its basic themes and portray its richness and resonance are central goals of this book, which is ultimately interested in explaining why early memory of the Nazi period took the forms it did and with what consequences.

The questions I ask therefore include the following: What issues concerning the Nazi past attracted the attention of German intellectuals, politicians,

38. See Olick, "The Guilt of Nations?"

and other leaders in the midst of their desolation? Why these issues and not others? What did they think had happened, and how could they explain it to themselves and to others? Who did they think was responsible? What did this responsibility entail? How relevant were these events for German national identity, German culture, and possible future German governments? Exactly what "events" were at issue? And how are we, who know the path of German history and memory after 1949, to assess the answers to these questions that were offered in this unusual period, frequently understood either as a mere prelude to what came later or as outside the continuum of normal history? Indeed, this last question highlights the relevance of this history not only to the future of German memory, but to subsequent moments elsewhere in which questions of "transitional justice" and collective memory have been key. In this regard, Germany is a—perhaps *the*—paradigmatic case.[39]

* * *

I begin the narrative, however, by tracing the origins and pathways of Allied occupation policy in wartime debates, for the rhetorical and substantive frameworks presented by the Allies, I argue, formed a powerful reference point for, and otherwise shaped, much of the German discourse. I start with the demand for "unconditional surrender," examine wartime public debates over German national character, and then challenge the commonplace view that U.S. policy planning was a struggle between a noble democratic vision (represented by Secretary of War Henry Stimson) and a desire (not incidentally Jewish in origin) for vengeance (represented by Secretary of the Treasury Henry Morgenthau Jr.).

The most visible manifestations of what was seen as the Western re-education agenda, of course, were the Nuremberg tribunals and the so-called "denazification" programs. These Allied-imposed frames were important for their practical effects on German society as well as for organizing German reaction. Discussion of these measures—and mostly rejection of them as illegitimate—led German commentators to articulate their own principles and understandings of what had occurred and what should be done about it. Nuremberg and denazification have often been the subjects of their own histories—and I draw on much of the outstanding work that has already been done on these issues—but my goal here is to place them in the context of other memory-political events and debates.

39. For an overview of the "transitional justice" literature, and an emphasis on Germany's place in it, see Kritz, *Transitional Justice*.

Indeed, the specific Allied frameworks—wartime writings, wartime and postwar military and political decrees, and postwar juridical measures—were by no means the only matters about which German commentators articulated interpretations. Much of the discourse did involve reactions to Allied policies—most importantly to denazification and removal of industrial equipment as reparations—and much discussion by Germans was framed by Allied institutions. But much was not. After chapters on the formation of Allied occupation policies, Nuremberg, and denazification, therefore, I analyze an array of German efforts to parse the burdens of the past, though also demonstrating the often surprising ways in which these German efforts were articulated in dialogue not only with each other and older German traditions, but with Allied discourses as well. These German debates include the following:

- first, an argument over the moral and political differences between exile and what came to be called "inner emigration" as responses to National Socialism, part of a vituperative public discussion over whether there was an "other Germany" not discredited by National Socialism, and who its proper representatives might be (a central focus of this debate in the immediate postwar period was the author Thomas Mann, though it had earlier and later versions);
- second, discussion over how much revision of German history the disaster of National Socialism required. How were historians and social scientists to interpret National Socialism without accepting the totalistic condemnations of German character and history charged during the war? Given the central role of historical references in national identity, the efforts of historians and social scientists to limn the boundaries of National Socialism's origins and impact, I show, were particularly telling.
- and third, a controversy over individual versus collective guilt, most prominently between the psychoanalyst Carl Jung and the publicist and children's book author Erich Kästner, a controversy that crystallized the sense that all Germans were being indiscriminately condemned and demonstrates to us what many Germans thought was at stake in such accusations.

I then turn to two institutional contexts that by necessity produced elaborate discourses about the German past and who was responsible for it: the churches and the political parties. Here the question of continuities with the past is especially prominent: What rights and burdens did these institutions assume because of their behavior in the past, and how did they frame

that behavior in light of their present ambitions? What sorts of acknowledgments did they think were necessary?

Finally, I turn to perhaps the most famous and most explicit statement
on German responsibility—*The Question of German Guilt* [*Die Schuldfrage*]
by the philosopher Karl Jaspers—and question, among other things,
exactly why it has been so significant in German and other memory of this
discourse, for indeed this work is substantially more prominent in cultural
and scholarly memory than almost any other statement of the postwar
years. In contrast to much of the extensive literature on this landmark
book, I place Jaspers's enduring and widely influential statement within not
only the highly personal context of his relationship with the philosopher
Martin Heidegger (as has often been done), but in the context of a wider
struggle with residues of an older German sensibility of proud rather than
repentant German identity; the operative question in Jaspers's account, I
argue, is whether the proper reaction for Germans is shame (preventing
acknowledgment) or guilt (requiring it). Here I challenge—or at least
refine—the conventional view that Jaspers represented a new political culture for Germany, by juxtaposing his arguments to what I show was an
equally influential and enduring alternative in the figures of Martin
Heidegger, Ernst Jünger, and Carl Schmitt, among others. However, by
taking up this difference only after considering the many other places in
which the German defeat was parsed, I argue, can we appreciate contours
and subtleties often missed in more focused accounts.

The Sociology of Memory

Approaching the formative period of West German memory in this way, I
also propose, helps avoid some of the more common problems in the sociology of collective memory, a burgeoning field of analysis in recent years that
I mentioned earlier in this chapter.[40] Sociologists of collective memory have
largely been concerned with explaining why we produce the images of the
past we do (and how different groups produce different ones) and, in turn,
with explaining the role such images play in other processes: In other words,
what affects collective memory and what does collective memory affect?
One of the main problems with sociological accounts of collective memory,
however, has been the tendency to reify it: that is, to treat collective memory
not only as singular (*the* collective memory), but to treat it as a thing rather
than a process. This is in some ways part of identifying it as a coherent

40. See note 9.

variable with causes and effects that can be measured. In truth, however, there is no such thing as memory; there is only the activity of remembering.

The tendency to reify collective memory is especially prominent when researchers focus on "official" sources, such as textbooks, encyclopedias, canonized artworks, government statements, public ceremonies, and the like, where images of the past are, sometimes literally, set in stone. Certainly one can, through content analysis and other methods, trace changes over time in images of the past in such media; but for any given moment, one is tempted to characterize a fixed image or set of images of the past that we call the "collective memory" of a society. Even when one notes contradictory images available in "official" sources at a particular point in time, these often come to be seen as the constitutive elements of a fixed discursive structure, a set of choices.

One solution to this has been to disparage such "top down" approaches as elitist, and to turn to public opinion and unsanctified popular sources as evidence of the multiplicity and fluidity of collective memory. This is sometimes called a "countermemory" approach.[41] The problem with that solution, however, is that it risks throwing the baby of cultural power out with the bathwater of elitism: there often do seem to be "regimes" or "discourses" of memory shaped by powerful cultural creators well placed to influence collective remembering at other levels and in other contexts; at very least, the relation between "official" and "popular" memory remains an empirical question, answerable differently for different times and places. The concepts of official and popular memory, it turns out, are as vulnerable to reification as is that of collective memory more generally.

Instead, my approach to what are largely "official" sources in what follows (in the sense that the interlocutors I examine were mostly both institutionally and culturally powerful and their statements were published or delivered in relatively sanctified forms)[42] seeks to avoid the problem of

41. The classic reference here is to Foucault, *Language, Counter-Memory, Practice*. For discussions of the countermemory approach, see Popular Memory Group, *Making Histories*; Bodnar, *Remaking America*.

42. There are numerous fields I will not present—such as professional associations (e.g., medicine and law), big business, art, film, historical preservation, and city planning, among others—not because they are not important and interesting, but because they are usually (though not always) more narrow in the collectivities they address than the kinds of discourse I do include. On big business and Nazi memory, see Wiesen, *West German Industry and the Challenge of the Nazi Past*. On historical preservation, see Koshar, *Germany's Transient Past*; Rosenfeld, *Munich and Memory*. On film, see Fehrenbach, *Cinema in Democratizing Germany*; Kaes, *From Hitler to Heimat*. On city planning, see Diefendorf, *In the Wake of the War*. These are only selected examples from enormous literatures.

reification by emphasizing fluidity even *within* culturally powerful discourses. In other words, I portray the discursive structures of the postwar intellectual, cultural, and political debates as works in continuous progress, rather than as fixed regimes and counter-regimes; my interest is in collective *remembering* rather than in collective *memory*. I work to capture transformations, multiplicity, and provisionality by emphasizing what literary analysts call "dialogical qualities," the ways in which every utterance is both a response to a partner and to a history of such responses. Doing this, it is important to note, does not deny structure—it merely redefines structure as a temporal process: *structuring*.[43] As I already pointed out, moreover, a dialogical approach attends not only to the different ways a past is remembered over time, but to the ways that remembering is part of an ongoing dialogue not only about the particular past, but about the different ways that past has been remembered in the intervening years. This later dimensions is what I mean by the "memory of memory."

The Agonies of German Defeat

The following pages thus tell the story of the public discourse about the Nazi past in the years 1945–49, though they also trace the origins of Allied framings during the war, especially from 1943 onward. The debates I examine are filled with familiar names of American and German culture— Franklin Roosevelt, Henry Morgenthau, Cordell Hull, Talcott Parsons, Margaret Mead, Thomas Mann, Carl Jung, Erich Kästner, Alfred Weber, Martin Heidegger, Ernst Jünger, and Friedrich Meinecke, to name only some. Most of these individuals, however, are much better known for their contributions in other areas. While many parts of this history have been examined before for other purposes, there are thus many surprises when one considers these materials together in the way that I do. The numerous debates among planners, intellectuals, politicians, and others about the meaning of National Socialism for German identity, it seems to me, formed as a series of *agonies*—in the classical sense of struggles—within and constituting a wider arena of political culture and collective memory. As with the gatherings in which the classical agonies were fought, these debates were part of a complex landscape of events in diverse arenas, yet in

---

43. The most significant literary theorist of "dialogism" is Mikhail Bakhtin. For an overview of Bakthin's work, see Morson and Emerson, *Mikhail Bakhtin*. For an application of Bakhtinian ideas to the sociology of German collective memory, see Olick, "Genre Memories and Memory Genres."

a delimited period and defined by common thematic materials and bound-aries and overlapping audiences. I treat the discourse, that is, as a complex, multivocal dialogue, because it makes sense to do so methodologically and because, I believe, that is the form it took.

The distinctive contribution of this book thus stems at least partly from its methodological premises: first, that examining the diverse memory debates in different fields on seemingly separate issues provides insights not available in broader cultural history, individual author studies, or analy-sis of one or the other of the debates alone; second, that treating the dis-course of German responsibility both before and after 1945 *together* yields insights not possible from separate studies of Anglo-American discourse during the war and of German discourse after 1945; and third, that high-lighting the dialogical qualities of this memory discourse helps avoid the pitfalls of episodic or emergentist approaches to this fascinating period and problem. The more mundane result of these methodological principles, however, is simply that my presentation itself will often be rather discur-sive, presenting as much of the actual dialogue as is possible without yield-ing too many diseconomies of presentation. Frankly, I was simply so often surprised by what I found in my reading that I want to share the reasons!

The goal of the pages that follow is thus to identify the terms—the sym-bolic and rhetorical tools—Germans developed in their moment of abjec-tion for handling the toxic materials of the Nazi past. These terms were part accommodation and part rejection of Allied frameworks, and the results of interpretive and political struggles over the value of German cul-tural and political legacies. This moral and political vocabulary, it is impor-tant to note, has been of enduring significance as a crucible of both German identity and contemporary political thinking about memory and justice more generally. The issues these famous figures debated—including how to treat a defeated enemy, how widely to draw the circle of guilt, how to place episodes within wider historical trajectories, how much to distinguish varieties of victimhood, whether to submit to the repetitive memory that defines trauma or to repress it—are clearly as pressing today as they were fifty years ago. The difference is that the ways we discuss them today are shaped, though not always in predictable ways, by these historical solutions to German dilemmas, by the memory, that is, German or otherwise, of German memory.[44]

44. For sources on and reviews of the problem of "transitional justice," see Kritz, *Transitional Justice*; and Olick, "The Politics of Regret."

PART I

The Victors

CHAPTER 2

Defining Defeat

May 8, 1945

The surrender of the German military to Allied forces took place at the Supreme Headquarters of the Allied Expeditionary Force (SHAEF) at Reims in the early hours of May 7, 1945. On April 30, Hitler and Goebbels had committed suicide, leaving Grand Admiral Dönitz as head of state; on May 1, the last remaining German forces in Italy capitulated; the following day General Weidling surrendered Berlin to Soviet general Chuikov, though Weidling stalled as long as possible to allow Martin Bormann and others to escape from Hitler's bunker;[1] on May 3, Hamburg fell to the British. By the first week of May, the endgame was played out, as had been inevitable all spring.[2]

Dönitz's immediate goal was to delay surrender as long as possible to enable German troops on the Eastern front to avoid capture by the Soviets. The German command believed that German soldiers and civilians could expect particularly brutal treatment by Stalin's forces. Indeed, when the German chief of staff, General Jodl, arrived at SHAEF to discuss surrender, he pleaded with the Western Allies to allow the German army more time, on the grounds that every troop saved from Soviet captivity (or worse) would be available for the coming struggle against the Communists. When Allied commanders insisted they would tolerate no further delays, Jodl sent a signal to Dönitz's headquarters in Flensburg asking for permission to sign the surrender documents. Dönitz responded at 1:30 A.M., at which point Jodl and his delegation sat before representatives of the Allied powers (though Supreme Commander General Eisenhower, out of disdain for the enemy, refused to be in the room) and signed four copies of the

1. Many years later, Bormann's remains were found in an underground tunnel leading from the bunker; Weidling's efforts were thus in vain.

2. See Beevor, *Fall of Berlin 1945*; see also Naimark, *The Russians in Germany, 1945–1949*.

surrender document, which set the end of the war for one minute after midnight British time on May 9. In a brief statement, Jodl expressed a sense of victimization by history that would be a hallmark of the postwar years: "With this signature the German people and the German armed forces are, for better or worse, delivered into the victor's hands. In this War, which has lasted more than five years, both have achieved and suffered more than perhaps any other people in the world. In this hour I can only express the hope that the victor will treat them with generosity."[3]

*   *   *

Neither history nor commemoration, it turns out, was nearly as final as this account suggests. Truman and Churchill had agreed with Stalin not to announce the Reims event until a parallel signing could take place in Berlin. Furthermore, the Reims document was not exactly the same one the Soviets had agreed to; the Soviet delegate Major General Ivan Suslaparov overstepped his authority when he signed the Reims agreement (he disappeared into Soviet custody immediately thereafter) and the Soviets threatened to repudiate it. By mid-afternoon on May 7, a press leak caused spontaneous celebrations in European capitals and on the East Coast of the United States before the Berlin ceremony took place, leading to accusations by the Soviets that the Western Allies were trying to cut them out of the victory (in truth it was likely more a matter of bungling than intention). In order not to appear to be latecomers, the Soviet leadership suppressed news of the Reims signing until after the Berlin ceremony, which was indeed grand in comparison to the one at Reims. The Soviet Union did not announce victory to its people until early on May 9. Interpretation of the victory was thus already divided at its birth.

Additionally, despite the celebrations of May 8 in the West and May 9 in the East, an undertaking as massive as World War II does not simply end. Fighting had ceased in some places months earlier, yet continued in others for several weeks after. The Allies allowed Dönitz's successor government to operate formally until May 23, when the British—under pressure from the Soviets and the French—arrested him. It was not until June 5 that the Allies assumed "supreme authority" in Germany, and exactly what that meant legally was ambiguous at best.[4] For most Germans, moreover, there was little

---

3. Quoted in Botting, *From the Ruins of the Reich*, 90.

4. As Theodor Eschenburg, among others, has pointed out, the legal meaning of this claim raised more questions than it answered. The Allies neither annexed Germany nor oversaw a

difference between the misery before May 8 (or 9) and after. Indeed, for those "ethnic" Germans in Eastern territories, new horrors of revenge and expulsion were just beginning; particularly in Berlin many German women (and girls) suffered brutal and repeated rapes at the hands of Soviet "shock" troops during these weeks; and many soldiers were dying of injuries or languishing in captivity (thousands of those in Soviet custody would remain there for many years). For complex reasons, many Germans (particularly leaders) have been heavily invested in seeing May 8, 1945, as a decisive rupture in history, a so-called "zero hour." Most Germans, however, experienced it as merely one day in the middle of an era of suffering begun at Stalingrad in 1943 and not to be over until the currency reform of 1948 (or, for some, not until the final return of POWs and sovereignty in 1955).[5]

Indeed, some sense of the extent of Germany's physical destitution (which does not minimize a sense of the destruction Germany wrought on its enemies) is essential for understanding the cultural and moral dilemmas of Germany's defeat. During the war, for instance, the Western Allies pursued an escalating strategy of carpet bombing that reached far beyond many definitions of military or industrial targeting. This air war left approximately six hundred thousand civilians dead, and wounded as many as nine hundred thousand more; more than 7 million Germans were left homeless at the end of the war (around 10 million people had been evacuated from the cities to avoid the bombings).[6] "Population transfers" from eastern Europe and the eastern parts of the Reich numbered as many as 12 million, and at least a half

---

puppet regime. Some theorists thus argued at the time that the occupation was technically illegal under international law; this legal vagueness, some argued, was a source of dangerous arbitrariness in Allied policy. Perhaps most important for later events was the question of the continuity of the German Reich. Technically, the German Reich did not cease to exist with the unconditional surrender. The question of the legal status of Germany thus remained open until the signing of a final peace treaty, which wouldn't take place for more than forty years. This legal continuity of the Reich was later an important technical argument in West German claims to represent the population of the German Democratic Republic and to refuse to recognize that regime as a legitimate government. See especially Eschenburg, *Jahre der Besatzung*, 23–24.

5. See especially Benz, *Die Vertreibung der Deutschen aus dem Osten*.

6. Memory of the air war against German cities has long been a complex and controversial topic, particularly in recent years. The fire bombing of Dresden, for instance, served both as an icon of German suffering and as the basis for an indictment of Allied policies (though that indictment can be independent—as in Kurt Vonnegut's novel *Slaughterhouse Five*—or as part of an effort to relativize German atrocities). In 1992, the unveiling of a statue of Air Marshall Arthur Harris (the campaign's architect, often referred to as "Bomber Harris") attended by the Queen Mother of England occasioned significant protests in Germany. More recently,

million ethnic Germans died or were killed in the process. More than 5 million German soldiers were killed in the war, leaving more than a million widows; the gender disparity after the war—more than two "marriageable" women for every man—was among the most significant demographic consequences of the war, which is to say nothing of the large number of fatherless or entirely orphaned children.[7] Just one consequence of the mass rapes of German women toward and after the end of the war and of the rampant prostitution and semiprostitution born of extreme necessity, moreover, was an astoundingly high venereal disease rate among German women (to say nothing of among Soviet and other soldiers).[8]

The physical, moral, and social devastation symbolized by May 8, 1945, was thus unprecedented and decisive, though its meaning remains disputed to this day. Was Germany defeated or liberated on May 8, 1945? Does that date mark a caesura in German and world history, or was it merely an arbitrary moment in a long historical process, one characterized as much by continuity as by rupture? These two questions—defeat versus liberation, rupture versus continuity—are no matters of mere historiographical pondering: They posed basic dilemmas for all Germans contemplating the future of their collective national existence, to say nothing of their personal and material circumstances. At the root of these dilemmas was the issue of whether, and in what ways, *all* Germans were responsible for National Socialism and everything it had wrought: Were ordinary Germans perpetrators, bystanders, or victims? To what extent was National Socialism a product of German culture and to what extent was it a deviation, accident, or even foreign plague?

While these questions were ultimately matters for the Germans themselves, how the Allies posed and answered them affected the course of the war and the nature of the occupation, and thus the contexts in which Germans confronted them in the moment of their abjection. The purpose of this and the following two chapters is to investigate both the evolution of Allied framings and the ways in which these framings have entered into collective memory, German and otherwise.

---

a lecture by the novelist W. G. Sebald ("Air War and Literature," in Sebald, *On the Natural History of Destruction*) as well as the publication of a best-selling book on the Dresden bombing by Jörg Friedrich (provocatively entitled *Der Brand* [The Fire] to evoke overtones of "holocaust") have generated renewed discussion about German suffering and the legitimacy of recalling it. See Kettenacher, *Ein Volk von Opfern?*

7. See especially Moeller, *Protecting Motherhood;* Heinemann, *What Difference Does a Husband Make?*

8. See Naimark, *The Russians in Germany*, 97–101.

Mythic Frameworks

The story of U.S. and British planning for the occupation of Germany is commonly told as a Manichean struggle between irresponsible Germanaphobes bent on vengeance and pragmatists who believed harsh measures were more likely to sow the seeds of a new war than to help avoid it. In this standard account, the U.S. treasury secretary Henry Morgenthau Jr. is the central figure. Labeled by the Nazi propaganda minister Joseph Goebbels as the "Jewish Angel of Revenge" (*jüdische Racheengel*), Morgenthau stands as the emblem of misguided policy. A witless lackey, according to the standard narrative, Morgenthau allowed himself to be manipulated by Jewish groups and Communist sympathizers, and called for the wholesale destruction of Germany; because of failing health, President Franklin Roosevelt momentarily went along, though he never would have let things go so far had he lived until the end of the war. In some versions of this story, the ultimate occupation statute—JCS (Joint Chiefs of Staff) 1067, which stated that "Germany will not be occupied for the purpose of liberation but as a defeated enemy nation"—was a last residue of Morgenthau's vision, to be undermined by all means; in others, JCS 1067 was a refutation of Morgenthau because it lacked some of his putatively more draconian desires, such as flooding the mines and dismantling all industry in the Ruhr and Saar regions. Either way, the story of the occupation of Germany is told as one of overcoming the vengeful impulses for which "Morgenthau" stood and developing the supposedly more level-headed policies that ultimately won the Cold War.[9]

There are many reasons why this account has dominated. Perhaps the most generous explanation would be in terms of the compartmentalization of historiography: for analysts of postwar Germany, or even of U.S. occupation policy after 1945, the complex story of the vicissitudes of American policy planning is a matter of prehistory, easily reduced to a few standard sentences. For historians of the occupation and of West Germany, "Morgenthau" has been useful as an emblem for a vast array of opinions, proposals, discussions, and theories from before the end of the war to be contrasted with what eventually happened. For Germans themselves during the occupation and afterward, "Morgenthau" was evidence of the Allies' punitive stance, the source of German suffering. Not only German commentators in the postwar period, but many scholars since then have thus referred vaguely

9. The latest, and in many ways most complete, version of this "standard account" is Beschloss, *The Conquerers.*

to Morgenthau and his plan to "dismember," "pastoralize," or "deindustrial-ize" Germany without further analysis; especially sophisticated accounts mention as well "Vansittartism," a label referring to the position articulated by Lord Robert Vansittart, a high-ranking British diplomat (commonly referred to as "the propagandist Robert Vansittart," as if that were a job description) who had opposed Prime Minister Neville Chamberlain's policy of appeasing the Nazis in the mid-1930s and who delivered important speeches during the war warning against a "soft peace." Rarely, however, are such mentions qualified by close analysis—or even reference to close analysis—of what exactly Morgenthau or Vansittart proposed, and why. "Pastoralization" and "Vansittartism" are thus convenient mythic emblems, often as much for historians as for political actors at the time.[10]

Another explanation for the persistence of this standard account has to do with the retrospective legitimation of U.S. policy in the Cold War. Here "Morgenthau" stands for those who did not recognize the threat the Soviet Union posed, and for the bankruptcy of accommodation. Particularly important here is the fact that Morgenthau's chief advisor (and principle author of the plan), Harry Dexter White, was accused in 1948 by Joseph McCarthy's House Un-American Activities Committee (HUAC) of being a Soviet agent; by implication, the only ones who would benefit from the rad-ical restructuring of the German economy for which Morgenthau called were the Soviets and their sympathizers.[11] The implication is that following Morgenthau would have spelled disaster for the West: we won the Cold War, in other words, because we chose the other path. As Michael Beschloss puts it, "History now shows that by destroying a barrier to Soviet power and alienating the Germans from Britain and America, the plan could have also opened the way for the Soviet Union to dominate postwar Europe."[12]

Such triumphal assessments of U.S. decisions at the end of World War II, of course, redeem the position of Morgenthau's opponents both leading up to and immediately following May 8, 1945. Though one could easily overlook them in the minimal standard references, however, there are other possible interpretations of Morgenthau's motivations and the poten-tial effects of having rejected his plan (as I show in chapter 4). While

10. See as well Greiner, *Die Morgenthau-Legende*; Später, *Vansittart*.
11. On White more generally, see Rees, *Harry Dexter White*. On the questions of White's alleged treason, see Boughton, "The Case against Harry Dexter White: Still Not Proven."
12. The logic here, however, is dubious. To say that the choice that contributed to bring-ing about the Cold War helped us win it proves nothing about what would have happened had the United States made a different choice.

"Morgenthau" has certainly long been iconic for those on the far Right, the myth is commonly assumed to be true across the spectrum; the only difference is in people's evaluations of how important it was that "Morgenthau" wanted to "pastoralize" Germany. The interesting point here is the myth's durability and its role in legitimating U.S. policy in the Cold War: it serves as the first chapter in the story of successful American Cold War strategy.

There is, however, a third and even more troubling explanation for the power and endurance of the "Morgenthau" myth, articulated most clearly in a recent book by the German historian Bernd Greiner, whose more critical take is already apparent in his title—*The Morgenthau Legend: On the History of a Disputed Plan.* "It is scurrilous," Greiner argues, "which names imprint on the collective memory and which not. Who recalls which politicians were in charge of the American War and State Departments as the bombs fell on Hiroshima and Nagasaki? In contrast, Henry Morgenthau is still fresh in memory here, even for those who think Henry Stimson is the quarterback for the Washington Redskins or James F. Byrnes is Clint Eastwood's double." For illustrative purposes, Greiner reports on an informal 1992 survey of seventeen high school students in Hamburg asking what the students associated with the name Henry Morgenthau. Fourteen replied, "Turn Germany into a cropland and grain silo for the USA," seven mentioned "American Jew," and two said "Jew, therefore extreme and adhering to thoughts of revenge."[13]

The *ad hominem* response to the Morgenthau plan, of course, was simultaneous with its formulation. As the Nazi propaganda minister Joseph Goebbels put it, "Hate and revenge of truly old-testament character are clear in these plans dreamed up by the American Jew Morgenthau. Industrialized Germany should be literally turned into a huge potato field."[14] This much was to be expected from Goebbels, who sought to use the image of a vengeful Morgenthau to encourage fiercer German resistance and to underwrite Hitler's "scorched earth" policy. Perhaps more troubling is that such *ad hominem* dismissals of Morgenthau's motives were also potent in the U.S. administration. Secretary of War Henry Stimson, for instance, believed that Morgenthau was "so biased by his Semitic grievances that he really is a very dangerous advisor to the President." For Stimson, the connection between Morgenthau's Jewishness and his policy ideas was more than obvious: "Morgenthau is, not unnaturally, very bitter and . . . it became

13. See Greiner, *Die Morgenthau-Legende*, 16.
14. Goebbels's statement came in an October 4, 1944, speech, quoted in Greiner, *Die Morgenthau-Legende*, 4, among many other places.

very apparent that he would plunge out for a treatment of Germany which I feel sure would be unwise." In a note to himself, Stimson wrote that the "objective of punishment is prevention but not vengeance. . . . Reason why Jew is disqualified." Nevertheless, Stimson found Supreme Court Justice Felix Frankfurter to be right-thinking because, "*[a]lthough* a Jew like Morgenthau . . . ," Frankfurter discussed the matter "with perfect detachment and great helpfulness" (emphasis added). Stimson's final assessment of Morgenthau's plan was that it "is Semitism gone wild for vengeance." In a discussion with Roosevelt, of course, Stimson was sure to refer to his "personal friendship for Henry Morgenthau who had been so kind to me when I first came into the Cabinet."[15]

For his part, Secretary of State Cordell Hull described events leading up to Morgenthau's attendance at the 1944 Quebec Conference, at which Churchill and Roosevelt temporarily approved a version of the plan, as follows: "[T]he President was *prevailed upon* to permit Secretary of the Treasury Morgenthau to attend the meeting. *Morgenthau and his friends* had been working for some time on a drastic plan for the postwar treatment of Germany, and the leaders of *groups who had been justly wrought up* by German outrages requested the President invite him to go to Quebec primarily to present his plan for Germany" (emphasis added). Later, Hull writes that "[t]he President was *induced* to permit Morgenthau to attend the conference, at which point he intended to advocate his extreme plan" (emphasis added).[16] This account, however, is not corroborated by most other sources. Hull himself had declined Roosevelt's invitation to travel with him to Quebec, and Morgenthau professed that he was more surprised than anyone by the last-minute invitation. Hull did, however, echo the charge that if the plan leaked out (which it did, most likely through Stimson's deputy and later high commissioner for Germany, John J. McCloy), "it might well mean a bitter-end German resistance that could cause the loss of thousands of American lives."[17] As we will see, however, such charges were leveled throughout the war for many different reasons, and are difficult to test.

The point here is not that Stimson, McCloy, Hull, and others were raving anti-Semites. They were very much within the norms of American

---

15. The cited remarks and statements are reported in Stimson and Bundy, *On Active Service in War and Peace*, 565–95.

16. Hull's wife, it should be noted, was half-Jewish, a fact he sought to keep out of the public eye, especially when he had presidential aspirations.

17. Hull, *The Memoirs of Cordell Hull*, 1602–22.

social prejudice at the time. The point is that associating Morgenthau's putative desire for vengeance with his Jewishness (whether or not there was a connection) made it easier for his contemporary rivals to dismiss his arguments. Indeed, this casuistry appears to have stuck. Nevertheless, as we will see, Morgenthau's proposals were not nearly as extreme and outside of the discourse as Stimson and others painted them. Additionally, from the perspective of memory, recalling the Jew Morgenthau as the emblem of revenge—an association to which Stimson as well as Goebbels contributed (though I certainly do not mean to associate Stimson and Goebbels with each other!)—blocks off a more serious inquiry into the wartime discourse about punishing Germany. As Greiner implies, identifying "harsh" proposals for Germany with a Jewish attitude makes such proposals easier to discredit retrospectively. The problem is that "Morgenthau" and Henry Morgenthau Jr. are not the same, and the realities of public discourse about Allied intentions are thereby distorted. In order to understand the genesis of the mythic figure "Morgenthau," it is thus necessary to trace out the dialogical development of Allied understandings, for they contributed at least in part to postwar German uses of this history as well. How did the "Morgenthau" myth come about? Was it merely a convenient emblem? And what other interpretations of his motivations are possible?

The Evolution of Allied Policy

We commonly remember World War II as "the Good War," in which, in Roosevelt's words, America served as the "arsenal of democracy."[18] From this perspective, it is perhaps surprising to recall not only the strong isolationist stance in the U.S. Congress throughout the 1930s but that the overwhelming majority of Americans opposed entry into the war, even after the fall of France and the bombing of Pearl Harbor. According to Richard Merritt's survey of public opinion data from the period, a 1939 Roper poll showed that only 3 percent of Americans wanted the United States to participate should a war break out between England and France and the "dictator nations," though 25 percent more were willing to enter if England and France would otherwise lose. The numbers supporting entry increased to only about one-third in 1941. None of this is to say that there was not a strong anti-German presentiment in the American population, focused particularly on the specter of German militarism from previous years. In 1939, more than 80 percent blamed Germany for the outbreak of war and

18. See, for instance, Terkel, *"The Good War."*

wanted England and France to win, though when asked which country they saw as "the worst influence in Europe," one-third named the Soviet Union.[19]

And what were U.S. and British war aims to be? Until 1941, Anglo-American thinking about peace had been guided by the desire for a return of the prewar *status quo*, albeit one cognizant of the putative failures of the Treaty of Versailles (which almost one-third of Americans blamed for German aggression). The main goal was to reestablish a balance of power in Europe by supporting moderate democratic forces in Germany. But through 1941, the extent of German aggression had become clearer; furthermore, with the alliance of the United States, Great Britain, and the Soviet Union, the geopolitical dimensions of any potential settlement were even more obvious than before.[20]

The essential conservatism of Anglo-American thinking at this early stage manifested itself when Franklin Roosevelt and Winston Churchill met "somewhere in the Atlantic" in August 1941. On August 14, they issued the so-called "Atlantic Charter," a vaguely Wilsonian document calling for renunciation of expansionist aims, the right of all peoples to "self-determination," and the final destruction of Nazi tyranny. These formulations were general enough that the Soviet Union issued a statement in September agreeing to them, but this consent was only hesitant, given the potential implication of "self-determination" for soviet interests in the Balkans. For his part, Churchill agreed only after obtaining a blanket exemption for the entire British Empire.[21] The Atlantic Charter did indeed remain a potent symbol for many Anglo-American policy-planners throughout the war and in efforts to establish a new international organization immediately afterward. But at this early stage, it could only serve as a general orientation, and not an unproblematic one at that. On what, then, could the new Allies agree?

Unconditional Surrender

By 1943, the lowest common denominator of Anglo-American and Soviet intentions seemed to be what Franklin Roosevelt called "unconditional surrender," a much more complex term at the time than it sounds in retro-

---

19. Merritt, *Democracy Imposed: U.S. Occupation Policy and the German Public, 1945–1949*, 23–48. See also Field and Van Patten, "If the American People Made the Peace."

20. See especially Graml, "Die deutsche Frage," in Eschenburg, *Jahre der Besatzung*.

21. See Gaddis, *The United States and the Origins of the Cold War*, 3.

spect. The formula appeared publicly for the first time at the January 24, 1943, final press briefing following Roosevelt and Churchill's summit at Casablanca, which Roosevelt at the time proposed naming the "Unconditional Surrender Conference." Critics immediately (and for many years thereafter, both in the United States and in Germany), however, charged that the statement was a huge mistake.[22] On the one hand, some agreed with the aim but thought stating it so baldly would provide a boost to the German propaganda machine (this was a similar argument to the one Hull later gave about the Morgenthau plan); Goebbels, they claimed, would be able to spur ordinary Germans to fiercer and prolonged fighting by painting the Allies as bloodthirsty and intent on destroying Germany once and for all.[23] On the other hand, others disagreed with the aim altogether. Many believed it discouraged opposition elements in Germany, with whom it might have been possible to negotiate if they succeeded in removing Hitler. For some of these critics, negotiation with the Germans was attractive because it would leave the German military deployed in the East as a bulwark against Soviet power, which eventually extended into the heart of Europe. Indeed, as one postwar critic of the critics has argued, "much of the adverse comment [on unconditional surrender was] made in the heat of the immediate postwar period, and seems to be directly related to the authors' satisfaction or indignation with postwar American policy in Germany."[24] (This point is analogous to my discussion above about the legitimation of U.S. Cold War policy by way of "Morgenthau.") This retrospective criticism of unconditional surrender, moreover, was especially strong among the Germans themselves: even during the war "unconditional surrender" served for many Germans as the first element in a narrative of Anglo-American vengefulness.

Was this interpretation justified? Did "unconditional surrender" cynically disregard the German opposition for geopolitical reasons? Did it prolong the war? Did it truly indicate a desire for vengeance? The record is indeed complex, but Roosevelt, Churchill, and their supporters believed they had very good reasons for their position. For Roosevelt, "unconditional surrender" harkened back to General Ulysses S. Grant. At Appomattox, Grant was so obstinate during negotiations with General

22. See, for example, Fleming, *The New Dealers' War*. See also John P. Glennon, " 'This Time Germany Is a Defeated Nation.' "

23. In fact, German propagandists did not immediately exploit the opportunity because at the time they were emphasizing dissention among the Allies.

24. Chase, "Unconditional Surrender Reconsidered," 258.

Robert E. Lee that he was nicknamed "old Unconditional Surrender." (The label for Grant had originated as early as 1863 during an attack against Fort Donelson in Tennessee, at which time Grant's demand for unconditional surrender was accepted; this was the first of a number of important victories for Grant, and contributed greatly to his heroic status.) One problem in 1943, however, was that Grant's sense of "unconditional surrender" had referred to a rather limited context, the siege of a particular fort or the end of a single battle, rather than to an entire nation. What could it mean to demand that an entire nation surrender "unconditionally"?[25]

In 1918, before the armistice, the term "unconditional surrender" had appeared in the context of a proposal by the German High Command for a negotiated settlement based on President Woodrow Wilson's Fourteen Points. Wilson responded to the Germans that surrender rather than negotiation would have to be the basis for any settlement. Generals Hindenburg and Ludendorff rejected this as a call for unconditional surrender, and thus an affront to their honor as soldiers. But their government was already committed to peace. To avoid problems, the words "unconditional surrender" were therefore scrupulously avoided at the Paris Conference, but they hung over the proceedings throughout. Indeed, the Versailles settlement was infamous, and served the Nazis well as a propaganda tool through which they were able to attract many who shared their outrage at the settlement and its imputation of guilt. The Nazis blamed the Versailles settlement on the treachery of Germany's hasty political leaders, denying that the military defeat had been absolute. (Memory of the Versailles Treaty generally, as we will see, was a potent specter for much of the Anglo-American planning as well.)

Clearly, the demand for unconditional surrender in World War II was profoundly shaped by the desire to prevent the emergence of any new "stab in the back" legends: defeat would have to be total so no one could later claim that better terms could have been negotiated or that a different outcome might have been possible. The demand at Casablanca, moreover, was also an important signal to Stalin, who was frustrated with the Atlantic Allies for taking too long to open a second front in the West: unconditional surrender was an assurance that the British and Americans would not make a separate peace with any elements within Germany.[26] Given all the

---

25. Accounts of this background to unconditional surrender can be found in Armstrong, *Unconditional Surrender*; Sherwood, *Roosevelt and Hopkins*.

26. For analysis of the strategic dynamics of American policy—the ways in which U.S. and British planning was a complex process of anticipating, reacting to, and heading off Soviet

potential points of disagreement among the "Big Three," unconditional surrender was thus a sort of lowest common denominator.

More immediately important for Roosevelt was the controversy during the winter of 1942–43 over dealings with the French. In order to secure the acquiescence of French forces in the North Africa campaign, U.S. officials had negotiated with discreditable figures from the Vichy regime. Subsequently, Roosevelt wanted to make clear that this embarrassing debacle was an exception, and that the Allies would under no circumstances negotiate peace with the Nazis. This explains the timing of Roosevelt's statement, though not its genesis or meaning.

At the Casablanca press conference, Roosevelt explained the historical derivation of the "unconditional surrender" formula, but he apparently left out the most important aspect of the Grant–Lee reference. When Lee hesitated to accept Grant's categorical demand, Grant told him that he would have to trust in his fairness. After submitting, Lee broached the subject of his officers' horses, most of which belonged to the officers themselves. Grant replied that they should keep their horses, which they would need for spring plowing. The obvious implication of the Grant reference for Roosevelt was thus *magnanimity in victory*, exactly the opposite of what many understood by "unconditional surrender."[27] It did not help matters that Roosevelt did not make this clear in the first statement.

Strangely, Roosevelt claimed after the fact that the "unconditional surrender" formula was spontaneous on his part. Churchill, as well, claimed he was surprised by Roosevelt's statement at the press briefing, would have chosen other words, but supported it in principle (though he revised his

---

plans (and vice versa), see especially Gaddis, *The United States and the Origins of the Cold War in Europe;* Deighton, *The Impossible Peace;* Eisenberg, *Drawing the Line.* These works are only selections from a vast literature.

27. In his revised account of the statement, Roosevelt advisor and biographer Robert Sherwood mentions—though without decisive evaluation—the argument of a critic of his book's first edition that one of the problems with "unconditional surrender" was that it could be translated in different ways. The Germans, this correspondent asserted, rendered it as *bedingungslose Übergabe* (unconditional surrender) rather than as *Übergabe ohne Bedingungen* (surrender without conditions). The argument was that Germans would have understood Lee's capitulation to Grant as a "surrender without conditions" rather than as an "unconditional surrender." The latter implied a level of humiliation that Grant did not imply, and that Germans in 1943 found unacceptable. The linguistic distinction is indeed subtle, but so are codes of military and political symbolism (Sherwood, *Roosevelt and Hopkins,* 932). As we will see in a later chapter, the sociologist Ralf Dahrendorf makes a similar argument about the concept of "collective guilt," which he argues sounds different—harsher—in German (Dahrendorf, *Society and Democracy in Germany,* 288–89).

claim to have been surprised in 1949). Roosevelt's advisor and biographer Robert Sherwood has speculated that FDR's claim to spontaneity was part of an effort to spare Churchill from responsibility for what was surely taken as a hard pill by ordinary British citizens, for whom unconditional surrender spelled out the struggle they still had in front of them.[28] Nevertheless, the term's use, as well as Roosevelt's intentions, were well prepared. In his January 7, 1943, State of the Union Address to Congress—thus directly in advance of his trip to Casablanca—Roosevelt had stated that he "shudder[ed] to think of what will happen to humanity, including ourselves, if this war ends in an inconclusive peace, and another war breaks out when the babies of today have grown to fighting age."[29] At the Casablanca press conference on January 24, in fact, Roosevelt carried notes with the following formulation (though he neglected to read from them):

> The President and the Prime Minister, after a complete survey of the world war situation, are more than ever determined that peace can come to the world only by a total elimination of German and Japanese war power. This involves the simple formula of placing the objective of this war in terms of an unconditional surrender by Germany, Italy, and Japan. Unconditional surrender by them means a reasonable assurance of world peace, for generations. Unconditional · surrender means not the destruction of the German populace, nor of the Italian or Japanese populace, but does mean the destruction of a philosophy in Germany, Italy and Japan which is based on the conquest and subjugation of other peoples.[30]

This formulation was the result of long and deliberate work in a number of different committees, and presaged later policies of radical demilitarization (and even deindustrialization, depending on how "total elimination" is to be understood) and, as we will see shortly, of "re-education."

Either way, claims that the demand for unconditional surrender indicated a vindictive posture on Roosevelt's part willfully distort the record. Following the statement, Roosevelt was at great pains to hammer home the idea that his posture was not vengeful. In an address to the White House Correspondents Association on February 12, 1943, Roosevelt stated that "[i]n our uncompromising policy we mean no harm to the common people of the Axis nations . . ." though adding that "we do mean to impose punishment and retribution in full upon their guilty, barbaric

---

28. Sherwood, *Roosevelt and Hopkins*, 930–32.
29. Here, again, the specter of the 1918 settlement was powerful.
30. Sherwood, *Roosevelt and Hopkins*, 665.

leaders." In an August 25, 1943, message to Congress, he stated, "Except for the responsible fascist leaders, the people of the Axis need not fear unconditional surrender to the United Nations.[31] . . . The people of Axis-controlled areas may be assured that when they agree to unconditional surrender they will not be trading Axis despotism for ruin under the United Nations." In his Christmas Eve 1943 radio address, Roosevelt stated again that

> [t]he United Nations have no intention to enslave the German people. We wish them to have a normal chance to develop, in peace, as useful and respectable members of the European family. But we most certainly emphasize the word "respectable"—for we intend to rid them once and for all of Nazism and Prussian militarism and the fantastic and disastrous notion that they constitute the "master race."

For obstinate critics, however, none of this added up to much. In his memoir, for instance, Secretary of State Cordell Hull wrote that "[t]he public statements made at different times by the leaders of the three major Allies to soften the interpretation of unconditional surrender did not conduce to the early surrender of Germany. The Nazi propaganda machine continued until the last to stress its drastic interpretation of unconditional surrender."[32] Both statements, of course can be true without being causally related: Roosevelt's efforts to make the magnanimity argument probably did not shorten the war; the Nazi propagandists certainly did try to make the most of it until the last, though this is unlikely to have made any real difference in the manic last months of fighting. The bottom line, however, is that it was not Roosevelt's goal to shorten the war. He believed firmly that the peace would only last if it was absolute. Roosevelt's desire for total defeat of Germany, therefore, was not primarily a matter of vengefulness (though, as we will see, his attitude toward Germany was not without a negative assessment of the German national character).

One reason for Hull's opposition to the demand was that he believed it would require the Allies to assume vast and long-term obligations in postwar Germany. Indeed, while Stalin supported unconditional surrender as a general principle (he declared this in his 1943 May Day Address), he too pushed for specification of the formula, though for different reasons than

---

31. At the time, this term referred to the Big Three (United States, Great Britain, Soviet Union) and their allies rather than to the international organization, which was not founded until after the war.

32. Hull, *Memoirs*, 1581.

Hull. Hull wanted to avoid all postwar entanglements for the United States; Stalin wanted to pin them down. Roosevelt, however, avoided the trap, and refused to specify any particular obligations or policies the United States would assume. As Roosevelt argued in a reply to yet another entreaty from Hull, "Whatever words we might agree on would probably have to be modified or changed the first time some nation wanted to surrender."[33] In this regard, the memory of Wilson's failure to attain congressional approval for the peace settlement he negotiated in 1919 was a potent warning for Roosevelt.

Indeed, as we will see, during the debate over the Morgenthau Plan in 1944–45, and in subsequent accounts of it, there was much frustration over Roosevelt's refusal to come down firmly, at least more than temporarily, on one or the other side—either for Morgenthau or for Stimson. In light of this debate with Hull over unconditional surrender, however, this may well have been a continuation of Roosevelt's desire not to commit prematurely to any particular course of action that would limit his room for maneuver after victory, and not, as it has usually been portrayed, a matter of Roosevelt's failing health and slipping grasp on the complexities. In fact, there is a remarkable (though usually unremarked) analogy between the situations. As we will see, after the Quebec Conference in 1944 Roosevelt denied to Stimson that he had intentionally agreed to the Morgenthau plan, a claim usually accepted as evidence of Roosevelt's declining mental grasp of events. Recalling that Roosevelt claimed that unconditional surrender had been spontaneous at Casablanca, however, one could reasonably conclude that Roosevelt was simply being true to form in 1944 after Quebec. Those who maintain that Roosevelt was enfeebled when he agreed to the Morgenthau plan, of course, have an interest in believing Roosevelt really did not mean it.

Regime, People, and Punishment

Beyond these strategic and tactical considerations, perhaps the most important facet of unconditional surrender was the underlying philosophy it indicated. For many Americans, the fight against Germany was a moral crusade. As Roosevelt had put it in his January 6, 1942, Message to

33. Roosevelt was also motivated partly by a commitment to "self-determination" as stated in the Atlantic Charter, and partly by the desire to avoid resistance among domestic Republicans, who he knew would balk at the prospect of a long involvement in Europe. See Gaddis, *The United States and the Origins of the Cold War*, 12–13.

Congress, "There has never been—there can never be—successful compromise between good and evil. Only total victory can reward the champions of tolerance, and decency, and faith."[34] Roosevelt and many others had long maintained the necessity of punishment. How far into the German population that punishment would extend, however, was unclear. The Allies certainly intended to purge the country not only of National Socialism, but of what they believed to be a pervasive culture of "militarism." In October 1942, for instance, Roosevelt stated, "The German people are not going to be enslaved—because the United Nations do not traffic in human slavery. But it will be necessary for them to earn their way back into the fellowship of peace-loving and law-abiding nations." Roosevelt, like many American leaders and ordinary people, regarded German *society* in its entirety, rather than just the temporary German leadership, as the source of trouble. Therefore, no easy distinction, so common in the history of modern warfare and essential to the identity of many Germans after the war, between regime and people was appropriate.

As a result of such a view, Vice President Henry Wallace said in a December 29, 1942, radio address—thus shortly before Roosevelt's trip to Casablanca—"The German people must learn to un-learn all that they have been taught, not only by Hitler, but his predecessors in the last hundred years, by so many of their philosophers and teachers, the disciples of blood and iron.... We must *de-educate* and *re-educate* people for democracy. ... The only hope for Europe remains *a change of mentality* on the part of the German. He must be taught to give up the century-old conception that his is a master race" (emphasis added).[35] This idea of "re-educating" "*the German*" was at the heart of debates, both governmental and public, over what the appropriate posture toward Germany should be, though not all formulations were as reductive as this singularization of "the German." It is important to note, however, that the refusal to distinguish between regime and people was consistent with the German theory of "total war," in which it was equally impossible to distinguish between combatants and civilians.

34. This and the following Roosevelt quotes are taken from Armstrong, *Unconditional Surrender*.

35. According to Theodor Eschenburg (*Jahre der Besatzung*, echoed in Bark and Gress, *From Shadow to Substance*), Wallace's ideas on re-education were influence by the German émigré journalist Leopold Schwarzschild, whose book *World in Trance: From Versailles to Pearl Harbor* we will encounter in the next chapter.

CHAPTER 3

Culture and Character

Public Opinion

According to opinion polling during World War II, the majority of Americans did in fact distinguish between the German people and the Nazi regime, though the tendency diminished after the invasion of Europe (the proportion of Americans agreeing that Germans would always be warlike went from 23 percent in February 1942 to 37 percent in December 1944; the proportion agreeing that Germans did not like war and were otherwise just like everyone else decreased in the same time frame from 45 percent to 26 percent). A February 1944 National Opinion Research Center (NORC) poll found that 64 percent of Americans thought that most Germans would like to get rid of the Nazis, though only 31 percent thought they were capable of doing so. This was in significant contrast to views on Japan, which were steady in their unwillingness to distinguish between the Japanese leadership and ordinary Japanese people (this skepticism extended to the loyalties of Japanese Americans).[1]

Regarding plans for the postwar treatment of Germany, most Americans believed ordinary Germans should not be held accountable "for the cruelties to religious groups, the mass killings in occupied countries, and the tortures in concentration camps," despite the fact that 76 percent believed that "the Germans have murdered many people in the concentration camps." The problem with interpreting this finding, however, is that it predated revelations about *extermination* of Jews and others, and only 18 percent of respondents estimated the total number of murders to be more than 1 million. For the postwar period, a majority of Americans thus recommended leniency, with a substantial minority recommending strict

---

1. Data in this and the next paragraph are reported in Field and Van Patten, "If the American People Made the Peace."

supervision. According to a January 1944 *Fortune* magazine poll, about 30 percent favored breaking up Germany into smaller states. Regarding postwar economic support, the comparison to Japan is again striking: almost twice as many Americans were in favor of food support for Germany as for Japan.

Attitudes toward Germany, unsurprisingly, were a good deal harsher in Great Britain, Australia, and even Canada. In the spring of 1943, for instance, a British poll reported that 43 percent of respondents either hated or had no sympathy for Germans. This fraction increased to 54 percent by February 1945. In a series of wartime polls, fully one-third of respondents called for revenge, and another third merely for preventing Germany from ever being able to make war again. According to British Institute of Public Opinion polls in 1944, large majorities of British wanted Germans to rebuild the countries their army had destroyed, demanded reparations, and supported partitioning Germany into numerous small states.[2]

In broader public discourse, support was available for virtually any position that could be imagined. Just like the policy planners, public commentators on Germany faced two basic sets of questions: First, to what extent did National Socialism express something authentic to the "German spirit" or emanate from German "national character"? Was National Socialism a new phenomenon, or did it fit with long-standing patterns of aggression and militaristic obedience? When in German history—and here the main options were Luther, Friedrich, Bismarck, and Hitler—did the problem emerge? Was there one Germany, that of National Socialism; or were there two Germanies, one National Socialist and the other the "true" Germany of culture (*Kultur*), humanism, and the Enlightenment? If there existed an "Other Germany," who were its proper representatives, how should they be treated, and what would their role be after the war? Second, given the answers to the first set of questions, what was to be done with Germany after the war? Had Germany forfeited its right to national existence? Was it enough to "decapitate" the regime and impose a democratic system? Or was more thorough "re-education" of Germany for democratic political culture appropriate? Was re-education enough, or was a genuine social revolution—one dismantling entrenched economic and political arrangements—required? If the latter, which elements of German society were most important, and what kinds of changes would be most effective, and how long would they take? Who should be in charge of instituting these transformations?

2. These data are summarized in Goldman, "Germans and Nazis," especially 157.

Vansittart and Gollancz

Other than the debate over the Morgenthau Plan in 1944–45 (which I consider in detail in the next chapter), perhaps the most significant discussion about the nature of the German problem and what to do about it after the war took place in Britain (though certainly noted by many in the United States) concerning the statements of Lord Robert Vansittart. From 1930 to 1937, Vansittart had been head of the British Foreign Office, where he warned repeatedly of the German threat, urging his government to rearm.[3] Despite being one of the most influential figures in government under two prime ministers (MacDonald and Baldwin), however, Vansittart's influence declined precipitously with Neville Chamberlain's election. Vansittart strongly opposed Chamberlain's efforts to "appease" the Nazis with territorial and other concessions. Too powerful to be pushed out entirely, however, Vansittart was appointed to a title designed just for him—Chief Diplomatic Advisor to the Government—which maintained his prestige, yet, because of the strictures on public advocacy by civil servants, severely constrained his ability to express his opinions. Upon his retirement in 1941, Vansittart took up a vigorous schedule of writing and lecturing, most of it on German issues.

As a young man, Vansittart had spent time in Germany, where he experienced anti-British attitudes and what he viewed as repulsive Prussian militarism. He wrote extensively of these experiences as a foundation for his understanding of Germany, in the process giving ammunition to critics. On this basis, many dismissed his opposition to appeasement and subsequent agitation against a "soft" peace as simple anti-German racism. In fact, "Vansittartism" took on a more generally negative meaning than anything specific to the writing and speeches of Vansittart himself, and he and his supporters were at best ambivalent about the term, which they had not coined.

At the very beginning of the war in September 1939, Prime Minister Chamberlain stated, "We have no cause for dispute with the German people other than that they allow themselves to be ruled by the Nazi regime." This did indeed remain a common sentiment, though seemingly less common than the contrasting views expressed by Vansittart. In February 1940, still in government service, Vansittart pressed for a pronouncement that those responsible for atrocities in Poland would not escape with their lives. As a result, on April 17, 1940, contrary to Chamberlain's initial statement

---

3. Important works on Vansittart include Später, *Vansittart*; Roi, *Alternative to Appeasement*; Rose, *Vansittart*; and Goldman, "Germans and Nazis."

(which he had in fact subsequently revised), a British, French, and Polish declaration laid responsibility on the entire German people. By the middle of 1940, early hopes for a compromise settlement had given way to an uncompromising stance. In August, Chamberlain's replacement—Winston Churchill—stated Britain's war aim as "total victory," which meant that there would be no armistice until Germany restored independence to all conquered lands and overthrew the Nazi regime. In effect, this demand was very little different than that for "unconditional surrender" at Casablanca nearly three years later.

In December 1940, Vansittart obtained permission to deliver a series of lectures on Germany to be broadcast on BBC overseas radio. Excerpts were carried in the *Sunday Times*, and then reprinted in 1941 as a best-selling book, *Black Record: Germans Past and Present*. There Vansittart identified the leading spirit in Germany as that of the "butcher-bird" that lives by preying on smaller, weaker birds. This creature, he diagnosed, was held aloft on the wings of envy, self-pity, and cruelty. Hitler, in this regard, was neither a novelty nor alien to most Germans. "The atrocities committed under this German Regime," Vansittart firmly believed, ". . . are no accidental and ephemeral outcrop. They are a reversion to something much further back than the Kaiser, or Bismarck, or Frederick, to the doings of a thousand, and two thousand, years ago."[4] As a result, "Nazism is not an aberration but an outcome."[5] Moreover, the few Germans not possessed of the butcher-bird spirit, whose existence Vansittart did acknowledge, he claimed had been entirely ineffective. Hitler, Vansittart charged, thus "gives to the great majority of Germans exactly what they have hitherto liked and wanted."[6] Vansittart's point in all of this was his belief that recognizing these characteristics of National Socialism's place in Germany was essential to the prospect of future peace. He was concerned that British propaganda was too soft; the BBC's effort up to that point to distinguish between Germans and Nazis, he believed, contributed to a sense of unaccountability among Germans, and was thus unlikely to hinder atrocities in the same way that assurances of being punished would. Apparently, Churchill did not disagree too vigorously. In a world broadcast in April 1941, Churchill stated, "There are less than seventy million malignant huns—some of whom are curable and others killable."[7]

4. Vansittart, *Black Record*, x.
5. Ibid., 45.
6. Ibid., 18.
7. Goldman, "Germans and Nazis"; and Friedmann and Später, "Britische und deutsche Kollektivschulddebatte."

Vansittart spent much of 1942 and 1943 expanding his views and defending himself against waves of criticism. A 1942 book by the exiled socialist Heinrich Fraenkel—titled *Vansittart's Gift for Goebbels: A German Exile's Answer to Black Record*—charged that Vansittart's position supported Goebbels's claim that ordinary Germans and the Nazis "must sink or swim together." Indeed, following the 1943 publication of Vansittart's *Lessons of My Life*, Goebbels wrote that "[t]his fellow Vansittart is really worth his weight in gold to our propaganda. After the war a monument ought to be erected to him somewhere in Germany with the inscription, 'to the Englishman who rendered the greatest service to the German cause during the war.'"[8] Of course, even claims that something was beneficial to propaganda were, in Goebbels's hands, themselves propagandistic.

In the same context, however, Frank Owen of the *London Evening Standard* charged in February 1942 along similar lines that Vansittart was driving thousands of potential anti-Nazi Germans back into Hitler's arms, enabling the Nazis to scare their population with an image of British vengefulness that had abandoned the Atlantic Charter. Vansittart's response was that he could not be uniting the Germans behind Hitler since they were already united (Churchill offered exactly the same defense to critics of unconditional surrender a year later). Most serious of the charges came in a *New Statesman* article arguing that Vansittart's indictment of German culture and character was a form of racism, making Vansittart "a kind of Nazi inside out." Vansittart responded repeatedly to such charges, insisting that he was no "racialist." In his defense, he distinguished between Germanaphobia based on the biological logic of heritable traits (a Nazi logic) and beliefs based on the experience of German behavior. For Vansittart, however, it *was* nonetheless legitimate to indict an entire nation. Against the charge that he advocated the wholesale extermination of the German people, he could only assert that this was a preposterous falsehood. Vansittart demanded a retraction by the *New Statesman*, though to no avail. (A lawsuit against *Time* magazine for attacking his record during the 1930s as a way of discrediting his position in the 1940s was more successful, evoking an apology from his friend Henry Luce.)[9]

An even more vituperative debate took place when Vansittart joined the House of Lords in March 1942. One of his primary opponents was G. K. A. Bell, bishop of Chichester. For Bell, the record of the German Protestant Church was a sure sign that not all Germans were Nazis. Bell also believed

8. Roi, *Alternative to Appeasement*, 11.
9. See Später, *Vansittart*, 137.

that the image of punishment would only serve to unite Germany. Another critic was the legislator Eleanor Rathbone, who argued that Vansittart expected too much from ordinary Germans when he pointed out the lack of significant opposition. The most vigorous attacks, however, came from socialists, among whom the publisher Victor Gollancz was perhaps the most significant. Gollancz's 1942 book—*Shall Our Children Live or Die?*—was an emotional argument against what he perceived as Vansittart's propagation of race hatred and blood lust. Gollancz dismissed Vansittart's claim that Germans are uniquely warlike as ridiculous, countering that "wars have been endemic in humanity.... It is vulgar," Gollancz thus argued, "to blame the German people—the toy-maker of Nuernberg or the steel-worker of the Ruhr—for something which lies deep in history."[10]

As a man of the Left, Gollancz's main objection was that Vansittart's account blamed the putatively aggressive German character, in the process distracting from the real cause—imperialism—which he argued was endemic to the capitalist West generally. Gollancz went so far as to deny that he hated even Hitler—it was right to hate Nazi crimes, but wrong to seek vengeance, Gollancz believed, since "every one of us is guilty."[11] During the war, the real damage, according to Gollancz, was the denigration of the exiles and of the internal opposition. In his above-mentioned book, for instance, Heinrich Fraenkel rested much on the observation that so many *Germans* had passed through concentration camps. The implication of this, for Fraenkel and Gollancz, was that denying the distinction between regime and *Volk* was blatantly unrealistic. For them, the German opposition was, as it was later called, an "alibi" for the nation, making collective condemnations—and policies based on them—illegitimate.[12]

In contrast, Vansittart had little sympathy either for the exiles or for Hitler's opponents in Germany. The former he believed were unrepentant "pan-Germanists,"[13] the latter Prussian militarists who would make very little difference indeed. Moreover, one should not, Vansittart warned, be "blinded by the side-shows of German literature, medicine, music, and philosophy."[14] Regarding the internal opposition, Vansittart was very much in line with Churchill's assessment: following the July 20, 1944, plot

10. Gollancz, *Shall Our Children Live or Die?* 32.

11. Ibid., 65, 72.

12. See Glees, *Exile Politics during the Second World War.*

13. As we will see shortly, Emil Ludwig made the same argument against German exiles in the United States.

14. Vansittart, *Black Record,* 56.

against Hitler and Hitler's brutal response, Churchill dismissively announced merely that the "highest personalities in the German Reich are murdering one another, or trying to."

On the basis of his assessment of German history and character, Vansittart supported a prolonged occupation of Germany and called for permanent disarmament, control and pruning of German industrial capacity (including prohibitions on machine tool manufacture, aviation, and oil refining), international control of the Ruhr Valley, and partition of Prussia (though not of all of Germany), though his economic proposals did not go quite as far as Morgenthau's later ones. Additionally, he was adamant that while Germans should not be starved, they should "not enjoy a standard of living higher than their victims."[15] In this his proposal matched Morgenthau's.

The debate over Vansittartism, however, did not end with the war. Indeed, it was particularly during the occupation that Gollancz's reputation truly flowered.[16] His attacks on what he saw as an inhumane occupation regime figured in German critiques and as "independent" proof of unnecessary German suffering. Following the war, Gollancz made the extent of his charges clear in the title of his book *Our Threatened Values*, in which he argued that the tradition of humanitarianism and respect for individual rights itself was at stake. He provided extensive detail of ordinary German suffering particularly in the two winters following the war, and laid blame for it squarely on the occupation authorities. It was indeed true that ordinary Germans experienced terrible hardships and dislocations during the occupation. Who was to blame and what could be done, however, were more complicated questions than Gollancz and his German admirers allowed.

In this context, Vansittart's reputation among Germans remained significant as well, albeit merely in the opposite direction. As during the war, "Vansittart" stood as an emblem of Germany's misfortune and Anglo-American misunderstanding. But what exactly that meant remained obscure. On the one hand, "Vansittart" was a simple bugaboo, divorced from any specific content. On the other hand, the course of the occupation ended up looking very much like what he had proposed during the war, though not always for the reasons Vansittart had proposed it. The point is that much of what was felt in Germany as harsh, punitive, or unconstructive was seen as continuous with a long-standing program of illegitimate

15. Vansittart's proposals for the occupation are stated most clearly in his *Bones of Contention*, 46–61.

16. See especially Farquharson, " 'Emotional but Influential.' "

Germany-baiting. As Michael Roi has argued in his study of Vansittart, however, "the evidence does not support the argument espoused by Vansittart's critics that his prescient assessment of the German menace in the 1930s sprang from the Permanent Undersecretary's ethnic prejudice against the Germans."[17]

That Vansittart fit the bill of an extreme German hater without a legitimate argument, that his utterances helped German propaganda, or that all the miseries of the occupation were the result of "Vansittartism" are highly questionable, though usually entirely unconsidered. Indeed, as German intellectuals and postwar opinion leaders debated the finer points of German accountability (or lack of it) for National Socialism, in the process reasserting at every opportunity the distinction between regime and *Volk*, Vansittart reflected on what his position entailed for postwar German discussions. Invited in 1949 by the editor of the *Wiener Library Bulletin*, Alfred Wiener, to respond to a collection on "Crime and Atonement" including statements by such prominent Germans as Protestant leader Pastor Martin Niemöller, Vansittart wrote that he did not expect Germans to be particularly repentant and did not assert a German collective guilt in the legal sense. Nevertheless, he was surprised and, even at that late date, disappointed with the evasions he noted in the postwar German discourse, though by 1949 this was already a minority position.[18]

The Journalistic Spectrum

The debate over Vansittartism, which had its peak in 1942–43, was only one focal point in a highly differentiated landscape of commentary. Lacking a galvanizing central figure like Vansittart, at least before the Morgenthau debate in 1944–45, the U.S. discourse was perhaps even more dispersed than the British, for whom Vansittartism was a central organizing referent. Nevertheless, the same questions of how well National Socialism fit with earlier German history, how responsible ordinary Germans were for it, and what should be done about it were operative throughout the Anglo-American public discourse, though in the United States there was more optimism about the project of reforming an entire nation with rational and scientific policy programs.[19] (Interestingly, the official

---

17. Roi, *Alternative to Appeasement*, 1. See also Später, *Vansittart*, introduction.

18. Vansittart, "Crime and Atonement," *Wiener Library Bulletin*, May–June 1949.

19. See, for instance, Reuther, *"Die ambivalente Normalisierung."*

discourse in Britain was harsher during the war, but denazification and other such measures were less stringent in the British zone after the war, in part because many British officials did not believe it was truly possible to re-educate an entire country.) While direct links between public commentary and policymaking are nearly impossible to demonstrate (only partly because in some cases there was no direct link), the available spectrum of argument is representative of the climate of opinion in which policymakers were working; many of the same themes occurred in both public discourse and policymaking, policymakers were indeed aware of their "audience," and commentators often had important insights into the policies under development. Furthermore, in a moment of total mobilization for war, many intellectuals were either directly or indirectly involved in policymaking and military administration. Not always being able to demonstrate direct effects thus does not prove that they did not exist or that indirect ones were not significant.

"Soft Peace"

Public commentary on Germany is usually characterized as having been divided between proponents of supposed "soft peace" versus proponents of supposed "hard peace," though this vocabulary is reductive and not always insightful. Among the most influential "softer" positions on postwar Germany was that of the Royal Institute of International Affairs in England. The report of their meeting at Chatham House in 1943 argued pragmatically that German national feeling would persist and thus that any efforts to disrupt it through partition or degradation would produce nothing but revanchism. For the authors of this study, Germany merely concentrated trends that were common to modern Western societies in general. In this regard, their interpretation was consonant with postwar interpretations by many German historians, which I examine in chapter 8. The message of the Chatham House report, however, was that nothing more than the principles stated in the Atlantic Charter of 1941 were necessary to guide judicious policy. The report supported re-education, but argued that this must be a German matter; the democratic nations could only help. Regarding industry, remembering how easily the Nazis had subverted Versailles, they argued that preventing rearmament was primarily a matter of convincing Germans not to desire it since almost all other measures could be evaded.[20]

20. Royal Institute of International Affairs, *The Problem of Germany*.

The influential American journalist Vera Micheles Dean, editor of *Foreign Policy Reports*, argued in an article asking "What Future for Germany?" along the same lines as the Chatham House report: "The German people," she wrote, "should be neither willfully humiliated nor indefinitely reduced to subjection," although she also believed they bore some responsibility for their continued support of Hitler at the time of her writing in 1943. Nevertheless, unlike some others, Dean resisted the idea of seeking an early peace, especially if it involved compromised elements like representatives of heavy industry or the *Junker* aristocracy. Again like the report of Chatham House, however, she also believed disarmament by dismantling industry was not likely to be helpful since it was the will to arms rather than the arms themselves that was responsible for war. On the other hand, Dean did prescribe, as a sort of penance, German labor battalions to rebuild areas the German army had destroyed. She believed such a gesture would enhance the distinction between regime and *Volk*.[21] For her part, the renowned journalist Dorothy Thompson, despite having been expelled from Germany for her prewar reports on Hitler[22] and having argued that Hitler expressed pathologies in German society, ultimately felt that the Germans were basically like other peoples. Thompson was substantially more sympathetic than many others to the German opposition and the idea of negotiated peace. She also believed partition would cause an unproductive backlash, and refused to treat the Germans as fundamentally evil.[23]

"Hard Peace"

In many cases, the "hard" positions at the other end of the spectrum were substantially more sensationalist; this was in the very nature of the position. However, that is not to say that there were not more and less reasoned versions of various arguments, and more and less acceptable proposals within

21. Dean, "What Future for Germany?" For a discussion of this and related works, see Lach, "What They Would Do about Germany."

22. In a famous 1940 *Foreign Affairs* article, Thompson wrote: "What frustration must be in this man . . . so sensitive, so cruel, so weak, and so aggressive! And those characters around him—perverts and adventurers, frustrated intellectuals who could not hold a job in any good newspaper or get their plays produced or their books published." Thompson, "The Problem Child of Europe."

23. It is interesting, in this light, that Vansittart dedicated *Black Record* to Thompson. See "Vansittart, Dorothy Thompson Argue the Hard Peace Question," *Newsweek*, October 9, 1944, 104–111.

the "hard" camp, though even calling it a "camp" is saying too much. Indeed, lumping together the wildly divergent versions of "hard" positions served the interests of those who sought to discredit the more reasonable versions with the taint of the more extreme ones.

Perhaps the most extreme bile-filled diatribe was Theodor Kaufman's unsubtly titled *Germany Must Perish!*, which received much more attention than it deserved in part due to its usefulness in German propaganda. The basic point of the book was that because Germany had started a total war, it had earned total destruction as a nation. However, the book was optimistic: it argued that with some application and commitment, it would be possible to sterilize all [*sic*] adult Germans in a mere three years! German land was to be divided among neighboring states, and those German people who survived extensive purges should be dispersed among other nations, where they would be forced to assimilate linguistically and culturally, thus solving the German problem once and for all. This self-published book by a New Jersey theater ticket salesman, however, caught the eye of the German propaganda machine, which falsely asserted that Kaufman was an agent of Roosevelt's, who, it was ridiculously claimed, had provided the book's argument. Richard Merritt has pointed out that rumor of this "Jewish manifesto" was raised at the Wannsee Conference, at which final plans for the "final solution" were formed.[24]

Unfortunately, Kaufman's was not the only such extreme formulation. Dorothy Snow Smith and Wilson M. Southam published a book in 1945, and again the title says all: *No Germany therefore No More German Wars*. Charles Braybook called his 1945 none-too-subtle diatribe *Here Is Your Hun: A Five Thousand Year Saga of Hun Wars, Murder, Rapine, and Savagery*. A book by the journalist Sigrid Schultz was perhaps more disturbing because the author was able to claim deep familiarity with German culture: she had a German father, grew up in Germany, and had served as Berlin correspondent for the *Chicago Tribune* from 1919 to 1941, and was thus a more creditable figure. Schultz's book, titled *Germany Will Try It Again*, placed particular weight on the role of a secret German General Staff after World War I, and claimed that plans were already in place to accomplish the same reemergence after World War II (the claim was not entirely unsubstantiated). As a dramatic warning, one chapter of the book was titled "Nazism Is Contagious." Interestingly, however, Schulz argued that National Socialism represented a recent deformation of the German character rather than being the manifestation of ancient yearnings.

24. Merritt, *Democracy Imposed*, 28.

Again, the false impression given by (well-justified!) critics of these arguments was that there was no basis whatsoever for punitive policies, and that anyone who offered such an argument was similar to execrable characters like Kaufman. Casual accounts of the Morgenthau Plan, for instance, often attribute to Morgenthau Kaufman's sterilization suggestion, among other measures Morgenthau never advocated. But there were quite a few reasonable and respected figures in the United States and Great Britain (aside from Vansittart and his direct supporters) who were still quite dubious about the quick rehabilitation of Germany, particularly of its economy. One of the earliest and best-informed anti-German accounts was that of the renowned American journalist, William L. Shirer, whose *Berlin Diary* was published in 1941. (Shirer's more famous *The Rise and Fall of the Third Reich*—perhaps the best known of all books about the Nazis—engendered significantly more controversy when it was published in 1960 and was vigorously attacked in West Germany as an anti-German diatribe.)[25] In *Berlin Diary*, Shirer did not prescribe any particular program for the postwar, since the war was far from won when he went to press. He did, however, offer a fairly negative assessment of German "national character":

> It is not correct to say, as many of our liberals at home have said, that Nazism is a form of rule and life unnatural to the German people and forced upon them against their wish by a few fanatic derelicts of the last war. It is true that the Nazi Party never polled a majority vote in Germany in a free election, though it came very close. But for the last three or four years the Nazi regime has expressed something very deep in the German nature and in that respect it has been representative of the people it rules.

Nevertheless, while Shirer's *Berlin Diary* does portray ordinary Germans as dangerously obedient to their leaders, according to Shirer there was not enthusiastic support for war in the general population. It is also important to note, however, that Shirer had almost nothing to say about Nazi policy toward the Jews, failing to comment on either the 1935 Nuremberg Racial Laws or on the events of November 9, 1938 (*Kristallnacht*).[26]

25. On the controversy, see Rosenfeld, "The Reception of William L. Shirer's *The Rise and Fall of the Third Reich*."

26. Quote from Shirer, *Berlin Diary*, 584. On Shirer's nonreference to Jews, see ibid., introduction by Gordon Craig.

The historian A. J. P. Taylor expressed a view similar to Shirer's.[27] In 1943, Taylor was commissioned by the British Foreign Office to write a chapter on the Weimar Republic for a handbook for future occupation troops. When his essay was rejected as too "one-sided and partisan," Taylor decided to make it the centerpiece of a book, which he published in 1945 as *The Course of German History*, next to Shirer's *Rise and Fall* perhaps one of the best-known works on National Socialism. In many ways echoing Shirer's earlier account, Taylor wrote that "[t]he history of the Germans is a history of extremes. It contains everything except moderation, and in the course of a thousand years the Germans have experienced everything except normality. . . . Only the normal person, not particularly good, not particularly bad, healthy, sane, moderate—he has never sat his stamp on German history." Taylor's indictment, moreover, did not focus, as did many other critical accounts, on the negative impact solely of Prussianism, but swept up even the failed liberal spirit of 1848 as in some sense both condemnable and typically German. Like many others, Taylor also asserted that National Socialism was "a system which represented the deepest wishes of the German people," which included the desire to enslave other peoples. Taylor went on, of course, to an enormously distinguished career as an historian, though never entirely free of controversy.

The Lifeboat of Exile

More difficult to characterize than straightforward "soft" and "hard" arguments was the more complex array of opinions among exiles.[28] The basic legitimating myth[29] of most exiles was the idea that there were two Germanies—the apparent Germany of Hitler and the "true" Germany of culture, humanism, and the Enlightenment—known as the "Other Germany"—the core of which they were preserving in the "lifeboat" of exile (exile was a lifeboat for them as individuals, but also for German culture).[30] An important early formulation of this claim was expressed by Klaus and Erika Mann (children of Thomas, winner of the Nobel Prize for

27. On Shirer and Taylor, see Friedmann and Später, "Britische und deutsche Kollektivschuld-Debatte."

28. See Radkau, *Die deutsche Emigration in den USA*.

29. Again, calling something a myth points out its organizing capacity, not necessarily its falsity. See Herz and Schwab-Trapp, *Umkämpfte Vergangenheit*.

30. In contrast, conservative exiles from revolutionary France had referred to exile as a "shipwreck." Fritzsche, *Stranded in the Present*, 73.

Literature and living embodiment for many of German humanism), who published a pamphlet in 1940 called *The Other Germany*, as well as profiles of various prominent exiles called *Escape to Life*.[31] Along similar lines, Frederick Foerster, a German educator who had become librarian of Columbia University, argued in his 1940 book *Europe and the German Question* that National Socialism was a significant departure from the course of German history. Others charged that those who believed there was no difference between the Nazis and the German people were playing into Hitler's hands, because Hitler also claimed there was no distinction between regime and *Volk*. Another prominent advocate of such a position was Ferdinand A. Hermens, a philosophy professor at Notre Dame who had been a member of the Center Party during the Weimar period. The title of his book says it all: *The Tyrants' War and the Peoples' Peace*. Hermens asserted that the idea that there was no distinction between regime and *Volk* was merely wartime propaganda. For his part, the Austrian socialist and journalist Julius Braunthal argued in *Need Germany Survive?* that fascism was no more a German phenomenon than capitalism an American phenomenon.[32]

Representatives of the "Other Germany" thus shared the conviction that Germans could not be collectively guilty, but they differed on why not and on what was to be done. While the range of positions and motivations within the exile "community" was broad ("communities" would be a more apt designation), their discourse can usefully be divided into a right wing and a left wing. By far, the largest single group of exiles was the socialists, but there were also numerous liberals (in the European sense of free market rather than the American sense of left wing) and even some older-style nationalists who had nonetheless fallen afoul of the Nazi regime. For the latter groups, all that was necessary was for the Nazi regime to be replaced, since most Germans, they asserted, had not wanted it in the first place. Sources of democratic tradition could be found in the

31. As we will see in chapter 7, their father did not entirely share their assertion of two distinct Germanies. According to Rebbeca Boehling, the term "Other Germany" (*andere Deutschland*) likely derived from the eponymous Weimer era German newspaper, which was associated with the interwar German peace movement and critical of Prussian traditions. Boehling, *A Question of Priorities*, 16. In contrast, the Israeli journalist Tom Segev ascribed the term "The Other Germany" to the newspaper *Haaretz*, which used it in 1933 to argue that "all Hitlers in the world cannot eliminate the names Kant, Goethe, and Schiller from German history." Segev, *The Seventh Million*, 17–18.

32. For a wider discussion of these works, see Lach, "What They Would Do about Germany."

memory of 1848 (despite Taylor's indictment) and the legacies of German culture, particularly Goethe. Members of the Association of Free Germans, for instance, asserted in a 1943 book (*Germany: To Be or Not to Be?*) that "democracy, though temporarily defeated, is by no means dead in Germany." Indeed, nonsocialist exiles, who included a number of prominent former political leaders and intellectuals, often saw themselves ready to step into the breach once the Nazis were defeated. Support for this interpretation could be found in organizations like the American Friends of German Freedom, which was formed in New York in 1936 by such well-known personages (some German, some not) as Paul Tillich, Lewis Mumford, and Reinhold Niebuhr. One of this group's main purposes was to counteract total condemnation of German culture by asserting the claims of the "Other Germany." In a collectively-authored book published in 1944, for instance, the organization stated that it was easy to understand why, given the brutality of the regime, many Americans were biased against all things German. But they nevertheless condemned as reverse racism the assertion "that the German people are different from all others, that there is a thousand-year history to prove the eternal evil residing in the blood and bones of the Teutonic race."[33] (In many ways, this sounded much like Frank Owen's charge against Vansittart discussed above.) A major concern of such groups was that a vindictive posture was negatively influencing the possibilities of resistance within Germany, which at very least could provide an organizational basis for reconstruction after Germany's defeat.

The other—in fact the larger—major constellation among exiles were the socialists, who were in a more difficult position vis-à-vis the exculpation of Germany. For socialists (as we already saw with Fraenkel and Gollancz) theories of collective guilt based on a putatively malevolent national character missed the point. The real problem lay in the social structure of Germany, and in the manipulations of it by particular powerful groups, namely, leaders of heavy industry, the military, and the *Junker* landed aristocracy. Socialists therefore rejected collective guilt and punitive policies toward ordinary people, but saw the situation as nevertheless demanding a thorough-going social revolution. For them, no simple replacement of leadership and top-down imposition of democratic institutions would suffice without major transformations in social structure. Of course, as long-standing advocates of such a position, they most often saw themselves as the right ones to lead the transition.

33. Ibid.

One particularly interesting and influential commentator on the variety of exile arguments—as well as on the German question more generally—was Emil Ludwig, an iconoclastic Swiss writer who published a number of noted works before the war in Germany and during it in the United States, testified before Congress on numerous occasions, and was involved in training army personnel to serve in the occupation. Ludwig argued, "It is both wrong and dangerous to accept a political distinction between Nazis and Germans, as German propaganda would have it." His book—*The Moral Conquest of Germany*—he characterized as offering "a case for the guilt of the German nation."[34] Ludwig reserved his most potent scorn, however, for the exiles in the United States and the theories of Germany they were propagating. "These exiles," Ludwig wrote,

> seek to make people in this country believe . . . that the good, democratic Germany whose spokesmen they used to be is still extant, impatient to call them home in a triumph matching Victor Hugo's return to Paris, Mazzini's to Rome, or Lenin's to Russia. . . . These émigrés have surrounded themselves with gullible American citizens, have set up committees, and published manifestos asserting that the Nazis, far from representing the whole nation, are but a tough gang which held up the German people and for eleven long years kept them gagged and bound. Once these gangsters are done away with, the "other Germany" will rise again, as the Liberals did in 1918.[35]

During the war, in his 1943 book *How to Treat the Germans*, Ludwig thus warned against choosing new leaders for Germany from exiles and other opponents of the regime, because "the martyr is not always an efficient political leader." His concern was that the distinction between opponents and Nazis was not nearly as sharp as the exiles claimed: "Too decent to be Nazis, they are as nationalistic as they ever were."[36]

Instead, Ludwig demanded the division of Prussia from southern Germany, removal of "the industrial clan which ruined the Versailles treaty and facilitated German re-armament," and that "[a]s an antidote against the insane race ideology they have been taught, German youth should be given the classic books of Goethe, Schiller, Herder, and Lessing."[37] This last point was because he believed that "the economic conquest of postwar Germany is secondary to its moral conquest. . . . [T]hrough nothing less than

---

34. Ludwig, *The Moral Conquest of Germany*. Both quotes from p. 7.
35. Ibid., 135.
36. Ludwig, *How to Treat the Germans*, 86.
37. Ibid., 91.

a temporary extinction of German political independence," he argued, "will this all-important rebirth of the German nation be accomplished."[38] Nevertheless, because he was concerned with the uses of such arguments for German propaganda, Ludwig strenuously urged U.S. officials to make as clear as possible to the German people what their intentions were; otherwise their fantasies, with a little help from Goebbels, would be counterproductive.

The Science of Re-education

With the exception of Kaufman and others beyond the realm of sober decency, and despite the sweeping tone of some accounts, even "hard peace" advocates were usually motivated by a constructive urge. The proximate goal was to prevent the recurrence of war, but the more exciting goal for many was the possibility of transforming an entire society guided by state-of-the-art social scientific theory. Particularly interesting in this regard was the work of the Joint Committee on Postwar Planning, which was supported by professional associations including the American Neurological Association, American Psychiatric Association, and the National Committee for Mental Hygiene. In the spring of 1944, the Joint Committee held a series of meetings in New York at the College of Physicians and Surgeons of Columbia University, the purpose of which was to bring to bear the resources of "the scientific disciplines which specialize in the study of human behavior and how it manifests itself under different conditions" on the question of planning for postwar Germany.[39] Participants included cultural anthropologists, psychiatrists, psychologists, sociologists, experts in education, economic, and political science, "and guests whose knowledge of the situation made their advice important."[40] Despite the diversity of participants, however, the organizing principle was "the psycho-cultural approach," which asserted that while political and economic dimensions were important, "the basic foundations of all social problems are how people feel, think, and act."[41]

The project's leader was the psychiatrist Richard M. Brickner, who in 1943 had published a widely noted book, *Is Germany Incur-*

---

38. Ludwig, *Moral Conquest*, 7.

39. Brickner, "Germany after the War," 381.

40. One guest worth mentioning was the Swedish writer Sigrid Undset. I later come back to Undset, who published an essay in 1945 characterizing German collective guilt. Undset's essay was the proximate spur for the philosopher Karl Jaspers to articulate his first public statements on the issue, which became his renowned book *The Question of German Guilt*.

41. Brickner, "Germany after the War," 381 ff.

able?[42] Brickner's thesis—which he developed under the tutelage in cultural matters of renowned anthropologist Margaret Mead[43] (who was also a central participant at the meeting)—argued that Germany possessed a "paranoid" culture characterized by "megalomania," "the need to dominate," a "persecution complex," and "retrospective falsification." Like many others, Brickner argued that "the Nazi movement and its leaders are symptoms, not causes, of Germany's trouble, the equivalent of scabs on the body of a smallpox patient." In contrast to those who called for regime change, Brickner continued the smallpox analogy: "To get rid of them [the Nazis] and let it go at that would be like treating the scabs and ignoring the disease itself."[44] Against all claims that there existed a distinction between regime and *Volk*, Brickner insisted that "the idea that militarists are a powerful influence in German life is wrong. The Germans and the militarists are one and the same." As a result, he warned against trials for the leaders because he believed this would both create scapegoats for the German population and "serve as rallying-points in the next frenetic development of German paranoia." Despite this harsh tone, however, Brickner differentiated his therapeutic approach:

> Victory for our side . . . carries huge responsibilities and an awkwardly large number of options. Having won, we can return to the principles used in the 1919 treaties; or, in a vengeful or precautionary mood, exterminate the Germans; or make a scientific effort to check Germany's paranoid trends. The first might be called the Versailles method, the second the Cato-and-Carthage method, the third the behavioral method.[45]

The purpose of the 1944 meetings of the Joint Committee, under Brickner's direction, was to specify this behavioral method, though Brickner himself believed that "since paranoia is fundamentally a psychiatric problem, not economic or political, only psychiatric methods will act as a pertinent protective device."[46] The point of the passage just quoted is that Brickner

42. According to Michael Beschloss, Eleanor Roosevelt had been reading Brickner's book in September 1944 when Morgenthau visited FDR in Hyde Park to discuss his proposals. The First Lady did not agree with Brickner's argument. Beschloss, *The Conquerors*, 103.

43. Both Mead and Brickner were also close correspondents of the anthropologist Ruth Benedict, who at the time was working on a report for the Foreign Morale Analysis Division of the U.S. Office of War Information, which would later become *The Chrysanthemum and the Sword*, a now classic work hypothesizing that the West is a guilt culture, whereas the East is a shame culture. I return to Benedict and her seminal distinction toward the end of the book to explore her idea's relevance for understanding postwar German political culture.

44. Brickner, *Is Germany Incurable?* 37.

45. Ibid., 297.

46. Brickner, "Germany after the War," 300–301.

distinguished his approach—"hard" as it might have been—from the "Cato-and-Carthage" approach, which was the term Secretary of War Henry Stimson would use to characterize Morgenthau's plan. Whether this distinction was justified for Brickner, and whether Morgenthau was more like Brickner (and thus not "Carthaginian") remains to be seen.

* * *

The idea of a directed re-education had been in play for some time. At the end of the previous chapter, we saw Vice President Henry Wallace's calling for it in his statement of December 1942. In the intervening years, there had been a fair number of proposals, some calling for international control of the German education system, others arguing that in order to be effective the process would have to be led by the Germans themselves. An important example of the latter argument is in a 1945 book by the exile philosophy professor (and former undersecretary in the Prussian ministry of education during the Weimer Republic) Werner Richter, *Re-Educating Germany*. Richter argues poignantly, however, that "one cannot simultaneously enslave a people and educate it for freedom."[47] Whether anyone to be taken seriously (as opposed to just Kaufman) was proposing enslavement, of course, is another question. Additionally, the pioneer of "field theory" in psychology, Kurt Lewin, in some contrast to many who were focusing on curriculum, argued that Germans needed training in the group processes necessary for democracy because they were familiar only with authoritarian group structures. Lewin argued that this kind of re-education could fruitfully be pursued through collaboration between Germans and Americans, a process he called "self-reeducation."[48] Another influential view was that of Leopold Schwarzschild, who concluded his book *World in Trance* with a stern warning much in the spirit of Vansittart and others, though he has been credited with introducing the language of "re-education" into the discourse.[49] "Dispelled forever," Schwarzschild wrote, "is the dream of 1918, that once Germany . . . is freed from its bad rulers, it will be saved and become like other nations. It will not. Not because of any unalterable racial characteristics, but because its spirit and instincts have

47. Richter, *Re-educating Germany*, especially chap. 8, which is an extended debate with Vansittart and others.

48. Lewin, "Cultural Reconstruction."

49. See Eschenburg, *Jahre der Besatzung*, 147–48; see also Bark and Gress, *From Shadow to Substance*, 156. Also see note 32 in the previous chapter.

been molded by an age-long education and tradition. . . . The products of education and tradition," Schwarzschild concluded, "can be changed only by new education and new traditions." In contrast to Richter, however, Schwarzschild did not believe this could take place among the Germans themselves, or within the short-term: "Before Germany can be called demilitarized," he argued, "generations will have to pass of which no one has ever held a gun in his hand, or crouched behind a machine gun, or served a cannon or a tank or an airplane, or had anything to do with the manufacture of weapons or the handling of troops."[50]

For Brickner and his conference interlocutors, however, re-education was to be simultaneously much more subtle than merely controlling Germany until a new generation grew up and much deeper than curriculum and exposure to democratic process. "Re-education" implied the sort of wholesale resocialization a paranoid undergoes in the course of effective psychiatric treatment. But what would this entail? One group of participants in the conference believed that because German national character was thoroughly authoritarian, there was very little that could be done. However, another group—led by Margaret Mead and the sociologist Talcott Parsons—believed that German culture historically contained both authoritarian and democratic elements. Indeed, they implied that this was true of any political culture; as a result, there was particular concern that fostering too brutal attitudes toward Germany might endanger *American* political-psychological health by producing feelings of guilt and efforts to repress it. The task, then, was to increase the power of the democratic impulse in Germany without endangering the self-image of American democracy.[51]

Indeed, in these matters, it was the sociologist Parsons who took the lead. Parsons was himself deeply familiar with German culture from his time as a doctoral student in Heidelberg in the 1920s, and was largely responsible for introducing many German ideas into American sociology, particularly the work of Max Weber through both Parsons's secondary elaboration as well as his translations of some of Weber's most important works. Since the advent of National Socialism, Parsons had been occupied with theorizing its rise and with specifying the unique features of German social structure that had allowed it.[52] As in his wider sociological approach, Parsons placed substantial emphasis on the unique configurations of what

50. Schwarzschild, *World in Trance*, 413.
51. See the discussion in Gerhardt, *Talcott Parsons*, chap. 2.
52. See the collection of Parsons's writings about National Socialism edited by Uta Gerhardt, *Talcott Parsons on National Socialism*.

he later referred to as "societal subsystems" like economy, polity, culture, and personality. Indeed, the theoretical sections of the Brickner conference report defining the "psycho-cultural" approach were largely Parsons's, and his work in this regard was seminal for what came to be known as the "culture and personality" approach in sociology and anthropology, a research program that sought to develop the idea that personality and social structure were integrally related phenomena. Exactly such a claim in fact was behind all theories of German national character, though rarely as thoroughly theorized as in Parsons's and Mead's hands, and often, as we have already seen, much less creditably.

In his efforts to theorize Nazi Germany—which he had been carrying on in study groups at Harvard and as an instructor at the School of Overseas Administration, which trained future military government officers—Parsons was never more impressed than by exiled German political scientist Franz Neumann's book *Behemoth*. That work was the definitive statement for a theory of National Socialism as a polycentric and ultimately chaotic political system, thus contrasting with accounts of Nazi Germany as a *Führerstaat*, or leader-directed state. The important elements held in uniquely destructive tension, for Neumann, were the Prussian-dominated ministerial bureaucracy, the Nazi Party hierarchy, the military, and monopolistic heavy industry. The constant struggle among these elements provided the unique opportunity for repression of the masses that was the hallmark of National Socialist rule. Neumann's identification of the unique "contributions" of these distinct power blocks was evident in Parsons's proposals for Germany, which included eliminating the Nazi party, dispersing the *Junkers* (by eliminating their control over the bureaucracy and dividing their estates), and disbanding the military.

However, in direct contrast to Brickner and some others at the conference (and as we will see to Morgenthau and his supporters), Parsons argued strenuously that German *industry* actually had the *most* potential for positive social transformation since economic logic was uniquely suited to what Parsons called "universalistic" and "achievement" orientations.[53] As a result, Parsons argued to Brickner that occupation policy should foster high productivity, full employment, and an expanding economy.[54] In part because of these differences, Parsons published a separate

---

53. At the meetings themselves in the spring of 1944, the Morgenthau Affair had not yet taken place, but by the time the report was in preparation it was headline news.

54. For an account of the Parsons–Brickner correspondence, see Gerhardt, *Talcott Parsons*, 105–18.

paper in the journal *Psychiatry* outlining his approach.[55] But his thinking was obviously central to the ideas published in the conference report, not least his emphasis on the autonomy of culture, which implied, again in some contrast to Brickner's tendency toward psychological reductionism, the importance of fostering certain cultural values, including those to be found in the Christian tradition and in the universities and sciences. An interesting connection here is that Parsons collaborated closely in the 1930s with his junior colleague Edward Hartshorne, who had published a book on the German university system and who subsequently became the U.S. Army officer in charge of supervising the reformation of the universities in the American sector.[56]

* * *

It is, as always, hard to say what direct impact, if any, the conference report had on the course of policy. There are, nevertheless, numerous reasons for discussing it at such length. First, it represents well the climate of opinion in which policy decisions were taken, and certainly contributed to it. Second, many of the conference participants were involved at the middle levels of preparing for occupation, among other things through the training of military government officials and the preparation of intelligence with which such officers entered Germany. Though Neumann did not participate in Brickner's conference, his theories, as we will see, provided a crucial justification for the U.S. approach to denazification. And third, the conference is particularly illustrative of the American eagerness to apply social science in the service of transforming an entire society. As the report stated: "We are primarily concerned with the question of how political, military, economic and other proposals for changing German national life can be utilized as vehicles or instruments for the modification of German traditional culture and for changing the dominant character-structure of the German people."[57] The conference thus well characterizes exactly the kind of American impulse that so many Germans found offensive insofar as they found this optimistic interventionism comprehensible at all.

55. The essay, titled "The Problem of Controlled Institutional Change: An Essay in Applied Social Science," is reprinted in Gerhardt, *Talcott Parsons on National Socialism.*
56. Hartshorne was shot and killed in 1945 while driving on the *Autobahn.* The few references to this bizarre event, however, deem it less mysterious than it sounds. See Tent, *Mission on the Rhine,* 97–98.
57. Brickner, "Germany after 1945," 385.

One further feature of the report is also interesting, in which the relevance of the psychiatric framing for the future of Germany is apparent:

> An essential step in the future development of Germany would be to create a situation in which Germans would have to react to the deeds committed by Germany during the war. It would be fatal to forget the barbarities, Rotterdam, Lidice, mass executions of Jews, the murders of war prisoners, and many other extreme atrocities which are too well known to require mention. Germans cannot be allowed to shrug their shoulders at these deeds, nor plead ignorance, nor find ways of blaming their enemies for them. These acts were committed by Germans in the name of Germany. *We have heard of little German protest against them.* The question of guilt feeling can be used to illustrate our main thesis. The German people, with the character structure we have described, will try to shirk responsibility for the injuries caused to other nations by the war, and blame others for their own sufferings. That is what happened after World War I; it was a uniform reaction of the whole people and not of a few leaders. It could be taken as a dependable sign of a real change in character if a cry should arise among the whole German people to try to make some recompense for the harm they have done. It is futile to say that the "Germans" were made helpless to protest by the "Nazis." . . . The Germans must be made acutely aware of what they have done and it must be made extremely clear that it is they who did it. *Strong motivation toward a change in character could come from powerful feelings of guilt over their own deeds.*[58]

Surely this was exactly the understanding, as we will see, that shaped the early days of the occupation, in which American authorities posed the issue of German collective guilt most vividly. Nevertheless, it is interesting to note that the conference report does not really distinguish between Germany's behavior in the two World Wars. The prediction of defensiveness, moreover, turned out to be quite accurate, though it is not clear one required psychoanalytic training to make it.[59]

58. Ibid., 440 (emphasis added).
59. For confirmation of the prediction, see Janowitz, "German Reactions to Nazi Atrocities."

CHAPTER 4

Woe to the Vanquished?

The Moscow Foreign Ministers' Meeting

Throughout World War II, the two central issues for those planning the occupation of Germany were the questions of punishment and partition, though these stood alongside several other, more specific questions, like those of reparations, the expected length of occupation, the appropriate economic level for postwar Germany, and controls of industry. Regarding punishment, as early as 1940 and 1941, the Polish and Czech exile governments prodded Britain and the United States to make statements warning Germany about war crimes and promising penalties. The Atlantic Allies did so, but more to placate the Polish and Czech exile leaders and to encourage occupied peoples than as a matter of the first importance. By 1943, however, continued pressure from the exile governments as well as increasing awareness of the extent of Nazi brutality led to further gestures and new institutional frameworks.

In October 1943, representatives of seventeen nations convened to set up the United Nations War Crimes Commission (UNWCC), which would serve as a crucible for developing legal structures to prosecute Nazi crimes. Nearly simultaneously, foreign ministers of Britain, the United States, and the Soviet Union met in Moscow and established the European Advisory Commission (EAC), which would work in London on detailed plans for the postwar administration of Germany, including structuring so-called "zones of occupation." At the start of the Moscow Conference, President Roosevelt cabled Secretary of State Cordell Hull asking him to push his colleagues to make a statement not just about past atrocities, but warning those who might perpetrate further ones. The final communiqué was the only official statement during the war by the Allies on the question of punishment. Its conclusion read as follows: "Let those who have hitherto not imbrued their hands with innocent blood beware lest they join the ranks of the guilty, for most assuredly the three Allied Powers will pursue them to the uttermost ends of earth and will deliver them to their accusers in order that justice may be done." However, how exactly that justice would be done—and how it would be done for those whose crimes were not in lands outside of Germany—remained undetermined, as did the question of postwar boundaries, which was the principal point of the meeting in the first place. The EAC, however, remained hamstrung throughout its existence by the reluctance of its members to develop policy, who were apparently content merely to have a podium for stating their established positions.

In the period leading up to the Moscow Conference, U.S. government planning for the occupation of Germany consisted largely of a series of working groups in the State Department, which produced numerous preliminary papers and proposals.[1] While State Department planners debated many points of view, their work bore the stamp of the general orientation of the Department and its head, Secretary Hull. In many respects, the wartime U.S. State Department was a bastion of establishment gentility. Not surprisingly, its old guard had long been staunchly anti-Soviet. Due to the department's limited resources, moreover, they turned to the Council on Foreign Relations for help, whose membership included prominent business and banking figures as well as academic specialists. The council's orientation was decidedly probusiness, though unlike some prewar conservative factions it was not isolationist. Hull himself was of a very modest background, the son of a Tennessee farmer, but had built his career in the House and Senate leading the movement for low tariffs, with the goal of stimulating international trade. Indeed, Hull believed economic nationalism was the single most important cause of war: "To me," Hull wrote, "trade dovetailed with peace; high tariffs, trade barriers, and unfair economic competition, with war."[2] His approach to the postwar order, therefore, aimed at the economic integration of Germany with other nations of the capitalist West through a multilateral trading order. A hard policy of vengeance, in this light, would be counterproductive. This very much fit the bill for business leaders.

Most State Department officials had been hostile to the New Deal and resisted government economic controls and redistributive measures, instead favoring moderate fiscal policy to ensure the expansion of markets. From this perspective, German industry would be an essential component

1. See Notter, *Post-War Policy Preparation*.
2. Quoted in Gaddis, *The United States and the Origins of the Cold War*, 19.

in the future economic and political security of Europe. The road these planners foresaw to such security thus involved a vigorous reconstruction of the German economy, and they were reluctant to prohibit any but the most obviously military industries. While State Department planners expected nations that had suffered at Germany's hands would demand reparations, the guiding principle of such reparations, they believed, should be economic usefulness to the victim nations, limited by the desire not to damage the German economy, as had the measures imposed at Versailles after World War I. They thus favored moderate reparations from production, rather than dismantling or expropriation of durable industrial resources. The point was to make the new Germany dependent in a beneficial way on the markets of Western Europe and the world. In order to accomplish this, moreover, rebuilt Germany would require a relatively centralized state.[3] These were the plans Hull carried with him to Moscow.

When Hull met with his counterparts Molotov and Eden, however, he intentionally soft-pedaled this essentially "soft-peace" position. Trying to sound tougher than his plan actually was, Hull highlighted the call for completely disbanding the German military, controlling industry sufficiently to prevent a future military capacity, and establishing a commission to facilitate reparations (though leaving vague what those reparations would be). With regard to punishment, Hull picked up on the spirit of the discussion on atrocities, during which Molotov had expressed a desire for swift justice for the German leaders. When it was his turn, Hull stated, "If I had my way, I would take Hitler and Mussolini and Tojo and their accomplices and bring them before a drumhead court-martial. And at sunrise the following day there would occur an historic incident." In his memoir, Hull expounded his view that a "fancy trial" would give the "archcriminals" the opportunity to propagate "a vast network of claims and pretenses embodied in a false and fraudulent defense," that would generate revanchist sentiments in their populations. Hull argued that the leaders of the defeated regimes should not be afforded the dignity of a trial; treating them poorly would have the highest symbolic value, reflecting the victors' disgust. However, he also denied having been opposed to the Nuremberg trial program once it came about.[4] Both positions, of course, were consistent with the idea of "decapitating" the regime and rehabilitating the people. Important to note here, as elsewhere, is the lumping together of the enemies; Germany was not, as of yet, viewed as an exceptional case defined by the extermination of Jews.

3. For a more detailed account of this process, see Eisenberg, *Drawing the Line*, 14–70.
4. Hull, *The Memoirs of Cordell Hull*, 1289 ff.

Nevertheless, Hull remained intentionally vague at the Moscow meeting on other key elements, such as exactly what he meant when he called for controls on "material essential for arms manufacture" and, in particular, when discussing the issue of partition. Hull's definition of the industries to be prohibited or controlled was likely much narrower than Molotov's. And his statements of his position on partition were much more ambiguous than he knew them to be: Hull conveyed that there had been a great deal of debate on the issue in his government, that many were favoring partition, though he himself was opposed to it. On the one hand, there had been a battle within the State Department over partition in particular and over the tenor of the planned settlement in general, and the harder version that would likely appeal to the Soviets had already been pushed out. On the other hand, Hull was unable to persuade Roosevelt of the softer plans his staff was pushing; Hull knew from a meeting prior to his departure for Moscow that FDR favored partition and a "hard peace" in general. For his part, Molotov was no amateur. Needing the Atlantic Allies to open a second front and not wishing to sow any dissent, he replied positively to Hull's proposals. Nevertheless, he did conclude by saying that his government would consider Hull's proposals a minimum, not a maximum.

Sumner Welles and the Liberal Alternative

The chief antagonist to "soft-peace" reasoning within the State Department was Undersecretary of State Sumner Welles, a friend of Roosevelt's since boyhood, chief architect of the U.S. "good neighbor" policy in Latin America, member of FDR's inner circle especially in foreign policy, and New Deal liberal.[5] As such, Welles's relations with Secretary Hull and his close deputies were often extraordinarily antagonistic. Yet Welles was a brilliant and effective statesman, and Roosevelt and his supporters considered him indispensable (some felt he should have been secretary of state, but Roosevelt needed the southern Democratic support Hull brought in). In 1943, in the midst of internal debates over Germany and other crucial issues, Welles's State Department rivals exploited rumors of his homosexuality to force him out.[6] Following his departure, however, Welles wrote a

5. For a sympathetic account of Welles, see the biography by his son Benjamin Welles, *Sumner Welles;* for an account of the complexities leading up to the scandalous removal of Welles, see Gellman, *Secret Affairs.* For a more critical account, see Fleming, *The New Dealers' War.*

6. In 1940, Welles had allegedly propositioned a number of porters on a train trip from a funeral in Florida. Roosevelt and FBI director Herbert Hoover managed to repress the

book outlining his vision of the future international order—*The Time for Decision*—which sold more than five hundred thousand copies, making it the number one bestseller.

Welles's chapter on Germany is worth considering in this context, in which we are interested in the origins of the memory of a putatively "vindictive" intent toward Germany in the United States. His position was in many respects the inverse of the plans Hull presented at the Moscow Conference, and indicates the internal struggle that took place between State Department conservatives and the major representative of Roosevelt's New Deal liberalism in the department; it is, moreover, another example of a "hard peace," demonstrating that Morgenthau's later position was not nearly as beyond the discourse as Stimson and other critics would imply, though Welles's and Morgenthau's views differed in some important respects. Welles's statement is also important because it clearly foreshadowed and by implication justified the notorious Potsdam Agreement, which mandated significant population transfers and became a key reference in the memory of German victimhood after 1945. In this way, it makes it harder to see Potsdam as an unprepared capitulation to Stalin.

The similarity of Welles's stance to other "hard-peace" arguments is already clear in the title of his chapter on Germany: "The German Menace Can be Ended." He began his chapter with the by-then standard condemnation of historical Germany: "During a period of some two hundred years, the Germanic peoples, and especially the Prussian people, have been a destructive force in the family of nations. Throughout that time they have never made any constructive contribution to regional or world peace."[7] Along similar lines as Sigrid Schultz (though, given the dates, the line of influence was likely in the other direction), Welles identified a conspiracy of the German General Staff to lie in wait for another chance for aggression. His greatest concern was that the democratic nations would once again be lulled into a sense that, with the war over, nothing more needed to be done to maintain the settlement. But in some contrast to other thinkers, Welles viewed German militarism as only one of two dangerous elements, the other being centralization. He thus stated that "[i]t is only because of my conviction that German unity means a continuing threat to the peace of the entire world that I have reached the conclusion that partition is the only

---

controversy for a time, but Welles's competitors in the State Department threatened to bring it out at a crucial moment. Hull himself was indeed jealous of Welles's influence with FDR, especially as that influence mostly worked in directions Hull did not approve.

7. Welles, *The Time for Decision*, 336.

way of offsetting the German menace in the future."[8] In particular, Welles proposed giving East Prussia to Poland while giving a piece of the old Polish Corridor to Germany.

As a result of this partition, Welles recognized, there would have to be enormous population transfers, with all the human problems they would entail. He argued, however, that this could be accomplished within the spirit of the Atlantic Charter—of which Welles was a principal drafter—because of its emphasis on self-determination. No individuals, he asserted, should be forced to move; by the same token, no one should be subject to the authority of a sovereign state to which he did not belong. Without this interpretation, Welles argued, the charter would in fact prohibit any solution to the problems that would face Central Europe after the German defeat. His justification, then, was a utilitarian one: "Any transfer of populations results in hardships, and in human suffering. But in such a case as that under consideration the eventual benefits to peace and stability of the whole of Europe would outweigh many thousands of times the temporary distress which might be created."[9] With all the disdain heaped on the subsequent Potsdam Agreement, it is notable that Welles has never received the sort of recognition in German and world memory as Morgenthau.

Roosevelt, Stimson, and First Formulations

Given his close personal relationship with Roosevelt, it is not surprising that Sumner Welles's approach to postwar Germany was consonant with the president's at this point. While the official State Department line emphasized economic reconstruction and political unity for Germany, Roosevelt believed that this solution would antagonize the Soviets. Moreover, Roosevelt's sentiments on Germany, partly shaped by his childhood memory of six weeks spent in a German boarding school, were not conducive to the separation of regime and *Volk* upon which quick reconstruction was premised. His experiences as assistant secretary of the Navy during World War I reinforced these memories, and he frequently spoke publicly of his disdain for Prussian militarism. One story he told repeatedly in later years was of his January 1919 trip with his wife to Germany, where American troops were not flying the American flag for fear of humiliating the Germans. The lesson for Roosevelt was that the United States would have to leave Germany in no doubt of its defeat in World War II. As he told

8. Ibid., 349.
9. Ibid., 356.

Congress on January 7, 1943, "by our failure, we have learned that we cannot maintain the peace by good intentions alone."

Roosevelt's very different view from Hull's was apparent when he met with Churchill and Stalin in Teheran in November 1943. There Roosevelt stated his belief that the very concept of the *Reich* had to be eliminated from German consciousness and language,[10] as well as engaged in further discussion about division. The main options at this point seemed to be partition (perhaps into three countries out of the Rhineland, Prussia, and Bavaria) or a more radical dissolution (some proposals included as many as seven units). The German term for the latter is *Zerstückelung*, which translates roughly as "dismemberment": the German interpretation of this plan, and the memory of it, are thus contained in the very language. Over a dinner in Teheran, moreover, Stalin apparently suggested summary execution of fifty thousand German officers; Roosevelt responded facetiously by offering forty thousand; Churchill left the room in disgust, though Stalin and Molotov chased after him, pleading that Stalin had not been serious. Whether serious about the large number or not, Stalin did intend at this stage a fairly extensive purge of German elites, military and otherwise. It is important to note, however, that neither Roosevelt nor Churchill was opposed at this point to summary execution of at least a small number of leading Nazis.

At this juncture, nevertheless, Roosevelt still stood by his reluctance to commit prematurely to any particular course of action. Beyond some form of partition, the president's ideas remained vague. As a result, by the time Eisenhower's forces landed on the European continent, his officers still had no specific guidelines for the coming occupation, which momentarily seemed like it might begin as early as the end of 1944. Indeed, they did not even know yet which portion of Germany they would be occupying. Military commanders thus pressed for guidance, often to the point of believing that any principle was better than none.

Until the middle of 1944, the War Department had, for a number of reasons, largely avoided questions of postwar planning. First, Secretary Stimson believed the principles stated in the Atlantic Charter were sufficient to guide Allied conduct in the war, and did not disagree with Roosevelt's reluctance to announce specific plans before the end of the war.

---

10. See Graml, "Die deutsche Frage," 290. According to Vice President Henry Wallace, Churchill was not at all happy with this demand, especially when Roosevelt added that not only *Reich*, but its equivalent in other languages (e.g., "empire"), must go as well. Blum, *The Price of Vision*, 283.

Second, at least according to his self-account, given his portfolio at the War Department, Stimson required himself to focus rather single-mindedly on the conduct of the war itself, rather than on any potential settlement. As the civilian leader of the military, he did not see postwar planning as within his purview. Rather, he understood his professional obligation to lie in extricating the military from responsibility once it had met its objective; the occupation, he expected, should be a civilian affair. In part for this reason, Stimson's wartime image of military occupation was that it would be brief, perhaps a matter of mere weeks. Nevertheless, during that period, most military leaders insisted they should be entirely free from civilian interference (which had been a problem in North Africa). These were the short-term considerations that shaped military planning.[11]

Despite Roosevelt's reluctance to commit to specific plans, in the spring of 1944 he appointed an interdepartmental Executive Committee on Economic Foreign Policy (ECEFP), including representatives from the Departments of State, Treasury, Agriculture, and Labor, among others, but not War. In the summer of 1944, the ECEFP produced a report largely consistent with the line the State Department had so far taken, which concluded that punitive policies would be counterproductive: "An indefinitely continued coercion of more than sixty million technically advanced people . . ." the report argued, "would be at best an expensive undertaking and would afford the world little sense of real security."[12] A main concern among these planners was that the Soviet Union, not Germany, would be the major threat to peace in Europe; the reintegration of Germany into the West would provide a significant limit to the Soviet Union's disruptive potential, much more so than if Germany were to be left hanging in the balance. (The U.S. representative to the EAC, Ambassador John Winant, shared this view of the Soviet Union.)[13] The report summarized the committee's philosophy as "Stern peace with reconciliation," though for critics this was a mere gloss on its "soft-peace" core.

At about the same time as the ECEFP was preparing its report, General Eisenhower established so-called "country units" at SHAEF facilities in England, and charged the Germany Unit with producing short-term spe-

11. Stimson described his thoughts on postwar planning up to that point in his memoir, *On Active Service in Peace and War,* by Henry L. Stimson and McGeorge Bundy, 565–67.

12. Cited in Gaddis, *The United States and the Origins of the Cold War,* 115–17. See also Eisenberg, *Drawing the Line,* 28–30.

13. The Treasury Department's representative on the ECEFP, Harry Dexter White, was at the time deeply involved in preparations for the Bretton Woods negotiations, and thus did not participate with his usual attention.

cific guidelines for the impending occupation. While military personnel had long focused on "military necessity" as the sole principle for what they hoped would be only a short-term occupation, however, the Civil Affairs Division of which the country units were a part was a largely civilian-staffed department; the resulting *Basic Handbook for Military Government of Germany* was thus significantly broader in scope than anything yet produced by the War Department. The *Handbook* assigned to the military governors the "main and immediate task . . . to get things running, to pick up the pieces, to restore as quickly as possible the official functioning of the German civil government," the latter because its authors assumed the German government and economy would still be functioning to some extent.[14] (In contrast, Eisenhower expected that, as Supreme Commander, he would have to assume more extensive responsibility for the economy than the report anticipated.) The *Handbook* instructed the occupation forces to reorganize the police force, control German finances, restore public utilities, promote agriculture, and employ German workers in order to minimize the unrest idleness would promote. It also instructed that the occupation force should aid in converting industrial plants from military to consumer production and assist in the reestablishment of foreign trade. Most significantly, the *Handbook* anticipated retaining the highly centralized German bureaucracy, maintaining all existing German regulations for the economy, and continuing production of such materials as ore and the processing of fuel at present levels. Despite the *Handbook's* presumption of a brief military occupation, these were obviously significant goals that would both take a long time and, if implemented, have an enduring impact. This, then, was the state of U.S. planning when Morgenthau's Treasury Department took the critical lead.

The Morgenthau Affair

According to Henry Morgenthau Jr.'s memoir,[15] before August 1944 the Treasury Secretary had not spent great energies on German questions, though this is strictly true only if one maintains a sharp barrier between "German" questions and those pertaining to the German treatment of Jews. Throughout 1942 and 1943, Morgenthau's family associate, Rabbi Stephen Wise, had been confronting Morgenthau with evidence of Nazi treatment of Jews and lobbying him to exert his influence with Roosevelt

14. Cited in Blum, *Roosevelt and Morgenthau*, 574–75, among many other places.
15. Ibid., 564.

to do something about it. (Wise also lobbied Roosevelt directly.) Throughout the war, Morgenthau had taken small steps to help Jewish refugees when possible. Beginning in January 1944, he finally overcame his reluctance to prevail on Roosevelt personally on "Jewish" issues, and brought to the president evidence of exterminations, along with specific requests for action. While he did not obtain the bombing of railway lines to camps like Auschwitz (War Department officials, particularly John McCloy, argued that such efforts would be ineffective and would consume resources that would otherwise speed victory, which, McCloy maintained, was the only feasible solution),[16] Morgenthau did extract a public statement from Roosevelt, issued on March 24, 1944: "In one of the blackest crimes of all history—begun by the Nazis in the day of peace and multiplied by them a hundred times in time of war—the wholesale, systematic murder of the Jews of Europe goes on unabated every hour. . . . None who participate in these acts of savagery shall go unpunished." Moreover, Roosevelt went so far as to implicate other nations for their complicity in deportation—"All who knowingly take part in the deportation of Jews to their death in Poland or Norwegians and French to their death in Germany are equally guilty with the executioner himself"—though Roosevelt assured Stalin and Churchill that he did not mean to signal any change in war aims (e.g., prevention of the "final solution" rather than "unconditional surrender"). Despite this statement, however, and despite the establishment of a limited refugee program, Roosevelt did little else on the matter.

Nevertheless, as stated in his memoir, it is true that Morgenthau had done little regarding the issue of postwar planning for Germany before an August 1944 trip to England. During his flight across the Atlantic, Assistant Secretary Harry Dexter White presented Morgenthau with State Department and ECEFP papers proposing the rapid reconstruction of the German economy and other "soft-peace" measures; upon arrival in England, Morgenthau's former advisor Colonel Bernard Bernstein (now working in the Civil Affairs Division of SHAEF) showed Morgenthau the SHAEF *Handbook*. During his stay in England, Morgenthau brought up the proposals with both Churchill and Eisenhower, and received, rightly or wrongly, the impression that both men supported a "hard peace."

16. On the controversy over why the United States did not bomb railway lines to Auschwitz, see Rubenstein, *The Myth of Rescue*. See also Beschloss, *The Conquerors*, 63–67, 88–89, particularly for his comments on McCloy's role. For a more general account of McCloy, see Schwartz, *America's Germany*.

(Eisenhower indeed felt quite bitter,[17] though he did not ultimately support the heart of Morgenthau's proposals; one reason he wanted to leave Morgenthau with the impression that he sought a "hard peace" was that Morgenthau had been a vigorous critic of the North African arrangements with the Vichy French that had preceded the Casablanca Conference, for which Eisenhower was ultimately responsible, and rather embarrassed.)

In a meeting with U.S. EAC representative John Winant, Morgenthau and White first described their intent to pursue a different course; Winant reacted negatively, arguing that restricting the German economy would push Germany toward dependence on the Soviet Union, and informed them that the EAC was working in other directions. Morgenthau also met with Herbert Pell, the U.S. representative to the UNWCC, who told Morgenthau of resistance there to deep legal measures against the Nazis. Morgenthau received ammunition, and some satisfaction, however, when British Foreign Secretary Anthony Eden told him of Churchill, Stalin, and Roosevelt's agreement at the Teheran Conference to move for partition. Morgenthau had not been informed on Teheran, and indeed Roosevelt had even refused to provide Secretary of State Hull with documents on, or even a vague description of, the Teheran meeting, knowing Hull would have opposed him on partition. For his part, Eden was surprised to learn from Morgenthau of the State Department and Army plans for reconstruction, as well as that Winant's work with EAC was also premised on rebuilding the German economy.

* * *

Morgenthau's approach to postwar Germany has often been portrayed as a direct emanation of his Jewishness, and of the efforts of Rabbi Wise and others to make him a point man in the administration for Jewish interests. The evidence Wise showed him of the unfolding Holocaust did in fact have the intended effect, though it is not clear why Morgenthau's personal reaction—he was sickened—has been an important part of the story: one hopes any observer would have been deeply affected (though apparently they were not always). But to locate the origin of Morgenthau's intrusion into the planning process as the result of a conversion experience (Morgenthau

17. The extent of his bitterness toward Germany can be found in a letter to his wife, in which Eisenhower wrote, "The German is a beast." Quoted in Gienow-Hecht, *Transmission Impossible*, 28. Also, as we saw, Eisenhower ultimately refused to be in the room when Jodl surrendered on May 7, 1945.

was the most secular of Jews, and did not want to be seen as Jewish first and foremost) is to downplay other, perhaps more ideologically charged motivations. (Morgenthau's conversion to interest in Judaism, moreover, was rather mild. Upon resignation from the Treasury Department, he did indeed become chairman of the United Jewish Appeal, but in significant measure because he had few other offers. Additionally, after his wife died, he remarried to a non-Jewish woman.)

Beyond the information he received from Wise and the mere fact of being Jewish, three salient background conditions must be included for a complete understanding of Morgenthau's perspective. First, having witnessed the Armenian genocide close-up as a young man (his father was at the time U.S. Ambassador to Turkey), Morgenthau was driven by the fear that, without the development of legal remedies, there was no way to prevent future atrocities. Second, as secretary of the treasury, Morgenthau was intimately familiar with the moral complicity of the German economy—expropriation of non-Aryan wealth, the effective subsidy by German industry of the Nazi police state, and the benefits to industry of slave labor. And third, though only a moderate in the New Deal liberal camp, Morgenthau counted among his successes cooperation with the Justice Department's "trust-busting" prosecutions of the 1930s. This last point has led one iconoclastic writer to portray the Morgenthau Plan as "a massive antitrust action to break up the entrenched monopolies and cartels that were a prominent feature of the German economy," an action "very similar to that which had been the legal backbone of the US department of Justice Antitrust Division's criminal indictments of major American companies during the 1930s."[18] This is perhaps an overstatement, but so are the majority of accounts that often discount these three salient background conditions in favor of emphasizing Morgenthau's "Semitic grievances."

Upon his return from England, Morgenthau was a man with what he saw as a moral mission. His first visit was to Hull on August 17, where he passed on Eden's report on Teheran; Hull was incensed, though it is not clear whether more by his exclusion than by Roosevelt's deal on partition. When Morgenthau asked Hull where he stood, Hull told of his toughness at Moscow, which indicated to Morgenthau his support for harsher measures, though it seems clear in retrospect that Hull's harshness was a matter of punishing the leadership rather than partition or restructuring the economy too radically (though he did support holding it down to a subsistence level in the short term).

18. Simpson, *The Splendid Blond Beast*, 150.

Next, on August 19, Morgenthau called on Roosevelt, who was chagrined to hear that Hull now knew about the results of Teheran. Morgenthau informed Roosevelt that the EAC was not working in the directions Roosevelt had agreed to at Teheran and that the panoply of planning efforts did not include much that expressed Roosevelt's predisposition. Morgenthau recorded that Roosevelt reaffirmed his intent to pursue a "hard peace" by saying, "We have got to be tough with Germany and I mean the German people not just the Nazis. We either have to castrate the German people or you have got to treat them in such a manner so they can't just go on reproducing people who want to continue the way they have in the past."[19] On this basis, Morgenthau appointed a Treasury committee to begin drafting his plan.

On August 23, Morgenthau met with Stimson to discuss what he had learned and to represent Roosevelt's opinion. For Stimson, this meeting was a wake-up call, for as noted earlier he had yet to give much thought to long-term planning for Germany. Nevertheless, when Morgenthau reported Roosevelt's assumption that there would be a long military occupation—perhaps twenty years, so that a new generation could come of age—Stimson quickly realized how serious their divergence was.

As a republican with a Wall Street law background, Henry Stimson had never been a part of Roosevelt's inner circle—a member of the New York elite, he was no New Dealer. But he and FDR got along cordially, despite Stimson's frequent frustration at what he believed was Roosevelt's inadequate administrative style (though Roosevelt's strategy of maintaining a tense environment of competing attitudes was quite intentional, if he was not always able to keep the competition in check, especially in his last years). Already well into his seventies, Stimson was the senior member of Roosevelt's cabinet, appointed after the fall of France in 1940 as an emblem of bipartisanship and for his vast experience in a number of administrations, including as secretary of war under President William Howard Taft, U.S. representative to Nicaragua, governor of the Philippines, and perhaps most importantly secretary of state under Herbert Hoover, during which appointment he dealt with what he saw as the very negative influence of the reparations imposed on Germany by the Treaty of Versailles. Stimson was no social liberal either, having supported the National Origins Act of 1939, which disadvantaged non-European immigrants in favor of European ones; but he was a strong interventionist and, on this basis, among others, was important to Roosevelt.

At their August 23 meeting, Morgenthau informed Stimson what he had learned on his trip to England, as well as conveyed his sense of Roosevelt's

19. Quoted in Blum, *Roosevelt and Morgenthau,* 572.

support for harder proposals than were embodied in the various State and War Department papers. Stimson replied that he doubted anything discussed at Teheran was at all final, though he did indicate that he had been surprised. Stimson agreed with Morgenthau that it would take a new generation—twenty years—before the Germans could be trusted, but he did not appear to support any particular program of re-education. In contrast, Morgenthau discussed removing children from their families, placing them in schools run by the Allies, though it is difficult to gauge how serious Morgenthau could have been about such a proposal. As for industry, Stimson consented that something should be done, and said he was particularly impressed by proposals to internationalize the Ruhr and Saar regions. Morgenthau liked the direction, but found it too moderate, and spoke of removing all industry from the region and refashioning Germany as a largely agricultural region of small landholders. Stimson expressed concern that such a plan might have been feasible in 1860, when there were only 40 million Germans, but that in 1945 it would entail removing large numbers of people from Germany. Morgenthau quipped that this was better than sending them to the gas chambers. Stimson and Morgenthau agreed, however, to suggest to Roosevelt a joint committee made up of Stimson, Hull, and Morgenthau to work toward resolving the matter as quickly as possible.

Two days later, Morgenthau again met with FDR, at which time he showed Roosevelt excerpts from the *Handbook*, in part to prepare the president for his meeting later that day with Stimson. In that meeting, Stimson made his case to the president, who remained cool. He also suggested the joint committee, which Roosevelt appointed without a moment's hesitation, later adding his closest advisor Harry Hopkins to represent the White House (as well as Navy Secretary James Forrestal when appropriate). The next day, however, Roosevelt dictated an angry letter to Stimson regarding the *Handbook*: "This so-called 'Handbook' is pretty bad. . . ." Roosevelt wrote. "It gives me the impression that Germany is to be restored just as much as the Netherlands or Belgium, and the people of Germany brought back as quickly as possible to their pre-war estate." In contrast, Roosevelt stated his belief that "[i]t is of the utmost importance that every person in Germany should realize that this time Germany is a defeated nation." He did not want them to starve, but "if they need food . . . they should be fed three times a day with soup from Army soup kitchens. That will keep them perfectly healthy and they will remember that experience all their lives."[20]

20. Ibid., 576–77.

Roosevelt rejected the idea that the Allies should attempt to rebuild Germany through social programs along the lines of the Works Projects Administration (WPA). He simply did not accept the theory of distinction between regime and *Volk* on which such programs would be premised: "Too many people here and in England," he argued, "hold to the view that the German people as a whole are not responsible for what has taken place—that only a few Nazi leaders are responsible." As Roosevelt saw it, this was simply not true. As a result, "[t]he German people must have it driven home to them that the whole nation has been engaged in a lawless conspiracy against the decencies of modern civilization."[21] Despite later vacillation over the Morgenthau plan, this statement leaves little doubt about the tenor of Roosevelt's view.

For his part, Morgenthau took this as encouragement to proceed with his plans, which he pushed his deputies to make as tough as possible. Indeed, despite later being charged with manipulating Morgenthau to a view so radical that it would serve only Soviet interests, Harry Dexter White urged Morgenthau to a more moderate formulation that would not include complete destruction of Ruhr and Saar industries, instead favoring internationalization; White wanted the plan to appear devoid of vengeful motives. Morgenthau, however, became only more confident, though it is hard to say when he was overstating his case for advantage in negotiations, when he was simply carried away, and when he believed sober judgment dictated the specifics proposals. Indeed, the tone of Morgenthau's 1945 book[22] (largely drafted by White), was surprisingly cool, containing little of the national character diagnosis to be found in Vansittart and others. For the moment, however, Morgenthau was positively triumphant at Roosevelt's letter to Stimson (which he had also copied to Hull, who was generally outraged at what he saw as encroachments on his territory). Over Labor Day weekend, Stimson recorded in his diary concern over what he saw as Morgenthau's "very bitter atmosphere of personal resentment against the entire German people without regard to individual guilt." Stimson was "very much afraid that it will result in our taking mass vengeance . . . in the shape of clumsy economic action . . . and will inevitably produce a very dangerous reaction in Germany and probably a new war."[23]

21. Ibid., 577.
22. Henry Morgenthau, *Germany Is Our Problem*.
23. Quoted in Beschloss, *The Conquerors*, 105; see also Blum, *Roosevelt and Morgenthau*, 578.

While Stimson entertained such thoughts, Morgenthau was meeting again with Roosevelt in upstate New York, at which time he presented the president with a draft of his plan. Roosevelt responded by asking for three things: Germany should be allowed no aircraft, all uniforms should be prohibited, and they were not to be allowed to march. It was in this context that Eleanor Roosevelt mentioned her lack of sympathy for Richard Brickner's diagnosis of collective paranoia.[24] Upon his return to Washington, however, Morgenthau instructed White to include these symbolic measures, and by the end of the day on September 4, a draft containing all the essentials of the final "Program to Prevent Germany from Starting a World War III" was complete.

Carthage and Quebec

The first meeting of the Stimson, Morgenthau, Hull, and Hopkins cabinet committee took place on September 5, 1944. As he had at Moscow, Hull had prepared a version of State Department plans that overemphasized the harsh elements in his department's work. Indeed, when Hull repeated his demand for a drum-head court-martial for the German leadership, Morgenthau pointed out to Hull that this was not at all what Hull's own papers contained, and Stimson too expressed frustration with Hull's seeming unfamiliarity with the work of his own department. For Hull, however, the most important issue was partition—which he opposed—but which he sought to hide behind a punitive sounding memo aimed at achieving some consensus. Particularly troublesome for Stimson was Hull's concurrence with Morgenthau that the German standard of living should be held down to "subsistence level." Hull discoursed on the similarities of his approach to what occurred in the American South after the Civil War, where "everything was destroyed in the South and it took the people 75 years to get back again." This was what Hull claimed to want for Germany, arguing that Nazism was deep in the German people "and you have just got to uproot it and you can't do it by just shooting a few people."[25]

While no longer surprised by Morgenthau, Stimson was aghast at Hull, and believed that he was very much alone on the committee, though in retrospect it is not really clear where Hull stood. In a preparatory meeting of the various deputies with Harry Hopkins on September 2, White had presented the Treasury plan, so Hull was certainly not surprised by it. In his

24. Beschloss, *The Conquerors*, 103.
25. Eisenberg, *Drawing the Line*, 38.

memoir, Hull characterized White's presentation as "a plan of blind vengeance . . . because it failed to see that, in striking at Germany, it was striking at all of Europe."[26] But this account was a retrospective one, when Hull was interested in portraying himself as having been clearly in line with Stimson the entire time. For his part, Stimson later recounted his realization before the meeting that "there was a strong divergence of view in Washington, between those who were in favor of a firm but discriminating treatment of Germany, looking toward her eventual reconstruction as a prosperous and peaceful nation, and those who frankly desired a Carthaginian peace."[27]

Indeed, in subsequent memory, this characterization of Morgenthau's plan as "Carthaginian" has defined one pole in what I described in chapter 2 as the portrayal of the struggle between Stimson and Morgenthau as one between vengeance and "firm but discriminating treatment." The "Carthaginian" label has stuck to the Morgenthau Plan since Stimson first employed it in this context. It is crucial to note, however, that this was not the first use of that label in regard to proposals for Germany. We saw it, for instance, when Richard Brickner distinguished between a "re-education" and a "Cato-and-Carthage" approach. And it first entered the discussion at least as early as the debate over unconditional surrender discussed in chapter 2. Carthaginianism, of course, refers to the Third Punic War, in which the Romans demanded "unconditional surrender" from Carthage as the price for sparing the city from annihilation. The Carthaginians refused, war followed, and the result was their complete destruction. The label "Carthaginian" had thus come to indicate a desire for vengeance beyond any sense of rational self-interest, sacrificing future peace on the altar of hatred. Precisely this charge was leveled at Roosevelt when he announced the demand for unconditional surrender at Casablanca in 1943, and now Stimson used the label to attack Morgenthau.

In his memoir, Stimson minimized the disagreement in the cabinet committee, singling out the treatment of industry as the only salient point of difference. The continuity of anti-Carthaginianism in Stimson's thought, however, indicates that his position was deeply rooted and broader than this effort at consensus implied, and he was clearly distressed at what became a very unpleasant meeting. On the one hand, Stimson's effort to narrow the difference to the treatment of industry shows how important economic philosophy was. Following the meeting, Hopkins and

26. Hull, *Memoirs*, 1606.
27. Stimson and Bundy, *On Active Service*, 569.

Morgenthau discussed Stimson, with Hopkins observing, "It hurts him [Stimson] so much to think of the non-use of property. He's grown up in that school so long that property, God, becomes so sacred. . . ."[28] On the other hand, the fact that all three secretaries agreed on September 5 to the complete demilitarization of Germany, the dissolution of the Nazi party and all affiliated organizations, the energetic punishment of war criminals, strong controls over communications and education, and the principle of reparations shows that not all of what critics (particularly in Germany) did not like about the occupation could be attributed to Morgenthau and his putative desire for "Carthaginian" vengeance. Of course, Stimson had also bristled at Hull's demand for summary executions, countering that he believed Germany should be treated with "Christianity and kindness."[29] For Stimson, legal procedures were absolutely necessary, and it was within his department, as we will see in the next chapter, that the most important thinking for Nuremberg took place.

On September 5, however, it was clear that there was a significant breach, with the issue of German industry in the Ruhr and Saar regions as its focal point. The three secretaries agreed that the only course of action was to submit separate memos to Roosevelt outlining the differences. Stimson's memo argued that the "need for the recuperative benefits of productivity is more evident now than ever before . . ." He warned that "speed of reconstruction is of great importance, if we hope to avoid dangerous convulsions in Europe." The convulsions he had in mind were largely those of socialist revolution. But the general point, extending beyond the Ruhr/Saar question, was clear. Regarding the level of the German economy, Stimson objected that "[t]his would mean condemning the German people to a condition of servitude in which, no matter how hard or how effectively a man worked, he could not materially increase his economic condition in the world. Such a program," he argued, "would . . . create tension and resentments far outweighing any immediate advantage of security and would tend to obscure the guilt of the Nazis and the viciousness of their doctrines and their acts."[30]

Following a meeting with Roosevelt on September 6, both Stimson and Morgenthau each submitted to him yet another memo. Morgenthau's emphasized the economic benefits to England of German dismantling. Stimson's only available response was to urge Roosevelt to postpone the

28. Eisenberg, *Drawing the Line*, 39.
29. Ibid.
30. Memo quoted in Stimson and Bundy, *On Active Service*, 571–73.

issue yet again, not to commit prematurely to anything irreversible, though he emphasized that he believed it was unthinkable to turn "such a gift of nature into a dustheap."[31] For his part, Roosevelt reiterated his interest in summary executions and indicated that he saw some merits in internationalization rather than dismantling of the Ruhr and Saar industries. Morgenthau argued, however, that internationalization would merely invite future German efforts to re-acquire the region through yet another *Anschluss* (the term used for the annexation of Austria in 1938).[32] In this regard, it is interesting to note that Stimson even opposed an independent Austria. Roosevelt, however, gave no clear indication of what he was planning to do—if anything in these regards—when he was going to meet with Churchill two days later in Quebec, though he repeated his invitation to Hull to accompany him (Hull declined, claiming fatigue).

To Quebec and Back

Settlement of the German issue was not at the top of the agenda at Quebec, though it should have been foreseeable that it would be a major point. Nevertheless, the road to the issue was circuitous, beginning when Churchill pushed the discussion toward postwar economic aid for Britain, which was nearly bankrupt. Roosevelt used this as an excuse to summon Morgenthau to Quebec, and Morgenthau seized the opportunity to push his plan. While Churchill was at first resistant, Morgenthau and Churchill's advisor Lord Cherwell (previously known as Professor Frederick Lindemann) sold the plan in terms of its economic benefits to England; dismantling of German heavy industry and closing of its mines would starkly increase demand for British exports, making Great Britain Europe's economic engine. Churchill worried that this would be like chaining England to a dead body,[33] but in the end he could not resist. In another concession to Britain, Roosevelt agreed to occupy the southern portion of Germany, leaving the northern regions to Churchill. At the meeting's conclusion on September 15, Churchill and Roosevelt thus initialed a confidential memorandum outlining their agreement to dismantle

---

31. Ibid., 572.

32. Indeed, after the war, German leaders across the political spectrum demanded, and succeeded in obtaining, the return of the Saarland (by way of a plebiscite). Moreover, while both Left and Right were prepared to accept some international cooperation in the regulation of the Ruhr, they vigorously demanded a leading German voice in that oversight.

33. We will see reference to this remark in the postwar political rhetoric of Konrad Adenauer in chapter 11.

war-making industries in the Ruhr and Saar regions as "part of a program looking forward to diverting Germany into a largely agricultural country." Churchill referred to Morgenthau's plan at that time as a call for "pastoralizing" Germany, a label that, accurate or not, has stuck. Their agreement at Quebec also included provisions for summary executions of the Nazi leadership.

Morgenthau, obviously, was elated. Matters had moved in his direction beyond his expectations, though it is important to note that the agreement only referred to dismantling military industries, which was not all Morgenthau had demanded. (This point—coupled with his pleasure—gives weight to the interpretation that the harder version of Morgenthau's plan was formulated with an eye toward negotiation.) Hull, again dismayed by his marginalization, converted quickly to Stimson's side, claiming in his memoir that he never could have approved any such program because "[s]eventy million Germans could not live on the land within Germany. They would either starve or become a charge upon other nations." The plan, he asserted retrospectively, "would arouse the eternal resentment of the Germans. It would punish all of them and future generations too for the crimes of a portion of them."[34] It is thus clear that for all his punitive talk, Hull had always been firmly in the "regime decapitation" camp.

When Stimson received notice of the agreement, Assistant Secretary of War McCloy was already drafting a third memo to Roosevelt for Stimson's signature. Though sensing its futility, Stimson went ahead and sent the memo anyway. Whether simply because of McCloy's pen or a tactical decision, this third memo was couched in substantially more emotional language than Stimson's previous efforts to sway Roosevelt (not that these had been entirely free of emotional rhetoric either). The Stimson/McCloy memo emphasized that, in Stimson's view, the Morgenthau Plan violated the principles of the Atlantic Charter. As stated in Stimson's memoir, "[t]he paper was designed to appeal from FDR., [sic] the hasty signer of ill-considered memoranda, to Franklin Roosevelt, the farsighted and greatly humanitarian President of the United States": "The question," the memo proclaimed, "Is not whether we want Germans to suffer for their sins. Many of us would like to see them suffer the tortures they have inflicted on others. The only question is whether over the years a group of seventy million educated, efficient and imaginative people can be kept within bounds on such a low level of subsistence. . . . I do not believe this is humanly possible." Regarding the supposed enforcement of poverty Stimson believed the

34. Hull, *Memoirs*, 1611.

plan demanded, "it destroys the spirit not only of the victim but debases the victor."[35] Foreshadowing relativizing arguments common in Germany after May 8, 1945 (and similar to statements we saw in reactions to Vansittart), Stimson went so far as to assert, "It would be just such a crime as the Germans themselves hoped to perpetrate upon their victims—it would be a crime against civilization itself."[36] By implication, the Jewish "angel of revenge" was thus employing the same logic as the Nazis.

The memo continued for pages, referring to "fundamental" American beliefs in freedom and the values embodied in the Atlantic Charter, warning against the "shortsighted cupidity of the victors" and that "the proposals would mean a forcible revolution in all the basic methods of life. . . ." Stimson's memo concluded with two historically interesting thoughts. First, he argued that the "total elimination of a competitor (who is always also a potential purchaser) is rarely a satisfactory solution of a commercial problem." The economic philosophy underlying Stimson's approach was, again, clear. And second, he sweepingly condemned the very sentiments behind Morgenthau's approach: "The sum total of the drastic political and economic steps proposed by the Treasury is an open confession of the bankruptcy of hope for a reasonable economic and political settlement of the causes of war." This certainly overshot the mark, to such a degree that one senses the explosion of dissatisfactions pent up since at least Casablanca.

From "Pastoralization" to the Occupation Statute

The seemingly decisive agreement at Quebec did not last long. The American press was highly critical when the plan was leaked, and the ensuing scandal played into the electoral contest for the presidency. Roosevelt's challenger, Thomas Dewey, claimed that the plan was being used by the Nazi leadership to spur the population to fight to the last (though we have seen this argument several times already). Under fire, Roosevelt temporized, arguing that he hadn't really meant Germany would be "pastoralized." Churchill as well retreated after his return to London, in part because of concerns for British POWs in German custody. But he maintained at least a general commitment to the idea of summary executions. Interestingly—and perhaps surprising to the Atlantic Allies—however, Stalin was already rethinking the idea of summary executions in favor of the propaganda possibilities of trials.

35. Stimson and Bundy, *On Active Service*, 578–79.
36. Ibid.

Given the hasty retreat from the Morgenthau plan, it was perhaps not predictable that the final Occupation Statute would end up reflecting Morgenthau's design as much as it did. As the post-Quebec controversy was unfolding, drafting of the urgently needed directive for the occupation forces continued in the War Department, largely under the direction of McCloy. McCloy's clever solution was to maintain most of the tone of the Morgenthau Plan while including greater autonomy for zonal commanders to respond to urgent necessities that might otherwise cause chaos, threatening military security. In other words, most of Morgenthau's plans applied unless the zonal commanders decided to neglect them with a thin justification. McCloy's solution, that is, was Morgenthau's symbolic tone combined with a huge loophole. A draft of the interim agreement was thus cleared by the Joint Chiefs of Staff on September 22, 1944, and recorded as JCS (Joint Chiefs of Staff) 1067 (Directive to SCAEF Regarding the Military Government of Germany in the Period Immediately Following the Cessation of Organized Resistance [Post-Defeat]).

The State Department made one more effort to undermine the plan by attempting to offer it as a proposal through Winant to the EAC, knowing that it would find no support there. But despite this, the September 22 draft received only minor modifications before Roosevelt's successor, Harry S. Truman, signed it on May 11, 1945, which Morgenthau recorded in his diary as "a big day for the Treasury."[37]

* * *

The continued influence of "hard-peace" objectives was apparent as well when Churchill, Roosevelt, and Stalin met at Yalta in the Crimea in February 1945. The meeting reaffirmed the general direction of Allied planning to this point, including unconditional surrender, total eradication of National Socialism, and demilitarization—precursors of the so-called "four D's" of occupation policy articulated more fully at Potsdam in July 1945 (demilitarization/dismantling, denazification, decentralization/democratization, and decartelization). (The idea of "the four D's" became a common trope of postwar analyses.)[38] Yalta produced agreement on a number of general principles, including that portions of Poland east of the so-called "Oder-Neisse line" would go to the Soviet Union (though where exactly that line lay was

37. Beschloss, *The Conquerors*, 233.
38. Speakers and historians frequently refer to the "four D's," but as just demonstrated there seem to be more than four and different stories highlight different ones.

WOE TO THE VANQUISHED? 87

less clear than one might imagine—there are two Neisse rivers—and became a point of contention at Potsdam); that Germany would be divided into "zones of occupation"; and that Germany would pay 20 billion dollars in reparations, half to the Soviet Union (this last point over the objections of Churchill, although the extraction was limited to ten years, and the concession was in truth not as bad as State Department planners had feared). The final communiqué, issued on March 12, 1945, moreover, provided a fairly stern statement on the imminent occupation, similar to the tone of JCS 1067, which asserted that Germany was not being liberated but would be occupied as a defeated enemy nation, prohibited "fraternization" with the "enemy," and included the symbolic restrictions on airplanes, uniforms, and marching that Roosevelt had sought: "It is our inflexible purpose," the Yalta communiqué stated,

> to destroy German militarism and Nazism and to ensure that Germany will never again be able to disturb the peace of the world. We are determined to disarm and disband all German armed forces; break up for all time the German General Staff that has repeatedly contrived the resurgence of German militarism, remove or destroy all German military equipment; eliminate or control all German industry that could be used for military production; bring all war criminals to just and swift punishment and exact reparation in kind for the destruction wrought by the Germans; wipe out the Nazi Party, Nazi laws, organizations and institutions, remove all Nazi and militarist influences from public office and from the cultural and economic life of the German people; and take in harmony such other measures in Germany as may be necessary to the future peace and safety of the world. *It is not our purpose to destroy the people of Germany, but only when Nazism and militarism have been extirpated will there be hope for a decent life for Germans, and a place for them in the comity of nations* [emphasis added].

Clearly, the Allies continued to see themselves at war with the German nation, and not merely with its Nazi usurpers; disentanglement of regime and *Volk*, the statement implied, was going to be very difficult.

Potsdam

Before drawing conclusions about this story for the emergent German mnemonic landscape, it is necessary to look briefly at the Potsdam conference, an event that has been treated as infamous in German memory. From July 17 to August 2, 1945, Truman, Stalin, and Churchill (the latter replaced after the British parliamentary election by new Prime Minister Clement Attlee) met in Potsdam outside of Berlin to negotiate the future of the geopolitical balance, and the future of Germany as its linchpin. Because the "Allies" no longer faced the common aim of defeating Nazi Germany, emerging perceptions of different interests created a more incipiently hostile tone than had prevailed at Yalta. Nevertheless, the meeting did yield concrete policies, the ramifications of which are felt to this day.

From the geopolitical standpoint, the most important result of Potsdam was the ceding of Polish territories to the Soviet Union and of German territory to Poland. While the Allies had in principle agreed to such an arrangement at Yalta, the details remained vague. In the final agreement at Potsdam, the territories released to the Soviet "sphere of influence" (a term just emerging during this period) included large portions of Silesia and Pomerania, and East Prussia, among others. The problem (as Sumner Welles had long foreseen) was that this meant millions of "ethnic" Germans would have to be forcibly expelled. According to article XII of the final protocol on the "Orderly Transfer of German Populations," "The Three Governments, having considered the question in all its aspects, recognize that the transfer to Germany of German populations . . . will have to be undertaken. They agree that any transfers that take place should be effected in an orderly and humane manner." This last normative statement was blindly unrealistic. Not only did such a transfer violate basic principles outlined in the Atlantic Charter (Welles's argument notwithstanding), it was an easily foreseeable practical humanitarian disaster, one which would serve important functions in German memory.

The Potsdam accord also included powerful programmatic statements to guide and define the occupation, in many ways reiterating earlier pronouncements and echoing aspects of JCS 1067, but in some respects going beyond them. In the section on political principles, the accord repeated that the goal of occupation was "to convince the German people that they have suffered a total military defeat and that they cannot escape responsibility for what they have brought upon themselves, since their own ruthless warfare and the fanatical Nazi resistance have destroyed the German economy and made chaos and suffering inevitable." (An important feature of JCS 1067 was the so-called "nonfraternization rule," prohibiting anything beyond official interaction with the German population; it was a thoroughly unworkable proposition.)[39]

The accord reached at Potsdam was a reminder, however, that the task was "[t]o prepare for the eventual reconstruction of German political life

---

39. On the fraternization question, see Goedde, *GIs and Germans*, which I also discuss in chapter 5.

on a democratic basis and for eventual peaceful cooperation in international life by Germany." Freedom of speech, press, and religion would be permitted, and religious institutions would be protected. Formation of trade unions would be allowed. Local self-government would be restored "on democratic principles." Political parties would be allowed to form, and public discussion would be permitted. More generally—and indeed shorter-lived—the "administration in Germany should be directed towards the decentralization of the political structure and the development of local responsibility." (This decentralization did not, however, fit emerging needs for consolidation in 1947–48, and thus retreated.)

Beyond political, institutional, and juridical matters (which included decentralization, demilitarization, denazification, and some aspects of re-education), the Potsdam accord also dealt with two economic topics: decartelization and reparations. "At the earliest practicable date," the final statement read, "the German economy shall be decentralized for the purpose of eliminating the present excessive concentration of economic power as exemplified in particular by cartels, syndicates, trusts and other monopolistic arrangements. . . . In organizing the German Economy, primary emphasis shall be given to the development of agriculture and peaceful domestic industries." (These measures, however, were never carried through to even part of the extent indicated here.)[40] While Germany would not be intentionally starved, the Allies aimed "to assure the production and maintenance of goods and services required to meet the needs of the occupying forces and displaced persons in Germany and essential to maintain in Germany average living standards not exceeding the average of the standards of living of European countries."

The winter of 1945–46 was harsh, and German suffering was great indeed; whether this suffering was a result of Allied policies and their putative vengefulness, however, is highly doubtful—people were hungry all over Europe that winter. The situation was certainly somewhat exacerbated by the extensive dismantling of basic resources under the rubric of "reparations," which the Western Allies conceded to the Soviets at Potsdam. Indeed, rightly or wrongly, Western forbearance of Soviet dismantling appears in German memory as evidence of the Atlantic Allies' willingness to sacrifice German interests on the altar of geopolitics.

Potsdam symbolized for many postwar Germans everything that was wrong with Allied occupation policy. Some of its provisions—like denazification and dismantling—were problematic but short-lived, nevertheless

40. Wiesen, *West German Industry and the Challenge of the Nazi Past.*

playing a large role in German memory of the period. Others, particularly the ethnic resettlements, were more enduringly significant and were seen in German discourse as the true punishment of Germany, becoming a rallying cry for claims of German victimhood and accusations of Allied duplicity. In some German formulations, the expulsion of ethnic Germans from Eastern territories approved at Potsdam was a crime equal to—and thus in many ways canceling out—the atrocities of the death camps. If December 7, 1941, is a day that has lived in infamy for Americans, Potsdam has thus achieved analogous iconic status in Germany. Indeed, May 8 and Potsdam are more significant referents in German memory than, say, January 30, 1933 (Hitler's seizure of power), or September 1, 1939 (the beginning of the war with the invasion of Poland). This fact is of substantial interpretive importance.

Assessing "Morgenthau"

According to an influential 1957 paper on U.S. planning for postwar Germany, there were three distinct schools of thought in 1944.[41] First, there was an "outlaw" theory that viewed a small clique as responsible for National Socialism, and thus called for regime decapitation. Stimson was certainly a prime exponent of this position, not only in his opposition to Morgenthau's economic proposals, but in his demand for criminal trials based on the individual's degree of complicity as well. Second, a "neo-Marxist" school of thought viewed National Socialism as the product of social tensions inherent in capitalism, and the collusion of industrial and aristocratic elites. The point of this perspective was that no mere regime decapitation followed by superimposition of democratic structures would solve the German problem because the social foundations for such a system did not yet exist. The only solution from this perspective was to disrupt entrenched patterns, to effect, that is, a social revolution of sorts. The third school of thought, according to this analysis, comprised "Vansittartists" of various color, those who adamantly denied any distinction between regime and *Volk*. For exponents of this third position, nothing short of a long-term re-education of the entire German people—whether it was to be political, cultural, or psychological—could prevent a resurgence of German militarism. Revolution would require significant disruptive measures before it could enter a more constructive phase.

41. Dorn, "The Debate over American Occupation Policy," 484–85. Dorn was denazification adviser to Deputy Military Governor Lucius Clay.

Under this analysis, Morgenthau belonged squarely within the third camp. This was how Stimson painted him when he characterized the plan as vengeful and Carthaginian. And this is how Morgenthau is most often remembered, as a pair with Vansittart. Given his Jewishness, how could he be motivated by anything other than pure Germanaphobia (though what explains Vansittart here remains open)? Nevertheless, there is an alternative understanding of Morgenthau that assigns greater weight to the distinction between the conservative economic interests Stimson, Hull, and McCloy represented and the New Deal liberalism of Roosevelt, Hopkins, and Morgenthau.

Evidence for Morgenthau's vengefulness was his putative desire to set the Germans back a hundred or more years by destroying their industry. But, as Warren Kimball has pointed out, "Although the Morgenthau Plan for Germany later received widespread condemnation as a design to starve the German people, that was not his intention. A gentleman farmer who loved the land (his early work with Roosevelt had been in agriculture), Morgenthau assumed that reestablishing contact with the land would turn the Germans into good, honest, democratic yeoman farmers, the Jeffersonian ideal."[42] In other words, Morgenthau's model for Germany was Denmark, not Siberia. Naïve perhaps, but not solely vengeful. Addressing the implication of such a proposal for the European economy more generally, Kimball argues that "[w]hether European economic prosperity depended upon German industrial recovery is both doubtful and moot; that equation became a self-fulfilling prophecy since American policy-makers ultimately acted as if that was the case." Kimball's conclusion thus emphasizes Morgenthau's partial membership in the second rather than third school of thought: "Taken as a whole, the Morgenthau Plan was a design for a radical reconstruction of Germany. Imbued with the belief of many New Dealers in the efficacy of grand plans as the solution to problems, it called for a total change in the occupations and life-styles of most Germans."[43] As Carol Eisenberg has argued, "To administration liberals, the overriding foreign policy objective was the obliteration of fascism—detested for its dictatorial, racist, and militaristic features. . . . From this perspective, the restoration of a capitalist Germany was an appalling prospect."[44] This will be important to remember when we observe later that it was the German Left that argued strongly that Allied re-education programs blocked an indigenous German reckoning with the Nazi past.

42. Kimball, *Swords or Ploughshares?* 25.
43. Ibid., 31.
44. Eisenberg, *Drawing the Line*, 32.

For his part, in his 1945 book justifying the plan, Morgenthau was clearly answering Stimson's character attack when he argued, "The elimination of German heavy industry is not a hate campaign. The world has seen enough of hatred. . . . It is, however, an essential preliminary to peace, to realization of the ideals for which the United States has fought, to the security of all nations (even including Germany), and to that better world which the sacrifices of all people have entitled them to expect."[45] Honest or not, a reflection of Morgenthau's intentions or White's tactics, Morgenthau's book is decidedly cool in comparison to many others mentioned in the previous chapter. The point here, however, is that interpretations of Morgenthau as a social reformer rather than as a vengeful Jew have remained marginal. In contrast, Michael Beschloss's Stimsonesque portrait of Morgenthau was required reading in the 2002 wartime Bush White House, and reflects the interpretative orthodoxy without acknowledging other possible interpretations.[46] I have already discussed the triumphalist motivations for such an account, which were even more important during the Cold War than after, or at least important in different ways.

*   *   *

Was U.S. policy for the occupation of Germany a triumph for Morgenthau? First, to make the case, the appropriate comparison is not between JCS 1067 (with McCloy's loopholes) and the Morgenthau Plan in its full bloom, but between JCS 1067 and the *Handbook* (even though the *Handbook*'s authors were already in the process of revising it when Morgenthau showed it to Roosevelt). In other words, the comparison is not between everything Morgenthau could imagine and what he got, but between what he got and what we would have gotten if he hadn't imagined anything at all. And second, one purpose of the foregoing chapters has been to situate Morgenthau within a wider context in which he was far from outside the spectrum of attitudes among serious people, ranging from Richard Brickner to Sumner Welles and ultimately to FDR himself. That Morgenthau's efforts were radical or, as Harry S. Truman called his plan, "crazy," is thus doubtful. Efforts to explain away Roosevelt's support for Morgenthau as indications of his dotage, moreover, are far from unproblematic.

Indeed, in part because many officials of the Military Government for occupied Germany (not least General Lucius Clay himself) viewed JCS

---

45. Morgenthau, *Germany Is Our Problem*, 28.

46. Beschloss, *The Conquerors*. The claim that Beschloss was widely read in the Bush White House was made by Nicholas D. Kristoff, *New York Times*, April 18, 2003.

1067 as unworkable and sought to subvert it in practice, the history of the occupation can be (and most often is) told as the story of the on-going abrogation of JCS 1067, an effort to overcome the influence of Morgenthau and Vansittartism more generally. Such a narrative fits as well with the idea that whatever support or good reasons there may have been for a "hard peace" outgrew their relevance very quickly as the possibilities for cooperation with the Soviet Union dried up. As Carolyn Eisenberg has pointed out, however, "Later it would be said that the rebuilding of West Germany was an unanticipated result of the Cold War. But the impetus for reconstruction predated the East–West rift."[47] This points to the usefulness for legitimating U.S. policy in the Cold War of portraying the struggle between Stimson and "Morgenthau" as a fight for the principles of American rule of law, economic freedom, and self-determination. As Warren Kimball concludes his revisionist reading, "When the American government finally threw out the Morgenthau Plan for Germany, it threw out the baby with the bath-water; for not only did the United States eschew a policy of revenge, but it also tossed away programs which could have established a truly neutral, disengaged Germany. That alternative might have, with relatively little risk, significantly diminished the tension and length of the Cold War."[48]

Conclusion

The foregoing should not be misunderstood as an effort to defend the Morgenthau Plan, the details of which made sense neither at the time nor retrospectively. But it is to show the differences between Morgenthau and "Morgenthau," and to uncover the mnemonic processes whereby the former became the latter. My purpose in the foregoing pages has thus not been to introduce new facts into what is a well-trodden historical terrain. Rather, it has been to retell this fascinating history from the perspective of an interest in the origins of memory of National Socialism. The story of Allied preparations (giving such predominance to the United States in large part because it was predominant in the actual history) is a crucial framework for the future dialogues of German memory, both because it provided a major reference and was an object of German memory itself. But I have also sought to tell this story as a dialogical set of struggles itself, the first decisive agonies of German defeat.

47. Eisenberg, *Drawing the Line*, 25.
48. Kimball, *Swords or Ploughshares?* 62. Indeed, that alternative would have been all the more likely had Stalin's proposals of the early 1950s to cede control over East Germany been more serious—a matter of much historiographical dispute.

From this perspective, we should remember three points. First, "hard-peace" approaches were not necessarily or solely vengefully motivated (there were "soft-peace" proponents who had vengeful instincts, "hard-peace" proponents who did not, and most people had at least some distaste for Germany by the end of the war). Second, even if vengefulness had a significant impact on American policy for postwar Germany, the causal connections between those policies and postwar German suffering are far from clear (the policy could have been ill conceived and vengeful, the Germans could have suffered, and these might have had little to do with each other; furthermore, identifying Anglo-American intentions rather than German Nationalist aggression as the source of German suffering has its own uses). And third, very little in these discussions had much to do with the truly novel aspect of National Socialism—its treatment of the Jews. In other words, none of the figures whose opinions and efforts we have examined in such detail thought that Germany was to be occupied and divided because of what it was doing to Jews; the crimes under consideration at this time were war crimes, and not the "crimes against humanity" taking place in the extermination camps: Germany was to be punished for undertaking an aggressive war and for the brutalities of occupation; "genocide" (a term coined during the war by Polish émigré legal scholar Raphael Lemkin and adopted by the United Nations in December 1946) was another issue not yet on the table.[49] Morgenthau certainly did not highlight it in his arguments or in his book. Again, it would take many years for the uniqueness of Jewish victimhood to crystallize (falsely) in German and world memory as the overriding motivation for, or at least benefit of, defeating Germany.

49. In his memoir of the Nuremberg trials, Telford Taylor reports that participants in the London Conference leading to the International Military Tribunal at Nuremberg (discussed below) began using the newly coined term "genocide" in late summer 1945. Taylor, *Anatomy of the Nuremberg Trials*, 103. "Crimes against humanity" referred at this point to crimes of Germans against Germans, and not to the exterminations of East European Jews in Auschwitz and elsewhere, which were generally understood as "war crimes." An interesting part of this story, as we will see, is the shifting division of reference between the concepts of "war crimes" and "crimes against humanity."

CHAPTER 5

Indictment

While occupation planning later appeared in German memory as a choice between "dismembering" Germany and "restoring" it, the previous chapters have shown that such an account portrays neither the planning nor its implementation accurately and underplays the more complex ambition of transforming (rather than destroying) German society. Between dismemberment and restoration, we saw, lay the idea of "re-education," born of a deep distrust of German culture but also of a pragmatic hope for the future. If Germany's reconstruction was to succeed, it would have to proceed through German recognition of responsibility and of the need for transformation.[1] In the early weeks and months of the occupation, this meant demonstrating to Germans both the extent of Nazi atrocities and that they were indeed responsible for them. This more complex ambition, of course, does not work as well mnemonically as the grand struggle between "dismemberment" and "restoration."

Though the Joint Chiefs of Staff occupation statute (JCS 1067) was a top-secret document and included loopholes that would allow more supportive measures for the German economy and society, the many wartime statements and the Potsdam communiqué, among other things, were all intended as a tough message to the German people. Any thoughts—like those expressed by the remaining German leadership after Hitler's suicide—that the Atlantic Allies would now join Germany in the fight against "Bolshevism" were to be nipped in the bud (in actuality, of course, "change of enemies" is exactly what happened, though perhaps not in the aggressive fashion the German military leadership had hoped, and not

---

1. For a general account of re-education policy, see Pronay and Wilson, *The Political Re-education of Germany and Her Allies after World War II.*

immediately).[2] Any sense, moreover, that ordinary Germans were not of a piece with the regime was to be refuted. Nevertheless, democratization was the overriding stated goal of all the Allies (though the Soviets understood it differently than the British and Americans). Even during the war, the Americans had been preparing their German prisoners for a new ideology in the so-called "barbed-wire colleges."[3] Training for the occupation forces, we also saw, was informed by the latest social and political science. In the Potsdam communiqué, positive measures for the occupation included reorganization of the universities and revision of school curricula with the intention of reworking the fundaments of German self-understanding. (Other plans for restructuring the German civil service, however, largely failed in the face of German recalcitrance.)[4] But before this could take place, many in the West believed—and early occupation measures and directives required—that Germans would have to recognize what had happened under National Socialism, and that they were the ones who, directly or indirectly, had caused it. Occupation policy on the ground was thus a complex amalgam of carrots and sticks.

For many Germans, however, the idea of re-education seemed arrogant and illegitimate. As we will see, many German intellectuals and politicians located the causes of National Socialism in generalized forces of Western history at large—including nihilism, secularization, and "massification." As a result, they rejected re-education and charges of "collective guilt" as efforts to make Germany the scapegoat for pathologies endemic to the West as a whole. Indeed, as we will see, they often characterized such thinking (without any indication of irony!) as "Pharisaical," referring to the ancient Jewish cult that, in Christian doctrine, represents hypocrisy.[5] Indeed, as we will also see, there arose a common equation between Germans and Jews, in which Germany was supposedly now suffering the same treatment as the Jews had. The implication of Pharisaism was that any charges against Germany without a corresponding inquiry into the guilt of the victors was unfair, perhaps even dangerous. Interestingly, this response was directed most vigorously at the West, for acts ranging from British Prime Minister Neville Chamberlain's attempt to appease Hitler by allowing the annexation of the Sudetenland, to

2. See Annan, *Changing Enemies.*
3. See Robin, *The Barbed-Wire College.*
4. See especially Frei, *Adenauer's Germany and the Nazi Past;* Diehl, *The Thanks of the Fatherland;* Hughes, *Shouldering the Burdens of Defeat.*
5. See Matthew 23:13 for the refrain: "How terrible for you, teachers of the Law and Pharisees! Hypocrites!" Also, the Parable of the Pharisee in Luke 18:9–14 gives the Pharisees as an example of "people who were sure of their own goodness and despised everybody else."

the firebombing of Dresden in the last months of the war. Because the Soviet approach was more directly political and less moralistic—sharing with German theories the diagnosis of problems not specific to Germany—defense against it did not have to be nearly so complex. Soviet motivations seemed clear. In contrast, whether the West was motivated by naïve optimism or festering anti-Germanism depended on one's point of view. The German Right was resentful but discredited and, at least temporarily, bitterly silent (though not as silent as one might imagine). On the Left, much was made of the Allies' putatively cynical lack of enthusiasm for the *Antifas*, or indigenous antifascist organizations, that cropped up during and following the defeat. These charges echoed the criticism of Anglo-American indifference to the German opposition during the war. The fiasco of denazification was widely seen to have preempted a self-motivated German political or legal confrontation with the Nazi past. Whether such a confrontation would have arisen, of course, is entirely hypothetical.[6]

Accusing and Denying

As noted above, overall planning for occupation was driven largely by geopolitical concerns about the balance of power and by the desire to prevent Germany from starting another war, rather than by moral concerns (though retributive and utilitarian, psychological and political motives are really only separable in retrospect). Nevertheless, advanced planning for how to treat the German population was overwhelmed in the first days by what the Allied soldiers found in Germany, and horror at the extent of Nazi cruelty shaped the first months of the occupation. The renewed harshness of the Potsdam statement at the end of the summer of 1945—including its more prominent than hitherto statement on the need to eliminate racist and politically discriminatory laws—was at least in part a reaction to reports from Germany. By the same token, the chaos of the early occupation strengthened the resolve of those who favored quick reconstruction (the early occupation of the city of Aachen was particularly notorious for its disorganization).

Despite this confusion, all of the Allies took measures in the first days to prevent ordinary Germans from evading "the truth."[7] These included

6. See especially Niethammer, *Die Mitläferfabrik;* Herz, "The Fiasco of Denazification."

7. There were, of course, important differences in the different zones. The Russians favored a more directly punitive approach, arresting larger numbers of people than the other Allies. The British, on the other hand, were less eager for punishment and re-education than the Americans. While there was some disagreement between the British and Americans, however, American strategies played a leading role.

forcing locals (most often élites, but frequently enough ordinary townspeople as well) to tour concentration camps,[8] to participate in burial and cleanup, and to answer accusations that they could not have been totally ignorant, and thus could not have been totally innocent, of "what had occurred."[9] In his history of the aftermath of the war, Douglas Botting illustratively quotes a speech given to mayors of Celle and surrounding towns on April 24, 1945, by a British Colonel at the beginning of a tour of the Belsen camp:

> What you see here is such a disgrace to the German people that their name must be erased from the list of civilized nations. You stand here judged by what you will see in this camp. It is your lot to begin the hard task of restoring the name of the German people to the list of civilized nations. But this cannot be done until you have reared a new generation amongst whom it is impossible to find people prepared to commit such crimes.[10]

Quite a number of American and British soldiers, moreover, reported surprise in the first weeks at what they saw as indifference of Germans to what many Germans claimed they were seeing and hearing for the first time. According to a 1945 study by the sociologist Morris Janowitz, most Germans he interrogated admitted knowing something about the concentration camp system, but denied knowledge of the atrocities committed in them. Moreover, his report points out, "Almost everywhere one encountered acceptance of the facts, although frequently in an automatic fashion which bespoke a lack of genuine concern."[11]

In many cities and towns, occupation authorities set up photographic displays of evidence. These were often accompanied by such slogans as "These Atrocities: Your Fault" (*Diese Schandtaten: Eure Schuld*) and "This is Your Fault" (*Das ist eure Schuld*).[12] Additionally, the Western Allies produced documentary films about the concentration camp system—the most promi-

---

8. Most of these tours, in Germany, were of camps that, while horrific, were concentration rather than extermination camps. As we will see shortly, this contributed to the overall despecification of Jewish victimhood.

9. See Marcuse, *Legacies of Dachau*, especially 55–59.

10. Botting, *From the Ruins of the Reich*, 45–46; also quoted (from Botting) in Bark and Gress, *From Shadow to Substance*, 37.

11. Janowitz, "German Reactions to Nazi Atrocities," 143.

12. Aleida Assmann argues that the impact of these photographic "placard actions" has been overlooked in the literature. She cites a directive to Allied press agencies stating that the goal of these demonstrations was to convince the German population of their collective guilt; this directive, Assmann (after Brink's work) writes, was rescinded because it hindered the emerging goal of democratization. Assmann and Frevert, *Geschichtsvergessenheit-Geschichtsversessenheit*. See also Barnouw, *Germany 1945*; Brink, *Ikonen der Vernichtung*.

nent of which was titled *Die Todesmühlen* (Death Mills)—and showed them widely throughout the Western Zones (*Todesmühlen* was released in the American Zone in January 1946, and was required viewing). There was no doubt about the accusatory stance of this "documentary": the narration concluded gruesomely, though sarcastically, by charging that the "farmers received tons of human bones as fertilizer . . . but apparently never suspected it came from human beings. . . . Manufacturers received tons of human hair . . . but apparently never dreamed it came from the heads of murdered women. . . . No nightmares haunted those who lived near concentration camps. . . . The cries and moans of the tortured were no doubt believed the wailing of the wind." The film ends with a crowd scene from the Nazi propaganda film *The Triumph of the Will*, thus implying mass German complicity.[13]

Nevertheless, the impetus to use these films and other devices to produce a feeling of collective guilt among ordinary Germans was not universally supported. Beginning in February 1945, for instance, the Psychological Warfare Division of SHAEF began a collaboration with the British to produce a film made from British, American, and Soviet footage of the concentration camps. The intent was to confront Germans with their guilt and humiliate them into submission, based on the assertion that blame could not be limited to the Nazi leadership or to the SS. But production of this film—labeled only "F3080" by the British archive that held it for decades—was delayed for a combination of mechanical, professional, and political reasons: there was trouble assembling and editing the materials; the Americans wanted Billy Wilder to direct it (he directed *Todesmühlen*) while the British ultimately asked Alfred Hitchcock for technical help; but, most important, the British military wanted to encourage a less harsh approach as a way of improving German cooperation with the occupation and reconstruction in their zone. The Americans withdrew from the project on July 9, 1945, shortly before the dissolution of the Psychological Warfare Division altogether. Given the less punitive British approach, the film was never shown in Germany, and first appeared publicly on PBS in the United States only in 1985.[14]

* * *

If imputations of collective guilt disappeared fairly quickly, the first months of occupation did pose the issue, though the answers were never entirely

13. Quoted in Fehrenbach, *Cinema in Democratizing Germany*, 57.
14. Historical information on the film is available at www.pbs.org/wgbh/pages/frontline/camp.

clear. As we will see, memory of these accusations played a central role in subsequent discourse. Their effects, however, were often the opposite of what was intended. Indeed, survey data and anecdotal evidence indicate that very few Germans denied the accuracy of the reports of the atrocities (though they did not accept personal or political responsibility for them), but many claimed not to have known, or at least not to have known the extent of, what had occurred in the camps. (As we will see later, the images of the camps were often of those that held German and other prisoners; when images were of camps whose inmates were mostly Jews, this fact was not highlighted.) While many German opinion leaders echoed claims not to have known, many others were perfectly clear that it would have taken significant self-deception truly to have missed what was going on, if not in the details at least in the outlines; moreover, when people claimed they did not know "what was going on," one had to ask what it was they did not know—that people were being killed in specific ways in specific places, or that the regime was terrorist and people were disappearing? Few specified. Surely, however, the overwhelming majority knew something. Others readily acknowledged they knew what had happened, but turned immediately to point out the ways in which Germans had suffered at least as much—and indeed were continuing to suffer.

All this, of course, should not be taken to imply that Germans did not suffer, that they were not also victims. The extent of physical and moral devastation in 1945 was truly unprecedented. For years, Germans had endured horrific bombing raids and the associated terrors of the shelters. German casualties were staggering, and manifested no real boundary between military and civilians. In some areas, in the last months of the war, repeated rapes by invading troops were common.[15] Physically, to speak of Germany as a ruin in 1945 is to romanticize it: "All the uncertainties of change in time and the tragedy of loss associated with the past" Georg Simmel wrote at the turn of the century, "find in the ruin a coherent and unified expression."[16] But Germany in 1945 was a wreck, not a ruin, devoid of coherent form, a rock-strewn landscape of disaster in which the dispossessed lived like mole people. Homelessness was rampant—the housing stock was substantially more than decimated. Moreover, estimates are that approximately 10 million people were expelled from the East, more than a million dying en route (the flight from the East had begun well before the end of the war, in large numbers as early as 1943, as

15. See especially Grossman, "A Question of Silence."
16. Simmel, "The Ruin," 260.

had the trope of *armes Deutschland* [poor Germany]). Conditions for German soldiers in U.S. army captivity were horrific, with severe food shortages and often inadequate or nonexistent shelter.[17] As many as 3 million German soldiers spent time in Soviet captivity. As many as a million died there, and tens of thousands did not return until well into the 1950s. Efforts to narrate May 8, 1945, as a liberation thus never spoke to the existential concerns of most Germans, though they had their political uses.

Nevertheless, many critics of Germany hoped for some recognition of the connections between early enthusiasm for National Socialism and what Germans were experiencing, as well as greater attention to the harms Germany had inflicted on others. In a much-quoted "Report from Germany," however, expatriate philosopher Hannah Arendt described the self-absorbed and defensive reactions she encountered when she revealed on a trip to Germany that she was a German Jew:

> This is usually followed by a little embarrassed pause; and then comes—not a personal question, such as "Where did you go after you left Germany?"; no sign of sympathy, such as "What happened to your family?"—but a deluge of stories about how Germans have suffered (true enough, of course, but beside the point); and if the object of this little experiment happens to be educated and intelligent, he will proceed to draw up a balance between German suffering and the suffering of others.

This report is from 1950; conditions immediately after the surrender and in the following winter were much more difficult for many Germans, and the self-absorption thus proportionally greater. Arendt's is only the most famous such report, and it is matched by many others.[18]

Different authors emphasize different elements of these German reactions to images of the camps. Some use the fact that "ordinary" Germans responded with horror as evidence that they rejected the implications of National Socialism; others point out that reactions of disgust only underlined ordinary people's sense that these atrocities had nothing whatsoever to do with them. People were repelled by what they saw, but often

---

17. Radical revisionists, however, have grossly exaggerated the extent of suffering and deaths of German POWs under American authority, as well as have bizarrely misread the evidence of General Dwight Eisenhower's motives for the U.S. army's treatment of POWs. For an incontrovertible refutation, see Bishof and Ambrose, *Eisenhower and the German POWs*.

18. See also Speier, *From the Ashes of Disgrace*.

complained that this was only half of the story: Germans too had suffered under a brutal dictatorship; had their cities devastated; lost homes, fathers, and brothers, to say nothing of their very pride both individually and collectively. From this perspective, the suffering of the Jews seemed nothing special to many Germans.[19] As Eugen Kogon wrote early in 1946:

> A people that had seen the charred remains of its women and children in every last corner of its bomb-ravaged cities could not be shaken by the amassed piles of naked corpses that were shown to it from the final phase of the concentration camps. . . . The policy of "shock" awakened not the powers of the German conscience, but the powers of resistance against the accusation of complete co-responsibility for the shameful misdeeds of the National Socialists.[20]

It is telling, however, that Kogon does not refer here specifically to Jews (we will see more of Kogon later, who was one of those most interested in this period in acknowledging Jewish suffering). Neither *Todesmühlen* nor F3080 referred to Jews either, naming only victims "from every European nationality." The last scene of *Todesmühlen*, moreover, even referred to the Calvary of the murdered victims: the Germans "bear heavy crosses now . . . the crosses of the millions crucified in Nazi death mills!" Whether the Jews who died in the camps thought they were being crucified is another matter altogether.[21] The point is that Jewish death was not viewed as distinct.

19. Public opinion data, for instance, show that Germans did in general support restitution to Jews, but they ranked Jews last on an ordinal list of who should receive financial help. Merritt, *Democracy Imposed*, 140–45.

20. Kogon, "Gericht und Gewissen." Translation adapted from Marcuse, *Legacies of Dachau*, 71. As Robert Moeller puts it in his incisive study of the postwar period, "By telling stories of the enormity of their losses, West Germans were able to reject charges of 'collective guilt,' briefly leveled by the victors immediately after the war, and claim status as heroic survivors. . . . In this abbreviated account of National Socialism, all Germans were ultimately victims of a war that Hitler had started but everyone lost." Moeller, *War Stories*, 3. Indeed, this "abbreviated account" is one of the founding myths of the Federal Republic. One possible point of dispute with this otherwise concise and trenchant analysis is that many Germans immediately after the war still excluded Hitler from culpability: The *Führer* was as much the victim of nefarious forces as were ordinary Germans. See Merritt, *Democracy Imposed*, 90–94. Moreover, according to a study based on reports from the British 21st Army Group in Germany, even in late 1945 and 1946 "Hitler towered . . . above every criticism." Marshall, "German Reactions to Military Defeat," 220. See also Kershaw, *The Hitler Myth*.

21. Fehrenbach, *Cinema in Democratizing Germany*, 57. See also Bloxham, *Genocide on Trial*, 81. Many years later, a similar elision was evident in Käthe Kollwitz's choice of subject for a statue in the *Neue Wache*, an East German shrine that according to the unification treaty was to be preserved after 1990 as a monument to the victims of World War II. Kollwitz sculpted a *Pieta*.

Jews and DPs

In the early months of the occupation, there were neither perceptual nor administrative distinctions drawn between Jewish and other "displaced persons" (DPs). As we just saw, non-Jewish Germans denied distinctions between their own suffering and that of their Jewish compatriots. When Jews were accorded some leeway or provided extra rations, this produced anti-Semitic jealousy.[22] Jews came to be seen as particularly adept at black-market activities, evoking the stereotype of cleverness and money changing, though they comprised only a small minority of black marketeers.[23] Indeed, this lack of distinction among political and religious victims, refugees, and the victims of racial persecution and attempted genocide was not restricted to the Germans. The overarching designation "DP" was a common term in the occupation lexicon and the situation of Jewish DPs was often not as immediately remedied as popular culture portrays. In June and July of 1945, for instance, Jews were classified in terms of their national origins and thus lumped in with their conationals (many of whom had sympathized with Nazi anti-Semitism).[24] Many occupation authorities expressed disgust at the chaos of the DP camps, often not free of dubious overtones of disdain for the people forced to live there. General George Patton even ordered erection of barbed-wire barricades to control the populations of various DP camps (Eisenhower later rescinded those orders). According to Zeev Mankowitz, the U.S. Army's policy was based on a logic "designed primarily to deal with the complex challenges of post-war Germany," which was "often at odds with the special needs of the many survivors who resisted the idea of repatriation." Perversely, at least part of the Army's failure to distinguish between Jews and other DPs was, according to Mankowitz, "the absence of a consensual view of the nature of the Jewish group and the fear that dividing them off would be seen as akin to the Nazi policies of separation and exclusion."[25]

The situation of the Jewish DPs was indeed woeful, misunderstood, and occasionally incendiary (there were numerous confrontations, some large,

22. See Marshall, "German Reactions to Military Defeat," 223.
23. One problem is that appearing Jewish provided a useful weapon against police intervention, so it was common for non-Jews to claim to be Jewish in order to evade official harassment.
24. British assessments of the specificity of Jewish victimhood were very much constrained by the situation in Palestine.
25. Mankowitz, *Life between Memory and Hope*, 13–16; see also Geis, *Übrig sein—Leben "danach"*; Königseder and Wetzel, *Waiting for Hope*.

some small, some between Jewish DPs and other DPs, some between Jewish DPs and Germans).[26] Aware of the situation, representatives of Jewish groups lobbied President Truman, as did Henry Morgenthau, to investigate the conditions of Jewish DPs in Germany and to issue new guidelines for the occupation authorities. Truman responded by commissioning Earl G. Harrison—U.S. representative on the Intergovernmental Committee on Refugees—to write a report on the matter. Harrison's report, presented on September 29, 1945, was scathing. Its conclusion raised the whole complex of issues surrounding Allied intentions and the powerful—and unprecedented—pedagogical role the occupation would have:

> There is the opportunity to give some real meaning here to the policy agreed upon at Potsdam. If it be true, as seems to be widely conceded, that the German people at large do not have any sense of guilt with respect to the war and its causes and results, and if the policy is to be "to convince the German people that they cannot escape responsibility for what they have brought upon themselves," it is difficult to understand why so many displaced persons, particularly those who have so long been persecuted and whose repatriation or resettlement is likely to be delayed, should be compelled to live in crude, overcrowded camps while the German people, in rural areas, continue undisturbed in their homes. . . . As matters now stand, we appear to be treating the Jews as the Nazis treated them except that we do not exterminate them. They are in concentration camps in large numbers under our military guard instead of S.S. troops. One is led to wonder whether the German people, seeing this, are not supposing that we are following or at least condoning Nazi policy.[27]

This equation of Allied and Nazi treatment of Jews is obviously an overstatement for rhetorical effect, though it is important to remember the goal of that misrepresentation; in comparison, Germans themselves offered a similar association between Allied treatment of Germans and

26. See especially Stern, *The Whitewashing of the Yellow Badge*, 106–11. In his memoir, U.S. Military Governor Lucius Clay confirms this attitude: "I was shocked with a German recommendation to lower the ration of displaced persons to the German level. It was necessary to remind the *Länderrat* (Council of States) that other nations were sending in the additional food for the displaced persons and that Germany was fortunate not to be forced to assume the entire burden of support for these unfortunate people who were there through no fault or desire of their own but as a result of ruthless Nazi action." Clay, *Decision in Germany*, 100.

27. Stern, *The Whitewashing of the Yellow Badge*, 72–82. Also see Bischof and Ambrose, *Eisenhower and the German POWs*, 3–4.

Nazi treatment of Jews in order to delegitimate occupation policy and to establish German national victimhood. Nevertheless, Harrison's report called for—and led to—recognizing the special status of Jewish DPs (Jews were already designated as "special victims" but without much institutional implication), thus giving official sanction to the specificity of Jewish victimhood. At this stage, however, the overwhelming problem of the German past was still the war; it would take more time for the problem of the German past to be identified with the memory of the genocide of the Jews.[28]

Indeed, these observations point to the danger of interpreting the postwar situation through contemporary eyes only. As Tony Kushner puts it:

> Historians and others have an enormous desire to believe that the liberation of the camps in spring 1945 exposed to the world the horrors of the Holocaust. In so doing they impose later perceptions on contemporary interpretations and provide a deceptively simple chronology on what was, in reality, a prolonged and complex process which is yet to be completed. The assumption that an immediate connection was made at the time of the liberation of the camps to what is known as the horrors of the Holocaust has rarely been checked by reference to detailed evidence. Surprise is therefore expressed when the reality turns out to be somewhat different from the expected pattern.[29]

This is particularly so in the memory of Nuremberg, which we may be tempted to see as the trial of those who ordered the Holocaust. In some respects it was, but that was not its main point.

Nuremberg

The mass extermination of Jews was structurally, at least, only a secondary issue for the International Military Tribunal at Nuremberg, the main event of which—the trial of twenty-two leading Nazi figures—was convened on

28. Truman went along on the matter, but his own views were quite different. While Truman has long been considered to have been receptive to "Jewish causes" because he supported the founding of the State of Israel, he was a social anti-Semite. According to a newly discovered diary from 1947, Truman recorded following a meeting about the DPs with Henry Morgenthau (who was at the time chairman of the United Jewish Appeal) that "[t]he Jews, I find, are very, very selfish. . . . They care not how many Estonians, Latvians, Finns, Poles, Yugoslavs or Greeks get murdered or mistreated . . . as long as the Jews get special treatment." Reported in the *New York Times*, July 11, 2003, A14.

29. Kushner, *The Holocaust and the Liberal Imagination*, 213.

November 20, 1945, and lasted until October 1, 1946.[30] As we have seen, throughout the war the Allies struggled with various ideas for punishment. While there had been, and would again be, significant questions about how far to pursue widespread complicity in Nazi crimes, no one was ever in doubt that something had to be done about the leadership. The question of how to treat the Nazi leaders was not to be conflated with questions about denazification or about how to deal with those who actually carried out atrocities (as opposed to those who designed and ordered them). This was clear already in the Moscow declaration of 1943, which concluded by stating, "The above declaration is without prejudice to the case of the major war criminals whose offenses have no particular location and who will be punished by a joint decision of the Governments of the Allies." The purpose of this statement was to preserve the Allies' prerogative to deal with leading Nazis without legal constraint, which at that point meant summary execution. At very least, however, the decision about how to handle the "big fish" would be a political one, not constrained by the work of the United Nations War Crimes Commission (UNWCC) to develop international law.

By the spring of 1945, however, Allied thinking had already moved beyond the idea of summary execution (though Churchill had moved only reluctantly). But exactly how a more legalistic proceeding might work was a very complex matter. In the first place, memory of the failure to hold German and Turkish leaders accountable after First World War I—which produced only a feckless set of trials in Leipzig and a toothless indictment of the kaiser—weighed heavily on the planners. Furthermore, foundations for such accountability in international law were not especially strong and would require substantial inventiveness.[31] The Hague Conventions of 1899 and 1907 and the Geneva Conventions of 1864 and 1906 provided some principles, but very little in the way of mechanisms for adjudication. The Kellogg-Briand Pact of 1929 seemed to some to provide new law rejecting war as a means for solving international disputes, but provided no obvious remedy. Clearly, the challenge of prosecuting National Socialist leaders demanded a legal *novum*, which has been taken simultaneously as the achievement and weakness of the "Nuremberg ideas."[32]

30. Twenty-four individuals were charged in the indictment, but Martin Bormann (tried *in absentia*) was not in custody (he was, it turns out, already dead), Robert Ley committed suicide before the trial began, and Gustav Krupp von Bohlen und Halbach was too ill to attend the trial.

31. For an analysis of precedents to Nuremberg, as well as refutation of the claim that Nuremberg was entirely novel, see Bass, *Stay the Hand of Vengeance*.

32. This term appears as a chapter title and theme in Taylor, *The Anatomy of the Nuremberg Trials*.

While legal planning for a prosecution of the Nazi leadership was already taking place in the U.S. War Department in the fall of 1944—resulting in an important memo of September 15, at the request of Secretary Stimson, by Colonel Murray Bernays—final hashing out of the details took place at the London Conference in the summer of 1945.[33] Aside from dealing with the more technical details, participants in the London Conference faced two major challenges: to find a way to hold Nazi leaders accountable both for what they had done before the start of the war and for acts perpetrated far down a chain of command; and to provide a basis for criminalizing large numbers of Nazis. Proving leaders responsible for specific atrocities was a difficult legal and evidentiary problem. The solution, following Bernays's original ideas, was to charge them as individuals with *conspiracy* to wage aggressive war and to murder large numbers of civilians. This also opened the possibility of holding them accountable for actions committed before 1939. Additionally, bringing to account the numerous lesser figures who had been instrumental in carrying out the atrocities appeared overwhelming. The solution was to indict entire organizations, and to hold individuals guilty "by association." These innovations, however, loom larger in memory than they were in the outcome of the trial.

* * *

On August 8, 1945, representatives to the London Conference signed the "Agreement for the Prosecution of the Major War Criminals of the European Axis," and the "London Charter" of the International Military Tribunal. The charter identified three kinds of charges: (1) crimes against peace (including "planning, preparation, initiation or waging of a war of aggression . . . or conspiracy for the accomplishment of any of the foregoing"); (2) war crimes (including "violations of the law or customs of war"); and (3) crimes against humanity (including "murder, extermination, enslavement, deportation, and other inhumane acts committed against any civilian population, before or during the war; or persecutions on political, racial or religious grounds").[34] It is important to note that this final formulation negated Bernays's original aim of using the conspiracy charge to provide a foundation for prosecuting Nazi atrocities against German Jews and

33. For the background negotiations over the tribunal, see the definitive account in Kochavi, *Prelude to Nuremberg.*

34. The indictment was divided into four counts: "common plan or conspiracy"; "crimes against peace"; "war crimes"; and "crimes against humanity."

other Germans both before and during the war (rather than just against Jews in occupied countries during the war, subsumed under war crimes). The idea had been that by coupling the right to prosecute such crimes (up to that point a matter of domestic law) with subsequent violations of international law was a way to hold the Germans accountable without at the same time opening up the possibility, for instance, of holding American leaders responsible for racial crimes in the United States: since those crimes did not lead to subsequent violations of international law, they were beyond the purview of international justice. As Telford Taylor, a member of the prosecution team, put it in his memoir, however, "[W]hile it might plausibly be argued that prewar anti-Jewish actions were a necessary part of a conspiracy to perpetrate greater atrocities after war came, it was difficult to argue that the prewar harassment of Jews was a necessary preparation for aggressive war.[35] Indeed, in its final ruling, the IMT held that atrocities against German Jews did *not* fall within the jurisdiction of the court:

> The Policy of persecution, repression and murder of civilians in Germany before the war of 1939 . . . was most ruthlessly carried out. The persecution of Jews during the same period is established beyond all doubt. To constitute crimes against humanity, the acts relied on before the outbreak of war must have been in execution of, or in connection with, any crime within the jurisdiction of the Tribunal. The Tribunal is of the opinion that revolting and horrible as many of these crimes were, it has not been satisfactorily proved that they were done in execution of, or connection with, any such crime. *The Tribunal therefore cannot make a general declaration that the acts before 1939 were Crimes Against Humanity within the meaning of the Charter.* [Emphasis added.]

On this basis, one could reasonably conclude that Nuremberg was more about dictatorship and aggressive war—that is, about "crimes against peace"—than about what would come to be known as the "Holocaust" or at least about the racial policies of Nazi Germany toward German Jews, though that is the opposite of how Nuremberg has been remembered.[36] The crimes of the concentration camps could be dealt with as war crimes, not as crimes against humanity. Nuremberg's contribution to the legal theory of "crimes against humanity" was thus purely rhetorical: it introduced the concept. In practice, the concept was less consequential than is remembered.

35. Taylor, *The Anatomy of the Nuremberg Trials*, 75–76.
36. As Daniel Levy and Natan Sznaider point out, "Calling up the original document on the internet reveals a 226-screen-long document [the indictment]. But only three are taken up with the extermination of the Jews." Levy and Sznaider, "Memory Unbound," 93.

The refusal of the court to connect Nazi Jewish policy before the war to the extermination camps, moreover, fit well with later efforts by some to portray the Jewish genocide as the *consequence* of a war of aggression, rather than as its cause or as a self-standing matter. Auschwitz, according to such an argument, was a sort of spasm in the throes of total war rather than the fulfillment of earlier racist ideology. According to the IMT, mass exterminations in Auschwitz and elsewhere were "war crimes." As Peter Reichel argues, "This had long-term consequences for the image of Auschwitz. One no longer distinguishes between war crimes and crimes against humanity. This extension of the expression war crimes to all sorts of criminal acts made the allied trials appear a matter of politics in the German public. The accused qualified as 'war condemnees.'"[37] In this way, all crimes committed in the Nazi period could be reclassified at least in ordinary understanding as individual acts rather than be seen as organized political crimes demanding collective resolutions, and were seen as the result of war.[38]

Additionally, according to Donald Bloxham's analysis, the very procedures and evidentiary forms deemed acceptable for the trial suppressed the centrality of crimes against the Jews:

> The disproportionately document-led approach, with its debt to technical anti-trust suits, set the tone for the IMT trial and beyond. It bored observers and simultaneously obscured some of the more extreme crimes of which documentary evidence had been destroyed or successfully concealed. Although the strategy was understandable and was predicated in part on practicality, it also slotted into a tradition of suspicion in Anglo-American officialdom of the evidence of victims, particularly Jews and particularly eastern Europeans. Furthermore, it was a means of marshaling identifiable strands of the recent past, some of which were ethnic-specific, for a liberal, universalist goal for the future: the juridical condemnation of aggressive war.

37. Reichel, *Vergangenheitsbewaeltigung in Deutschland*, 44. Additionally, Harold Marcuse makes a related point concerning the meaning of "crimes against humanity." "From its first use at Nuremberg this English term was officially mistranslated into German as 'crimes against humaneness' [*Verbrechen gegen die Menschlichkeit*], instead of *Menschheit*). This euphemism has been used ever since in essentially all German books on the subject, even critical works." Marcuse takes this as evidence of "German inability or unwillingness to conceive of what had transpired" (Marcuse, *Legacies of Dachau*, 90). Further, "In official communications and publications in the fall of 1948 the term 'war criminals' was first set in quotation marks and then progressively euphemized from 'war condemnees' to 'military condemnees' to 'condemned soldiers' to 'war-imprisoned Germans' to 'Landsberger' (after the prison where they were being held)" (ibid., 98).

38. Jeffrey Herf notes the same defect, but sees it as less consequential than Reichel and Marcuse do: "Although the concept of 'war crimes' played a far greater role than 'crimes

As in the debate over the Morgenthau Plan, there was thus a desire to keep the proceedings free of any appearance that they involved a *particular* complaint. As Bloxham writes, "The unwritten rule that the Nuremberg case could in no way be seen to be influenced by Jewry appears to have been a pre-eminent check, a view buttressed explicitly by the long-standing mistrust of the 'objectivity' of 'Jewish' evidence and the traditional Christian stereotype of the vengeful Jews. . . ."[39] As an illustration of this, Bloxham points out that Chief Prosecutor Robert Jackson's response to Jewish groups who wished representation on the prosecution was significantly different from the response he gave to Poles and others. To Poles he referred to logistical difficulties. To Jews, he said he wanted to "get away from the racial aspects of the situation."[40]

The general result, according to Bloxham and others, was that "the crimes against the Jews were subsumed within the general Nazi policies of repression and persecution."[41] This is perhaps an overstatement given the record the trials created of the systematic nature of the extermination program. But it is certainly true that the trials, because they centered on the perpetrators rather than the victims, and because—relatedly—they employed only documentary rather than testimonial evidence, generated a very particular picture of Nazi crimes. These procedures, moreover, expressed the underlying understanding of the prosecution team—again, that the extermination of the Jews was an outcome, not a chief purpose of National Socialism.

*   *   *

In the end, the IMT handed down eleven death sentences, seven prison sentences, and three acquittals (the latter meeting with confusion in the German public, and dismay by the Soviet authorities). The conspiracy charges held up (though conspiracy to wage aggressive war, not to perpetrate genocide).

---

against humanity,' a great deal of testimony regarding the persecution of European Jewry was presented at Nuremberg." Furthermore, Herf argues, "If the Germans focused more on postwar suffering but conveniently forgot its antecedents, the Nuremberg judgments accentuated the causal connection between the aggression and crimes of the Nazis and postwar German misery. . . . The Nuremberg Trials repeatedly turned causal historical narratives back to the consequences of 1933 and to what the Germans had done to others before 1945." Herf, *Divided Memory*, 207. As Robert Moeller argues, most Germans were unwilling or unable to accept these arguments because doing so would call into question perceptions of their own victimhood (which for many was an extremely effective defense mechanism). See Moeller, *War Stories*.

39. Bloxham, *Genocide on Trial*, 66.
40. Ibid., 67.
41. Ibid., 57.

Charges against six criminal organizations were more problematic, and the court dismissed charges against three. In its ruling, moreover, the tribunal held that any subsequent hearings to determine involvement of individuals with the condemned organizations would have to show that the individual had known of the organization's criminal goals when he joined and that he had participated voluntarily. The organizational guilt innovation thus did not entirely serve its purpose of easing evidentiary burdens.

Following the trial of major war criminals, the United States held twelve subsequent trials at Nuremberg, including prosecutions of SS leaders, doctors, judges, industrialists, and army generals, among others. Out of more than five thousand indicted, slightly more than eight hundred received death sentences, of which approximately five hundred were carried out.

Reception and Legacies

The legacies of the Nuremberg system for German memory are in many ways highly contradictory, partly because of the unreconciled diversity of intentions and partly because of the multiplicity of its messages. In his landmark history of the occupation years, for instance, Theodor Eschenberg writes in regard to Nuremberg that "[c]ollective guilt was not the theme. It wasn't the official British and American doctrine. Nor did it appear in the Potsdam Protocol. There *responsibility* was spoken of."[42] On the other hand, the American historian of the trials, Bradley Smith, writes that "[f]or the system to work as intended, the prosecution had to convince a court, which was trying to appear legally respectable, that it should overlook shaky evidence, as well as its scruples, and condemn millions of organization members on the basis of collective guilt."[43] In an influential letter to Chief Prosecutor Robert Jackson (associate justice of the U.S. Supreme Court and at the time chief American delegate to the London Conference), Telford Taylor (later to become chief prosecutor in the secondary trials), however, wrote:

> It is important that the trial not become an inquiry into the causes of the war. It cannot be established that Hitlerism was the sole cause of the war, and there should be no effort to do this. . . . The question of causation is important and will be discussed for many years, but it has no place in this trial, which must stick rather rigorously to the doctrine that planning and launching an aggressive war is illegal.[44]

42. Eschenburg, *Jahre der Besatzung*, 57 (emphasis added).
43. Smith, *The Road to Nuremberg*, 249.
44. Taylor, *The Anatomy of the Nuremberg Trials*, 51.

In his opening statement at the trial, Jackson nevertheless stated:

> We would also make clear that we have no purpose to incriminate the whole German people. . . . If the German populace had willingly accepted the Nazi program, no storm troopers would have been needed in the early days of the Party and there would have been no need for concentration camps or the *Gestapo*. . . . The German, no less than the non-German world, has accounts to settle with these defendants.[45]

Indeed, the trials faced a number of very serious criticisms from both Germans and others. These included that the tribunal applied *ex post facto* law, prosecuting individuals, that is, for violating laws that did not exist at the time of their acts (the legal principle is *Nullum crimen, nulla poena sine lege:* No crime, no punishment without law);[46] that the tribunal dealt only with crimes on the German side, thus condemning itself to the appearance of victors' justice;[47] that individuals could not be held accountable for acts of state; that only German courts had jurisdiction; that charges against entire organizations violated the principle of individual guilt; and that because of the military situation, prosecution and defense did not have equal power. Interestingly, there is a discrepancy between elite commentary at the time and the data of public opinion. As Richard Merritt has shown in his study of the Office of Military Government in Germany–United States (OMGUS) surveys, public opinion data indicated not only that the German population followed the trials (closely at beginning and end, less so in the middle), but that the vast majority (79 percent) thought that the trials were fair. Of course, they drew diverse lessons from the spectacle: 30 percent thought the lesson was not to follow a dictator; 26 percent thought it was never to start a

---

45. Quoted in Taylor, *The Anatomy of the Nuremberg Trials*, 118.

46. As we will see later, one of the most vigorous proponents of this argument was the legal theorist Carl Schmitt, whose significant role in the National Socialist intellectual pantheon and whose anti-Semitism have been downplayed by postwar proponents on both the Right and the Left. This argument, we will also see, reversed Schmitt's earlier position. He formulated the argument in a legal brief defending the industrialist Friedrich Flick, who was tried at the industrialists' trial (one of the secondary Nuremberg proceedings), which he wrote in the summer of 1945, before Schmitt himself was arrested and evaluated as a possible defendant for the trial of the judiciary at Nuremberg. See chapter 13.

47. Critics took particular umbrage at the idea of Soviet participation, though there were also calls for equal treatment of such acts as the fire bombing of Dresden. Indeed, during negotiations in London leading to the charter, the Soviets insisted that the title of the document—"Agreement for the Prosecution and Punishment of the Major War Criminals of the European Axis"—include those last four words so as not to leave open the possibility of charges against the victorious powers.

war again. Only 3 percent thought the main lesson concerned justice, and only 2 percent referred to human rights.[48]

The trial thus rejected collective guilt, but condemned entire organizations. The Allies chose the appearance of legal rigor, but chose to pursue it in Nuremberg, the now devastated site associated with Nazi Party congresses and the notorious racial laws of 1935. The trial sought to demonstrate the rule of law, but did so on highly dubious legal foundations. And it argued that Germans had accounts to settle among themselves, but preempted them from doing so.

Not surprisingly, Chief Prosecutor Robert Jackson—while aware of the possible faults—focused more on the positive promise in his opening remarks at the trial: "Civilization asks whether law is so laggard as to be utterly helpless to deal with crimes of this magnitude by criminals of this order of importance."[49] In 1962, however, philosopher Karl Jaspers attempted to reconcile the two views—his excitement that the Nuremberg idea marked a new era in political accountability (one in which individuals could no longer escape responsibility for their acts by appealing to the authority of the state) and his concern with the trial's faults (during the trials, Jaspers was more willing than he was later to judge Allied acts differently from German acts because they were committed against citizens of a criminal state). Where Jaspers first warned against dismissing the trial as a show or mere appearance of justice, however, he later concluded that there was a significant difference between the idea of Nuremberg and its realization: "The Anglo-Saxon idea was outstanding. It seemed to us at that time that something glimmered out of the future that would change mankind." Nevertheless, "[i]t was, in effect, a singular proceeding of the victors against the vanquished, in which the foundation of a shared legal understanding and legal intention of the victorious powers was absent. It therefore achieved the opposite of what it should have. Law was not made, rather mistrust of law increased. The disappointment is, in light of the importance of the matter, crushing."[50] And this is the assessment of one of Germany's most liberal, Western-oriented thinkers.

* * *

48. Merritt, *Democracy Imposed*, 150–62.

49. Quoted in Taylor, *The Anatomy of the Nuremberg Trials*, 171.

50. This rethinking appears in the 1962 afterword to Jaspers's 1946 *Die Schuldfrage* [The Question of German Guilt], which I will examine in significant detail below. In 1946, Jaspers praised the Allied goals as outstanding (*grossartig*), promising a new world order based on the rule of law, one in which avoidance of responsibility for one's own acts through appeal to the authority of the abstract state would be impossible. At the time, Jaspers's positive

Among the greatest legacies of the Nuremberg system is the wealth of specific knowledge about the Nazi regime that the prosecution generated, a perhaps unprecedented historiographical resource of its kind. This is the case even if "crimes against humanity" remained a nebulous concept, with the court, as we saw above, unable to rule in this way. Additionally, while legal scholars have debated the jurisprudential plausibility of the Nuremberg ideas, the IMT redeemed Jackson's hope that it was possible to hold leaders accountable for their actions, a powerful precedent in spirit if not in detail for future international justice.[51] Some did hold the exercise to have been victor's justice, but such judgments, while accurate in minor points, failed to appreciate the dignity with which the trials met the challenge. Jackson and others felt this was a unique opportunity for re-education by demonstrating once and for all—by representing the diversity of the Nazi leadership and the extent of the crimes they led Germans to perpetrate[52]—to bring about the reorientation of Germany necessary for preventing a recurrence. As émigré writer Alfred Döblin put it, ambiguously, Nuremberg was thus a "pedagogical trial" (*Lehrprozess*). Over time "Nuremberg" became, even in German discourse, a metonym of justice, in the same way that "Auschwitz" became the metonym of atrocity, even if it was received more ambiguously at the time.

On the negative side, it is not clear that the trials in the short run had the pedagogical effect the Allies hoped for (though of course different Allies hoped for different effects). For much of the main trial, most Germans paid little attention—it was long, and most of it quite dull. Moreover, the conflation of war crimes with crimes against humanity—the failure to separate out genocide from war of aggression—led in subsequent years to conflations in memory.[53] Additionally, as Theodor Eschenburg points out, "For some, who had assumed no leadership or key positions, of course the delusion may have appeared that through the Nuremberg verdict the guilt was now atoned and the level of their co-responsibility had sunk."[54] Indeed, the

---

assessment was motivated by the thought that perhaps Allied acts like the bombing of Dresden could not be judged by the same measures because the ordinary people who were the victims of such acts were citizens of a state that was motivated by criminal intentions. At a distance of fifteen years, Jaspers was less willing to qualify the principle in this way.

51. For a longer-term perspective, see Maguire, *Law and War*; Bass, *Stay the Hand of Vengeance*.

52. Such considerations were involved in the selection of defendants.

53. See note 37.

54. The decline in public approval of the verdicts in the subsequent lesser trials support this interpretation. Eschenburg, *Jahre der Besatzung*, 59.

relatively large numbers who were listening carefully to the remarkable last day of the main proceeding (August 31, 1946)—during which the defendants were permitted to make brief statements to the court—found a ready lexicon of exculpation which likely resonated with many private sentiments and could be heard in much coming public rhetoric from more respectable figures.[55]

Hermann Göring, for instance, condemned the "terrible mass murders" and summed up by asserting that "[t]he only motive which guided me was my ardent love for my people, its happiness, its freedom, and its life." Rudolf Hess claimed to be "happy to know that I have done my duty to my people, to my duty [sic] as a German, as a National Socialist, as a loyal follower of my *Führer*."[56] The assertion that he was only doing his duty for his fatherland Hess shared with most of the other defendants. Taking another tack, Joachim von Ribbentrop—Hitler's foreign minister—denied responsibility for his deeds: "I am held responsible for the conduct of a foreign policy which was determined by another." Furthermore, Ribbentrop raised the specter of Versailles as a motivation: his actions as foreign minister (now his actions, not Hitler's) were directed at overcoming "the consequences of Versailles." Arthur Seyss-Inquart—governor of the *Ost-Mark* (Austria)—questioned the legitimacy of the tribunal's accusations by arguing that similar charges could be levied against the victors (and not just the Soviets). Referring to his previous testimony, he argued on this last day that "[t]hese statements can no more serve as evidence of the intention to wage a war of aggression than the decisions of Teheran concerning the German Eastern territories."

Field Marshall Keitel, in yet another vein, said he "believed" but "erred": "It is tragic to have to realize that the best I had to give as a soldier, obedience and loyalty, was exploited for purposes that could not be recognized at the time, and that I did not see that there is a limit even for a soldier's performance of his duty. That is my fate." This was indeed a standard defense of even the most ordinary low-ranking soldier; if it works for Keitel, surely it works for the draftee! Indeed, Jodl sought explicitly to defend the military leadership, and ordinary soldiers by implication: "They did not serve the powers of Hell and they did not serve a criminal, but rather the people and their fatherland." Of course, he did not mention that

55. On the exculpations employed by the Nuremberg defendants, see as well Overy, *Interrogations*.

56. Hess was quite probably insane, and this was a rare moment of relative clarity in an otherwise rambling address.

soldiers swore a personal oath to Hitler, not to the German people. Grand Admiral Dönitz, on the other hand, said he would do everything the same had he to do it over. Grand Admiral Raeder described his error as not conceiving his duty more broadly: "If I have incurred guilt in any way, then this was chiefly in the sense that in spite of my purely military position I should perhaps [sic] have been not only a soldier, but also up to a certain point a politician, which, however, was in contradiction to my entire career and the tradition of the German armed forces."

Identification of other causes was plentiful as well. Ernst Kaltenbrunner referred to insidious forces "threatening the world" (i.e., the Soviet Union). Hans Frank—after a jailhouse conversion—asserted that he now saw that "Hitler's road was the way without God, the way of turning from Christ, and, in the last analysis, the way of political foolishness, the way of disaster, the way of death." Nevertheless, this testimony (in the religious sense) did not prevent him from claiming that all German guilt had already been wiped clean by the "crimes" perpetrated against Germany by Poland, Czechoslovakia, and the Soviet Union (referring to the Potsdam expulsions). Wilhelm Frick (interior minister), in contrast, asserted the value of his oath as a civil servant: any deviation from obedience would have constituted treason. Julius Streicher and Walter Funk merely asserted that they, like all Germans, simply had not known what Himmler was doing.

Finally, several defendants plead for the future of Germany. Hans Fritzsche, after accepting his (pending) conviction "as a last sacrifice on behalf of my people," stated:

> It is quite possible, perhaps even understandable, that the storm of indignation which swept the world because of the atrocities . . . should obliterate the borders of individual responsibility. . . . It may be difficult to separate German crime from German idealism. It is not impossible. If this distinction is made, much suffering will be avoided for Germany and for the world.

And Julius Streicher concluded with the following: "I have no request to make for myself. I have one for the German people from whom I come. Your honors, fate [sic] has given you the power to pronounce any judgment. *Do not pronounce a judgment which would imprint the stamp of dishonor upon the forehead of an entire nation*" [italics added]. Indeed, the claim that this was done at Nuremberg and throughout the occupation years was one of the hallmarks of emerging West German discourse.

CHAPTER 6

Nurembergs of the Common Man?

From the perspective of ordinary people in the victorious nations, Nuremberg was a sort of final reckoning with the Third Reich; from the German perspective, it was in many ways merely the first such reckoning.[1] Indeed, the Joint Chiefs of Staff occupation statute (JCS 1067) called not only for the prosecution of the leaders of National Socialism, but for a widespread purge of complicit individuals from public life. How to accomplish this, however, was at least as problematic as the question of how to deal with the leaders.

Like the prologues to Nuremberg, discussion about how to treat lower-level Nazis and ordinary Germans was structured by contrasting historical, political, and strategic understandings, both within the West and between East and West. First, for those who viewed the Third Reich as the result of historical contingencies exploited by pernicious (even devilish) individuals, responsibility resided only with the leaders. This was the popular view in Germany both during the occupation and for many years after: "Hitler and his henchmen" formed a "seductive clique" who misused the German people; since ordinary Germans ended up suffering great losses, they could not at the same time be considered perpetrators of their own destruction! While perhaps not quite as directed at exculpation, many outside Germany as well subscribed to some version of this "outlaw" theory. From this perspective, the goal was to eliminate the Nazi elite from power once and for all and then to rehabilitate the German population.

---

1. As Jeffrey Herf puts it, however, "As the Cold War refocused Western attention on what the Soviet Union had done after May 8th, 1945, the Nuremberg narratives became an increasingly dissonant and uncomfortable but never extinguished counterpoint." Herf, *Divided Memory*, 208.

Second, as we saw, on the other side were those who argued that Germans manifested collective pathologies and a defective political culture. From this perspective, not all the blame could be laid on the leadership: the Nazis had—at least until Stalingrad—enjoyed widespread support, and ordinary Germans had participated enthusiastically in all aspects of collective life. No mere symbolic prosecution of notorious personalities would address the profound extent of collective responsibility (in some versions, collective guilt) borne by wide segments of the population. Indeed, this latter view had at least momentary support in American public opinion, particularly after reports of atrocities perpetrated against American soldiers at Malmedy, for example, or during the Battle of the Bulge. In both JCS 1067 and the Potsdam Agreement, a version of this more thorough-going accusation against the German population predominated.

Nevertheless, there were significant differences even within the argument that responsibility extended beyond the demonic powers of seductive leaders. According to the Soviet version (with some sympathy on the Western Left), the "cause" of National Socialism (understood as but one variety of fascism) was economic, broadly understood. Only by eliminating the weaknesses of the Weimar Republic, which were understood to be primarily social-structural rather than legal or political, could a repeat of 1933 be prevented.[2] "Denazification"[3] in the Soviet zone therefore placed most of its emphasis on land reform and the socialization of heavy industry. Wide segments of the Nazi leadership were indeed removed with comparative alacrity. But ordinary members of the party and so-called "fellow travelers" (*Mitläufer*) were to be rehabilitated. One former minor Nazi party member captured the political essence of the Soviet solution in a much-quoted off-the-cuff remark: at an assembly to generate support for the SED (Socialist Union Party) among former Nazis, he shouted out, "Long live the SED, big friend of the small Nazis."[4] Indeed, a common complaint by many German intellectuals and leaders to the Western Allies was that such Soviet measures would drive many into the Soviet camp; and Western occupation authorities were in fact sensitive to the competition of public relations, more so over time.

Nevertheless, the West had the advantage that it resisted most ideas for structural transformation in the form of socialization of industry or redis-

---

2. See Kleßmann, *Die doppelte Staatsgründung*, 80–84.

3. According to Theodor Eschenberg (*Jahre der Besatzung*, 112), the term, though not the idea, originated in Eisenhower's staff.

4. Reported in Leonhard, *Die Revolution entlässt ihre Kinder*, 553.

tribution of wealth (with a few exceptions, most prominently a later measure to "equalize burdens" for "expellees" and "war-damaged").[5] While "intentionalist" theories focused on the culpability of powerful individuals and "functionalist" theories (Soviet or otherwise) highlighted structural problems, Western occupation policy pursued a sort of mass intentionalism for functionalist reasons: National Socialism was the product of the complicity not just of the leadership but of wide segments of the population; but that complicity was a matter of individual error rather than class structure.[6]

As already mentioned when discussing the roles played by Talcott Parsons and Richard Brickner (see chapter 3), perhaps the single most important architect of American denazification policy was the political scientist Franz Neumann. Neumann had been an associate of the "Frankfurt School," a critical social science research institute from the later Weimar years whose members, mostly Jewish, all loosely Marxist, escaped to exile largely in the United States. He was later recruited to work for the U.S. Office of Strategic Services (predecessor of the Central Intelligence Agency) by Col. William "Wild Bill" Donovan. As we saw, Neumann was the author of one of the earliest and still most important studies of National Socialism—*Behemoth: The Structure and Function of National Socialism, 1933–1944*—in which he argued that power in the Third Reich was divided among various sectors, including the military, industry, civil service, and the Nazi party and leadership (thus contradicting depictions of the Nazi state as a "*Führer*-state" directed by a few powerful individuals). On the basis of this understanding, Neumann developed the outlines of American denazification policy, arguing that the only way to eliminate Nazi influence was to remove completely from public office and from important private enterprises all those who had been involved in the Nazi Party, in other National Socialist organizations, or in other powerful complicit enterprises. Indeed, JCS 1067 and American policy more generally demanded removal of large numbers of individuals, and acknowledgment in the wider population of political and moral responsibility. Denazification, as one characterization had it, was thus to be a "Nuremberg of the common man."[7]

5. On the "equalization of burdens," see especially Hughes, *Shouldering the Burdens of Defeat*.

6. It is important to note, however, as Donald Bloxham does, that "[c]ontrary to popular perception, the disagreement between intentionalists and the various shades of functionalist has not been over the role of antisemitism." Bloxham, *Genocide on Trial*, 205.

7. Friedrich, *Die kalte Amnestie*.

Grand Designs

On July 7, 1945, the American Military Government (AMG) issued a clarifying directive that included a long list of organizations whose members were by definition suspect. The directive distinguished between "active" and "nominal" participants: the former were to be arrested automatically, the latter after some determination of the nature of their involvement. A further directive, AMG Law No. 8, issued on September 6, 1945, called for all active National Socialists and Nazi sympathizers to be prohibited from anything but menial labor. The result of these measures was that by the end of 1945 more than 250,000 people had been arrested and many others assigned work restrictions, producing what a popular slogan referred to as "full camps, empty offices."[8] Many prominent Germans railed against these measures, some going so far as to claim the tactic was reminiscent of the *Gestapo*. (Among the critics was Theophil Wurm, Evangelical Bishop of Württemberg, who compared "persecuted Nazi Party members and their sympathizers" to the victims of terror in the Third Reich. Later, in a *New York Times* interview appearing on July 28, 1946, Wurm went so far as to disparage denazification in general because there "is something Bolshevistic about it."[9])

From the perspective of later debates in the history of the Federal Republic, one resonant aspect of Law No. 8 was that it divided those who had joined the party before May 1, 1937, from those who had joined after that date. This was an expansion of earlier plans (e.g., a SHAEF directive from November 9, 1944) that identified January 1933 as the cut-off.[10] The U.S. position was that those who had joined before 1937 were the true hardcore Nazis and thus likely to be ideologically intractable and potentially dangerous; those who had joined later had done so only out of fear or under pressure. Strangely, German leaders argued exactly the opposite—that those who joined earlier were starry-eyed idealists who may not have understood where things were going, while those who joined later were distasteful opportunists who understood better exactly what they were supporting. Similarities to Hans Fritzsche's remarks (quoted at the end of the previous

8. Kleßmann, *Die doppelte Staatsgründung*, 87.

9. Quoted in Bower, *Blind Eye to Murder*, 187. Referring to the situation of teachers who had joined the Nazi Party, a more moderate strand of critique inspired by future federal president Theodor Heuss stated, "How most of these unfortunates had waited for the collapse of Nazi domination. They hoped for freedom and law again finally. Now they have been dismissed and have nothing."

10. See Gimbel, *The American Occupation of Germany*, 101.

chapter) about German idealism and German crime being distinct—which he would make in his closing statement at Nuremberg—are striking. Of course, Fritzsche was a leading Nazi criminal. Those who argued with the AMG about dates of joining the party were leading politicians of the emerging new Germany. The question of when one joined the party was an important issue on several occasions later in the history of the Federal Republic, perhaps most prominently in the case of Chancellor Kurt-Georg Kiesinger (1966–69), who had joined in 1933. The point here is that if the German argument was not merely obstructionism (and in part it was), it demonstrates a basic feature of German political culture at that time—a greater preference for even delusional grandeur than for *Realpolitik*.[11]

* * *

Perhaps the greatest problem with this first ("automatic arrest") phase, however, was that there was no quick way to determine who had been an active, and who merely a nominal, participant; the Americans erred on the side of quick arrest (the British were a bit more generous, in part because they were substantially less sanguine about the possibility of "cleansing" German society without thoroughly disrupting it). Mere membership in condemned organizations, of course, was not the only relevant criterion of complicity. Some members of such organizations had indeed been only nominal participants, while others who had not been members of any particular condemned organizations may nevertheless have been substantially complicit. Only a small percentage even of active Nazi supporters, moreover, were guilty of criminal acts.

The AMG thus introduced new procedures. Allied Control Council Directive No. 24, issued on January 12, 1946, expanded the denazification program to include all those who sought public responsibility or who had business with the occupation authorities, and required all such individuals to fill out a survey—known in German and among occupation authorities as the *Fragebogen*—asking 131 questions about their affiliations, activities, education, background, and so on. The program reflected the almost missionary zeal with which many American officials approached the task of

11. As we will see later, this issue is particularly relevant in evaluating the role of leading conservative intellectuals—like Martin Heidegger and especially Ernst Jünger—who had early on enthusiastically supported the Nazis but later broke with them. The postwar reconstruction of conservatism involved a positive evaluation of the fervor that led such figures to early enthusiastic support of the Nazis; such support was seen as positive because it was coupled with a supposed sober realization and responsible break, just in time. As such, so they claimed, conservatism was untainted by developments it did not intend.

"re-educating" Germans and of transforming their political culture. Indeed, this shift from automatic arrest to a more differentiated and individualized assessment was seen as a positive change by many Germans. Practically, however, the occupation authorities saw themselves faced with a task of insurmountable proportions (by the end of the *Fragebogen* phase of the U.S. denazification program in March of 1946, nearly 1.4 million people had filled out the questionnaire), and inconsistencies in administration led to much indignation on the German part.

In fact, despite the perceived improvement from mass arrests, the *Fragebogen* became a popular topic of ridicule, particularly through the bestselling eponymous novel of Ernst von Salomon, which satirized the very idea of imposed denazification as well as the ignorance of German life displayed by some of the questions.[12] In many histories of Germany, the novel is mentioned in passing to illustrate German mockery of denazification, and is even taken as a valid demonstration of the program's problems; the book is rarely read anymore (seemingly even by those who refer to it). But the reality of the book should be more problematic in the historical literature. According to Hans Habe, whose journalistic influence we will examine later, "When in 1951 Ernst von Salomon, one of the [1922] assassins of [German Foreign Minister] Walther Rathenau and now a respected and best selling author, published his novel *Der Fragebogen*, it described nothing but the tortures inflicted upon him by German Jews in American disguise."[13] According to Goronwy Rees's introduction to the American edition, to those "humane and liberal Germans who still dare to believe . . . that Germany may yet redeem the errors of the past . . . *Der Fragebogen* must seem like a calculated blow in the face, and its popularity in Germany a proof that even now their countrymen have learned nothing and forgotten nothing." As Salomon wrote about denazification, in whose web both he and his Jewish mistress were temporarily entangled:

> When the Americans decided to pass the contents of the pot— in which everything had been stewed up together—through the sieve, they found in their sieve as many categories of man as there had been in that other pot, the Jewish one. It was the second greatest crime of the *terribles simplificateurs* that they had not attempted to pass the contents of the Jewish pot through the sieve, their greatest being that they had simply destroyed the whole brew.[14]

12. Salomon, *The Answers of Ernst von Salomon*. Quotation from the preface by Goronwy Rees, vii.

13. Habe, *Our Love Affair with Germany*, 124.

14. Salomon, *The Answers of Ernst von Salomon*, 514–15. Also see the discussion in FitzGibbon, *Denazification*, 168–69. FitzGibbon was the translator of the English edition of Salomon's book.

It is not quite a direct equation between the Nazis and the Americans (the Americans, after all, were not committing the greatest crime, only the second greatest), but the implication is clear.

It is interesting to recall in this context that many complained about what they perceived to be an obvious and inappropriate "Jewish influence" over Allied policy. Perhaps surprisingly, it was an American church official—Bishop Alois Muench of Fargo, North Dakota, who was brought in to improve AMG communication with the Catholic Church—who objected most vocally to what he saw as the putative overabundance of Jews in the AMG intelligence service, leading to what Muench considered an attitude of vindictiveness in the occupation government. As Frederic Spotts put it in his study of the churches in postwar Germany, "there was apparently a not uncommon feeling among the German population shortly after the war that there were 'too many' emigres, including Jews, in the military government. To this extent Muench was registering the privately held view of some Germans—and of some American officers."[15] As we will see later, the legal theorist Carl Schmitt's complained about being interrogated by Robert Kempner, a Berlin Jew who had become an American and was one of the lead prosecutors at Nuremberg.

Revisions

Obvious differences in application both within the American zone and among the American, French, and British zones as well contributed to the widespread impression that the entire enterprise was arbitrary. And the Germans were not the only ones complaining: U.S. General George S. Patton Jr. publicly ridiculed the idea of denazification and the way it was being carried out. With characteristic disregard for diplomacy, Patton went so far as to compare membership in the Nazi Party to membership in the Republican or Democratic Parties in the United States. (This was the straw that broke the camel's back, costing him his job.) This kind of sentiment—a refusal to recognize important differences—led many Germans in the 1950s to a thorough skepticism toward political involvement in, and commitment to, emerging democratic structures: if "honest participation" could have been so misused and condemned once, one should not risk political involvement again.[16] In the 1950s, this sentiment congealed into

15. Spotts, *The Churches and Politics in Germany*, 83–84.
16. A prominent sociologist, writing about the 1950s, referred to a "skeptical generation." See Schelsky, *Die skeptische Generation*.

the popular slogan *ohne mich* (without me), which some have used as an indicator of the dangers of "too much memory."

More important, U.S. Military Government officials responsible for the program despaired of being able to process so many cases, and were becoming increasingly frustrated by German efforts to subvert the process. By early 1946, American officials believed the process was fairly well stymied, and began pressing for greater German involvement in its administration. This move should not be misunderstood, as it sometimes has been and was by many at the time, as a loss of patience on the part of U.S. authorities with denazification *per se* (though some of them had indeed lost patience). One frequently finds statements in subsequent discourse claiming that even the Americans saw that the program was a total failure (thus legitimating German assignment of the event to the negative side of memory). Deputy Military Governor Lucius Clay had long opposed what he saw as the destructive implications of the Morgenthau Plan and of JCS 1067, and had worked hard to build up rather than to hold down the German economy. But he was always a strong proponent of denazification, and saw German involvement not as a way to hand off the problem but as an opportunity for building German democratic responsibility. Indeed, when frustrated by what he perceived as inadequate compliance, Clay repeatedly threatened to take back control rather than to allow denazification to fail.

After much negotiation and significant pressure from the Americans, on March 5, 1946, the newly formed German Council of States (*Länderrat*) thus passed the "Law for the Liberation from National Socialism and Militarism," which put denazification largely in German hands. The signing ceremony took place in Munich because of the symbolic weight of ending National Socialism where it began. On that occasion, Bavarian Minister-President Wilhelm Högner stated, in the name of the *Länderrat*, "We are fully conscious of the difficulty of our task. Without a thorough purging, no democratic reconstruction and no re-education of the German people will be possible." The degree of his actual commitment to this idea, or how representative it was of the views of his colleagues or of the German people at large, however, is highly questionable. In his remarks (made on behalf of his boss, General McNarney), Clay made the following statement:

It has been a basic policy and is a basic policy of Military Government to eliminate National Socialism and militarism—to that we are pledged. It has never been our desire to accomplish that by arbitrary methods. The responsibility for self-government of a people carries with it the responsibility for determining those who would destroy self-government and for taking measures which would prevent its ever happening again.[17]

The new phase of denazification required all Germans over the age of eighteen to fill out a new *Meldebogen* (registration form), enforced by making ration cards dependent on submission. Of 13 million *Meldebogen* filed, 3.5 million were deemed to require further examination, which was to take place in so-called *Spruchkammern* (hearing panels) run by Germans. The result of these hearings was a classification of the examinee into one of five categories: major offender (*Hauptschuldig*), offender (*Belastete*), minor offender (*Minderbelastete*), follower or fellow traveler (*Mitläufer*), and exonerated (*Entlastete*). Punishments for those not exonerated (the largest group was exonerated) ranged from minor fines to up to ten years in work camps.

Retrenchment

By the summer of 1946, however, the new German-administered system was mired in corruption. There were glaring inconsistencies in the procedures and verdicts in different panels. Deceit, back-room dealing, mutual back-scratching, and even outright bribery were fairly open secrets.[18] Lack of support for the process by many involved in its administration led to foot-dragging. And a good proportion of the decisions involved reducing earlier classifications. In one of the most important characterizations, the entire enterprise was becoming a *Mitläuferfabrik* (fellow-traveler factory), meaning that many people who should have been classified in higher categories of complicity were reformed with this relatively innocuous designation: the *Spruchkammern* were turning guilty parties into mere "fellow travelers."[19] As Harold Marcuse notes, early metaphors of delousing quickly gave way to new ones of whitewashing.[20] One way of securing

17. The quote is from Clay's self-report in his memoir *Decision in Germany*, 99. Clay includes the Högner quote there as well, indicating that he thought it was an honest statement: he says he "congratulated the minister-presidents on their sincerity and courage."

18. The right-wing weekly *Der Stern* published an article series in 1952 detailing the criminal history of *Spruchkammer* judges themselves. The series was called *Der grosse Schwindel* [The Big Swindle]. The point of the series was to further delegitimate the entire enterprise, even in retrospect. See Habe, *Our Love Affair with Germany*, 31.

19. Niethammer, *Die Mitläuferfabrik*.

20. Marcuse, *Legacies of Dachau*, 91. Another such observation is from the American political scientist John H. Herz, writing in 1948: "While at first signifying the elimination of Nazis

exoneration or mild judgment was to produce testimonials from people with unassailable credentials. These were known as *Persilscheine:* a *Schein* is a certificate; *Persil* is a brand of laundry detergent known for eliminating brown stains (brown being the color of the early Nazi uniforms). The most valuable *Persilschein*, of course, was from a Jew or a politically persecuted German; the easiest to come by were from priests, whose vigorous opposition to denazification led them to produce such exonerations prolifically (one bishop even had forms printed, with a blank for the name).

By the end of fall 1946, General Clay was extremely frustrated by the course of events, but still believed in the merits of the effort. At a meeting of the *Länderrat* in Stuttgart on November 5, 1946, he expressed his consternation: "We are sorely disappointed with the results and we have yet to find the political will and determination to punish those who deserve to be punished. . . . I do not see how you can demonstrate your ability for self-government nor your will for democracy if you are going to evade or shirk the first unpleasant task that falls upon you."[21] The urgency in this statement was profound, given recent events: on September 6, 1946, Secretary of State James Byrnes had delivered a speech in Stuttgart announcing a major shift in U.S. policy. In contrast to the harsh tone of JCS 1067 and the Potsdam Accord, the United States, Byrnes announced, now envisioned a quicker reconstruction of German economic and political life, even possibly in the form of a Western German state. While not yet aggressively anti-Soviet, the speech charged that Soviet extraction of reparations had inflicted excessive hardships on Germany and had hindered its capacity to rebuild. Byrnes indicated as well that the United States intended to maintain its military presence on the European continent. These statements reflected the change in American attitude, both influenced by and represented in George Kennan's famed February 1946 cable from Moscow warning of Soviet expansionist aims and unreliability. Most important from the German perspective, Byrnes announced:

> It is the view of the American Government that the German people throughout Germany, under proper safeguards, should now be given the primary responsibility for the running of their own affairs. More than a year has passed since hostilities ceased. The millions of German people should not be forced to live in doubt as

---

from public life, it [denazification] has now in everyday German language come to mean the removal of the Nazi stigma from the individual concerned." Herz, "The Fiasco of Denazification in Germany," 569.

21. Quoted in Bower, *Blind Eye to Murder,* 188.

to their fate. . . . Freedom from militarism . . . will give them the opportunity to show themselves worthy of the respect and friendship of peace loving nations, and in time, to take an honorable place among the members of the United Nations.[22]

This was in effect something of a prescription for future West German politics. In the 1950s, demonstrating that the new West German state was meeting all the requirements for reentry to the "community of nations" was a major feature of Konrad Adenauer's rhetoric as chancellor. Another interesting feature of Byrnes's statement in 1946 is that "militarism" was the problem: Germany's exclusion from the "community of nations" was the result of aggressive war, not first and foremost anti-Semitism and mass exterminations.

The more immediate point, however, is that when Clay expressed his dissatisfaction with the way the Germans were running denazification—thus raising questions about their ability to govern themselves on the basis of clear acknowledgment of the problems of the past—the stakes were high indeed. Clay's commitment was clear in his sharp rebuke to the German leadership: "Regardless of its effect on German economy, regardless of the additional time which it may take, if this will [to denazify] does not develop, Military Government will necessarily have to take measures to see that denazification is carried out in that zone of Germany. . . . Let us have no misunderstanding. Denazification is a 'must.'"[23]

Modifications

Despite criticisms of denazification and complaints about its corrupt implementation, General Clay remained convinced that the problems were largely practical rather than with the idea—or the German willingness to live up to the idea—itself. He thus supported a number of pragmatic revisions, including two amnesties (one in June, one for Christmas 1946) excluding all those born after January 1, 1919, and all those who had had annual incomes during the Third Reich less than 3,630 marks. When German officials complained that they could not find enough people willing to serve in the *Spruchkammern*, Clay instructed them to draft participants. That this complaint was at least in part a ploy to encourage the AMG

22. Department of State, *Documents on Germany*, 91–99.
23. The connection between Byrnes's speech and Clay's subsequent remarks on denazification—including the possibility that it was Clay who had written Byrnes's speech—are discussed in Gimbel, *The American Occupation of Germany*, 106–110.

to allow the scale to be reduced rather than to provide more support, however, is clear from the statement of a leading German official who referred to the drafting of participants as "a sort of kidnapping."[24] Of course, the reason the German authorities could not find enough people was not merely the large numbers necessary—ultimately there were 545 *Spruchkammern* with 22,000 members—but that qualified people were afraid of repercussions or would have to pass up more remunerative opportunities elsewhere; many, of course, simply did not approve of the process, and thus avoided participating.

Nevertheless, by the spring of 1947, both public opinion and foreign policy in the United States had taken on a new tone, manifest most prominently in the articulation of the Truman Doctrine (containment of the Soviet Union) and announcement of the Marshall Plan (economic aid to bolster Western European resistance to the Soviet Union). As part of the reorientation of policy that had been gaining ground since Byrnes's speech and was now nearly complete, JCS 1067 was replaced with a new statute— JCS 1779—calling for German self-sufficiency, new industrial targets, and a revision of the reparations list. The difference was apparent in the rhetoric of the JCS document itself: "As a positive program requiring urgent action the United States Government seeks the creation of those political, economic and moral conditions in Germany which will contribute most effectively to a stable and prosperous Europe." This was two short years (or long years, depending on one's perspective) from JCS 1067's proclamation that Germany was not being liberated, but occupied as a defeated enemy nation, that the main concern was to prevent Germany from causing more trouble, and that "fraternization" with the German public was strictly prohibited.

As part of this geopolitical maneuvering, the Soviet Union announced in August 1947 their intention to end denazification in their zone, at least in part to curry favor with ordinary Germans (including low-level Nazis), from whom they hoped to gain political support. Soviet denazification thus ended on February 27, 1947. In reaction, the U.S. Defense Department (the postwar name for the War Department) instructed Clay to move quickly toward an end to the program in the Western zones. When Clay suggested May 8, 1948 (a date heavy with symbolism three years after the unconditional surrender), however, the German minister presidents and their "liberation ministers" were outraged, as were many public commentators. The *Spruchkammern* had been working through the simpler cases

24. Kleßmann, *Die doppelte Statsgründung,* 89.

first, purportedly motivated by the desire to clear low-level Nazis of the work prohibition imposed by Law No. 8.[25] Individuals with more to lose had realized they might benefit from delay; with more resources at their disposal, many such individuals had appealed their automatic classifications and dragged out the process with a sort of paper war (indeed, the number of appeals of the *Spruchkammern* hearings was vastly higher than even the German authorities had predicted). Their gamble paid off, serving at the same time to discredit the entire operation: "small fry" were often punished more harshly than "big fish," since the will toward harshness diminished over time. Ending the program in 1948 would thus have been a symbolic disaster.

The German program dragged out until the *Bundestag* (the lower house of Parliament of the Federal Republic) finally declared denazification complete on December 15, 1950, though the effort had been in disarray for years by that point. In the end, of the more than 3 million *Meldebogen* that indicated chargeable offenses, 930,000 were left after amnesties and other reductions. More than 1,500 were found to be major offenders, 21,000 offenders, 104,000 lesser offenders, and 475,000 followers. Slightly more than 9,000 received prison terms, 30,000 received special labor, 22,000 were declared ineligible for public office, 122,000 had their employment restricted, 25,000 had property confiscated, and 500,000 paid fines. Many of these rulings, however, were later swept away when the new German government (as well as the churches) demanded reduction of punishments and general amnesty as a major bargaining chip in debates over rearmament in the Cold War context.[26]

Whether the numbers are high or low depends on one's perspective, as does whether the punishments were sufficient. Moreover, the effort's legacies are ambiguous: at the founding of the Federal Republic, a great deal of rhetoric was aimed at rejecting putatively false distinctions between "two classes of people in Germany: the politically unobjectionable and the objectionable."[27] Ending denazification was a declaration that this kind of judgment would not continue. On the other hand, equally vigorous arguments were aimed at avoiding the insufficient differentiation of collective guilt.

25. For this and other reasons, according to Tom Bower, "Politically Law no. 8 was an appalling mistake. . . . It gave both respectability and massive support to the opponents of denazification." Bower, *Blind Eye to Murder,* 171.

26. See especially Brochhagen, *Nach Nürnberg;* Frei, *Adenhauer's Germany and the Nazi Past.*

27. This quote is from Konrad Adenauer's first Government Declaration (*Regierungserklärung*) as chancellor in September 1949. See chapter 11.

Assessing Denazification

Evidence on which to evaluate denazification and to determine its impact is contradictory. Many later critics have argued that the real problem was that the occupation authorities squelched indigenous efforts to cleanse German society. The Allies, these critics charge, repressed German antifascist or so-called *Antifa* committees that sprung up as defeat approached, bemoaning that Germany did not have a chance to denazify itself. Some point as well to opposition plans during the last stages of the war, arguing that the idea for a purge of Nazis was originally a German one. Putative support for this reading is found in public opinion data, which demonstrates relatively strong support in the German population for some kind of denazification. From October 1945 to September 1946, for instance, three quarters of those knowledgeable thought it was justified. These positive attitudes continued until 1949, though dropping off somewhat with more experience, and precipitously after 1949. Indeed, other data qualify a reading of support, which was much lower at higher income and educational levels. Furthermore, survey responses indicating support were often based on ignorance of the details. In March 1946, for instance, only a third of respondents could describe the current program accurately. Moreover, other surveys show that 40 percent of respondents in 1946 believed National Socialism was a good idea poorly executed; by 1948, the proportion that agreed with this outlook had climbed to 55 percent.[28] So when respondents indicated that they supported denazification, it is unlikely they supported anything as thorough as what was in the works.

Public commentary, moreover, was largely negative. We have already seen indications, for instance, of the negative assessment of the Evangelical leadership, which was shared by Catholic leaders. Perhaps one of the principle motivations behind clerical rejection of denazification was fear of communism, but both Protestant and Catholic leaderships refused even to rebuke their own clergymen who had been Nazis. Bishop Wurm and others complained bitterly about the retrospective application of law, and argued that it would be impossible to convert the German people to democracy if they were shackled to the past. Even Pastor Martin Niemöller—one of the leading moral authorities in postwar Germany—ended up calling his followers to passive resistance. One argument Bishop Wurm gave is that punishment of earlier enthusiasms denied the value of a change of heart through contem-

28. Merritt, *Democracy Imposed*, 97.

plation. (I examine the attitudes of the churches in greater detail in chapter 10.)

The political parties in formation at this point, with the exception of the Social Democrats, also argued that accusations that were too widespread would not generate allegiance to democracy. Indeed, as ordinary people came to realize that denazification meant examining *everyone's* possible role, the demand for denazification began to sound to many much like a charge of collective guilt (though the direction of denazification's development in fact looked less and less like collective guilt as it became increasingly differentiating). The procedure of the *Spruchkammern* was indeed problematic in this regard, insofar as the burden of proof was on the defendant. Because only those who had received a nonexonerated classification appeared before the *Spruchkammern*, they were the ones required to disprove their guilt.

The Right to a Political Mistake

From the point of view of resonance in subsequent years, perhaps one of the most interesting cases in the history of denazification was that of Minister President Reinhold Maier of Württemburg-Baden (as it was called at the time), one of the *Länderrat* members who signed the Liberation Law. To his surprise, Maier, along with Culture Minister Wilhelm Simpendörfer, was called to answer before a *Spruchkammer* because he had been a member of the *Reichstag* in 1933 and had signed the notorious Enabling Act (*Ermächtigungsgesetz*—the law granting Hitler dictatorial powers). Though not a Nazi, Maier was charged with having contributed decisively to Hitler's seizure of power, was to be classified as a "major offender," and was to be considered unsuited for public responsibility in the new Germany. Maier defended himself vigorously. In a much-noted speech, he argued that merely signing the Enabling Act was not evidence of complicity in the Nazi rise to power. Maier and his defenders argued that the Enabling Act was meaningless for the rise of National Socialism:

Everything would have happened just the same, with or without the Enabling Act. If the Enabling Act had not been passed, the *Reichstag* would have immediately gone up in smoke [*schonungslos aufgeflogen*] on that day. On the 23rd of March, 1933, the question was solely whether the *Reichstag* would later be able to regain its influence. Whoever sat in the *Reichstag* and saw these things in front of his eyes had to say to himself: If only a single last vestige remains, so that all the institutions of the constitution, *Reichspräsident, Reichsrat* [upper house], *Reichstag* [lower house], could be maintained even as a hint and a remnant, one had to support it.[29]

Part of the public controversy concerned accusations that denazification was being used for domestic political purposes. Indeed, the prosecutor in the Maier case was the licensee of the *Stuttgarter Zeitung*, the city's major newspaper, and had already been quite critical of Maier. The case became an issue in the *Länderrat* at the instigation of the SPD and communists, who argued that signing the Enabling Act was more than sufficient to exclude one from political life. Maier succeeded, however, in establishing his claim: the legal brief of the *Länderrat* came to the conclusion that signing the Enabling Act was indeed an extraordinary contribution to National Socialist domination, thus meeting the criterion of the Liberation Law; but the individual's intention was held to be ultimately more important: Did the individual want to establish the Nazi dictatorship? Since Maier claimed that this had not been his intention, he was exonerated. Early enthusiasts, as we saw, were not accountable because they were seen as idealists who perhaps withdrew their support; now those who took concrete action were not responsible because they had not been enthusiasts. Culpability was thus restricted to those unreconstructed enthusiasts who also made a concrete, rather than merely intellectual, contribution, and who refused to repent. In retrospect, the pragmatic bargain seems clear: the past should not matter so long as one agrees to cooperate with the new regime; this was indeed the attitude of the Adenauer government, for which generating a new base of loyalty was the overriding concern. Indeed, as already discussed, many later commentators on both the Left and the Right have agreed with this political assessment—that oblivion served the purpose of legitimation—disagreeing only on whether this was the right choice for the long-term political health of the country.[30]

Significantly, one of Maier's major defenders in the scandal was future federal president Theodor Heuss, who went so far in a radio address as to call the prosecutor (confusingly named Franz Karl Meier) the "Robespierre of Ochsenhausen" (Ochsenhausen was the local area where the charges were filed) and even further to attack him personally. At least part of the explanation for this reaction from a figure hailed in memory (as well as in scholarship) as a moral beacon was that Heuss too had signed the

29. On this affair, see Fürstenau, *Entnazifizierung*, 193–97. See also Kittel, *Die Legende von der "Zweiten Schuld,"* 34–35. For Maier's political perspective, see Maier, *Ein Grundstein wird gelegt*, and *Die Reden*, vol. 1. More generally, see Matz, *Reinhold Maier*.

30. See especially Dubiel, *Niemand is Frei von der Geschichte*; Schwan, *Politik und Schuld*.

Enabling Act, and rightly saw himself in a struggle for his political existence. Indeed, Federal President Heuss spoke repeatedly and at length about his "political stupidity" in 1933.

The question of accountability for such "stupidity" was also the topic of one of the most influential essays of the time, Eugen Kogon's "The Right to the Political Mistake."[31] Kogon, himself a survivor of Buchenwald whose position we will examine more thoroughly below, used the affair to articulate a ruthless critique of the denazification program and Allied re-education goals more generally:

> The form in which one has tried for more than two years to free the German people from National Socialism and Militarism has contributed much to the thoroughly chaotic condition in which we find ourselves. The result is fore-most—everyone who is informed knows it—*less denazification than renazification.* The nasty saying is going around: "The more we bask in the democratic sun, the browner we get." German deficiencies and Allied mistakes have complemented each other with disastrous certainty, as if they were in cahoots [*aufeinander abgestimmt gewesen wären*] and have to this point stymied all efforts of the judicious [*Einsichtigen*]. . . . One has regarded the entire German people with a Nazi lens. As a result, one has accused it as a collectivity. [Emphasis added.]

Like many later speakers—particularly his Catholic co-religionist Konrad Adenauer—Kogon agreed that the guilty must be punished, but that the circle of "the guilty" is rather small:

> Whoever acted culpably is punishable; whoever acted negligently is responsible for the damages and must under certain circumstances be punished; whoever made a mistake and sees the consequences will voluntarily do what is in his power to contribute to reparation; he can also be justly required to do so if he does not feel compelled on his own; the opportunists one should sensitively absolve, drastically and noticeably. The other way, which began with one wanting to treat everyone the same has led, even with the improvements that were later made, to a chain of inefficiencies, errors, injustices and political absurdity. There is little positive here worth mentioning.
>
> The demand to put an end to it is justified. Of course, not everyone has a right to make it.

This conclusion that who you are limits what you can demand is an interesting and important moral point, unusual in a culture prone to accusing

---

31. The essay, originally published in 1947 in the *Frankfurter Hefte*, is excerpted in Kleßmann, *Die doppelte Staatsgründung*, 387–88.

others of Pharisaism. More important for the Maier affair, for Heuss and other signatories of the Enabling Act, and for a wide variety of successors, however: "It is not a crime to have made a political mistake. . . . [P]olitical error belongs before neither a court nor a *Spruchkammer.*"

As we have seen, immediate reactions to, and subsequent memory of, denazification were almost entirely negative. Much of the criticism was factually justified: presumption of guilt, uneven verdicts, corruption, and arbitrary amnesties are, to be sure, troubling matters. But whether the judgment was (and is) warranted that some peace with the perpetrators was a necessary condition for establishing democratic legitimacy is at least equally as troubling. On the one hand, former President Herbert Hoover, returning from a trip to occupied Germany, was of the opinion that "[y]ou can have vengeance or peace, but you can't have both."[32] On the other hand, this is a rather Manichean formulation. Is it always vengeance to hold large numbers of people responsible for "political mistakes"? And is the quiescence achieved through amnesty or silence the same thing as peace? On the basis of a more differentiated understanding, one can wonder—as many Germans and others have done[33]—about short-term versus long-term costs and benefits.

In the immediate context, however, it is worth pointing out, as two American historians of Germany do, that "[d]enazification had many faults, but it put on the record that to have been a devoted follower of Hitler was to have supported crime and violence on a massive scale."[34] This message was certainly received by the producers of official memory in the Federal Republic of Germany.

From Allied Frameworks to German Discourse

I will return to some further considerations on military government in 1948–49, but it is worth remembering here that looking solely at Nuremberg, denazification, and Allied policy more generally as self-contained matters to which Germans merely reacted can give undue support to a "zero hour" or "caesura" interpretation—an interpretation, that is, in which all German trajectories were stopped dead and the situation was redefined from outside. This was certainly not the case, or at least not as completely the case as some accounts would have it. German intellectual, political, and cultural elites were by no means merely passive recipi-

---

32. Quoted in Bark and Gress, *From Shadow to Substance*, 29, among many other places.
33. See especially Schwan, *Politik und Schuld.*
34. Bark and Gress, *From Shadow to Substance*, 86–87.

ents of re-education. A vibrant public discussion (and not just one of complaint about Allied policy) began emerging even before the end of the war, and a number of important public debates garnered significant attention at the time and provided terms, frameworks, and materials for future discourse.

For the time being, it is important to note the political value of the zero-hour trope, as well as the dangers of taking it too literally as a category for scholarly analysis. For many Germans in the immediate aftermath of the war and later, the zero hour—for all its sense of the nadir of German existence—implied that the slate was wiped clean, that postwar Germany was to be completely distinct from National Socialist Germany. At a logical level, of course, this claim fits uneasily with the claim that Germany was "liberated" on May 8, 1945, which indicates continuity with a pre-1933 Germany, not a radically new entity. The "liberation" claim was useful because it made the Germans seem like victims who were not to be identified with the regime, even if it did not represent common sentiment.

The main point of the zero-hour trope in German discourse is, nevertheless, to claim that the emerging political order bore none of the defects or tendencies of the previous one. Critics of the trope use continuities in personnel to charge that the new system was not different enough from its predecessors. Defenders of the trope claim that though some people may have resumed careers the new institutional contexts made them very different actors (of course, defenders also denied that the most prominent of the individuals who returned to power had actually been complicit in the defects of the previous regime).

Certainly, many ideas as well as institutions were reexamined during this period. Within the reexamination of German identity that took place, however, many commentators drew both implicitly and explicitly on German traditions they claimed had retained—even increased—their legitimacy since the advent of National Socialism. Zero hour or not, the degree to which those connections to older ideas are to be understood as restorations, reconstructions, or rejections is an important interpretive question, one that requires a close reading of indigenous German efforts.

PART II

The Vanquished

CHAPTER 7

Other Germanies?

If the victorious powers faced the issues of German guilt out of a (certainly well-justified) concern for geopolitical security, the issues looked very different to the Germans themselves. Indeed, a vibrant public discourse emerged rather quickly in the postwar period, one constituted—for obvious reasons of access and legitimacy—by individuals and groups who had not actively supported the Nazis and who were dismayed—to greater and lesser degrees and for diverse reasons—by the regime, the war, and the atrocities of the concentration camps.[1] (As already seen, persecution of Jews was not yet considered to have been the distinctive feature of the concentration camp system; many of the Germans speaking with public authority at this point had themselves been persecuted in various ways, some even in camps, though not usually in the "extermination" camps.)

The scholarly literature and public discourse refer to a "guilt debate" of 1945–47.[2] This debate, however, was not focused simply on the questions of criminal or political responsibility being addressed at Nuremberg and in the *Spruchkammern*. Indeed, despite Karl Jaspers's famous book title *The Question of German Guilt [Die Schuldfrage]*—there were quite a few distinct *questions* of German guilt. These included the role individuals played in *supporting* the Nazi regime (materially, morally, politically, socially, or otherwise), which is different from asking whether one *perpetrated* specific

1. As we will see in chapter 13, certain discredited figures—such as philosopher Martin Heidegger, writer Ernst Jünger, jurist Carl Schmitt, writer Gottfried Benn, and sociologist Hans Freyer—were able to maintain an alternative discourse on the margins and in private, though not without effect on the immediate and subsequent discursive trajectories at the center of public life.

2. The secondary literature on the so-called "guilt debate" has grown in recent years. Before that, virtually the only comprehensive study was Eberan, *Luther? Friedrich "der*

crimes or was an active Nazi. They also included questions about how one should have reacted if one did not support, or claimed not to have supported, the regime; here the issues of exile (forced or voluntary), accommodation, silence, or active opposition were potent. There was the further question of what one should do after the fact to atone for or expiate the atrocities: Does one acknowledge personal guilt or merely responsibility through a collectivity, and what does that acknowledgment entail? And there was also the question of how to understand the meanings of German history, whether National Socialism was a final consummation of long-standing pathologies or whether it was an aberration, and what this meant for the future (these questions looked rather different to Germans within Germany after the war than they did to British and Americans during the war). For practical purposes of securing political existence, what remained of German identity and traditions, and what was gone forever? How could Germany and Germans find their way again after the rupture?[3]

The emergent discourse in different parts of the guilt debate was, as we will see, characterized by some vigorous defenses and, in retrospect, unexpected omissions. Why? Part of the German reaction was indeed nothing more than defensive attempts to deny—to themselves as much as to others—their implication as individuals and as a collectivity in what had happened. (The form of the referent "what happened," of course, could be filled with several different contents, and often with no specific content at all.) The sense of German victimhood—at the hands of the Nazis, the Allies, and fate itself—was often overwhelming. Certainly some of the German reaction can be understood in light of hunger and privation, conditions that do not often support a sense of just desert or sympathy for others. But to stop at labeling German confrontations with the legacies of National Socialism in a coherent "guilt debate" as defensive and self-pitying is to abdicate the need for sociological explanation—which consists of more than noting how hard

---

Grosse?" Wagner? Nietzsche? Wer war an Hitler schuld? More recently, see Steinle, *Nationales Selbstverstaendnis nach dem Nationalsozialismus;* Wolgast, *Die Wahrnehmung des Dritten Reiches.* Numerous more general works on the immediate postwar period include briefer analyses of the guilt debate. Additionally, countless institutionally focused studies (such as of the churches or parties) analyze attitudes toward the past in these circumscribed institutional contexts.

3. Questions of how to go on after the rupture were distinct for individuals and for the collectivity. The former involved personal and psychological matters, the latter political and economic ones. Moral questions arose at both levels, but how an individual should deal with the fact that he had fought for a reviled regime, for instance, is a different question than what the collective identity should mean in the future. Whatever the distinctions, of course, there were also numerous ways in which these dimensions were inextricable.

it is to recognize guilt when you are hungry—as well as to trivialize the very serious reflection and debate that did occur. Despite the differences in perspective from different fields, these defenses and blind spots were remarkably consistent, parts of a distinctive political cultural profile.

Identifying a "guilt debate of 1945–47" at all, of course, risks lending more coherence to a diverse discourse than it actually merits: this "debate" included approaches from existential, cultural, psychological, historiographical, philosophical, and religious perspectives, among others. Again, relatively distinct "agonies"—including the agonies of the Allies and now of the Germans—together constituted a complex discursive landscape. Sometimes arguments from different perspectives and centered on different themes did in fact address each other directly, but often not. This should not be surprising, though perhaps the extent to which identical terms and even syntax reappear is remarkable.

German public identity in this period was in many ways profoundly up for grabs. What is interesting is that many public Germans, whether literary, philosophical, or political figures, were grabbing in the same directions. If future commentators refer retrospectively to a debate with greater coherence than it actually had, moreover, that is in itself a matter requiring explanation. In this case, it was part of characterizing the questions of guilt as belonging to the first hour, asked and answered. Keeping in mind the central goal of understanding the dynamics of German collective remembering, the task here is to describe the variety of first formulations of public memory—diverse as they were—and to understand why they took the forms, and addressed the issues, that they did.

The Conditions of German Discourse

The conditions for German public discourse after May 8, 1945, were, to say the least, highly unusual. First, the Nazi regime had expended great effort controlling (indeed strangling) public opinion, which they accomplished by co-opting near total control of organs of information under a central command (though this is not to suggest that public opinion would necessarily have been uniformly opposed to them). While during the 1930s there were isolated pockets of limited independence (though highly scrutinized and thus risky), by the early 1940s there was no reasonable mechanism for disseminating anything but official doctrine. As always in dictatorships, there were informal networks and very precarious private areas, and significant numbers of people did risk tuning in to overseas broadcasts. But the centralization of the Nazi information apparatus—its elimination of public discourse—in many ways made the Allies' control easier after victory.

In their planning for the occupation, the Western Allies had originally intended to effect a news blackout that would keep the German population totally dependent on direct military authority. After a period of "purification"—a response to what planners saw as the successful misuse of radio and press as instruments of Nazi propaganda—they intended to school the Germans gradually in democratic journalism. These intentions, however, proved unworkable because of the time it took from the first victories on German soil until the fall of the regime, which was longer than anyone had anticipated. The U.S. Army, therefore, began publishing notices in German as early as the end of January 1945, although German radio and the national party newspaper—*Der Völkische Beobachter*—continued until the very end. After a period of dual sources before the surrender, in the first weeks after May 8 the only information to be had thus came from the Army's notices and seized radio stations (though many Germans had lost the ability to receive radio when their homes were destroyed).[4]

The numerous local "notices" were coordinated under a centralized editorship in Bad Nauheim. Nevertheless, the Western Allies began granting licenses to German editors very quickly (the first license went to a German editorial team for the *Aachener Nachrichten* on June 27, 1945, the second to the *Frankfurter Rundschau*, which began publishing on August 1). One interesting proviso for licensing newspapers and magazines was that their boards had to represent a diversity of political orientations. Thus, many of the first boards included a communist. This was intended to break the long tradition of overt partisanship in German journalism, as were prescriptions for separating "news" and "editorial" content. Until September 1945, the Allies exercised direct censorship over the content of German publications; after that, the primary mechanism of control was the granting or revocation of licenses. Radio was more directly controlled by the occupiers, and was later organized regionally as decentralized public enterprises.

Within the Psychological Warfare Division (which later became the Information Control Division), which was responsible for the publication of the local notices, there was substantial skepticism about the wisdom of allowing independent German efforts right away, even if closely monitored. Following ideas of "re-education"—in the formulation of which a number

4. On Allied press policy and the emergence of German journalism after the war, see Flanagan, *A Study of German Political–Cultural Periodicals;* Gienow-Hecht, *Transmission Impossible;* Hurwitz, *Die Stunde Null der deutschen Presse;* Mosberg, *Reeducation.*

of the PWD's officers had been involved—many believed German journalists and opinion leaders needed to be trained in the principles of democratic journalism and discourse, both by doctrine and by example in practice. The chief advocate of this stance was Captain (later Major) Hans Habe, who was the coordinating editor in Bad Nauheim of the Army notices. Habe was certainly one of the most colorful—and indeed significant—figures in the occupation story. Originally named János Békessy, Habe was born in 1911 in Budapest, the son of a successful Jewish editor (though the father often denied being Jewish). The family moved to Vienna when Habe was a child, where, at age nineteen, he briefly joined the Austrian fascists. At twenty-one, he became the youngest editor-in-chief in Europe at Vienna's *Der Morgen*. Habe's major prewar claim to fame was that in 1935 he discovered that Hitler's family name was Schickelgruber (he later joked that he had thereby single-handedly delayed the *Anschluss*). After the Nazi take over, Habe went first to Paris to join the French army, and then, following the fall of France in 1940, emigrated to the United States. Habe was, by all accounts, a notorious playboy and dandy, and married into substantial American wealth and power (his wife was the daughter of Joseph Davies, former U.S. ambassador to the Soviet Union, and granddaughter of Charles W. Post, the owner of General Mills). During the war, Habe was involved in military intelligence training in Maryland, where he developed ideas along the lines of the re-education plans discussed by Richard Brickner, Margaret Mead, and Talcott Parsons, among others. During the war, he even toured the country advocating the formation of an "American Educational Expeditionary Force," which would consist of one hundred thousand academics charged with teaching the Germans democracy.[5]

Concerned about handing over control to Germans without a tutorial period, Habe vigorously pushed plans in June 1945 for a single newspaper for the American zone. He argued that it would "take many years before we have out of the mental bewilderness [*sic*] of Germany, [and] created an aristocracy which than can really lead Germany into the family of free people."[6] This made clear his intentions for what became *Die Neue Zeitung* (the New Newspaper), "an American newspaper for the German public." The first issue was published on October 18, 1945, and included the following statement by General Eisenhower: "The *Neue Zeitung*, although it is published in the German language, in no way attempts to be a 'German'

5. See Geinow-Hecht, *Transmission Impossible*, 18–21; and Habe's own account, *Ich stelle mich*.

6. Quoted in Gienow-Hecht, *Transmission Impossible*, 24–25.

newspaper. . . . . Militaristic ideas must be erased from the German mind. For all civilized nations on this earth, aggresion [*sic*] is immoral; the Germans, however, have to be educated to this self-evident truth." This was not at all the program or tone Habe had in mind, however, and this divergence was the source of much trouble for Habe and his colleagues. Like many émigrés, Habe very much believed in distinguishing between "good" and "bad" Germans (indeed, his staff included a number of rather marginal figures, himself included). His goal—which he in fact managed to fulfill for several months, much to the consternation of his superiors—was to provide a forum for discussion of German values and thereby a model of democratic discourse. Habe was frequently accused of being too pro-German, though, as we will see, this was not an accurate characterization.

Die Neue Zeitung's two central (related) preoccupations under Habe's direction (he resigned under pressure in March 1946) were the role of the exiles and the question of collective guilt. Regarding the former, he and his colleagues (émigrés as well as so-called "inner emigrants" among them) made special efforts to present German ideas and culture that had been crushed by the Nazis. The newspaper was thus filled with essays by and commentaries on exile literature, Nazi-prohibited traditions, as well as serious discussion of the role of writers. Most prominent of these discussions was that concerning Thomas Mann, to which I turn below. (In chapter 9 I explore more direct discussions of collective guilt, which took place both in the *Neue Zeitung* and in many other literary, intellectual, and political journals that were born [and often died] in the immediate postwar years.)[7]

The Mann Affair

As we have already seen, the central legitimacy claim of German exiles was that there were two Germanies, the manifest Germany that was not the real Germany and the latent Germany rescued by the lifeboat of exile, the "Other Germany." However, while many exiles thus felt themselves to be morally superior to their compatriots who stayed—whether they supported the regime, merely accommodated it, or resisted either actively or passively—the idea of exile was a problematic notion for many Germans. Indeed, for many,

---

7. One of the reasons so many journals were born and died in this period was another of the peculiar conditions of the—supposedly short-lived—intellectual renaissance after 1945: printed matter was one of the very few items not rationed. Because of the Nazi regime's inflationary economic policies, many Germans had more cash than they could spend, since almost nothing was available; within the limits of paper shortages, therefore, printed matter sold unusually well before the 1948 currency reform.

there seemed to be something discreditable about it. Not least of the reasons for this discredit was that most exiles were Jews. Even more, the very idea of exile was associated not just in practice but in principle with the Jewish people, for whom the diaspora was such a central experience. Wandering, in other words, was for Jews, not Germans. This is not to say that all Germans dismayed by the regime but who nevertheless remained did so because of the association between Jewishness and exile. An additional factor was the sense that one does not abandon one's country *especially* in times of difficulty. For those of the latter view, the sense that they represented an "Other Germany" of "inner emigrants" was thus a central part of their self-understanding. In later years, there would be much debate about the relative moral merits of "inner emigrants" versus active members of the opposition. In the immediate postwar period, however, the operative distinction was between exiles and "inner emigrants" as representatives of the "Other Germany." *Die Neue Zeitung* provided perhaps the central forum for working out the status, meaning, and legacies of both exile and "inner emigration."

* * *

The prismatic case for establishing and parsing these issues was the debate over Thomas Mann.[8] One of the most prominent and active German exiles, the renowned author was Weimar Germany's preeminent man of letters and thus a major propaganda thorn to the Nazis. During the war, Mann published numerous critical essays, delivered important speeches, nurtured contacts with circles close to President Roosevelt, and eventually became an American citizen. At the same time that he was a leading symbol of the "Other Germany," however, Mann harbored reservations about the very idea. Among exiles, as we already saw, there was a fundamental split between those who defended German culture to the last, believing the current regime had no roots whatsoever in the authentic German traditions of humanism and Enlightenment, and others for whom the Nazis signaled profound flaws in the German tradition, which would require an internal battle to remedy, one in which one spirit must conquer the other.

Thomas Mann fell into neither of these camps—was neither an attacker of all things German nor a defender of an unsullied "Other Germany."

8. The account I present here draws on the following literature: Glaser, *The Rubble Years*, 73–81; Hermand and Lange, *"Wollt ihr Thomas Mann wiederhaben?"*; Kurzke, *Thomas Mann*; Sontheimer, *Thomas Mann und die Deutschen*. Useful texts are included in Mann, *Fragile Republic*.

Indeed, in 1939, Mann had published an essay in *Esquire* magazine titled "That Man Is My Brother," referring to Hitler: "A brother—a rather unpleasant and mortifying brother. He makes me nervous, the relationship is painful to a degree. *But I will not disclaim him.*"[9] In August 1943, at a meeting in Los Angeles that Mann attended along with a "who's who" of famous exile German politicians, writers, artists, and scientists, the National Committee for Free Germany issued a declaration asserting the difference between the Hitler regime and its supporters on the one hand and the German people as a whole on the other. Mann first signed the declaration, but a day later removed his signature, arguing that the declaration was too patriotic.

In perhaps his most famous speech, at the Library of Congress in May 1945, Mann stated, "Any attempt to arouse sympathy, to defend and excuse Germany, would certainly be an inappropriate undertaking for one of German birth today." On the other hand, "[t]o play the part of judge, to curse and damn his own people in compliant agreement with the incalculable hatred that they have kindled, to commend himself smugly as 'the good Germany' in contrast to the wicked, guilty Germany over there with which he has nothing in common,—that too would hardly befit one of German origin." Most important and unusual for one with easy recourse to an identity-saving claim, Mann went on to argue that "[t]here are *not* two Germanys [*sic*], a good one and a bad one, but only one, whose best turned into evil through devilish cunning." For Mann, the German tradition was a complex contradiction: "Wicked Germany is merely good Germany gone astray, good Germany in misfortune, in guilt, in ruin."[10]

This ambivalence was emblematic of Mann's personal position, manifesting his feelings about his own exile. Indeed, Mann was highly conflicted about his decision to leave Germany, which was almost accidental. While abroad on a lecture tour, he was warned that it was not safe to return. Even so, he agonized about not returning, and more than once contemplated seizing an opportunity to slip back in. Mann shared the sense of irony about German exile. As early as July 1934, he had noted what would become a common association: "Perhaps history has in fact intended for them [the Germans] the role of the Jews, one which even Goethe thought befitted them: to be one day scattered throughout the world and to view their existence with an intellectual proud self-irony."[11]

9. Mann, "That Man Is My Brother" (emphasis added).

10. "Deutschland und die Deutschen," *Addresses Delivered at the Library of Congress, 1942–1949*, 48, 64.

11. Mann, *Past Masters*, 220. For the complex issue of Mann's putative anti-Semitism, see Kurzke, *Thomas Mann*, 188–215.

This "intellectual proud self-irony" seems to have been Mann's hope for himself, though he was often unable to maintain confidence in that position. In key moments, he admitted feeling denied his destiny as Germany's literary "preceptor."

Nearly all of these themes, and Mann's entire approach to exile and to the question of guilt, are summed up with the literary mastery for which he is famous in the conclusion to his novelistic reflection on National Socialism—*Doctor Faustus*. Indeed, the Faust story struck many as the obvious literary metaphor for what had occurred in Germany, with its theme of bargaining with the devil and losing one's soul for practical conquests. The key passage is worth quoting at length as one of the most important and lasting statements on the German tradition and condition:

> Our thick-walled torture chamber, into which Germany was transformed by a vile regime of conspirators sworn to nihilism from the very start, has been burst open, and our ignominy lies naked before the eyes of the world. . . . I repeat, our ignominy. For is it mere hypochondria to tell oneself that all that is German— even German intellect, German thought, the German word—shares in the disgrace of these revelations and is plunged into profoundest doubt? Is it morbid contrition to ask oneself the question: How can "Germany," whichever of its forms it may be allowed to take in the future, so much as open its mouth again to speak of mankind's concerns?
>
> One can call what came to light here the dark possibilities within human nature in general—but it was in fact tens of thousands, hundreds of thousands of Germans who committed the acts before which humanity shudders, and whatever lived as German stands now as an abomination and the epitome of evil. What will it be like to belong to a nation whose history bore this gruesome fiasco within it, a nation that has driven itself mad, gone psychologically bankrupt, that admittedly despairs of governing itself and thinks it best that it become a colony of foreign powers, a nation that will have to live in isolated confinement, like the Jews of the Ghetto, because the dreadfully swollen hatred all around it will not permit it to step outside its border—a nation that cannot show its face. . . .
>
> . . . Was not this regime, both in word and deed, merely the distorted, vulgarized, debased realization of a mindset and worldview to which one must attribute a characteristic authenticity and which, not without alarm, a Christianly humane person finds revealed in the traits of our great men, in the figures of the most imposing embodiments of Germanness?[12]

This passage contains many important tropes—including "the vile regime of *conspirators*," "epitome of *evil*," "a nation driven itself *mad*," the analogy

12. Mann, *Doktor Faustus*, 505–6.

(paraphrasing Goethe) of Germans and Jews, and reference to "the Christianly humane person"—which we will encounter again elsewhere and examine in more detail where they reappear. But the immediate point we should note is that Mann was arguing that good Germany and bad Germany are not alternatives, but mere moments in a dialectic: in a clear rebuke to his fellow exiles, he argued that to "proclaim that such a state was forced upon us as something without roots in our nature as a people, something totally alien to us . . . would, so it seems to me, be more high-minded than conscientious."[13] The charge, seemingly, applies even more to those who had stayed. No easy defense that National Socialism perverted the true "Other Germany," whether by exiles or "inner emigrants," Mann thus argued, is possible.

Despite the subtleties of Mann's arguments, nevertheless, many of his contemporaries read him as an advocate of collective guilt and as a traitor to his people. In a radio broadcast of January 16, 1945, Mann had declared, "Let us not speak of guilt. That is a name for the fatal concatenation of consequences of a tragic history, and if it be guilt, it is intermixed with a great deal of guilt belonging to the whole world."[14] Nevertheless, highly differentiated arguments did not work well in this context, despite charges by Germans against the occupation authorities that their treatment of Germany rested on *insufficiently* differentiated understandings. The question was obviously one of the kind of differentiation.

Exile versus "Inner Emigration"

These reflections burst the bounds of politically engaged *belles lettres* (if they were ever really within those bounds)[15] in August 1945, within the context of debates sponsored by Habe's journalistic "school." It was in the *Münchner Zeitung* (one of Habe's enterprises) that Walter von Molo published a letter of August 8, 1945, to Thomas Mann. Von Molo, who had been president of the poetry section of the Prussian Academy of the Arts from 1928 to 1930 and who had remained in Germany during the Third Reich, called upon Mann to return to Germany. Mann, who according to von Molo represented the best of the "Other Germany," was to tend to his countrymen like a "good physician," proving to the world that in its "innermost core" the German people really had nothing in common with the "misdeeds and

13. Ibid., 506.
14. Mann, *Addresses Delivered at the Library of Congress.*
15. In Germany, in part because German identity had traditionally been understood as a primarily cultural identity, the field of *belles lettres* and the political field were never as clearly distinct as they were in some other places.

crimes, the horrible atrocities and lies." In the last analysis, so many had "remained reasonable people" despite the "slogans" and "humiliations" of the occupation [*sic*—the occupation, not the regime], these "Germans who yearned and yearn for the return of that which gave us respect in the counsel of nations." "Please come back soon," von Molo wrote, "and give to these crushed souls consolation through humaneness; revive their faith that justice does exist, that it is indeed wrong to split humanity so cruelly, as has been done here in our recent, gruesome past." Mann represented German humanism, and with him on the scene no one would be able to deny that this was a core German virtue. Mann was living proof of the difference between regime and *Volk*. As the last quoted sentence indicates, von Molo saw the same logic at work in Nazi distinctions "in our recent, most gruesome past" and contemporary undifferentiated condemnations of Germany and the emerging classificatory schemas of denazification, which produced the above-mentioned "slogans" and "humiliations."[16]

As already clear from Mann's statements at the Library of Congress and the passage from *Doctor Faustus* (which Mann had been working on since 1943 but which was not published until 1947), von Molo's letter was anathema to Mann's argument that Nazi Germany was not something separate from an "inner core" of German identity, but a pathological emanation of it. On less of a theoretical and more of a visceral foundation, however, Mann found distasteful the idea that an exile like himself had anything in common with self-styled defenders of German humanism who had remained in Germany, like von Molo. Indeed, Mann had specific occasion to respond to that association because of an article following von Molo's by Frank Thiess, a writer who had been editor of the *Berliner Tageblatt* from 1915 to 1919. Thiess's article was titled "The Inner Emigration," thereby coining a term that would appear throughout subsequent discussions.[17] Thiess claimed a unity of exiles and "inner emigrants" as representatives of the "Other Germany," on the basis of which German identity could be rehabilitated, new (old) foundations strengthened, and collective accusations repudiated.

Thiess's argument, however, was not only not modest, it was supercilious. Responding to the question as to why he too had not emigrated, Thiess wrote: "If I were to succeed in surviving this terrible epoch . . .

16. Crucial passages from von Molo's letter, as well as from that of Frank Thiess to be discussed below, along with Mann's response, are reprinted in Glaser, *The Rubble Years*, 73–77, among many other places. Mann's complete response is reprinted in Mann, *Fragile Republik*, 23–36.

17. See also Paetel, *Deutsche innere Emigration*.

I would gain thereby so much for my intellectual and human development that I would emerge richer in knowledge and experience than I could possibly become by observing the German tragedy from seats in the loges or orchestra stalls of foreign countries." Thiess went so far as to argue that it was more difficult—and thus a more worthy achievement—to preserve one's character in Germany than it was "to send messages to the German people from over there, which fell on deaf ears while we knowledgeable ones always felt ourselves many lengths ahead." Comparing leaving Germany during the Third Reich to leaving one's mother in her sickbed, Thiess nevertheless condescended on behalf of the "inner emigrants" that they "expect no reward for not having left Germany. It was natural for us that we stayed by it." Reproducing a rather nationalistic claim, Thiess argued that Germany, after all, lay more on the ground than it ever had in its "thousand year history." He thus warned Mann and other exiles not to wait so long that they lose their linguistic, and by implication, cultural credibility. Thiess and many others clearly saw themselves as generous, allowing those who abandoned Germany in its time of need to return and participate in the recovery: "That is not to say that I want to rebuke anybody who did leave," Thiess offers backhandedly.

Thiess and von Molo, it is important to note, were not without good reason for their defensiveness. In his wartime speeches, Mann had argued that German intellectuals were partly responsible for the Third Reich since they had failed to resist, especially in the form of a "general strike." In particular, Mann had criticized Ernst Jünger, perhaps the leading conservative writer of the Weimar period, who had been an early enthusiast for National Socialism. Mann charged Jünger with more responsibility for his early flirtations with the Nazis than Jünger and others were prepared to accept after they had withdrawn their support; whether or not Jünger and others had eventually withdrawn their support, their nationalistic "saber rattling" was, for Mann, a serious indictment. For Jünger, in contrast, Mann was a traitor for giving speeches while German cities were going up in flames. In a notorious 1973 interview, Jünger stirred controversy when he criticized Mann for abandoning Germany, fully aware that Mann would have been imprisoned had he stayed: for Jünger, that was a cost Mann should have been willing to bear.[18]

Mann struggled with the issue for many weeks, finally responding to von Molo in October 1945. He gave three reasons for not returning

18. See the discussion in Neaman, *A Dubious Past*, 104–7. Jünger will appear again in greater detail in chapter 13.

to Germany. First, as he had already stated during the war, he was disappointed that Hitler's seizure of power in 1933 had not led to a general strike of all intellectuals. Second, Mann argued that one could not simply forget the horrors of what followed. And third, he had become an American citizen, he admired the United States, and his children had become assimilated there. More emphatically, Mann rejected the charge that he and his co-exiles had comfortably observed Germany from afar and thus had not suffered for their views. Thiess and others, Mann argued, did not appreciate the psychic trauma of exile.[19] Mann did not explicitly use Thiess's term "inner emigration" so as not to credit the claim: "I confess," Mann wrote, "I fear . . . that in spite of everything, understanding between one who experienced the witches' Sabbath from outside and you who joined in the dance and served Herr Urian [the name of the devil in Goethe's *Faust*] would be difficult." Although he later regretted doing so, Mann went so far as to dismiss all intellectual work produced during the Third Reich—the legitimacy claim of the "inner emigrants": "It may be superstition, but in my eyes books that were even printed in Germany between 1933 and 1945 are less than worthless and should not be touched [*nicht gut, in die Hand zu nehmen*]. An odor of blood and shame clings to them: They should all be pulped." Despite this indignant rejection, Mann ended the letter by assuring von Molo that he had never stopped seeing himself as a German writer and that he remained true to the German language. More important, he had always sympathized with those who were condemned by an "undifferentiated Anti-Germanism."[20] The positive benefit, for Mann, of not distinguishing a good, "Other Germany" from the bad was that one could, on that basis, reject judgments of Germany as purely bad; the good and the bad together constitute Germany, preventing collectivistic accusations as well as collectivistic defenses. Neither absolute innocence nor absolute guilt is a justified claim.

As could be expected, Mann's response caused a storm of indignation, and the newspapers were filled in the months that followed with letters and articles addressing Mann's arguments. Mann himself expressed no interest in modifying his position, though very little of the reaction was even

19. The literature on the exile experience, both autobiographical and scholarly, is extensive. See especially Jay, *Permanent Exiles;* Coser, *Refugee Scholars in America;* Heilbut, *Exiled in Paradise;* Anderson, *Hitler's Exiles;* Köbner, Sautermeister, and Sigrid Schneider, *Deutschland nach Hitler;* Mann and Mann, *Escape to Life;* Reuther, *"Die ambivalente Normalisierung";* Wiggershaus, *The Frankfurt School;* Zuckmayer, *Als wär's ein Stück von mir.*

20. This statement can be compared to Chancellor Konrad Adenauer's later remark that two kinds of Germans were being illegitimately distinguished from one another.

remotely sympathetic to him. One of the only examples of public support for Mann was from Hermann Hesse, who had survived the war in Switzerland.[21] Hesse addressed the question of what a "right-minded decent German should have done in the Hitler years." He rejected those responses focused only on the latter years, that is, on what one should have done after 1938 or later. To those who argue that resistance was dangerous, Hesse asked "why they first discovered Hitler in 1933" rather than since at least the Munich *Putsch* (1923); why instead of supporting the Weimar Republic they had voted for Hindenburg and Hitler, who were the ones who made it life-threatening "to be a right-minded decent person." The attack on conservatives who had been early Nazi supporters is thus clear.

Regarding "inner emigration," to those who defended their actions in the Third Reich by saying they always had one foot in the concentration camp, Hesse quipped that he only trusts "those who had two feet in the camps, not one foot in the camps, the other in the Party." Most important, Hesse rued the fact that of all the people who were writing to him, none admitted to having been a Nazi and now saw things differently. We should recall that Hesse was writing around the same time that leaders of the Evangelical Church in Germany were decrying denazification because it denied people the right to a change of heart. According to Hesse's evidence, no one was acknowledging a change of heart because no one was admitting to having been a Nazi in the first place. For Hesse, the question of political responsibility extended far back into the Weimar Republic, associating early origins and ultimate ends in a more direct fashion than those who focused only on the war did.[22] The real question for German society was one Allied soldiers had been asking as they marched through Germany: Where were all the Nazis? They did not reemerge as a political force until several years later, when they lobbied for the restoration of civil service protections, pensions, and the like.

The Gift of Goethe

This was by no means the end of the Mann affair, which continued actively into 1947 when Mann traveled to Europe but refused to visit Germany,

21. The text of Hesse's letter is reprinted in Kleßmann, *Die doppelte Staatsgründung*, 442–44.

22. Later, we will see the philosopher Martin Heidegger's antithetical response in his notorious letter to his former student, Herbert Marcuse, that one should not "judge the beginning of the National Socialist movement from its end." Reprinted in Wolin, *The Heidegger Controversy*, 162.

calling forth a new public discussion of the role of exiles.[23] Mann and, by implication, others who had "abandoned" Germany or who had even fought against it were roundly condemned as traitors, as despicable figures who had sullied their own nest (*Nestbeschmutzer*). Indeed, the Mann affair had echoes later in the history of the Federal Republic, particularly in the 1960s debates over SPD chancellor candidate (and chancellor from 1969 to 1974) Willy Brandt, who had spent the war in Scandinavia and who had at that time given up his German citizenship (and his birth name—Herbert Frahm—as well); Brandt was seen by some conservatives as a traitor. In contrast, Chancellor Konrad Adenauer referred repeatedly to his own experience as an "inner emigrant," though his comparison was not to exiles but to those who had participated actively in one or another opposition group.

The complexities of the "Other Germany" and the difficult reception of the German opposition were certainly a part of the subsequent history of German memory. More immediately important in the Mann affair, however, was the question of German humanism: Was the "Other Germany"—whether literary (best represented by Mann), philosophical (best represented, as we will see, by Karl Jaspers), religious (best represented, as we will see, by Martin Niemöller), or political (represented by a number of figures, though perhaps best by Theodor Heuss and Kurt Schumacher, though in different ways)—able to "protect" something of value that could now serve to rescue Germany from the abyss? What value was there to be found in German traditions? And what were those values?

Such questions were prominent when Mann finally did return to Germany in 1949 for the bicentennial of Goethe's birth. For Germans in the immediate postwar, Goethe stood for the untouchable, untarnished essence of an "Other Germany," the Germany of humanism, Germany as a "people of poets and thinkers" rather than of "judges and executioners."[24] For Mann as for many Germans, Goethe was Germany's gift to the world. In his speech at Frankfurt after receiving the 1949 Goethe prize, Mann stated, "The 'good Germany' is the strength that is blessed by the muse,

23. Concerned about the controversy, as well as hopeful that it would provide a unique window on attitudes, the U.S. authorities undertook surveys and focused interviews to gauge reactions to the question of whether Mann and other exiles should return. For transcripts of these interviews and a more detailed account of the entire controversy, see Hermand and Lange, "*Wollt ihr Thomas Mann wiederhaben?*"

24. In German these two slogans rhyme, the second a play on the first; "Ein Volk von Dichtern und Denkern" versus "Ein Volk von Richtern und Henkern."

moral greatness. Thus a German could become exemplary, not only the model and completion of a people, but of humanity."[25]

This is not to say that there were no critical voices. Once again demonstrating the dialogical intricacies of memory, philosopher Karl Jaspers's Goethe prize speech had engendered controversy two years earlier with the statement that Goethe could not merely be imitated or held up uncritically as a model. There was a danger, Jaspers argued, that in lesser hands all that Goethe stood for was susceptible to debasement. Jaspers noted a fine line between "the depth of Goethean thoughts" and "the obscurity of blurred thinking," between "real soaring of Goethe's wisdom" and "the indecisiveness of insubstantiality. . . . It is the doom of German education after Goethe that the latter paths were traveled. . . . Goethe served as the reason and excuse for everything." Jaspers therefore warned against a "cult" of Goethe.[26] The speech was vigorously attacked in 1949, when it was published as a small book, by Jaspers's long-time acquaintance Ernst Robert Curtius. Curtius charged Jaspers with using an unjustified smear of the Goethe legacy to burden Germany with a religiously inspired guilt. Many of Jaspers's colleagues rejected the *ad hominem* attack on him, but rejected as well Jaspers's critique of Goethe, in the process reinforcing Jaspers's conviction that German culture was more slavish than reflexive.

How accurate Jaspers's description of the politicization of German culture was is evident in the extent to which German public culture embraced the Goethe bicentennial in 1949 and in the debate that ensued when Mann followed his appearance in Frankfurt with a trip to Weimar—Goethe's birthplace, now in the East. Critics charged that Mann was debasing Goethe's humanist legacy by not acknowledging its putative abrogation by the communists. On their side, communist critics charged that the challenge to Goethe's humanism came from the Western critics who maligned the "antifascist" foundations of the East. But the idea that Hitler had nothing to do with Goethe, that Goethe rather than Hitler represented the "true" Germany, was common in the political as well as cultural discourse more generally.

* * *

25. The speech is reprinted in Mann, *Fragile Republik*, 74–90.

26. An essay version of Jaspers's address was printed in *Die Wandlung* in 1947 as "Unsere Zukünft und Goethe," and in 1949 as a small book. For Jaspers's comments, as well as a description of the event, see Glaser, *The Rubble Years*, 314–18. Also see the discussion in Kohler and Saner, *Hannah Arendt–Karl Jaspers: Correspondence, 1926–1969*, 714–15.

Outside of Germany, such debates may appear as tempests in teapots. But it is difficult to overstate the importance of such matters for German identity, particularly at this delicate stage of national insecurity. Moreover, the problematic relationship between intellect (*Kultur*) and politics was a long-standing theme in German commentary. The standard argument was that because Germany was unsuccessful for so long politically, it had developed as a cultural nation (*Kulturnation*). This simultaneously attributed to intellectuals and artists virtually the entire responsibility for German identity while freeing them of any responsibility for practical affairs, which gave rise to a peculiar form of impractical idealism. Mann's own transformation—from claiming to have been an unpolitical man[27] to this symbolic demonstration of the importance of culture for politics—was thus in many ways emblematic of the transformations through which German self-understanding would have to pass.

A vivid example here is the contrast between Mann and a conservative figure—Gottfried Benn. Benn, who had remained in Germany, offered his diagnosis of the vexed relation between the German intellect and state: "In my view, the West is doomed not at all by the totalitarian systems or the crimes of the SS, not even by its material impoverishment or the Gottwalds and Molotovs, but by the abject surrender of its intelligentsia to political concepts. The *zoon politicon*, that Greek blunder, that Balkan notion—that is the germ of our impending doom."[28] This contrasts with the diagnosis that because intellectuals had remained aloof from politics, they had rendered themselves susceptible to the seductions of National Socialism and other aestheticized political impulses. As Wolf Lepenies puts it, Benn "did not deplore the aloofness of Germany's intelligentsia from the public realm which had made them easy prey for the Nazis—he pretended that the intellectual had failed to remain unpolitical and had thereby contributed to a political catastrophe."[29] This was, according to Lepenies, a further misdiagnosis of the German spirit, yet another grand illusion: "[C]ulture always came first, politics followed. The contrary was true. To survive the civilizational break it had inflicted upon Europe, Germany would have to give up the most German of all ideologies: the illusion that culture can compensate for politics." The process, Lepenies points out, would take a long time.

27. *Observations of an Unpolitical Man* was the title of a book by Mann published during World War I.

28. Benn, "Letter from Berlin, July 1948," 80. I examine in detail the conservative constellation of which Benn was a part in chapter 13.

29. Lepenies, "The End of 'German Culture.'"

Mann provided a major first step in rethinking the relationship, but what Lepenies calls a "blurring of genres" between exile and "inner emigration," effected by the reaction against Mann, delayed the transformation.

For many contemplating their nation in ruins and spurned by the world, however, Goethe, Schiller, and Beethoven were all that Germany had left to save their modern Sodom and Gomorrah from collective denunciation; their celebration, many believed, could serve as beacons in the effort to reground German values, leading Germany back onto the right path it had originally formulated so well. This was certainly the case among many German historians, to whom I turn before returning to the question of collective guilt proper.

CHAPTER 8

The Meanings of German History

Much of the wartime writing on Germany, as we saw in chapter 3, can be divided between those who understood National Socialism as deeply rooted in German history (essentialists) and those who thought of it as a contemporary aberration (aberrationists). For both groups, however, the fact of National Socialism required explanation with the resources of history and social science: for essentialists, the historiographical portrait of Germany required wholesale revision; for aberrationists, it was nonetheless necessary to explain how, despite three hundred years of humanism, this "industrial accident" (*Betriebsunfall*) could have occurred. In the immediate aftermath of the war, therefore, historical reflection on National Socialism would clearly be a key arena for reconstructing German identity, whether this required reassertion, revision, or replacement.

The Limits of German Revisionism

Some revision, obviously, was necessary, but how much, and by whom? A particularly zealous defense against wholesale condemnation was mounted by Gerhard Ritter, one of the most prominent of the national conservative historians from the Weimar period, and certainly one of the most important after 1945. In contrast to some other conservatives, Ritter was able to defend this position and German national history somewhat more vigorously because of his persecution as a member of the opposition. Like many conservatives, of course, Ritter faced the problem that he had shared with the Nazis nationalist frustration with the Versailles settlement, and had thus been willing to follow them up to a point. Indeed, despite the requisite total rejection of National Socialism after 1945, Weimar-era conservatives were often unwilling to abandon even Prussian nationalism, which they argued was a German achievement—in contrast to National Socialism, which, as we will see, was often regarded as a "foreign plague." The national-conservative tradition in German historiography, after all, was defined in part by its celebration of the German (read Prussian) *state*.[1]

For Ritter, there were real dangers in allowing wholesale condemnations to stand, whether or not some revisions were necessary. And here the dialogical quality of the discourse is particularly relevant: Ritter addressed his remarks on revision directly against Robert Vansittart and others. Ritter warned his opponents vigorously against what he saw as a facile diagnosis of the "errors" of German history. To condemn all of German history for a twelve-year aberration—and Ritter argued that it *was* an aberration, in which even the Prussian military tradition could not be implicated—was to invite undifferentiated and premature final judgment (the historiographical version of "collective guilt").

Ritter and others were particularly concerned with the fact that such criticisms came from outside. He warned that foreign demands for German guilt far exceeded what one could reasonably expect, and would lead to a dangerous humiliation:

> Premature historical accounts, summary judgments, vague collective conceptions of the German past are not at all useful for our orientation, but lead us astray to new missteps; what we need is the most careful critical differentiation, conscientious consideration of the overall direction, as well as of individual steps, above all: not passionate chatter but unwavering pursuit of the unvarnished historical truth and justice.[2]

While Germany needed to avoid "arrogant over-confidence" (*Selbstüberhebung*), it should not replace it with "undignified self-deprecation" (*würdelose Selbstentehrung*). The warning was clear: total condemnation would yield the opposite of what the accusers claimed to want.

The Historical Situation of Opposition

One source of potential confidence for conservatives—indeed for all historians and for ordinary Germans as well—was the opposition movement (or, more precisely, movements), particularly that which sponsored the July 20,

---

1. For general accounts, see Iggers, *The German Conception of History;* Berger, *The Search for Normality;* Breisach, *Historiography.*
2. Quoted in Schulze, *Deutsche Geschichtswissenschaft nach 1945,* 59.

1944, assassination attempt against Hitler.[3] Interestingly, however, despite his personal experience it was not Ritter who published the first major study of the German opposition, but Hans Rothfels, a returned German Jewish exile who published a book in Germany in 1949 based on a lecture he had given at the University of Chicago in 1947.[4] Rothfels also had German nationalist tendencies, though bitterly disillusioned ones: despite his authentic German nationalism, his conversion from Judaism had failed to protect him, and he was forced to flee.

Rothfels's account of the opposition was hagiographic and fundamentally exculpatory, and he was explicit in siding for Victor Gollancz against Vansittart, which he did in a section titled "Obstacles on the Road to Truth":

> While all available evidence and any sober examination are calculated to show that modern mass civilisation generates a reservoir of evil forces whose release spells naked barbarism and while it should be similarly clear that potential torturers as well as martyrs are present in every nation, a policy of hate and revenge has decreed that this should be overlooked. This has happened as a consequence of total war, but also as a result of the picture of the "eternal" German propagated in the main by Vansittart and underlying the Morgenthau Plan.[5]

Like Ritter, Rothfels dismissed attacks on Prussian militarism as misplaced, and warned against "Pharisaism," charging that "the men of the German opposition were entitled to look on . . . support from outside [for Hitler from appeasers and admirers] as a real stab in the back"[6] For Rothfels, Prussian military men and their national conservative associates represented the very best of Germany and gave their lives to provide a "bulwark against nationalistic and demagogic excesses." As we will see when considering Rothfels's colleagues, his view that "National Socialism can be considered as the final summit of an extreme consequence of the secularization movement of the nineteenth century" rather than as a particularly German

3. The literature on the opposition is enormous. On the *memory* of the opposition, however, see Steinbach, *Widerstand in Widerstreit*; Holler, *20. Juli 1944*; Large, *Contending with Hitler.*

4. Rothfels, *The German Opposition to Hitler.*

5. Ibid., 20.

6. "The book," Rothfels writes in the preface to *The German Opposition to Hitler,* "abstains from any kind of Pharisaism, for no one has the right to pass facile judgment on conflicts of conscience and the possibility of unqualified resistance who has not himself fully experienced the trials of life under a totalitarian system" (7). For "stab in the back," see ibid., 25.

phenomenon is quite common. "What triumphed after the pseudo-legal revolution of 1933," Rothfels wrote, "was in fact and to a great extent the dark forces forming the sediment of every modern society."[7]

In this first major work on the opposition, it is important to note, Rothfels provided comparatively little space (four pages) to left-wing opposition circles or to ordinary people. In the 1960s, this almost exclusive acknowledgment of conservative military opposition in the official rhetoric of the Federal Republic would become a major target for attack. These generals, it would be argued, were certainly not motivated by any desire to save the Jews, nor were they liberal democrats. For New Left critics, the July 20 conspiracy was a reactionary coup attempt in a fascist state, and thus not praiseworthy. (This was also the view of Kurt Schumacher, the first leader of the postwar Social Democratic Party.) By the 1990s, following unification, a more differentiated portrait emerged, one which could appreciate the heroism and sacrifices of these individuals (whose families were often treated poorly even in the 1950s, tainted as they were with a lingering stench of treason even after the so-called "zero hour") while noting their political identity by including equal attention to other opposition circles. In the immediate aftermath of the war, however, even national conservative opposition had, for many, an odor of disloyalty about it, to say nothing of leftist opposition.

Literary figures as well addressed the issue of complicity and resistance. In particular, Carl Zuckmayer, who had spent the war in Vermont, raised the issue powerfully in *The Devil's General* [*Der Teufels General*], a stage play that was performed widely in the late 1940s. The story was about a German officer who had joined the air force out of love for flying, subsequently recognizes his criminal complicity, and finally sees the only solution to the conflict between his oath of allegiance and his conscience in suicide. Nevertheless, the status of opposition—was it treason or courage?—was at this point deeply problematic: If one praised opposition—particularly those who were a part of the July 20, 1944, conspiracy to assassinate Hitler—was one not thereby discrediting the "ordinary soldiers" who fought to the bitter end on the Eastern front? Establishing the existence of a vital opposition thus provided an alibi for the nation while accusing its citizens. Resolving this aporia took a great effort in the 1950s, particularly by Federal president Theodor Heuss, whose speeches shaped early images of the opposition. And again, these were the complexities of dealing with conservative and military opponents, not opponents whose patriotism was more easily (though not necessarily justly) questioned.

7. Ibid., 21, 41.

Dresden, 1945. The city was destroyed by Allied firebombs; similar scenes of devastation characterized many German cities.

Berlin, May 1945. Photo: Keystone.

General Alfred Jodl *(center)* signs the capitulation of the German armed forces in the War Room at Allied Headquarters, Reims, May 7, 1945. Also seated at the table are Major General G. S. Wilhelm Oxenius, Jodl's aide *(left)*, and Admiral General Hans Georg von Friedeburg of the German Navy *(right)*. Allied Supreme Commander Dwight Eisenhower waited in his office down the hall.

German officials prepare to sign ratified surrender terms at the headquarters of the Soviet forces in Berlin-Karlshorst, May 8, 1945. *Seated, left to right:* General Hans-Jürgen Stumpff of the Luftwaffe; Field Marshall General Wilhelm Keitel, chief of staff of the German high command; and Admiral General Hans Georg von Friedeburg of the German Navy. Photo: Keystone.

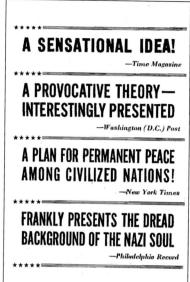

Front and back covers of "the book that Hitler fears," published in 1941 and written by a New Jersey dry goods salesman. German propagandists attributed surreptitious authorship to President Roosevelt and exploited the book as evidence of a Jewish-led American desire to destroy Germany.

Not yet the Jewish Angel of Revenge, Treasury Secretary Henry Morgenthau Jr. is shown awash in taxpayer funds. *Time*, January 23, 1943.

In 1945, Morgenthau published an elaborate justification of his original plan for Germany, including a reprint of his "Top Secret" proposal. *Germany Is Our Problem* was received with much public acclaim as well as some scorn.

German citizens view American placards of wartime atrocities, part of the short-lived program to awaken feelings of collective guilt.

An American poster, similar to many displayed in the first weeks of the occupation, accuses the Germans: "These Atrocities: Your Fault! You watched quietly and silently tolerated. . . . That is your greatest guilt—You are co-responsible for these atrocious crimes!"

Many Germans were required to watch films in U.S. Army theaters documenting German atrocities.

The main proceeding at the Nuremberg war crimes trials. Photo: Keystone.

MG/PS/G/9

MILITARY GOVERNMENT OF GERMANY

FRAGEBOGEN

PERSONNEL QUESTIONNAIRE

WARNUNG. Im Interesse von Klarheit ist dieser Fragebogen in Deutsch und Englisch verfasst. In Zweifelsfällen ist der englische Text massgeblich. Jede Frage muss so beantwortet werden, wie sie gestellt ist. Unterlassung der Beantwortung, unrichtige oder unvollständige Angaben werden wegen Zuwiderhandlungen gegen militärische Verordnungen gerichtlich verfolgt. Falls mehr Raum benötigt ist, sind weitere Bogen anzuheften.

WARNING. In the interests of clarity this questionnaire has been written in both German and English. If discrepancies exist, the English will prevail. Every question must be answered as indicated. Omissions or false or incomplete statements will result in prosecution as violations of military ordinances. Add supplementary sheets if there is not enough space in the questionnaire.

A. PERSONAL
PERSONNEL

Name / Name — Zuname / Surname — Middle Name — Vornamen / Christian Name — Ausweiskarte Nr. / Identity Card No.

Geburtsdatum / Date of birth — Geburtsort / Place of birth

Staatsangehörigkeit / Citizenship — Gegenwärtige Anschrift / Present address

Ständiger Wohnsitz / Permanent residence — Beruf / Occupation

Gegenwärtige Stellung / Present position — Stellung, für die Bewerbung eingereicht / Position applied for

Stellung vor dem Jahre 1933 / Position before 1933

B. MITGLIEDSCHAFT IN DER NSDAP

1. Waren Sie jemals Mitglied der NSDAP?

Ja ___ Nein ___

2. Daten
3. Haben Sie jemals eine der folgenden Stellungen in der NSDAP bekleidet?

(a) REICHSLEITER oder Beamter in einer Stelle, die einem Reichsleiter unterstand? Ja ___ Nein ___
Titel der
Stellung ___ Daten ___

(b) GAULEITER oder Parteibeamter innerhalb eines Gaues? Ja ___ Nein ___
Daten ___ Amtsort ___

(c) KREISLEITER oder Parteibeamter innerhalb eines Kreises? Ja ___ Nein ___
Titel der
Stellung ___ Daten ___ Amtsort ___

(d) ORTSGRUPPENLEITER oder Parteibeamter innerhalb einer Ortsgruppe?
Titel der
Ja ___ Nein ___ Stellung ___
Daten ___ Amtsort ___

(e) Ein Beamter in der Parteikanzlei? Ja ___ Nein ___
Titel der
Daten ___ Stellung ___

(f) Ein Beamter in der REICHSLEITUNG der NSDAP? Ja ___ Nein ___
Titel der
Daten ___ Stellung ___

(g) Ein Beamter im Hauptamte für Erzieher? Im Amte des Beauftragten des Führers für die Überwachung der gesamten geistigen und weltanschaulichen Schulung und Erziehung der NSDAP? Ein Direktor oder Lehrer in irgendeiner Parteischulungsschule? Ja ___ Nein ___
Titel der
Daten ___ Stellung ___
Name der Einheit oder Schule

(h) Waren Sie Mitglied des KORPS DER POLITISCHEN LEITER?
Daten der
Ja ___ Nein ___ Mitgliedschaft ___

(i) Waren Sie ein Leiter oder Funktionär in irgendeinem anderen Amte, Einheit oder Stelle (ausgenommen sind die unter C unten angeführten Gliederungen, angeschlossenen Verbände und betreuten Organisationen der NSDAP)?
Ja ___ Nein ___
Titel der
Daten ___ Stellung ___

(j) Haben Sie irgendwelche nahe Verwandte, die irgendeine der oben angeführten Stellungen bekleidet haben?
Ja ___ Nein ___
Wenn ja, geben Sie deren Namen und Anschriften und eine Beschreibung deren Stellung ___

C. TÄTIGKEITEN IN NSDAP-HILFSORGANISATIONEN

Geben Sie hier an, ob Sie ein Mitglied waren und in welchem Ausmasse Sie an den Tätigkeiten der folgenden Gliederungen, angeschlossenen Verbände und betreuten Organisationen teilgenommen haben:

B. NAZI PARTY AFFILIATIONS

Have you ever been a member of the NSDAP? yes, no. Dates.

Have you ever held any of the following positions in the NSDAP?

REICHSLEITER or an official in an office headed by any Reichsleiter? yes, no; title of position; dates.

GAULEITER or a Party official within the jurisdiction of any Gau? yes, no; dates; location of office.

KREISLEITER or a Party official within the jurisdiction of any Kreis? yes, no. title of position; dates; location of office.

ORTSGRUPPENLEITER or a Party official within the jurisdiction of an Ortsgruppe? yes, no; title of position; dates; location of office.

An official in the Party Chancellery? yes, no; dates; title of position.

An official within the Central NSDAP headquarters? yes, no; dates; title of positions.

An official within the NSDAP's Chief Education Office? In the office of the Fuehrer's Representative for the Supervision of the Entire Intellectual and Politico-philosophical Education of the NSDAP? Or a director or instructor in any Party training school? yes, no; dates; title of position; Name of unit or school.

Were you a member of the CORPS OF POLITISCHE LEITER? yes, no; dates of membership.

Were you a leader or functionary of any other NSDAP office or units or agencies (except Formations, Affiliated Organizations and Supervised Organizations which are covered by questions under C below)? yes, no; dates; title of position.

Have you any close relatives who have occupied any of the positions named above? yes, no; if yes, give the name and address and a description of the position.

C. NAZI "AUXILIARY" ORGANIZATION ACTIVITIES

Indicate whether you were a member and the extent to which you participated in the activities of the following Formations, Affiliated Organizations or Supervised Organizations:

Der Fragebogen (the questionnaire), 1946, a central pillar of denazification in Germany. Those who sought public office or who had business with the American occupiers were required to fill out the survey, which asked more than a hundred questions about affiliation, activities, education, and background.

Kurt Schumacher, Prussian leader of the Social Democrats, delivering a speech, Munich, November 24, 1946. Photo: Keystone.

Cardinal Josef Frings *(left)*, archbishop of Cologne, and German Chancellor Konrad Adenauer *(right)*, on the occasion of Frings's seventieth birthday, February 1957. Each of these Catholic leaders in his own way rejected all accusations of collective guilt during the occupation. Photo: Keystone.

Philosopher Karl Jaspers lecturing in the Alten Aula of Heidelberg University, August 11, 1946. Heidelberg University Archives.

Writer and army staff officer Ernst Jünger *(left)* and Catholic intellectual and legal theoretician Carl Schmitt *(right)*, Paris, 1942. Whereas Jünger quietly turned against the Nazis and was hailed years later by political leaders in the Federal Republic, Schmitt never broke with the regime, was imprisoned by the Americans at Nuremberg, and remained a subterranean (though not inconsequential) figure.

The *German* Catastrophe

There were, of course, important differences of perspective in the discussion among historians, even among national conservatives, concerning both the oppositions and the meaning of National Socialism overall. Nevertheless, given that statements came from many (though by no means all) corners of the intellectual-political spectrum—including Marxist, liberal, Christian, and conservative—the commonalities across the immediate postwar diagnoses are impressive.

On the one hand, as already noted, in contrast to some exiles and to the many British and American writers mentioned in chapter 3, there was almost complete consensus among the German historians and social scientists offering interpretations in the mid 1940s that National Socialism was an error, German history derailed rather than fulfilled. Most German intellectuals were reluctant to throw what they saw as the baby of German humanism and culture out with the bath water of National Socialism. Many thus turned to a selective reappropriation of German traditions for consolation, for a sense that the Germany they loved endured. Once again, then, the failures of German politics seem to have thrown Germany back on the ideal realm of culture: Goethe, Schiller, and Beethoven. As in the Mann debate, few were willing to question the value of that culture, though different historians located its origins and effects differently.

On the other hand, a major difference was where they placed the beginning of the perversion of German history. Some placed it as early as the Thirty Years War, others—like Ritter—dated it to January 30, 1933. Still others were excited by the early years of National Socialism, becoming disenchanted over time, particularly as the war progressed; these Weimar ultraconservatives, we will see, thus faced unusually complex problems of self-justification after 1945.[8]

Whenever the beginning, however, all agreed that National Socialism was a perversion, a plague, a catastrophe, and finally a tragedy. But the language goes beyond the realm of political responsibility and error: Hitler and his henchmen were evil seducers and usurpers, who exercised *demonic* qualities. It was by no means unusual that Mann should have found the Faust story to be an appropriate narrative framework for understanding what had happened, referring as we saw to "the vile regime of conspirators" and to National Socialism as "the epitome of evil." Friedrich Meinecke, in what is

8. See especially van Laak, *Gespräche in der Sicherheit des Schweigens*, as well as my discussion of ultraconservatives in chapter 13.

perhaps the best-known work by an historian in the immediate postwar period (*The German Catastrophe*) saw German history as a catastrophe and as a tragedy, "the essence of [which] consists above all else in the fact that the divine and the demonic in man are indissolubly linked together." This sense of the demonic in politics led Meinecke to characterize the Third Reich as "a period of inner foreign rule" that preceded "the postwar period of external foreign rule."[9] The Third Reich, in this view, thus came from outside, and was not really German at all. This uncritical equation of National Socialist rule with the postwar occupation is, moreover, emblematic.

Those raised on the values of Goethe and Beethoven thus often stood in simple disbelief and denial. At very least, the Nazis were obstreperous vulgarians; one was grateful for the return of "sobriety."[10] Making clear that they understood National Socialism as a profound challenge to their historical worldview, many authors employed an almost funerary vocabulary, even in the titles of their works. Alfred Weber (an "inner emigrant" who shared with his more famous deceased brother Max a liberal nationalist position) titled his book, written before the end of the war, *Farewell to European History*; Alexander Abusch (a Marxist writing in Mexican exile), called his book *Missteps of a Nation*; Wilhelm Röpke (a leading designer of the currency reform of 1948, central figure in the so-called "economic miracle," and ideological contributor to the notion of a "social market economy," the organizing principle of center-right politics in the emerging Federal Republic) authored *The Solution to the German Problem*. Perhaps most famously, as we just saw, Friedrich Meinecke (who according to a cliché of the secondary literature was "the doyen of German historians") titled his well-known pamphlet *The German Catastrophe*. Numerous other less influential and less remembered works refer to the "detour" (*Irrweg*), "error" (*Irrtum*), "catastrophe" (*Katastrophe*), "abyss" (*Abgrund*), "calamity" (*Tragik*), "tragedy" (*Tragoedie*), "ruins" (*Ruinen*), and "collapse" (*Zusammenbruch*), among others, of German history.[11] How much or what kind of valediction these works actually implied, however, remains to be seen.

This negative consensus on the part of intellectuals should not be mistaken as evidence that no one really supported or found anything positive in National Socialism. National conservatives like Ritter, who had found something positive in the Third Reich's nationalist aims, certainly faced

9. Meinecke, *The German Catastrophe*, 108, 103.

10. See the discussion of Wilhelm Röpke below.

11. Among the most thorough secondary accounts of this literature is Schulze, *Deutsche Geschichtswissenschaft nach 1945*. See ibid., 46–47, for a list of other such immediate postwar

dilemmas. Those who might have had something different to say, moreover, were either not allowed to publish, did not dare to publish, or did not dare to admit to themselves how much they had found positive (though the conditions for articulating other views changed over time). The possibility that many were unable to acknowledge what they had found attractive about National Socialism led the psychoanalysts Alexander and Margaret Mitscherlich to their famous diagnosis in the 1960s of a German "inability to mourn" in the first decade after the war.[12] The object of this missing mourning, of course, should not be misunderstood—as it sometimes was in public by people who had not read the book—as the Jews; rather, the Mitscherlichs argued, Germans were unable to mourn Hitler, whom they had loved, because they were not allowed—and did not allow themselves— to acknowledge that they had indeed loved him. A central myth of the occupation period was that no one had ever really supported or been a Nazi. As we saw in exploring the reactions to denazification, most thought the sense of complicity and, by implication, responsibility was vastly overblown.

In most historiographical and political accounts from the immediate postwar discourse, the point was that National Socialism was something that happened *to* the German people, who were its first victims. All other experience was derivative, when mentioned at all. This was, after all, the *German* catastrophe. Indeed, Wilhelm Röpke reflected widespread sentiments when he argued that

> it should be clear to everybody that Nazism began its march of conquest in Germany itself, that the Germans were the first victims of that barbarian invasion which poured over them from below, that they were the first to be overwhelmed by terrorism and by mass hypnosis, and that all that the occupied countries had later to endure was suffered first by the Germans themselves, including the worst fate of all, that of being impressed or seduced into becoming tools of further conquests and oppression.[13]

As a result, Röpke went on to argue vehemently, "The guilt of the Germans is different from that of the National Socialists; it is the guilt of the

revisions of German history. For additional discussions, see Müller, *Another Country*, 21–31; Fulbrook, *German National Identity after the Holocaust*, 107–18; Glaser, *The Rubble Years*, 99–102; and the ubiquitous Eschenburg, *Jahre der Besatzung*. Published too recently for me to draw on in researching and drafting this chapter is Berg, *Der Holocaust und die westdeutschen Historiker*, though my much briefer account is confirmed in Berg's much more detailed study.

12. Mitscherlich and Mitscherlich, *The Inability to Mourn*. The German original was published in 1967.

13. Röpke, *The Solution of the German Problem*, 14.

seduced, not of the seducers, the degradation of the violated, not the infamy of the violators."[14] Recalling that Röpke was to become a major ideologist and advisor for the new West German state, one cannot write off such comments as unusually nationalistic sentiment from the delegitimated margin.[15]

Most historians and public commentators in the immediate postwar years thus protected German history from being consigned to the dustbin by characterizing National Socialism not as the realization of a German *telos* but as its perversion. The most common mechanism for doing so was the old trope of German historiographical discourse noted at the end of chapter 7: the separation of culture from power. In earlier accounts, understanding Germany as primarily a *Kulturnation* (a "cultural nation" unified by ideas rather than by institutions, in which membership flows from language, culture, and blood) was associated with dissatisfaction that it was not at the same time a *Staatsnation* (a "state nation" unified politically and capable of exercising real power on the world stage): Germany, that is, had a right to political power commensurate with its cultural and other contributions. Now, however, this distinction between nation and state and between culture and power was associated with the idea that Germany only got into trouble through its political aspirations, which were marked by failed democratization and domination by a brittle aristocracy and military class (the *Junkers*).

Such dichotomous thinking is a long-standing hallmark feature of "German thought," whether it took the form of Immanuel Kant's distinction between "noumena" and "phenomena" or Max Weber's distinction between "technical rationality" and "value rationality," whose disjunction, some retrospectively read Weber as saying, would lead to disaster.[16] No one, of course, addressed the potential contradiction between this blaming of the militaristic state and the appeal to the July 20 conspiracy—a largely aristocratic and military affair—as an alibi for the nation. This perhaps explains Ritter's and Meinecke's relatively stronger defenses of the Prussian military tradition: their associations with the opposition—in Ritter's case landing him in prison—allowed them to maintain their prewar national conservative thinking, where others judged Prussianism more harshly.

The implication of this defensive portrait, however, was that Germany was not to be identified by its failed political institutions—which came and

14. Ibid., 42.
15. In a letter of 1946, Konrad Adenauer reported being very impressed with Röpke's book.
16. See Bauman, *Modernity and the Holocaust*; Rubenstein, *The Cunning of History*.

went—but by its *Volk* and *Kultur*. Indeed, these accounts often associate the distinction between power and culture with that between regime and *Volk* drawn on by "inner emigrants" and representatives of the "Other Germany," be it one of exiles, members of various opposition circles, or "ordinary patriots." Like German humanist culture, the German people were misused and nearly destroyed by the false appropriation of their name by the crass, alien power of the state and its ruthless leaders. Nevertheless, these authors argued, the destruction of German culture was not complete. Out of the "ashes of disgrace,"[17] Germany could find redemption by recovering its *cultural* essence. The path to rebirth, in other words, was through immersion in the German *Geist* (spirit), the authentic embodiment of the Christian Occident.[18] Historiographical discourse thus mirrored that found in the debate over Thomas Mann.

At the end of *The German Catastrophe*, Meinecke suggested that an important road to German salvation would be the establishment of "Goethe communities" that would meet every Sunday afternoon to read German poetry and listen to German music.[19] Indeed, besides the title, this seemingly trivializing suggestion is often all that appears in scholarly and public representations of Meinecke's book. Given the long historiographical tradition of distinguishing between *Geist* (spirit) and *Macht* (power), however, the suggestion does not appear to be such an unmotivated avoidance of Germany's situation: an avoidance it is, but unmotivated by a tradition of discourse it is not.

Meinecke, of course, was by no means alone in his prescription for the preservation of German identity through culture. In *Farewell to European History*, Alfred Weber put his stock in more rigorous humanistic education as a way out of the oversimplifications of Nazi ideology: reducing class sizes and extending the ideas of the *Gymnasium* (humanistic high school) to wider circles, he argued, would reestablish the foundations of a German humanist culture more resistant to incursions. Ritter among others called more generally for a return to the idea of Germany as a *Kulturnation*, which in emerging political rhetoric meant preserving *German* culture by

17. This is the title of autobiographical reflections by the sociologist Hans Speier. Speier, *From the Ashes of Disgrace*.

18. We will encounter the same issue in chapter 10, though with a different solution, in the context of religious confrontations with the Nazi past. Protestants in particular argued that they were mistaken when they submitted to political authority to preserve their spiritual freedom; the Reformed Church would not let spirit take the leading role, even dictating political activity.

19. Meinecke, *The German Catastrophe*, 120.

embedding it in *European* politics.[20] This appeal to the *Kulturnation* fit well with Konrad Adenauer's later policy of Western integration and European unification throughout the 1950s.[21] In Karl Jaspers's version, this restriction of German identity to the *Kulturnation*, we will see, was simultaneously a deep loss and a profound opportunity.

European Dimensions

A second major feature of immediate postwar "explanations"—even more directly exculpatory than the first—was that what had happened to Germany was by no means unique to Germany. Alfred Weber thus called his book *Farewell to European History*[22]; Gerhard Ritter titled one of his books from this period *Europe and the German Question*. In many of the major intellectual statements from this period, Germany was merely the most extreme manifestation of wider trends. Writing during his Mexican exile, for instance, the Marxist historian Alexander Abusch argued that National Socialism was the manifestation of fascist tendencies within capitalism; as a result, there was nothing unusual other than the extremity of the German case. Abusch thus rejects the *Sonderweg* (special path) thesis, which before the war had supported a myth of German superiority and after the war was used to explain why Germany had failed where other nations had succeeded in developing democracy.[23] Abusch's account is one of the repeated conquest of negative militaristic and capitalist forces over those of progress. Abusch is thus more critical than most of the liberal and conservative authors, arguing that it was false to consider most Germans victims of National Socialism. He even includes a fairly vivid description of the concentration camps: "The huge ovens and dark chimneys of the 'death factories' in which millions of human beings were suffocated under exact scientific control. . . . Maidanek, Auschwitz, Mauthausen, Buchenwald, Bergen-Belsen, Dachau, and the

20. In later years, however, Ritter worried that this turn toward Europe had became a flight from the nation: "Today the debate with non-Germans is less urgent than the confronting of a tendency which is noticeable especially in the younger generation of German intellectuals . . . the tendency . . . to turn away from the idea of the nations as a historically bound and binding community. [W]e must do whatever we can to keep alive . . . the interest of the German public in our national past." Ritter, *The German Problem*, vii–viii.

21. See Poppinga, *Konrad Adenaur*; Foschepoth, *Adenauer und die deutsche Frage*.

22. In the German original, the book was titled *Abschied von der bisherigen Geschichte*, which translates more directly as "Farewell to History Up to Now," but the reference to European history in the English translation captures the spirit of the argument fairly.

23. See especially Blackbourne and Ely, *The Peculiarities of German History*; Berger, *The Search for Normality*.

other extermination camps together form a picture that will not be erased from German history."[24] Nevertheless, despite a gruesome portrait of stacked corpses and emaciated survivors, Abusch does not specify who the victims were or why they were killed. And his account shares with the others the implication that this was not the *true* path of German history.

In substantive but not formal contrast to Abusch's Marxist "fascism" theory, Ritter assigned the cause of National Socialism—which as an example of totalitarianism was "not a specifically German development"—to the rise of "mass society": "The possibility . . . is given everywhere where, after the destruction of all traditional authority, there is an attempt at the unmediated popular domination of the 'uprising of the masses'. . . ."[25] Despite the fact that Meinecke and Ritter are usually seen as opponents in the historiographical agonies of the occupation, Meinecke makes a similar claim:

> The Machiavellian, amoral element in the Germans of Hitler's day was not limited to Germany alone but was part of the general fermentation in a monstrous process, whether of the decline or of the transformation of the West into new forms of life. . . . Only the general picture of a development which leads from the culture of the few to the unculture of the masses can explain it. It cannot be explained by the individual peculiarities of the German development, nor even by the unique historical circumstances, events, and decisions which at clear and definite points have perhaps definitely [*sic*] determined its course.[26]

For Weber as well, like for Meinecke, the problem was a rising tide of "nihilism" in culture; for both Abusch and Ritter, despite the one being a Marxist and the other a conservative, the problem was "massification" in society and a deviation from Germany's historical destiny. For all, however, this was part of the pathologies, extremisms, and failures of the nineteenth century in Europe at large.

* * *

For Röpke, like for Ritter, nihilism, massification, and demonic powers were summed up as "totalitarianism," which subsequently became the dominant interpretive frame for the first decade of official memory in the Federal Republic: Here Röpke was both substantively and personally

24. Abusch, *Der Irrweg einer Nation*, 242–43. Translation of this passage is from Herf, *Divided Memory*, 62.

25. Ritter, *Europa und die deutsche Frage*, 193–94. Also quoted in Fulbrook, *German National Identity after the Holocaust*, 113.

26. Meinecke, *The German Catastrophe*, 53.

the forerunner of future official rhetoric, especially given his role in policymaking in the 1950s. From the Left, "fascism" refers specifically to forms of despotism and political criminality that are seen to be an extreme outgrowth of capitalism; as such, fascism is a product of the decadent West and can be cured only with communism. For many in the West, however, both in anticipation of and during the Cold War, totalitarianism provided a conceptual umbrella that joined together National Socialism and communism as mere varieties of the same force, a force clearly distinct from capitalism, the core individualism of which protects against the imputed violations of the human spirit represented by "totalitarian" systems.

In the immediate aftermath of the war, Röpke thus warned against invidious distinctions and self-righteousness, for the problem was not confined to German history: "[S]ince these two chief varieties of collectivism—National Socialism and communism—were rivals who very naturally fought bitterly against each other and who, as tricksters who saw through each other's methods, had every reason to be afraid of each other, neither of them missed any opportunity of turning the free opinion of the world in its favor and against each others." As a result, Röpke argued, "It remains a serious fault that the world should have allowed itself to be so led astray in its judgment and its moral susceptibilities by this playing off of communism against National Socialism."[27]

However, not only was the world deceived by this false opposition, it also suffered the same temptations and had indeed itself given birth to the phenomenon:

> If National Socialism is essentially a particular form of totalitarianism, the story of its intellectual birth must to that extent be also that of totalitarianism. . . . [T]he very circumstance that German totalitarianism was preceded by the Russian and Italian forms shows to how great an extent Nazism took over and worked out with German thoroughness ideas that were by no means of German origin.[28]

After listing such foreign sources as Georges Sorel, Vilfredo Pareto, and the Bolsheviks, Röpke argued it is only fair to conclude that "the outer world worked just as ardently on the building of the intellectual foundations of the Third Reich as did Germany herself."[29] Not only was the idea of totalitarianism not uniquely or originally German, it was thus the West's

---

27. Röpke, *The Solution of the German Problem*, 8.
28. Ibid., 25.
29. Ibid., 26.

moral, intellectual, and political failure not to recognize the disease that had attacked Germany from outside:

> If we consider all this soberly and with scientific objectivity, we can no longer doubt that the world-wide catastrophe of today is the gigantic price the world has to pay for its deafness to all the warning signals that prophesied with ever increasing shrillness from 1930 to 1939 the hell the satanic forces of National Socialism were to let loose, first against Germany herself and then against the rest of the world. The horrors of the war correspond exactly with those that the world permitted Germany to suffer, while it actually maintained normal relations with the Nazis and organized with them international festivals and congresses.[30]

For Röpke, not only were the sources of National Socialism not uniquely German and not only did its extreme extent in Germany result from the failures of the West to stop it, but these combined to indicate that the rest of the world suffered from the same disease as well:

> [I]t would also be an error to see in Nazism nothing more than the sudden madness of a single nation in the midst of an entirely healthy world, and to forget that it was the special German form of a tendency that was of an international character. The Third Reich was the German form of the social and administrative system that we know as totalitarianism; and just as that system is not the mark of a nation but of a period, it came into existence in Germany owing to conditions that can be shown to have existed throughout the civilized world. For reasons peculiar to Germany, she succumbed to germs of disease from which other countries were not free, but against which they were able to set greater powers of resistance. The disease obtained an exceptional hold over Germany because in that country national characteristics, international infection, and the exceptional circumstances of the time made up a particularly dangerous combination. . . . The world could not have had so appalling a degree of complicity in German totalitarianism and its career if it had not already been itself infected.[31]

One might have hoped that German intellectuals—particularly those claiming not to have been "infected" with National Socialist ideology—would by then have avoided such disease rhetoric (a staple of Nazi ideology).[32] But we should take care within the normally forward-looking theory of totalitarianism—which encourages continuation of the fight against the Nazis now against the Bolsheviks—not to miss the retrospective exculpation:

30. Ibid., 13–14.
31. Ibid., 17.
32. We might recall here Richard Brickner's smallpox metaphor as well. See chapter 3.

"It would be a misjudgment of the German problem," Röpke argued, "if we were pharisaically to ignore the share of guilt that has to be borne by the world outside Germany." Moreover, Röpke concluded his introduction:

> Every society, however civilized and Phaeacian it may seem to us, conceals in its depth a sewer of subhuman types, which must be kept firmly closed like the fisherman's bottle in the Arabian Nights. In other words, the powers of evil lurk everywhere, awaiting their chance from some earthquake or conflagration, revolution or war. Bore into these depths and it will be seen how masses of the dregs of humanity are hurled into the air. Ask the French with their bloodthirsty militia of the Laval regime, the Norwegians with their hirden, the Dutch, the Croats, the Hungarians, or the Austrians, and let not the Englishman or American be too sure that "it can't happen here." Instead, let them be glad that they have been spared that experience so far. And we will not be so tactless as to ask how things are in Russia.[33]

Instead, we must always remember, as he reminds, that "Nazism is no fabulous monster, no dragon found only in the primeval forests of Germania."

What Is to Be Done?

As Mary Fulbrook puts it, the dominant strategy of this historiography was "to condemn Nazism and Hitler as evil, while at the same time asserting that Nazism neither arose from long-term trends in German history, nor had any intrinsic relationship with the German people, who appear simply to have bumped into it and been blown off their proper course."[34] This is perhaps something of an overstatement, but one is certainly struck by a sort of macrohistorical exculpation in these arguments. Nevertheless, by asking how much revision of German historical self-understanding the "ignominy" of National Socialism necessitated, these authors were attempting to locate the relevance of their immediate past for the future: What explanation of Germany's present circumstance could be found in the past, and what of that past could serve as a guide for the future? While the problems of fascism, nihilism, and massification took a particularly virulent form in Germany, these authoritative intellectuals insisted, they were not specifically German problems. For many of them, therefore, one had merely to recover the German humanist tradition from before the corrupting second half of the nineteenth century, for the German Imperial Age was not the fulfillment of humanist trajectories, but their desecration. No radical revision was appropriate.

33. Röpke, *The Solution of the German Problem*, 45–46.
34. Fulbrook, *German National Identity after the Holocaust*, 114.

For philosophical support of his position, Meinecke turned to the philosopher of nationalism Johann Gottfried von Herder, who had argued for the indissoluble unity of nationalism and humanism: Every nation, according to Herder, had its own unique essence; the humanist tasks of the Occident could be achieved only with mutual respect for these differences, which could only be achieved when each was given free expression. Indeed, Meinecke referred to a "German *Character indelebis*": "The German spirit, we hope and believe, after it has found itself again, has still to fulfill its special and irreplaceable mission within the Occidental community." In a statement richly redolent of Herder, Meinecke wrote: "For it is a fact that precisely the cultivation of our own peculiarly individual German spiritual life is what can bind us in the purest and most natural way with the spiritual life of other nations." It would be a devastating error, it follows, to abandon German identity for a rootless cosmopolitanism (one of the central Nazi characterizations of Jewish intellectuals). In repudiating National Socialism, "[i]ts place does not have to be taken by pale, empty, abstract cosmopolitanism, but by a cosmopolitanism which in the past was formed by the cooperation of the most individual German contributions and which is to be further formed in the future."[35] We will see shortly how a strong defense against collective guilt involved the argument that collectivistic thinking was incoherent (indeed a residue of Nazi ideology). But the claim that all guilt was individual apparently did nothing in this context to discredit the principle of national identity: individualism had its uses, but national identity was as yet untouchable if it was now to be expressed in different institutional forms—namely, a Europe of united yet still culturally distinct nations.

Meinecke and other historians who represented the German humanist tradition thus believed the road to inner recovery (for the recovery must be one of inward renewal more than outward reconstruction) was through contemplation of "the truly good" in German culture, "the most vital evidences of the great German spirit," which are to be found in the music, poetry, and art of pre-Bismarck eras."[36] This is partly why the debate surrounding Thomas Mann was so important. Though it was not part of public discourse in the strict sense, moreover, composer Richard Strauss's reaction to the German catastrophe was in many ways emblematic of this understanding: Strauss, the living embodiment of bygone German romanticism, had assumed the presidency of the *Reichsmusikkammer* in 1933 but resigned in part over the prohibition against the playing of music by Mendelssohn and

35. Meinecke, *The German Catastrophe*, 117, 119, 121.
36. Ibid., 120.

other Jewish composers (though even after the war Strauss described various Nazi leaders as men of culture).[37] Upon the destruction of the Munich Opera, Strauss began to sketch out a composition that he described as a "mourning for Munich." In 1945, the octogenarian composer again took up what would become his *Metamorphosen* [Metamorphoses] for twenty-three solo strings. He titled the piece so not because it described its musical form but because the term came from Goethe, whom he had been reading in the midst of destruction as a source of consolation. This musical masterwork includes numerous references to Wagner (particularly *Tristan*), but the core of the piece (which Strauss denied was intentional) is a repeated near-direct borrowing from Beethoven's *Eroica* Symphony, namely, from the funeral march in the second movement. The last time the passage appears in the score, it is superscribed with the epitaph "In memoriam!" The historians were not so final, but they shared Strauss's sense of loss.

*   *   *

According to Meinecke, and to many of his colleagues, the task for historians in this dark hour of the German soul was thus "to give evidence of both love and severity for our past and to proceed to the task of maintaining what was truly good in it, recognizing what was valueless, and taking warning from it when one has to take action."[38] Indeed, as a result of its unique experiences, Germany might eventually once again even assume a position of moral leadership.[39] For the moment, however, Germany had to recover from the catastrophe—an ineluctable force of nature—that had befallen it. It is important to note, again, that the "catastrophe" for Meinecke and others is May 8, 1945—the onset of external foreign rule—and what came after, not January 30, 1933—the commencement of inner foreign rule and what it brought. Here one might comment as well on the similarity with Thomas Mann, for whom the focus was on Germany's loss of "face," in which Germany's "ignominy lies naked before the eyes of the world." *This* is the real tragedy of German history. Very little of this, of course, has anything to do with the Holocaust.

While Meinecke argued that there is nothing left but to work with the occupation authorities—for this is Germany's sorry lot—good Germans

37. See Klaus Mann's report to his father upon visiting Strauss in May of 1945, quoted in Glaser, *The Rubble Years*, 123.

38. Meinecke, *The German Catastrophe*, 108.

39. This can be contrasted to Mann's question about how Germany would ever be able to speak again. Meinecke's answer is that it will be able to do so *because* of its travels through the

like himself and his readers must help the occupiers to a differentiated view, preventing them from "schematic exaggerations and mistakes," because "embitterment might spring from a feeling of being treated unjustly, might hinder our inner recovery, and might make Germany into a center of disease of the worst sort."[40] Most public intellectuals of the first hour thus did call for introspection and the acknowledgment of responsibility "where it is appropriate." But reconstruction had to be judicious lest the essence of German history be misused again.

The Irritation of Anti-Semitism

An additional major feature these historical arguments share is their evaluation of the place of anti-Semitism in National Socialism and of the "final solution" in the *German* catastrophe. Like the emerging political rhetoric we will examine later, historians and literary intellectuals maintain what in retrospect appears as an eerie silence on the implications of the German catastrophe for Jews or of the centrality of the Holocaust for the diagnosis of German history. It is important to remember, however, that few either in Germany or elsewhere had yet begun to theorize the civilizational rupture we now see as the main characteristic of National Socialism, at whose center rather than periphery stood the extermination of nearly an entire people with the greatest technical capacities of the supposedly most philosophically advanced nation. In fact, German historians in the immediate aftermath of the war shared a belief in anti-Semitism's peripheral, derivative role, one hardly worth mentioning.

Meinecke, for instance, made only the briefest mention of anti-Jewish racism, and none directly of the "final solution." In his account, hatred of the Jews was merely incidental: "The raw material of [Hitlerism] consisted to a certain degree of racial ideology with its central point of hatred against the Jews. Of this there was already a certain amount in every country, or it could be simulated." Here Meinecke was addressing the possibility of "Hitlerism" as a potential "export article," since he viewed it as possible throughout the

---

abyss. As we will see, philosopher Karl Jaspers makes a similar point when he described German identity as a "community of guilt." This idea presages the claim made by the German Left in the 1960s and 1970s that Germany's unique historical experiences and willingness to face up to their legacies provides unique insights, thus enabling Germany to lead other nations morally. Echoes of this attitude also occurred in the 1990s in debates about German participation in the Gulf War, the Somalian conflict, and in Yugoslavia. See Olick, "What Does It Mean to Normalize the Past?"

40. Meinecke, *The German Catastrophe*, 104.

West. In such a scenario, "[w]hen the racial ideology and hatred of the Jews was somewhat ineffective as raw material for the needs of the masses, some other ideology, hatched by theorists or sects, could be substituted for it and duly pumped up."[41] Anti-Semitism was thus not the decisive feature of Hitlerism. Meinecke's few remarks on Jews reflected traditional—though perhaps not fully blown Nazi—prejudices: "The Jews," Meinecke wrote, "who tend unreflectively to enjoy the favor of the economic situation once it smiles on them, have caused considerable annoyance since their emancipation. . . . Many Jews were also among those who raised to their lips, much too hastily and greedily, the cup of power which had fallen to them."[42]

In *Farewell to European History*, Alfred Weber dismisses (with characteristic bombast) the entire matter as a stupidity, though not merely a German one: "The idea of race, introduced into history with so much blood and beastliness, with its 'one-times-one' table of heredity like a grotesque diagram imposed on a mystery as completely inexplicable now as then, is only the acme of bathos attained by the West after all its failures in profundity, the peak of pseudo-scientific tomfoolery."[43] We will see a similar approach later, when we turn to the self-defense of ultraconservatives, who often claimed that it was precisely this addition of biological racism to a more defensible core of political values that baffled them and contributed to their turn away from National Socialism.

Röpke wrote:

Even the racial mania that seems to be an exclusive domain of German totalitarianism was presented to the Germans by foreigners—particularly by the French writer Gobineau, who himself simply elaborated the idea which dates back to the eighteenth century. The racial delusion may be described as a cross between those foreign germs and the specifically German ethical romanticism that will occupy us later. While these and other precursors of the Nazi racial doctrine have nothing in common with the appealing delusionary character of that doctrine, the fact remains that that is the abyss into which we are inevitably plunged in the end if we once pursue the mistaken path of the biologism of which Darwin and his school laid the foundations. The Nazi racial doctrine is the final putrid product of the decay of an intellectual process by which in the course of the nineteenth century man was degraded, with the zeal of a misunderstood science, to a subject of zoology and stud farming; but in this process all the principal countries of the West took part.[44]

41. Ibid., 91, 92.
42. Quoted in Stern, *The Whitewashing of the Yellow Badge*, 201–2.
43. Weber, *Farewell to European History*, 156–57.
44. This and the next quote are from Röpke, *The Solution of the German Problem*, 26.

Röpke did, however, offer a direct reference by name to the extermination camps of the Third Reich: "The death chambers of Auschwitz and Maidanek are the final gruesome result of certain scientific ideas having ultimately found their way in the course of a century to the morally and mentally lowest levels of humanity, to a group that then, through a social catastrophe of inconceivable dimensions, became the rulers of a great people." Here one senses the neoliberal Röpke's nostalgia for the aristocracy—similar to the disdain others like Theodor Heuss would express for what they saw as the crass, shrill, lower class, mob mentality symbolized by the "Austrian Corporal" (Adolf Hitler). What is required, more than anything, is a "return of sobriety." The point here, however, is that the "destruction of the European Jews" is a symptom of other trends, which are not specifically German. We have already seen how even the Marxist Abusch avoided identifying Jews as the quintessential victims; while Abusch did include anti-Semitism in a long list of factors contributing to the rise of National Socialism, even there it was only one part of a much larger constellation. This is consistent with East German doctrine, which saw fascism as an extreme outgrowth of capitalism, in which anti-Semitism is only an incidental feature and Jews random victims.[45]

This silence about Jews for the interpretation of German history, however, has one fascinating exception: for many figures in this period, the example of the Jews provides a framework for understanding *German* suffering. In other words, for many German intellectuals and politicians of this period, as we will see in even greater detail later, there was a remarkable effort to understand Germans as the new Jews, a pariah people serving as the scapegoats for the sins of civilization.[46] We saw this already (chapter 7) in the passage from Mann's *Doctor Faustus*, when he portrays Germany as "a nation that will have to live in isolated confinement, like the Jews of the Ghetto, because the dreadfully swollen hatred all around it will not permit it to step outside its border." The dramatist Carl Zuckmayer claimed it as well when he wrote, "We Germans share with the Jews a certain unpopularity in the world that always distorts other people's views of us."[47] The

45. For a survey of East German approaches to history, see Dorpalen, *German History in Marxist Perspective*.

46. As I discuss in chapter 12, Anson Rabinbach's brilliant reading of Karl Jaspers highlights Jaspers's projection of this Jewish status onto Germans. This projection, however, was not limited to Jaspers but, as we are seeing, was pervasive, though with different inflections. See Rabinbach, *In the Shadow of Catastrophe*.

47. Quoted in Marcuse, *Legacies of Dachau*, 298.

analogy is implied in Meinecke where he mourned that National Socialism and Germany's defeat took "the last breath of Western Christian cultured behavior and humanity," when it was really the last breath of Jewish culture that was extinguished. The peculiar identification of Germans and Jews, of course, is to be found in Goethe as well, belying Röpke's claim that German anti-Semitism was merely the misapplication of pseudo-scientific doctrine. As Röpke himself put it:

> Let us hold on to the fact that the Germans, who today have become *odium generis humani*, are a people with whom fate has played a more evil game than with any other—fate and their own failure. What is worst of all is that this unique history . . . has left deep traces in the German character that have made the Germans one of the most complex and problematic and, in the end, one of the most hated of all nations. Thus, on top of all their other troubles, they have to bear the dislike of the rest of the world, which still further worsens their situation. *In this, as in so many other things, they strikingly resemble another tragic nation of world history, the Jews.*[48]

Röpke was thus certainly correct when he continued by identifying "a peculiar relation between Germans and Jews." His own work manifests that peculiarity. Nevertheless, as we will see in abundant detail in the following chapters, this projection of Germans into the status of the Jews is widespread, even the norm. Clearly, there was something quite deep here, to which we will return later.

The analogization of Germans to Jews in the immediate postwar period, however, was only possible because of (though by no means fully explained by) the general lack of differentiation among kinds of victims and kinds of suffering. Non-Jewish Germans who had been persecuted in the camps served as spokesmen for the experience despite the important differences between even a place so horrible as Dachau and Auschwitz. As Mary Fulbrook argues, "even those Germans who had themselves experienced life inside a concentration camp as political prisoners were less than fully aware of the true extent and character of the extermination camps and the Holocaust proper. Thus Eugen Kogon's path-breaking early anatomy of the "SS state" was deeply rooted in his own experiences as a German political prisoner in a concentration camp designed primarily for detection rather than extermination."[49] Kurt Schumacher (future leader of the Social Democratic Party, and most important critic of the early Adenauer govern-

---

48. Röpke, *The Solution of the German Problem*, xii–xiii (emphasis added).
49. Fulbrook, *German National Identity after the Holocaust*, 116.

ment) was another such figure representing universal suffering. After long imprisonment at Dachau for his political activities, Schumacher spoke often and passionately about the situation of the Jews *and* of the Social Democratic opposition.

An even more complex example is Pastor Martin Niemöller, whose moral authority in the late 1940s was unparalleled. Niemöller was the father of the "Stuttgart Declaration" of the Evangelical church, in which protestant leaders confessed their shared guilt (I examine this in greater detail in chapter 10). While Niemöller had suffered for his opposition to the Nazis, he had nevertheless been associated in the 1920s and 1930s with strongly nationalistic and even anti-Semitic camps. When some of his writings from those years became known to his American boosters in the late 1940s, much of their support dried up. For many Germans, this kind of (mis-)judgment was characteristic of indiscriminate foreign attitudes that, again, were likened to the Nazi treatment of the Jews. Now the Germans suffered the same fate.

* * *

Much has been made of a so-called "philo-Semitism" that emerged during the first years of the Federal Republic, an uncritical continuity in singling out Jews for special treatment, if now with the signs reversed.[50] This construct did indeed become a powerful principal later in terms of practical imperatives in international politics, but an argument could be made that some of the construct's appeal is for the moral stature that accrues to pariahdom, and Jews merely as examples of this status. So while certain segments of the German Left in the 1980s and 1990s, for instance, practically fetishized elements of Jewish culture—like Klezmer music—at least part of this "philo-Semitic complex" can be attributed to the authority of victimhood; thus, when Jews seemingly lost their pariah status in the Six Day War of 1967, for instance, sympathy with the new pariahs—the Palestinians—allowed a disdain if not for the Jewish people then at least for the Jewish state. Again, the distinction between people and state allows much. The deep cultural message here, however, is that while just as in philo-Semitism the evaluative sign has changed (anti to philo), and for the Germans the same thing has happened (thousand year *Reich* to *Pariah-volk*), the principle of identification itself has remained the same.

50. See especially Stern, *The Whitewashing of the Yellow Badge;* Jesse, "Philosemitismus, Antisemitismus und Anti-Antisemitismus"; Kaunders, "History as Censure."

Reflections

The major message of immediate postwar historiography was thus that the German catastrophe was merely the first and worst manifestation of civilization's universal faults. Given that, Germany's exclusion from the "community of nations" was an unjust deflection of critical insight from the West as a whole. In this the historians were in line with the critics of Nuremberg (in fact, sometimes they were one and the same) who argued that Germany's crimes were essentially no different from the war crimes of other nations that now stood as Germany's judges. Germany's feeling of special exclusion—its claim to pariah status—depended on the belief that Germany was being charged collectively, condemned without regard to internal differences or level of responsibility. (Of course, the flip side to this charge of insufficient discrimination in judgment was the argument against invidious distinction: on the one hand, collective guilt accusations were seen as indiscriminate; on the other hand, division of Germany into two categories—"the politically acceptable and the politically unacceptable," as Konrad Adenauer would put it in his first parliamentary statement in 1949—was seen as invidious—in other words, too discriminate.)

While the consensus may have been that *some* critical reflection on German history was necessary, in this context many agreed with Wilhelm Röpke's warning that, though critical reflection is important, "[i]t is quite a different thing . . . to establish a collective responsibility of all Germans in the sense of a real partnership in a punishable crime for which we assume them to be guilty because they happen to have this passport and this domicile." Here Röpke was able to draw on the common argument that undifferentiated condemnations of the Germans employ the same logic as undifferentiated condemnations of the Jews, thus equating the Western Allies with the Nazis and the Germans with the Jews: collective guilt, he argued, "is simply a barbaric notion that would lead us back to the darkest periods of mankind when group responsibility still took the place of personal responsibility. As Christians we ought to know that it is nonsense to speak of 'collective guilt' because guilt is always personal."[51] For Gerhard Ritter, discussions of German guilt published in Hans Habe's *Neue Zeitung* were "a true hailstorm of new propaganda of domestic and foreign origin, a propaganda of equally significant passion, amateurish sloppiness and

51. Röpke, *The Solution of the German Problem,* 85.

recklessness as that which preceded it."[52] Again, the Germans suffer as the Jews did.

* * *

The relationship between historical and legal-political arguments should thus be fairly clear. Seen cynically—as many critics in the 1960s did—the individual and historical here served as each other's alibis: the existence of good Germans who preserved the essence of humanism rescued German culture from the verdict of history, while the ineluctable force of history exculpated the individuals who were caught up in events beyond their control. In this light, there are implicit analogies among the compulsion of history, the oath to Hitler, and the duty to obey orders. Individuals are nothing in the face of such pressures. Seen more generously, the perversions of history did indeed confront individuals with impossible choices and magnified their effects to ends many did not want; that others were not faced with those choices, seen from the perspective of the individual, is a mere accident, and thus precludes recrimination. The question is how ordinary Germans, to say nothing of their leaders, could process these realities. For answers, many turned to the churches for leadership. Psychology and philosophy as well offered answers, though often not the ones people wanted to hear. These answers are the subject of the next chapters, which examine those works that take on the concept of "collective guilt" even more directly.

52. Quoted in Steinle, *Nationales Selbstverständnis nach dem Nationalsozialismus*, 42.

CHAPTER 9

The Psychology of Guilt

Whether in the context of the Thomas Mann affair or in historiographical assessments of the German past, the central intellectual and cultural issue in postwar Germany seems to have been that of boundaries: What categories were relevant, and who belonged in which ones? What kinds of distinctions were legitimate, which were not? In the Mann affair, the question was whether "inner emigrants" and exiles together constituted the "Other Germany" or whether the "inner emigrants" belonged to the larger culpable mass. For historians, the question was whether German history—and its production of National Socialism—represented a unique path and pathology, whether it could be resected from the history of Western civilization generally. If it could be, then Germany was indeed burdened, its right to continued existence quite questionable; if it wasn't, then the rest of the world was being "Pharisaical" to think themselves not in the same boat. As we will see in this chapter, the boundary issue is of utmost importance in the psychological context as well. Who is guilty? Who is not? What kind(s) of guilt require what kind(s) of responses, and from whom? How widely should the circle of guilt be drawn?

The overriding fear of many German commentators, regardless of field, was the possibility of a "collective guilt," though what exactly that might mean, was far from clear. Most German commentators at the time, however, believed that they were being accused of something unbearable, and this perception has remained axiomatic in German public memory—that Germany was indiscriminately and inappropriately charged with collective guilt in the first years of the occupation. This perception is not entirely unreasonable: the occupation statute of the Joint Chiefs of Staff (JCS 1067) and other official documents often referred to Germany and "the Germans" as a whole; as we have already seen, placard actions and documentary films were intended to awaken not only disgust (which they did), but a sense of responsibility and even guilt (which, as we also saw, they usually did not, producing instead more vigorous boundary work: this is the work of monsters, not of us!); denazification formally placed all German adults under suspicion until they could be classified; the Morgenthau myth raised the possibility of destroying German political and cultural unity once and for all; Thomas Mann called for all intellectual works produced in Germany between 1933 and 1945 to be pulped; and public opinion in the United States and Britain remained anti-German, with an expectation of inflicting punishment.

Particularly disturbing to some German commentators was that so many of the accusations were psychological or even psychoanalytic in nature. We already saw Richard Brickner's psychiatric approach in chapter 3, and the widespread use of terms like "mentality" and "character." Such approaches, of course, were not limited to non-Germans. Max Horkheimer and Theodor Adorno, for instance, collaborated with colleagues in the mid-1940s on *The Authoritarian Personality*, which proposed a "F" (for fascism) scale—a measure of the psychological propensity of the people in particular nations to succumb to authoritarian demagoguery. According to such theories, the roots of German susceptibility could be traced to the authoritarian structure of the Prussian family, with its distant father and ineffectual mother. Siegfried Kracauer, in his book *From Caligari to Hitler*, argued that German cinema of the Weimar period provided a perspicuous window into the deficits of the German soul: Kracauer discerned a propensity toward self-pity, retrogressive resentments, and submission to authority in the collective subconscious that film is so well suited at expressing. In 1936, the renowned psychoanalyst Carl Jung addressed National Socialism in terms of collective psychopathology; in 1945, an interview and essay by Jung offered a sweeping diagnosis of collective guilt, in the process making Jung a favorite whipping-boy for German public discourse, a symbol for everything that was wrong with the "foreign" intellectual response. (Jung is often credited with being the first to use the term "collective guilt" [*Kollektivschuld*], though individuals like Thomas Mann had already referred to a "common" or "aggregate" guilt [*Gesamtschuld*]. It is an interesting question, which I explore shortly, why Jung's particular formulation both caught on and was seen as so problematic.)

This diagnostic psychiatry of the German soul, of course, was no mere matter for intellectuals. The Western Allies sent teams of psychiatrists to examine the Nuremberg defendants and sought all sorts of social scientific measurements and assessments of the German population more widely.[1] As we saw earlier, moreover, Hans Habe's journalistic program was subordinate to the U.S. Army's *Psychological* Warfare Division.

By the same token, the occupation authorities were by and large careful, after the first weeks, to avoid vigorous accusations of collective guilt in their official rhetoric. Robert Jackson's clear statement in November 1945 that the Nuremberg tribunal had nothing to do with collective guilt was at least partly in response to the vituperative debate about the subject, which I examine in the following pages. In a similar vein, the newspapers edited by Hans Habe explicitly did not advocate collective guilt, even if their pages did provide a central forum for German and other intellectuals to debate the issue.

Habe's own views on the matter are especially interesting, and nowhere near as straightforward as the accusations that he was too pro-German implied. Indeed, Habe put on the record his opposition to accusations of collective guilt.[2] He believed they were counterproductive: "The declaration of collective guilt," Habe wrote in 1953, "was impractical," creating many problems, not least of which that "[w]e couldn't turn to the 'good Germans' for we had claimed that they do not exist." Even worse, because of the reversal in Anglo-American policy with the advent of the Cold War, Habe believed that the memory of collective guilt accusations made the inconsistencies in Anglo-American policy even more clear: "When five years later we needed the Germans to fight communism, we had to retract everything we had previously said. Because we overstated our case first, we had to apologize in the end."[3]

This does not mean, however, that Habe did not think the Germans *were* collectively guilty:

According to American and English standards, they were [collectively guilty]. They had voted a raving maniac into power. He might have falsified majority into unanimity, the majority still existed. They had allowed him to abuse the institutions of democracy in order finally to destroy them. He had met no resis-

1. See Aycoberry, *The Nazi Question*, 109–24. See also Kershaw, *The Nazi Dictatorship*; Overy, *Interrogations*.

2. Habe, *Our Love Affair with Germany*, 2–3.

3. Ibid., 3. In his 1945 book *Crusade in Europe*, General Eisenhower wrote that "the *Wehrmacht*, and especially the German officers corps, had been identical with Hitler and his exponents of the rule of force." By 1951, under pressure to secure a German military contribution to the Western defense, Eisenhower recanted publicly, issuing a statement proclaiming that "there is a real difference between the regular German soldier and officer and Hitler and his criminal group."

tance in his days of glory and very little in his days of doom. They actively sustained, silently tolerated or irresponsibly overlooked the most abominable
crimes ever committed in the history of mankind. They openly prepared and
happily pursued a war, and only objected to it when it was lost.

Nevertheless, Habe argued, "In fact, if the Germans were collectively
guilty, we should have concealed it from them." His reasoning was partly
that the accusation misrepresented Anglo-American war aims: "We were
not waging war to eliminate evil from the face of the earth. . . . We fought
Germany because the military, political and economic plans of Hitler's
regime endangered our security and our way of life." (This is not, of course,
how World War II has entered into collective memory.) Habe concluded
this line of reasoning by arguing, "The idea of a collectively guilty nation
itself tends to defeat any and all purposes of a crusade. Crusades are fought
for the liberation of a people or a country; they are not punitive expedi-
tions." Mostly, however, Habe believed that overt accusations would not
produce the kind of introspection and re-education he believed was so
necessary.[4]

Again, while the pages of Habe's newspapers provided one of the central
forums for the discussion of German guilt, their editorial policy was nevertheless substantially less accusatory certainly than the "placard actions"
(discussed in chapter 5) and other early condemnatory measures. Extreme
ideas (rightly or wrongly) associated with the Morgenthau Plan, moreover,
had not carried the day unmodified. While rejecting the "inner emigrants,"
Mann also rejected "undifferentiated anti-Germanism." And despite negative opinion polls, Germany's desperate food situation produced an historically unprecedented and extensive response from abroad in the form of
CARE packages and other personal aid. Regarding denazification, it was
true that the entire adult population was technically under suspicion; by the
same token, the fact that the overwhelming majority were classified as
"unburdened" could have been, but was not, interpreted as a rather generous exculpation.

In what sense, then, was Germany truly accused of collective guilt? In
some ways, it does not really matter. There were enough reasons for either
interpretation in the early months. The more interesting questions are
whether most Germans felt accused, why they felt that way, and how they
reacted to their perceptions. Given that evidence for genuine accusations
was harder to find after the first postwar months, however, the German

4. Habe, *Our Love Affair with Germany*, 2–3.

reaction to collective guilt theory must be understood as a traumatic memory.[5] Indeed, a sense of trauma is apparent throughout the discourse. As Eugen Kogon, the former Buchenwald inmate whose reactions to re-education we encountered in chapter 5, put it in 1946, "While it was still half-dazedly struggling for the first consciousness, a chorus of accusatory voices of repugnance and resentment crashed over the German people. It received nothing else to hear except the thousand-fold cry: You, you alone are at fault! All you Germans are guilty! The heart of the people was confused, in many it hardened."[6] For many at the time and in later decades, the validity of Kogon's perception was taken for granted.

Another of the most important intellectual voices of the time was that of Erich Kästner, a world-renowned children's book author both before and after the war, whose adult books were burned and banned during the Third Reich and who spent the war as an "inner emigrant," suffering numerous arrests by the *Gestapo*. As the war came to an end, Kästner assumed one of the most influential positions in the Allied-sponsored discourse as editor of the arts and ideas (*Feuilleton*) section of Habe's *Neue Zeitung*. As one who had suffered (though mildly in comparison with many) under the regime, Kästner was particularly struck by any implication of German collective guilt, which he perceived as adding insult to injury. For this reason, Kästner expressed personal relief at Chief Prosecutor Robert Jackson's opening remarks at Nuremberg. According to Kästner, "The ranks laden with grief, distress, and worry breathed a sigh of relief, because a just thinking man took a remaining burden from them, which they perceived had been unjustly loaded on them. Their burden is still heavy enough. But hope, while still small and timid, patters alongside and helps carry it a bit."[7] For Kästner, this was no mere observation of his compatriots. As we will see shortly, it is clear that he took the accusation—whatever it may have been—quite personally.

For both Kogon and Kästner, and for many others, American re-education policy was based on an arrogant misunderstanding of German experience and culture and, no matter how it was packaged, reflected a deeply held accusatory attitude. According to Kogon:

> To awaken the powers of contemplation in the German world was the task of a far-reaching *Realpolitik* of the Allies. It was included in the program of "re-education." And it stemmed from the thesis of a German collective guilt. The

5. Aleida Assmann makes a similar argument. See Assmann and Frevert, *Geschichtsvergessenheit-Geschichtsversessenheit.*

6. Kogon, "Gericht und Gewissen," in Kogon, *Die unvollendete Erneuerung*, 7.

7. Kästner, "Die Schuld und die Schulden," in Kästner, *Splitter und Balken*, 501.

THE PSYCHOLOGY OF GUILT 185

shock of accusation, that they were all complicit [*mitschuldig*], was supposed to bring the Germans to the realization of the true causes of their defeat.

Instead, the accusation produced the opposite: "Because of the awful clamor around it and because of its own blindness they [the German people] wanted to hear nothing more of self-examination. The voice of their conscience did not awaken." "A justified feeling of millions defended itself against the collective accusation, which had a leveling [*egalisierend*] appearance."[8] This sense that Allied policy was responsible for whatever "repression" or "silence" about the Nazi past existed was to become a pillar of Leftist critiques in the 1960s.

Kogon, it is important to note, was no apologist. In rejecting collective guilt both on principle and for its effects, he warned his compatriots not to use its rejection as an argument against individual guilt, which many were doing with ever more elaborate schemas. For Kogon, who was a devout Catholic, guilt was both solely individual and the right of God alone to judge. He duly chastised those who defended Germany with the argument that the Allies were no better and thus in no position to accuse Germany: "Many today in Germany say: Where do the Allies get the right to sit in moral judgment of us? Is their history free from violence and atrocities?" Kogon responded that who is doing the accusing has no bearing on the accuracy of the accusation. To illustrate this, however, he chose a telling analogy: "To this moral question the Bible has already answered, insofar as the prophet named the dictator Nebuchadnezzar the 'servant of God' who was sent by him to lead the people of Israel out of error." According to the analogy, Germans are the people of Israel who erred, and the Allies are Nebuchadnezzar. This is an interesting reversal, consistent with the theory that Germany is the new pariah, just like the Jews. Nevertheless, according to Kogon, whoever examines his own conscience in all honesty does not care where the impulse came from; he makes a virtue out of necessity: "The others are servants of God to him, whether just or unjust; he allows them the victor's triumph, even when they have gone the same or similar way that has made him guilty, and does not consider himself the toll collector: 'Lord, I thank you that I am not like that *Pharisee* over there!' "[9]

Kogon's argument, religiously inspired, is that we all, Germans or Allies, answer to a higher authority: "Most of them [the Germans] sensed that a higher judge would not set them in the same dock with the criminals and

8. Kogon, "Gericht und Gewissen," 10.
9. Ibid., 89 (emphasis added).

activists of the Nazi Party—to say nothing of the countless noble and fearless fighters or at least respectable and effective carriers of the inner opposition against the regime, as of yet so unknown abroad." Again, the insult of being charged indiscriminately as a collectivity was responsible for the unwillingness of Germans to face their *individual* guilt: "Had one allowed the yearning expectation of at least half of the German people finally to be freed from the terror of National Socialism, which they could no longer shake off alone, to rise to the heights of true excitement, then the unveiled concentration camps would have become landmarks of German self-reflection, of a deep horror towards the abyss into which the nation had sunk."[10] Whether Kogon's optimism was justified about the preparedness of many Germans to engage in this reflection (if only it weren't for the insult of re-education), however, remains an unresolvable counterfactual.

*   *   *

Central to Kogon's argument (and to its echoes in the political discourse of West Germany, particularly in the 1960s) is thus the claim that it was Allied programs that produced resistance and closed off German introspection. There is evidence both for and against this claim. It is certainly true that there were some early efforts to come to terms with collective guilt, and that they retreated very quickly with the justification that re-education was insulting, denazification was, as Kogon and others referred to it, a "fiasco," and the occupation in general was too indiscriminately punitive. The question, however, is at least partly one of causation: Was occupation policy the cause of the retreat or merely a justification for it?

Again, the evidence is mixed. Given the efflorescence of intellectual journalism in 1945–47 (which, again, was at least partly supported by the peculiar combination of rationing with a large money supply), virtually every conceivable stance was visible, as a quick survey of journals shows.[11] For instance, writers in *Aufbau*, a journal with a largely Marxist orientation, argued that National Socialism was the result of a trajectory at least five decades long, and required a wholesale conversion of the German population. The basis for such a conversion was to be found in German classics and the humanist tradition. In particular, Germany had to go back and redeem the promise of 1848. As a result of this line of thinking, the edito-

10. Ibid., 11.
11. See especially Flanagan, *A Study of Political-Cultural Periodicals from the Years of Allied Occupation*; Eberan, *Die Debatte um die Schuldfrage*. See also Ewald, *Die gescheiterte Republik*.

rial staff of *Aufbau* supported the Nuremberg program because it identified the usurpers who had led Germany astray from its core values. Johannes Becher, one of the principle editors, even accepted a *Mitschuld* (co-guilt) of the German people in his early essays, though he also wrote extensively of the opposition. Other writers in the journal argued, following the religious tone of the wider debate, the necessity for an inner acknowledgment of guilt by every individual, citing Luther as inspiration. One contributor referred to the "transient" guilt of individuals, thus highlighting the healing, transformative role of confession (we will later encounter a similar argument by Karl Jaspers).[12]

In one of the most noteworthy early contributions to the journal, Georg Lukacs wrote that although not all factions of German society supported the Nazis, silence was also a form of culpability. Nevertheless, Lukacs denied the equation of regime and *Volk*, and, as time went on, other contributors moved away from the early acceptance of collective guilt to blaming leaders. The retreat is especially clear in the essays of Becher, who by 1947 was restricting guilt to the leaders and portraying the Germans as their victims. He even went so far as to equate the suffering of the Germans with that of the Jews: "What was done to the Jews was done to us."[13] This was, however, one of the few references to Jews in the pages of *Aufbau*, although Lukacs addressed racism in general terms, seeing it—authentically to Communist doctrine—as an outgrowth of other, more fundamental developments (his language was similar to that of Alfred Weber, dismissing racism as an idiotic calculus).[14]

A similar dynamic (though very different tone and position), was evident in *Ost und West*, edited by the Jewish communist Alfred Kantorowicz, who had worked in the United States for CBS during his exile. Like many others, Kantorowicz also prescribed a broad cultural renewal, though he was clear that this responsibility rested on the Germans themselves. Kantorowicz emphasized the importance of German thought developing independently, though he had gained an appreciation for the West during his years in exile. A particular complaint was against the Allied press policy, which he accused of licensing German thought by controlling publication and always threatening revocation of licenses to publish (a case of which we

12. On Becher, see Flanagan, *A Study of German Political-Cultural Periodicals from the Years of Allied Occupation*, 52–68.

13. Quoted in ibid., 37.

14. In September 1946, Lukacs also participated in an important meeting, the so-called "Rencontres Internationales de Genève," where he discussed these and other issues with Karl Jaspers, Stephen Spender, Julian Benda, and others, again illustrating the direct as well as indirect dialogism of these statements.

will see shortly). Though eventually licensed by the Soviets, Kantorowicz warned against allowing Germany to be pulled too clearly into either power block, advocating instead a search for a "third way," a concept that had a long history in German thought, the Nazis being not the shortest chapter in that history. Kantorowicz's primary emphasis, however, was on literature and culture, rather than on politics.[15]

Ost und West nevertheless published increasingly virulent (and sometimes irresponsible) attacks on re-education and on American society generally, charging that Allied policy was encouraging the persistence of fascist ideology in the West. One contributor emphasized that many returning students at the re-opened universities were Nazis, and argued that re-education "was an unfortunate term. The first step is not re-education but consciousness [*Besinnung*]," which had to be an independently German affair. In a letter to the journal, the writer Arnold Zweig wrote that he hated the term "re-education" "because the powers that prescribed it for the Germans were themselves not well-educated."[16] By 1948, the journal had become increasingly partisan toward the Soviets, repeating (false) rumors of American plans to destroy Berlin, which the journal justified because such rumors, they argued, were illustrative of a general destructive attitude in the United States, representing a turn from Roosevelt's social programs to those of his successors, who supposedly destroyed his legacy (though there was hope in the figure of Henry Wallace, whose contributions on re-education were nevertheless not mentioned in this context).

That intellectual arguments were in transition through this period is clear in comparing a relative latecomer to the scene, *Der Monat*, which did not begin publication until October 1948. *Der Monat* very much embodied the neoliberal orientation that underlay centrist political thinking in the very late 1940s and early 1950s (though it represented a diversity of opinions). Its contributors included F. W. Hayek, Wilhelm Röpke, Hans Kohn, Arnold Toynbee, Stephen Spender, Bertrand Russell, A. J. P. Taylor, and Hannah Arendt, among other famous figures, and represented the growing intellectual reaction to Soviet "totalitarianism" (many of the contributors became members of the Congress of Cultural Freedom). The first issue included an inscription committing the journal to freedom of expression and open discourse, which most contributors viewed as hallmarks of Western political culture. In addressing National Socialism, many of the

15. On Kantorowicz, see Flanagan, *A Study of German Political-Cultural Periodicals from the Years of Allied Occupation*, 75–111.
16. Ibid., 90.

contributors emphasized commonalities with Soviet communism. German collective guilt was not a central theme, though a review of Arnold Zweig's book *The Axe of Wandsbeck* [*Das Beil von Wandsbeck*]—which described the Germans as having become "innocently guilty" (*schuldlos schuldig*)—was highly positive, describing the book as "the first great representation of this German tragedy."[17]

Perhaps the greatest contrast, and most notorious case in the early history of postwar German journalism, is that of *Der Ruf*. *Der Ruf* grew out of a prison camp circular for German POWs in American captivity, edited by Alfred Andersch, Hans-Werner Richter, and Walter Kolbenhoff, among others. Andersch in particular was a self-styled "inner emigrant," though it is not entirely clear that the term applies. He started out a communist, though he later dropped out of the Party. He was twice imprisoned by the Nazis, eventually served in the *Wehrmacht*, and ultimately deserted in Italy. As part of wartime re-education in the so-called "barbed-wire colleges," the original *Ruf* was published from March 1945 until April 1946. During that time, the editors took classes at Fort Kearney, Rhode Island, where they were imprisoned, many of them taught by Harvard professors committed to the idea of re-education. There they acquired a largely positive attitude towards FDR's liberal policies. Upon their return to Germany, Andersch and Richter applied for and were granted a license from the Americans for a journal under the same name (*Der Ruf*—roughly, The Summons).

The authorities expected the journal to represent the American values the editors had supposedly learned in captivity. But Andersch and Richter's different intention was already apparent in the reconstituted journal's sub-title: "Independent Pages of the Young Generation." Indeed, Andersch and Richter's personal identification with young soldiers (rather than primarily with the writers of the "inner emigration"), who they believed had borne the brunt of National Socialism's burdens without having had any real responsibility in bringing it about, gave the journal its unique identity. The editorial program of *Der Ruf* was to advocate "socialist humanism," which meant for Andersch and Richter absolutely rejecting the collective guilt thesis, mostly on the grounds that these charges did not apply to the younger generation.

Der Ruf was also consistently anti-American, and with its sympathy for the seemingly paradoxical Social Democratic resistance to Western integration in the name of national unity, the editorials took on a nationalistic tone. They condemned what they took to be the misuse of German virtues

17. Ibid., 121.

by the Nazis and the destruction of German honor this implied. For this, they blamed the top leaders. For the younger generation (a new "Front Generation"), they asserted innocence. In their attacks on the occupation, they argued that re-education was "not a nice term (*kein schönes Wort*), at any rate not much nicer than the National Socialistic term re-orientation (*Umschulung*)." They complained bitterly that Nuremberg was an affront, that it should have been a purely German affair. Regarding denazification, they claimed that any transformation had to be one's own achievement (though such transformation was not a pressing goal for the younger generation), and, referring to the "thousand year Reich," they quipped that "the Nazis were there for 12 years, the denazification for 988."[18] They campaigned vigorously for the return of German soldiers in captivity, arguing that they were hostages.

Der Ruf enjoyed enormous support and circulation, limited only by difficulties in obtaining paper. After sixteen issues, however, in April 1947, the AMG authorities revoked *Der Ruf*'s license, accusing the editors of "nihilism" and "nationalism." This prohibition nevertheless seemed to have the opposite effect from what was intended: it proved to be a rallying cry for younger intellectuals. Andersch and Richter took the opportunity to create one of the most significant cultural institutions in the history of the Federal Republic, the so-called "*Gruppe 47*," whose annual meeting at Richter's country house in Bavaria became the proving ground and rite of passage for virtually every important West German writer for decades to come. Its legacies, however, are mixed. While praised by the New Left of the 1960s (many of whose intellectual beacons were lit by *Der Ruf* and *Gruppe 47*), the scandal over *Der Ruf*'s de-licensing was a foundational moment for a new German sensibility, one which placed all the blame on a corrupt older generation and on the fascist West overall, while claiming for a new generation the legacies of a moral nation, one superior in some ways to the corrupt old world. Nevertheless, in a recent critique, the novelist W. G. Sebald argued, "The articles written by [co-editor Hans-Werner] Richter and Andersch derive their inspiration almost without exception from the period before 1945. . . . *Der Ruf* is a positive glossary and index of Fascist language."[19] This is a powerful challenge to the Left of the 1960s, who saw *Der Ruf* as an example of critical thought not complicit with the policies of the Allies that, because they perceived it to be mainly capitalist in character with an authoritarian cast, the Left rejected as continuous with

18. Ibid., 162 ff.
19. Sebald, *On The Natural History of Destruction*, 125.

fascism. Sebald's claim, in this light, is similar to that of Jürgen Habermas in the 1960s, when he broke with the student movement, charging it with fascist tactics.[20]

Subjective Guilt

While Eugen Kogon's confidence rested at least in part on his unassailable credential as a former concentration camp inmate and Alfred Andersch's rested on a (dubious) identification with the younger generation (and an even more dubious association with the "inner emigration"), Erich Kästner's response was in many ways more telling—a better representation of the "inner emigrants." It is worth considering even more closely his important journalism from the first years, which was more subtle than much of that in Der Ruf and better represented the attitudes of many in the older generation, whose non-Nazi members would lead the early Federal Republic.

As we have already seen, Kästner was indeed quite defensive about perceived accusations. Given the discursive context, it is not surprising that this would be so; the "inner emigration," much to Kästner's dismay and incomprehension, had been impugned by no less a moral authority than Thomas Mann. In many ways, Kästner's attitude was typical of the "inner emigration," if not quite as strident as Frank Thiess's, as we saw (chapter 7) in the response of Thiess to Thomas Mann. Explaining why he did not emigrate, for instance, Kästner wrote, "A writer wants to and has to experience how the people to whom he belongs bears fate. To go abroad just then is only justified through acute mortal danger. Otherwise it is his professional duty to accept every risk if by doing so he can remain an eyewitness and someday provide written testimony."[21] And this testimony he does indeed provide. For Kästner, the most remarkable accomplishment of the Nazi regime was the reversal of values and the misuse of character they extorted from the population:

> For here, in the area of conscience and character, lay the most terrible, the most frightening malediction of those twelve years. The men in power and their party systematically aspired to the biggest, most devilish spiritual corruption of all time.... The disorientation [Ratlosigkeit] of conscience, that was the worst. The lack of escape out of a muddy labyrinth into which the state had driven a people and at whose exits the executioner stood.[22]

20. See Habermas, Toward a Rational Society.
21. Kästner, "Wert und Unwert des Menschen," in Kästner, Gesammelte Schriften, 61–65.
22. Kästner, "Unser Weihnachtsgeschenk," in Kästner, Splitter und Balken, 515.

Clearly, Kästner saw good Germans like himself as victims of the Nazi state, and drew a sharp line between regime and *Volk*. The perversions of National Socialism, moreover, were no special fault of Germans, "who were not better or worse than other people on earth." The warning is clear: "Whoever did not experience it, whoever was not despairingly caught up in this labyrinth throws the first stone at this people [*Volk*] too easily." As for Thomas Mann, Kästner had unbounded respect for Mann the writer; for Mann the man he had none: "It was foolishness to call him. Instead, one should have asked him for goodness sake to stay over there!"[23]

Diagnosis and Denial

The full brunt of his scorn, however, Kästner reserved for the Swiss psychoanalyst Carl Jung. Indeed, Jung has served—much as Morgenthau and denazification have—as a mnemonic imago of collective guilt theory: Jung is considered to have introduced the term "collective guilt" into the discourse (this is unlikely to be true)[24] and to have proffered a most vicious version (also, as we will see, not exactly true). This imago is partly due to Kästner's response to him.

With the exception of Sigmund Freud, who had died in 1939, Jung was perhaps the most famous psychiatrist in the world, and enjoyed an exceptional international reputation for his theory of "archetypes" and of the "collective unconscious," to say nothing of having introduced the terms "complexes" and "free association" into everyday language.[25] Unfortunately, Jung had also flirted with the Nazis in the first half of the 1930s, seeing an opportunity to establish the predominance of his own views against those of his former friend Freud, who was Jewish. Jung collaborated with the psychotherapist Matthias Göring, the brother of Hermann, in the formation of a psychotherapeutic society free of "Jewish influence" and in the editing of its

23. Kästner, "Über das Auswandern," in Kästner, *Gesammelte Schriften*, 90–92. In some ways, Kästner's reaction to the Mann affair is similar to that of Hannah Arendt, who commented on the matter in a letter to Karl Jaspers (January 29, 1946): "It really is absurd to take him [Thomas Mann] seriously politically, important as he is as a novelist—except that he does exert a certain vague influence. The correspondence between him and Walter von Molo of all people borders almost on the comic." Lotte and Saner, *Hannah Arendt–Karl Jaspers*, 32.

24. Jürgen Steinle traces earlier uses to the post–World War I era. See Steinle, *Nationales Selbstverständnis nach dem Nationalsozialismus*, 70. Other terms, moreover, clearly stand for the same concept.

25. Biographical assessments of Jung's contributions include Bair, *Jung*; Hayman, *A Life of Jung*; McLynn, *Carl Gustav Jung*.

international journal. In 1933, Jung also gave an interview on Berlin radio in which he seemed to endorse the *Führer* principle. Indeed, Jung entertained a fascination for the occult dimensions of National Socialism that was more than purely opportunistic; also it is likely that he personally was not entirely free of anti-Semitic prejudice.[26] So it is not completely incomprehensible why a diagnosis of German collective guilt by Jung would rankle the sensibility of a German opponent of National Socialism like Kästner: If ever the label "Pharisee" applied, it seemed this was just such a case.

In February of 1945, Jung gave an interview to a Zurich newspaper in which he stated that "the popular sentimental distinction between Nazis and opponents of the regime" was illegitimate. In the interview, Jung referred to the "general psychic inferiority of the Germans" and to a "national inferiority complex," for which, he argued, they had tried "to compensate by megalomania."[27] Elsewhere, Jung argued that all Germans were either actively or passively, consciously or unconsciously, participants in the atrocities, that the collective guilt of the Germans was "for psychologists a fact, and it will be one of the most important tasks of therapy to bring the Germans to recognize this guilt." Jung acknowledged that this might seem unfair, particularly to those Germans who believed themselves to have opposed the regime: "It may be objected that the whole concept of psychological collective guilt is a prejudice and a sweepingly unfair condemnation. Of course it is, but that is precisely what constitutes the irrational nature of collective guilt: it cares nothing for the just and the unjust, it is the dark cloud that rises up from the scene of an un-expiated crime."[28] These statements were reprinted in Habe's *Neue Zeitung* where, again, Kästner was a top editor.

Kästner's response to Jung was withering. Whether or not one accepts Kästner's arguments, one cannot fail to appreciate that this literary master brought to bear here his prodigious talents as a stylist. Throughout, Kästner refers to "the researcher of the soul [*Seelenforscher*] Prof. Dr. C. G. Jung," as if Jung's reputation as an insightful observer were a huge joke,

26. Jung's attitude toward Jews is a much-debated issue in the secondary literature. Understandably, a loyal following minimizes and even denies that Jung was anti-Semitic.

27. The actual content of the interview is much disputed. Jung denied that he said some of the things he was quoted as saying, and believed that he had been misrepresented, and certainly mistranslated into English (the English translation of Jung's interview occasioned a debate in addition to that we will examine below in Germany). The quotes here are taken from Erich Kästner's response, *Splitter und Balken*. In his essay, Kästner refers explicitly to the debate over Jung's interview in the United States, particularly a response in the *American Journal of Psychiatry*. On the dispute and the accuracy of the interview quotations, see Bair, *Jung*, 509–15.

28. Quotations are from Jung's essay collection, *The Psychology of Nazism*, in this paragraph from 72 and then 52–53.

since no one with any insight could possibly have uttered such nonsense as Jung did. For Kästner, however, the issue concerned more than just Jung, who was important not only because of his fame but because his arguments were indicative of an ill wind indeed: "If even one of the most famous judges of the soul in Europe doesn't understand us, one can count on even less understanding from the overseas victors."[29] But this is unfathomable to Kästner, because less understanding seems to him hardly possible.

The real tragedy for Kästner is that German opponents of the Nazis, who had "for twelve long years resisted the greatest malice," had dared "to count on a bit of consolation and help, encouragement and sympathy. . . . They were, God knows, not proud but tired. A drop of understanding would have been an immeasurable gift for them." Instead, they received the reproach of "the researcher of the soul Prof. Dr. C. G. Jung."[30] For Kästner, "It sounded as if the important man had swallowed the trumpet of final judgment." The result for those such as himself was devastating:

Then the poor, exhausted opponents of the regime sunk into themselves without a word. Granted, they had not been able to overcome the Genghis Kahn of Inn [Hitler was born in Branau am Inn] and his bronzed horde. But they did try to withstand the demons of torture and bloodlust, the furies of the gas chambers and crematoria, the vipers of surveillance, blackmail and dispossession. Not every one of them could be so valiant and incorruptible as the researcher of the soul Prof. Dr. C. G. Jung most certainly would have been if he had been in their position rather than living in Switzerland. . . . So the opponents of the defeated regime silently covered up their pale, tired, starved heads. The "popular sentimental distinction" between them and the Nazis was not permitted. The researcher of the soul Prof. Dr. C. G. Jung was decidedly against it and informed the entire world of his expert opinion.[31]

For Kästner, Germans like himself had a right to expect more than this slap in the face.[32]

The charge was even more outrageous because it came from one who himself was not free of guilt. Jung had tried to avoid the charge that such a psychoanalytic diagnosis as his was born of self-righteousness by invoking the New Testament teaching: "[T]ake the log out of your own eye first, and

29. Kästner, *Splitter und Balken*, 520.
30. Ibid.
31. Ibid., 521.
32. One is reminded here of Frank Thiess's claim that as an "inner emigrant" he did not expect exceptional praise as a hero, but at least did not anticipate being accused and spurned by Thomas Mann.

then you will be able to see and take the speck out of your brother's eye" (Matthew 7:5), and saying that "[w]e love the criminal and are ardently interested in him because the devil lets us forget the log in our own eye in the examination of the speck in someone else's." Kästner responded:

> Too bad that Jung didn't send his log in a special freight train to Germany. The log could have provided many opponents of the regime and their freezing families with a warm oven for months this winter. But unfortunately Jung does not belong to those who make "that sentimental popular distinction" between opponents and the Nazis. And so he didn't grant us his log.[33]

Kästner thus argued that any accusation of collective guilt is not only one further humiliation good Germans like himself had to suffer, but that the charge is incomprehensible. In comparison to the religiously inspired Kogon, however, Kästner was less primarily concerned with individual contemplation of guilt. Kästner's evaluation of Nuremberg, for this reason, was thus more positive: the big fish are the true criminals. Indeed, he was particularly disgusted with those defendants who, having once claimed to be the masters of German destiny, now claimed to have been caught up in a system beyond their control.[34] Without Kogon's religious devotion, Kästner was less confident of a higher judge, or at least more concerned with the court of public opinion.

One can appreciate Kästner's feeling that accusations of collective guilt did not fairly account for individuals like himself who had never wanted National Socialism's widely praised first triumphs, much less its disastrous outcomes. What is more difficult to appreciate is that Kästner deliberately refused to consider Jung's motives and that he misrepresented Jung's argument, in part by responding only to Jung's interview and not to the more considered essay by Jung that was reprinted from a Zurich newspaper in the *Neue Zeitung*. Jung's argument is in fact not nearly as outrageous as Kästner made it out, though it is rather shrill in places.[35] The crucial questions are

---

33. Kästner, *Splitter und Balken*, 523–24.

34. In this context, it is important to point out that Kästner's disdain was not for a psychoanalytical approach *per se*. In an essay entitled "Nuremberg and the Historians," Kästner remarked positively on the ideas of the psychoanalyst Alexander Mitscherlich. Mitscherlich argued that a more interesting outcome of Nuremberg would have been to encourage the defendants to undergo psychoanalytical inquiry without overt resistance. Doing so would have produced invaluable knowledge, which could then have been used to prevent future such crimes. Kästner entertained this idea because, consistent with his own view, it drew the circle of guilt narrowly.

35. In fact Jung justifies his essay by pointing out the "the spoken word very quickly gives rise to legends." Jung, *The Psychology of Nazism*, 50. See note 27.

thus why Kästner responded as he did, whether Kästner's reaction was representative, and why his reading appears to have stuck in popular memory.[36]

* * *

Jung began by making a crucial distinction between a psychological guilt and a moral or criminal one: "The psychological use of the word 'guilt' should not be confused with guilt in the legal or moral sense. Psychologically, it connotes the irrational presence of a subjective feeling (or conviction) of guilt, or an objective imputation of, or imputed share in, guilt." Jung argued that "[g]uilt can be restricted to the lawbreaker only from the legal, moral, and intellectual points of view, but as a psychic phenomenon it spreads itself over the whole neighborhood. A house, a family, even a village where a murder has been committed feels the psychological guilt and is made to feel it by the outside world." Indeed, Jung warned that "[n]aturally no reasonable and conscientious person will lightly turn collective guilt into individual guilt by holding the individual responsible without giving him a hearing. He will know enough to distinguish between the individually guilty and *the merely collectively guilty*."[37]

This last turn of phrase is perhaps the crux of the dispute: for Kästner and many of his compatriots, collective guilt was in many ways a much

36. Kästner, it is important to note, was by far not the only one in the German discourse—to say nothing of the U.S. discourse referenced above—to address Jung's argument directly. Wilhelm Röpke dismissed Jung's accusation of collective guilt at length in *The Solution of the German Problem*, arguing that Jung was a hypocritical anti-Semite who had collaborated with the Nazis. Röpke charged that the accusations of Jung and others constituted "a theory which is bound to be fatal to any solution of the German problem today." Röpke also attacked the Protestant theologian Karl Barth, whose arguments we will explore in detail in the next chapter. See ibid., 15–16. Less polemically, the British journalist Stephen Spender also addressed Jung's argument in his 1946 memoir *European Witness*, 160–65. Spender began more sympathetically, appreciating Jung's very generalized concept of guilt: "[I]t would do little harm," Spender wrote, "and might do a lot of good if everyone all over the world examined his or her conscience and seriously asked himself whether he was in any degree indirectly responsible for Nazism and all its consequences." But, he argued, "[i]f such a self-examination were made, I think that a few Germans . . . would be as guiltless of creating the Nazi regime as anyone else in the world. At the same time," he continued, "I agree with Jung that there is a special kind of German suggestibility." He concluded judiciously that "[t]here is guilt of the German people, and every German has a certain relation or responsibility for that guilt. That is the sense in which the phrase 'Collective Guilt' is true. It does not mean that every German is equally guilty but that every German should be conscious of guilt."

37. Quotations from Jung, *The Psychology of Nazism*, 51, 53 (emphasis added).

more serious matter than mere individual guilt; because the latter (individual guilt) clearly does not affect them, only the former (collective guilt) is a real challenge. Interestingly, a related issue lies at the heart of an exchange between Hannah Arendt and her former teacher Karl Jaspers, to whose work on *The Question of German Guilt* we will turn shortly. Responding to Jaspers's definition of Nazi policy in terms of criminal guilt, Arendt wrote, "The Nazi crimes, it seems to me, explode the limits of the law; and that is precisely what constitutes their monstrousness. For these crimes, no punishment is severe enough. It may well be essential to hang Göring, but it is totally inadequate. That is, this guilt, in contrast to all criminal guilt, oversteps and shatters any and all legal systems." In response, Jaspers expressed concern about the implications of Arendt's formulation:

> You say that what the Nazis did cannot be comprehended as "crime"—I'm not altogether comfortable with your view, because a guilt that goes beyond all criminal guilt inevitably takes on a streak of "greatness"—of satanic greatness—which is, for me, as inappropriate for the Nazis as all the talk about the "demonic" element in Hitler and so forth. It seems to me that we have to see these things in their total banality, in their prosaic triviality, because that's what truly characterizes them.[38]

This exchange is fascinating in itself for its depth and for its documentary value regarding two great minds struggling with important issues. It is also interesting because it shows the possible origin of Arendt's famous emphasis on the ordinary rather than demonic qualities of the Holocaust in her best-selling 1963 book, *Eichmann in Jerusalem: A Report on the Banality of Evil.* Jaspers's rejection of "all the talk about the 'demonic' element in Hitler" is also an important rejoinder to his historian colleagues, whose ideas we explored in the chapter 8. Here, however, the important point is that Jaspers's concern that discussion in terms of anything beyond an individual criminal guilt risked an apocalyptic implication is similar to Kästner's charge that Jung sounded as if he had "swallowed the trumpet of final judgment"; in contrast, however, Jaspers, as we will see, shared with Jung—at least at the most general level—an openness to nonjuridical understandings of guilt. For Jaspers, the mechanism for doing so legitimately is to draw a sharp distinction between criminal and political guilt on the one hand (which are public), and moral and metaphysical guilt on the other hand (which are private). For Kästner, however, any imputation of a guilt beyond the criminal risked placing him in community with the Nazis when he and others had

38. Kohler and Saner, *Hannah Arendt–Karl Jaspers*, 54, 62.

already paid a tremendous price to maintain the distinction; he thus felt any imputation of collective guilt—whether an accusation that he shared in this objectively or a diagnosis that he must *feel* guilty for having been present at the scene of the crime—was unacceptable; Kästner denied not only that he was guilty (individually or collectively), but that he should feel guilty if he hadn't done anything punishable. The latter seems to be the implication of both Jung's diagnosis of psychological collective guilt as well as of Jaspers's discussion, which we will see later, of a "metaphysical" guilt.

A related explanation of the gulf separating Kästner and Jung comes from the sociologist Ralf Dahrendorf, who attributes the debate over collective guilt to linguistic and cultural differences, emphasizing the different ways different societies draw the boundaries between public and private:

> Collective guilt has a very different, much more "external" connotation for Anglo-Saxon ears schooled in public virtues than it has for Germans. "Guilt" (*Schuld*) in German always has an undertone of the irremediable, incapable of being canceled by metaphysical torment; *Kollektivschuld* binds every individual as such for all time. On the other hand, one of the corollaries of collective guilt is the notion of reparations or, more generally, of making up for past failures; what is meant is a collective responsibility that forces those responsible to answer by common effort, that is, in political and economic ways, for the damage they have brought about. Such guilt does not really involve the individual as a person, as a human being—as one would say in the language of private virtues—but in his membership role, thus as a German national. In principle, one can cast off the guilt with the role.[39]

Whether it is individual guilt or collective guilt that is *"mere"* is thus of the essence. While Jung was certainly not the least bit "Anglo-Saxon," there may well be something to Dahrendorf's explanation. Again, Kästner felt himself accused personally by collective guilt when Jung claims he did not mean it that way. Just as Jung refused to acknowledge the distinction between Nazis and opponents, Kästner was unable to understand the difference between individual and collective guilt, as Dahrendorf's explanation predicts. Kästner appears to have taken collective guilt as a deeply *private* accusation.

*　*　*

What, then, can be said for Jung's diagnosis? His assessment of German collective guilt draws on his theory of the "shadow," his belief that each individual is in some way exactly what that person has no wish to be:

39. Dahrendorf, *Society and Democracy in Germany*, 288–89.

"Everyone harbours his 'statistical criminal' in himself, just as he has his own private madman or saint."[40] An individual is healthy not because he conquers his shadow, but because he understands and has integrated it; the shadow is most dangerous when it remain unconscious. Indeed, this concept of the shadow helps Jung explain National Socialism. Hitler, Jung argued, symbolized something in every individual: "He was the most prodigious personification of all human inferiorities. . . . He represented the shadow, the inferior part of everybody's personality, in an overwhelming degree, and this was another reason why they fell for him." For Jung, National Socialism as a mass movement was an unconscious compensation for the universal chaos of the twentieth century that was "merely" much worse in Germany: "The Germans wanted order, but they made the fatal mistake of choosing the principle victim of disorder and unchecked greed for their leader."[41]

But the "shadow" also explains Jung's diagnosis of collective guilt in postwar Germany: "The wickedness of others becomes our own wickedness because it kindles something evil in our own hearts. The murder has been suffered by everyone, and everyone has committed it: lured by fascination of evil, we have all made this collective psychic murder possible; and the closer we were to it and the better we could see it, the greater our guilt."[42] Clearly, then, Jung's charge of collective guilt was not meant in any conventional sense. His point was to understand the ways in which one can feel badly for an act that one has not in fact committed, both because no one can honestly claim never to have had a bad motive and because one is always stained by the very proximity to its realization: "Since no man lives within his own psychic sphere like a snail in its shell, separated from everybody else, but is connected with his fellow-men by his unconscious humanity, no crime can ever be what it appears to our consciousness to be: an isolated psychic happening." Collective guilt is thus "a state of magical uncleanliness," but it is also "a very real fact."[43]

In an essay entitled *Die Schuld und die Schulden* (a virtually untranslatable formulation, roughly "The Guilt and the Debts"), Kästner addressed exactly the same issue that informed Jung's discussion about the feeling of guilt spreading out over a neighborhood: "If I had a brother who had robbed someone, and someone came and said I was guilty, that would be unjust. But if

40. Jung, *The Psychology of Nazism*, 55.
41. Ibid., 6.
42. Ibid., 54.
43. Ibid., 53.

he said that because the thief was my brother I should help the victim get his property or its equivalent back, I would answer without hesitation: "That I will do." The guilt I must reject. The debts I would recognize."[44] As Dahrendorf implied, for Kästner a debt is payable, but guilt is permanent, like original sin or, perhaps, the guilt of the Jews for allowing Christ's crucifixion.

Kästner, we should recall, was indeed a remarkable individual. Unlike many compatriots who looked away when confronted with Nazi atrocities, Kästner was genuinely struck by the horror of it all. Tasked with reviewing *Die Todesmühlen*, for instance, he was baffled by the defenses of his compatriots, and grew so upset that he was unable to produce his review: "I just can't manage writing a coherent article about this unimaginable, infernal insanity. . . . What happened in the camps is so terrible that one can neither remain silent nor speak about it. We Germans will certainly never forget how many people were killed in these camps." Nevertheless, consistent with his feeling of victimhood, he added: "And the rest of the world should every now and then remember how many Germans were killed there."[45]

One is tempted to say, then, that Jung's diagnosis of a *feeling* of collective guilt has some merit, redeeming itself not only in the worst dregs of German society but here in its best representative. This is exactly the kind of defense Jung's theory expects, a "me too" claim of victimhood. Jung's argument certainly takes on a patronizing tone, particularly when he claimed he did not wish to excite the hysteric and, as a physician, was merely telling his patient the hard truth. But instead of examining the argument, Kästner dismissed it from the outset with sarcasm. Instead of engaging with the theory—which was well-rooted in Jung's theoretical system—Kästner attempted to delegitimate it via *ad hominem* critique: an early Nazi sympathizer himself, Jung had no right to cast the first stone. (Of course, if one followed Kogon's Christian ethic of introspection, it should not matter where the accusation comes from.)

* * *

Ultimately, it is impossible to determine whether Kästner was correct in labeling Jung a hypocrite; loyal secondary literature on Jung, understandably, argues that his work on Nazi Germany was a genuine attempt to confront *his* own shadow. Either way, it is important for evaluating the validity

44. Kästner, *Die Schuld und die Schulden*, 502.
45. Kästner, *Wert und Unwert des Menschens*, 64. Also, see the discussion in Barnouw, *Germany 1945*, 2–3.

of Jung's thesis to appreciate the lengths he took in order to avoid the charge of Pharisaism: in direct contrast to the dominant German trend, Jung included himself and his Swiss countrymen within the community of guilt. Jung referred to a "participation mystique with events in Germany," that caused him "to experience afresh how painfully wide is the scope of the psychological concept of collective guilt." He claimed to have approached the problem "certainly not with any feelings of cold-blooded superiority, but rather with an avowed sense of inferiority." He did offer psychiatric advice to the German national patient: "If a German is prepared to acknowledge his moral inferiority as collective guilt before the world, without attempting to minimize it or explain it away with flimsy arguments, then he will stand a reasonable chance, after a time, of being taken for a more or less decent man, and will thus be absolved of his collective guilt at any rate in the eyes of individuals." This is because Jung, as a psychiatrist, believed that "[w]ithout guilt, unfortunately, there can be no psychic maturation and no widening of the spiritual horizon."[46] Here we can recall Richard Brickner's conclusion that acknowledgment of guilt can have a salutary effect on the paranoid patient. This argument had clear implications for future German political culture: the road to strong identity and healthy democracy is through, not around, the past. As we will see in chapter 10, it also matches the Christian notion of redemption through confession. Nevertheless, it is hardly surprising that such a formulation from the pen of Jung would evoke the kind of reaction it did. As we will see, it did not fare much better from the pulpit.

Jung did, however, warn the Swiss not to feel as if this crime had nothing to do with them: "The fact that one member of the European family could sink to the level of the concentration camp throws a dubious light on all the others. Who are we to imagine that 'it couldn't happen here'? . . . Do we seriously believe we would have been immune?" He vigorously warned against self-righteousness, arguing that most of us are tempted by the nefarious pleasures of sanctimony: "[W]hen the crimes mount up, indignation may easily get pitched too high, and evil then becomes the order of the day." The message for the victors is clear:

> Now we knew for certain where all unrighteousness was to be found, whereas we ourselves were securely entrenched in the opposite camp, among respectable people whose moral indignation could be trusted to rise higher and higher with every fresh sign of guilt on the other side. Even the call for mass executions no longer offended the ears of the righteous, and the saturation bombing of German cities was looked upon as the judgment of God.

46. Jung, *The Psychology of Nazism*, 51, 53, 72.

Small wonder that Jung is identified only as the originator of an illegitimate charge of collective guilt. Engagement with his arguments would have required more sacrifice than was politically feasible by the Allies or was psychologically bearable by Kästner.[47]

While a Swiss may feel a world of difference between his own country and Germany, Jung pointed out that this distinction would appear ridiculous should the Swiss try to make the argument outside of Europe: "The moment we so-called innocent Europeans cross the frontiers of our own continent we are made to feel something of the collective guilt that weighs upon it, despite our good conscience." Jung is clear that the collective mental condition he diagnosed extends to the whole of Europe. As such, the "world sees Europe as the continent on whose soil the shameful concentration camps grew, just as Europe singles out Germany as the land and the people that are enveloped in a cloud of guilt; for the horror happened in Germany and its perpetrators were Germans. No German can deny this, any more than a European or a Christian can deny that the most monstrous crime of all ages was committed in his house." Indeed, the value of Jung's diagnosis is perhaps clearest when he applied it to the churches. In his main essay, he demanded that the churches acknowledge the role of Christianity: "The Christian Church should put ashes on her head and rend her garments on account of the guilt of her children. The shadow of their guilt has fallen on her as much as upon Europe, the mother of monsters." In an epilogue meant to respond to critics such as Kästner, Jung even argues that "[a]nyone who wishes to get a vivid picture of the workings of psychopathic inferiority has only to study the way in which responsible Germans—i.e., the educated classes—react to the *faits et gestes*."[48] As his demonstration example, Jung chose the discussion in the German Protestant church regarding the question of guilt. It is, he found, perfect proof of his hypotheses.

47. Ibid., 56, 55.
48. Ibid., 52, 86.

CHAPTER 10

The New Political Theology

The ways in which the German churches confronted the question of guilt in the immediate postwar period is perhaps even more significant than is remembered in subsequent discourse, which ritually refers to the Protestant "Stuttgart Declaration of Guilt" of 1945 as an important example of German acknowledgment of responsibility, but does not recall much else. In fact, the complexities of debate over the Stuttgart and other declarations were great, and shaped subsequent discourse in ways that memory of the declaration does not fully capture. This is at least in part because of the unique structural position of the churches in 1945: they were the only major institutions that had largely maintained their institutional identities and structures from before the Nazi period. Moreover, the Western Allies approached church leaders with a fairly traditional respect (occupation directives instructed military leaders not to interfere with the activities of religious organizations). Additionally, there was a widespread religious revival in Germany in the immediate aftermath of the war, borne in part of spiritual desolation, in part out of desire for a few hours in a heated building, and in part because of a reflexive return to more "traditional" cultural values after the Nazi experiment. Along with the absence of any real governmental institutions in the early months and of national ones later, these factors combined to place the churches in an unparalleled position to speak for the German people and to exercise power culturally, politically, and even economically.[1]

1. One of the best histories of the churches in the postwar period remains Spotts, *The Churches and Politics in Germany*. A useful overview and documentation of the Protestant Church is Greschat, *Im Zeichen der Schuld*. A useful overview of the guilt debates in the Catholic and Protestant Churches can be found in Wolgasst, *Die Wahrnehmung des Dritten*

While the West German political parties departed significantly from German tradition by abandoning sectarian identities (as we will see in the next chapter), the ways in which each church confronted the *Schuldfrage*—the question of guilt—had profound legacies for the development of, and indeed cleavages within, subsequent political discourse. The situations of, and trajectories within, the Protestant and Catholic Churches, of course, differed historically, institutionally, theologically, as well as politically. The discussion in the Protestant Church provided a more explicit set of terms and touch-points than that in the Catholic Church; but the more silent legacy of the Catholic Church was equally important, especially in the figure of Konrad Adenauer, whose worldview was in many ways directly in line with official Catholic positions.

The Protestants

Background

The situation of, and discourse in, the Protestant Church was in many ways more complex than for the Catholic Church. The roots of the differences are deeply historical. The Lutheran break with papal authority in the sixteenth century was fundamentally important here, in large part because it altered the political status of religious authority. Where the Catholic Church was a significant independent power—indeed greater than any local political power—Protestantism (including Calvinism) was decentralized; in each German state, Protestant authorities were thus subordinate to local political authorities. As a result, local church structures depended on local political structures, and had to accommodate to them. This created two characteristics of German Protestantism: it was comparatively non-hierarchical and it was comparatively variable politically, depending on local pressures. As Frederic Spotts puts it, "German Protestantism itself emerged from the Reformation era territorially fragmented, confessionally divided, organizationally bound to the state, and psychologically tied to the status quo. [And it] has never succeeded in fully liberating itself of these characteristics."[2]

_____

Reiches in der unmittlerbaren Nachkriegszeit. An interesting historical source is the 1947 report of the Council of Foreign Relations, Price and Schorske, *The Problem of Germany*, chap. 10.

2. Spotts, *The Churches and Politics in Germany*, 5.

During the Weimar years, the majority of Protestant organizations and policies were highly conservative and nationalistic, in line with the traditional subordination to the state. The perceived chaos of the Weimar Republic was thus often met with a demand for order and retrenchment. As such, a significant proportion of the Protestant clergy saw the advent of National Socialism as a positive development. Even before the Nazi seizure of power (*Machtergreifung*), Nazi supporters in the Protestant establishments formed the German Christian Faith Movement, more informally known as the "German Christians." With the seizure of power, this movement produced the German Evangelical Church, which was a fairly extensively Nazified organization, taking control of all but three provincial church structures. Ultimately, about 10 percent of the Protestant clergy became members of the Nazi Party, and almost one-third were associated with the German Christians.

A major objection to the German Christians was their challenge to the traditional regional autonomy of the provincial churches. This was a hallmark of the Nazi strategy of *Gleichschaltung*, the penetration of all intermediate associations by the doctrines of the state, and the centralization of control of such organizations by the party. The Protestant church, as we just saw, was traditionally fractured and nonhierarchical. One of the most important developments was thus the founding in 1933 of the Pastors' Emergency League by Martin Niemöller, and the subsequent Reich Synod held in the town of Barmen in 1934. The so-called "Barmen Declaration" was a radical departure from Protestant traditions up to that point insofar as it challenged the conventional subservience of the churches to the state and asserted the supremacy of scripture as a bulwark against political vicissitudes. As such, the Barmen Declaration was a decisive shift in the history of German Protestantism.

For many, but not all, of the Barmen participants, however, the motivation was theologically founded repugnance not only for National Socialist *organizational* interference, but for *content* as well. The practical result at Barmen was the establishment of the Confessional Church (*Bekennende Kirche*), whose members ranged from radical opponents of the regime on substantive grounds to those who merely resented the challenge to church autonomy. On the more radical side were such famous names as Karl Barth, Dietrich Bonhöffer, and Martin Niemöller.

Official Protestantism in the Third Reich was thus highly fractured, and included Nazi supporters in the German Evangelical Church, moderate to radical opponents in the Confessing Church, and a substantial middle group who sought coexistence without accommodation.

A New Church?

The first postwar convocation of Protestant leaders was called by Bishop Theophil Wurm—head of the Württemberg church since 1929, a nationalist but clandestine leader of an opposition group during the war, and, as we will see, an outspoken critic of the Allies after the end of the war—and met at Treysa in August 1945. There the Protestants sought to bind up their internal wounds by establishing the Evangelical Church in Germany (EKD) as an umbrella organization, with Wurm, Pastor Niemöller, and theologian Karl Barth constituting the leadership, thus giving the majority (Niemöller and Barth) to members of the Confessing Church. One of the first tasks was to overcome the legacy of the Nazi German Evangelical Church, which the EKD accomplished by treating that organization as illegal; in December of 1945, Wurm obtained the cooperation of the Allied Control Council, which annulled the law that had established the German Christians. One additional result of the Treysa accord was to reconfirm the autonomy of the regional churches, thus establishing a confederate structure for Protestantism in the new Germany.

Given the influence of Niemöller and Barth at Treysa, it is not surprising that the conference statement included remarks on the need to reflect on the guilt of the church. While some, like Bishop Otto Debelius—who in 1933 had warned, in Hitler's presence, against the dangers of dictatorship—wanted the church simply to take up where it had left off in 1933, Niemöller and Barth argued that a more thorough inquiry into the failures of the church was warranted. A major part of the problem, these critics argued, was what they believed to be an inappropriate historical relationship of the church to political authority. Their statement to parishes read: "Long before churches sank in ruins, pulpits were profaned and prayers silenced. . . . Long before the specious order of the Reich collapsed, law had been falsified. . . . Moral standards do not suffice to measure the depth of the guilt which our nation has brought upon itself. . . . We acknowledge our guilt and are bowed by the weight of its consequences."[3] Clearly, this was a fairly radical statement, implying a new, more politically engaged role for the church.

Conservatives, in contrast, saw the national disaster as a matter of God's inscrutable Will, and thus did not think it was appropriate to break with the church's pre-Nazi past, either institutionally or doctrinally. As we will see, these positions struggled with each other in important ways over the next years, contributing to significant shifts in German political and religious

3. Quoted in ibid., 11.

culture. But the Treysa statement was intended as, and remained, an inner-church matter, in contrast to the Stuttgart Declaration, which followed in October 1945.

The Moral Theology of Karl Barth

Perhaps the major intellectual—to say nothing of political—source for the more critical stance taken toward the churches was the theologian Karl Barth, who had spent the war in Switzerland (he possessed dual citizenship). As already noted, Barth was one of the major inspirations for the establishment of the Confessing Church at Barmen in 1934, and remained an important voice during the war. In January and February of 1945, Barth repeatedly delivered a lecture in Switzerland (entitled "The Germans and Ourselves"), which, along with an essay for the *Manchester Evening News* (entitled "How can the Germans be Cured?") and texts of two letters from critics (with his replies), he published together as *The Only Way*. This short work is one of the strongest statements on German guilt, and it is worth noting not only for its influence on the debate, but because the differences between Barth's views and more standard fare bring into stark relief exactly what that standard fare was. It provides, moreover, an interesting comparison with Jung's ideas, and the reactions they evoked.

In "The Germans and Ourselves," a lecture to his Swiss compatriots, Barth characterized the historical location of National Socialism, predicted German reaction to accusations against it, expressed his hopes, and instructed the Swiss and, by implication, others on how they can help. As for the historical location of National Socialism, Barth rejected any short-term horizon, much like the Anglo-American writers who identified National Socialism's deep historical roots and connection to German culture: "The achievement of Frederick the Great and Bismarck," Barth stated, "could not be brought to a more logical conclusion nor to more complete destruction than it has been done by Adolf Hitler."[4] By the same token, the question of German guilt was, for Barth, a matter for the long-term:

We have to reckon with the possibility that the great majority of Germans even now scarcely realize in what collective madness they have lived so long, with what deep-seated and justifiable consternation Germany is regarded, what a responsibility they assumed when they supported first Bismarck, then

4. Karl Barth, *The Only Way*, 83.

Wilhelm II, and last of all, Adolf Hitler, and willingly and patiently did all they were told; and that especially they have no inkling of the horror and loathing with which the German name has been surrounded in the last twelve years.[5]

Where Thomas Mann and others spoke of the dark possibilities of the German soul hidden behind its humanist countenance, Barth was comparatively more brutal. Asking whether Germans should be considered supporters of the Nazis (as some exile writers like Emil Ludwig argued) or whether they were victims (as, for instance, the Socialist opposition or even the "inner emigrants" believed), he wrote:

> Or is a third version correct, which claims that the German is in a quite peculiar way a being with two completely different mentalities, so that in every German one would have to look simultaneously for something of Friedrich Schiller and Matthias Claudius as well as something of Joseph Goebbels and Heinrich Himmler, something of the spirit of Weimar as well as the spirit of Potsdam? But over and above all that, there seems to be something like a spirit—represented by not a few Germans—of Oradour and Oswiecim.[6]

Even Auschwitz cannot be disavowed, and this is so for all Germans, not just the defendants at Nuremberg. There can, as a result, be no relativization of damages:

> In spite of all the sympathy we have for the German victims, we simply cannot admit that the annihilation of the peasants of Oradour and of the Jews, in Auschwitz, falls into the same category with the bombardment of the German industry and communication centers in the interest of winning the war by trying to break the impetus of attack and resistance in a nation mobilized for total war.[7]

Indeed, Barth was ready for every equivocation (and was in fact betting correctly on what the discourse would look like). He referred, rather crudely, to "the great German art of intellectual evasion," and to "the fact that the Germans love to meet every political accusation with an immediate counter-accusation and with indignant counter-claims."[8] Barth also diagnosed a peculiarly German denial of personal responsibility:

5. Ibid., 104–5.
6. Ibid., 72–73. Oradour-sur-Glane was a French village whose inhabitants were massacred by German troops on June 10, 1944; "Oswiecem" is the Polish name for Auschwitz. See Farmer, *Martyred Village*; Dwork and van Pelt, *Auschwitz*.
7. Barth, *The Only Way*, 53.
8. Ibid., 107, 105.

The fact that individual responsibility for political situations is alien to them explains why it is so difficult to make them understand that they cannot simply be cleared of all charges brought against the Nazi system and all its consequences, but that they must be held responsible for all that has been done to them and to the rest of Europe.[9]

There is, of course, no real evidence that such tendencies are peculiarly German—though there is something to be said for the German "virtue" of duty and the blurred distinction between public and private to which Ralf Dahrendorf referred (chapter 9)—and one would expect quite a visceral reaction to such statements; strangely we have no single document, comparable to that of Erich Kästner against Jung (chapter 9), for Barth, who was treated with respect even by critics.[10]

Other predicted and disallowed equivocations included a false "religious profundity of the Germans, which," Barth said, "all too willingly avoids acknowledgment of their own concrete guilt by pointing out the great truth that before God in the last resort all men and nations are alike guilty and alike need forgiveness for their sins; thus the bold conclusion is drawn that a particular German repentance is obviously unnecessary and absolutely uncalled for."[11] As we have already seen, and will see again, Barth was right on the mark here. He also argued that explanations blaming particular groups are not useful:

This is not the time to search for all sorts of scape-goats—officers, Prussian Junkers, landowners, great industrialists, etc.—There are, of course, more or less "guilty" groups. Of course, there are conceptions and systems which, considering what happened, should not only be fought, but uprooted; there are individuals who should vanish from the face of the earth, in the interest of the majority. But the only pertinent and constructive question concerns the guilt in which all groups were involved—the Communists as well as the Christian Church. There is one point in the question of guilt where all anger against one another is senseless,

9. Ibid., 7.

10. In *The Solution of the German Problem*, Wilhelm Röpke was critical not only of Barth but of the reverential and, he believed uncritical, attitude with which his argument was received: "It may be astounding for some people to hear the story of the famous Swiss theologian Karl Barth. He is now passing as one of the great and unbending anti-Nazis, and lately he has been lecturing as such very much and very severely on the Germans in Germany." For Röpke, however, such attacks could only mean can mean only one thing: "[I]t goes almost without saying that Karl Barth is now bending his knees to the Russians." Röpke, *The Solution of the German Problem*, 16–17.

11. Barth, *The Only Way*, 106. Jung as well, as we saw in the chapter 9, predicted similar equivocations.

where all Germans belong together, and they should openly or silently agree on it;
I mean: in a word, *all Germans failed to a certain extent—not only some of them, not only
this one or that one, because they allowed things to go as far as they have gone.*[12]

No more bald statement of German collective guilt is to be found anywhere in the literature, short perhaps of Robert Vansittart! In response to a
letter asserting that "[t]here is no such thing as collective guilt of the German people for National Socialism, and therefore should be no question of
collective punishment,"[13] Barth argued:

> Comparatively few Germans must have taken part in the crimes themselves. But
> they all took the road leading to these crimes, either in the form of actions or
> negligence, of direct or indirect participation, of explicit or tacit consent, of
> unequivocal, active or "pro forma" party membership, of political indifference
> or in the form of all kinds of political errors and miscalculations.

Barth was thus "very much in favor of the Germans, and I mean all Germans, admitting their responsibility for all that which happened since
1933." All attempts to avoid doing so he characterized as "brain acrobatics,
meant to provide a way to escape reality. It could not possibly be of any real
help to the German people." His hope was that, instead of focusing on the
faults of others, the Germans would "have the grace to admit that today the
responsibility of others does not concern them in the least. They should
have the grace of not thinking today in terms of Europe or the globe, but
merely in terms of Germany."[14]

What, then, is to be done? Or, as Barth put it, "How can Germans be
cured?" The first question here is *who* can help. "What the Germans need
is friends," Barth argued. But one could not expect the Allies or victim
nations to fill this role:

> The Russians, the English, the Americans, the French and the smaller nations so
> badly treated by the Germans, together with the Jews, cannot be expected at this
> moment to offer them such a friendship, although they, too, will one day have to
> see that the German peril can be finally and decisively removed only in this way.
> But it is to be expected of us Swiss, because we are Swiss and because (I must now
> make express use of the presupposition) we are *Christian* Swiss.[15]

12. Barth, *The Only Way*, 13–14 (emphasis added).
13. This statement, with its defense against "collective punishment," is an indication of
why for many Germans the concept of collective guilt—which would justify collective punishment—was to be rejected. Ibid., 25.
14. Ibid., 34, 31, and 10.
15. Ibid., 96.

As well-intentioned as Allied plans may be, they are ill-conceived:

> In the United States they are supposed to be all ready to deliver after the war a whole cargo of teaching facilities to Germany, in order to inculcate in the barbarians (after so much Wotan worship,[16] nihilism, and rifle-practice) human brotherhood, democracy, respect for law, love of peace and (instead of the vile *Horst Wessel Lied*),[17] *Onward Christian Soldiers*. The intention is admirable but it can never work. The Germans, however bad their state, will retreat into themselves, like an oyster into its shell, before all who approach them as teachers, and German youth will defend itself against them tooth and nail. They will treat all who approach them in the guise of teachers as people who are against them, and much more against them than those who came earlier in aircraft and tanks.

Re-education is thus an enterprise doomed in its very conception, though Barth did assert that "[t]he more thoroughly that Germany is unbuilt, the better—above all for themselves. We could not help them to escape the expiation and restitution and complete reorientation that are now necessary."[18]

Interestingly, however, Barth did not believe, as many Germans argued, that the tasks of judgment should be left to the Germans themselves. This, he argued, would lead to "a split between Germans and Germans; that is, between the 'innocent' and the 'guilty,' the 'honest' and the 'dishonest' . . . so that, in the end, the Germans should also fight against each other." Thus, where Kästner and others worked with all their strength to build up a symbolic barrier, here Barth rejected it out of hand. Where critics of denazification resented Allied intrusions and blamed the Allies for pre-empting a self-cleansing of German society, Barth saw this as dangerous: "it will lead either to civil unrest or it will not confront real responsibility as widely as it exists."[19]

Germany's friends, Barth argued, must avoid the danger of self-righteousness, though of course self-righteousness is not the word Barth chose: "It will not be easy to make clear to them that we mean them well, that we are turning to them without conditions, that we want to meet them not as the *Pharisee* did the publican, and that nevertheless, in this respect, we cannot yield them an inch." More programmatically, "All is lost if we

---

16. There is good reason to believe that this reference is to Jung's 1936 essay, "Wotan."

17. Horst Wessel was a figure in Nazi political mythology, and the (explicitly anti-Semitic) song in which he figures as a martyr was a major feature of the Nazi political liturgy, sung virtually everywhere.

18. Barth, *The Only Way*, 103.

19. Ibid., 11, 12.

meet them in *Pharisaic* fashion."[20] Interestingly, though, Barth was quite typical in that he uses the "Pharisee" label only as a warning to foreigners approaching Germany with charges; for the potential mutual recrimination of German against German—one might imagine Kästner against not the "inner emigrants" but Nazi functionaries—"Pharisee" does not seem to fit; this is so even when Barth argued that the Germans cannot themselves reckon with the criminals because doing so will exacerbate invidious (dare one say, Pharisaical) differences in the population. Again, this does not appear to be a mere preference for impressive vocabulary. As Barth stated, "The Germans are there, as the Jews are there, with whose nature and destiny they have so much in common."[21]

Despite all this, then, Barth did not issue a call for eliminating Germany; rather, he asks for Germany to "retire" from the stage of history, just as the Swiss, another unusual people, had done. In Jungian terms, one might be tempted to diagnose a widespread "complex" here involving the desire to achieve the status of the Jews; as we saw, however, Jung himself shared in this complex.

* * *

Obviously, Barth's was a rather unusual charge for the discourse, though, as we have just seen, it shares in rather common language. Important differences in Barth's argument, however, include not just the extremity of the condemnation—which dismisses all boundary distinctions as "mental acrobatics"— but the moral reasoning reflected in the language. Over the course of examining numerous controversies in the previous pages, we have already encountered enough examples of what I think of as a "grammar of exculpation," ways of framing the problems of the German past so that they appear less burdening. Examples of this include not specifying what crimes one is talking about; avoidance of anti-Semitism as a causal factor; careful distinctions between "us" and "them" deployed with as much precision as variability; metaphorical language of demons, madmen, and villains; and, overwhelmingly in political rhetoric, passive and vague constructions—"the crimes that were committed," "what happened in those years," and many others.[22]

I introduce the idea of "grammars of exculpation" here because Barth revealed an important formula by reversing it. I am speaking here of what I

---

20. Ibid., 104, 107 (emphasis added).
21. Ibid., 120.
22. For a useful analysis and typology of apologetic language, see Tavuchis, *Mea Culpa*.

would term an "inevitable *aber*." *Aber* is the German word for "but." The standard formulation is "The Germans did this (more commonly 'This was done by Germans,' or merely 'This happened') *but* others did things as well." Barth, however, turned the order around: "Others did things, *but* Germans did things too." If the act comes first and the qualification second, the effect is exculpatory; if the qualification comes first and the act second, there is more a sense of accepting responsibility, no matter what the circumstances. This is, as we have just seen, how Barth put it in the passages above. In the statements he negotiated with adversaries in the church, however, some of the content remained the same, but, as we will see, the grammar was more exculpatory. Even so, the debate over the official statements to which he contributed called forth virtually all of the defenses he predicted. Whatever one makes of the arguments, Barth thus revealed himself as an insightful prophet of moral language.

The Stuttgart Declaration of Guilt

The genesis of the Stuttgart Declaration of Guilt (*Stuttgarter Schuldbekenntnis*) is extraordinarily complex, and it is not possible here to unravel all its tangled threads. What is most important for present purposes is for us to note that how the Declaration is remembered is not a straightforward product of its contents. The lesson for the sociology of collective memory is that memory is often a winner-takes-all proposition: in German memory, the Stuttgart Declaration was unequivocal; in reality it could not have been more equivocal. The point, however, is not merely to state that memory is selective, but to explain why what is selected to be remembered is chosen over other possibilities.

Competing scholarly accounts of the declaration's genesis argue over the motivation behind the document. Some have maintained that the real impetus was pragmatic, that it was a response to pressure from outside Germany. The occasion was a first meeting between members of the International Ecumenical Council and leaders of the EKD. Representatives of the council expected some kind of declaration from the Germans as evidence of their change of heart, though they did not want it to be coerced. As the general secretary of the Ecumenical Council, the Dutchman Willem Visser't Hooft, put it, "Help us so that we can help."[23] Following the earlier meeting at

---

23. Cited in Wolgast, *Die Wahrnehmung des Dritten Reiches in der unmittelbaren Nachkriegszeit*, 242. In his fuller statement, however, Visser't Hooft attributed this particular formulation to his colleague Pierre Maury.

Treysa, it was clear that the EKD would offer some statement, but exactly what it would look like was highly contested.

At one extreme were ultraconservative Lutheran traditionalists who rejected any such declaration. More significant was the position represented by Bishop Theophil Wurm that while some declaration might be theologically founded, it would be politically misused to Germany's disadvantage. Wurm led a vigorous opposition to Allied occupation policies; he was thus concerned that any declaration of guilt would damage German national honor and that, furthermore, German crimes were matched by crimes against Germany, particularly the expulsions from Eastern territories. Among those strongly in favor of a declaration were Bishop Hans Asmussen and Pastor Martin Niemöller, who nevertheless differed on the degree to which a declaration should have political implications in addition to its theological content, and whether the subject of the declaration should primarily be the German people as a whole or merely the church. (Another important figure in these discussions, in many ways sympathetic to Niemöller and the need to confess guilt, was Gustav Heinemann, who would later be a member of Adenauer's cabinet, would resign as a moral protest against rearmament and strategies of Western integration in the 1950s, switch to the SPD, and later become president of the Federal Republic in the morally charged atmosphere of the 1960s.)

The declaration that was finally approved, after numerous drafts and heated discussion, had all the hallmarks of a forced compromise. Its most important section reads as follows:

> We know ourselves to be with our nation not only in a great community of suffering but also in a solidarity of guilt. With great pain we say: because of us, infinite suffering has been brought to many peoples and countries. As we often testified to our congregations we now declare in the name of the entire church: Even though we fought over many years in the name of Jesus Christ against the spirit that found its terrible expression in the National Socialist reign of violence; we condemn ourselves because we did not believe more courageously, did not pray more devotedly, did not believe more joyously, and did not love more deeply.[24]

The impact of this statement, however, was substantially greater than that which was intended, at least by some of its authors (and certainly by its opponents). Perhaps most decisive for the impact was that, for reasons that remain unclear, a number of newspapers reported—with large headlines—

---

24. The full text of the declaration is reprinted in Greschat, *Im Zeichen der Schuld*, 45–46, among many other places.

"Evangelical Church Acknowledges War Guilt" and other slight variations. Whether, and in what way, this was an accurate description is not entirely clear from the text just quoted. Indeed, if this was the result of Barth's work, it must in many ways have been his worst nightmare, for many of the equivocations he warned against are there in grammar and substance.

Indeed, many features of the Stuttgart Declaration are usually glossed over. The statement begins with *German* suffering. The declaration claims that its authors are not guilty of not having done anything, for they say that they *did* preach to their congregations and *did* fight the evil: the guilt is for not having done so *even more vigorously*. With the reproach for not having believed more courageously, prayed more devotedly, believed more joyously, and loved more deeply, it thus sounds as if their only failure was not having been saints. In this light, one should recall Barth's reply to one of the letters reprinted in *The Only Way*, in which the writer implied that one would have had to have been a hero to avoid the charge of guilt. In response, Barth wrote that he did not agree "that the German nation would have had to consist only of heroes, in order to avoid the National Socialist catastrophe. It would have had to consist merely of politically reasonable citizens ready to act, or of citizens quietly remaining in their places."[25]

Furthermore, the declaration is ambiguous because it is not entirely clear who "we" refers to: it seems as if the "we" and "us" refer to the clergy, but not to the German people at all.[26] In fact, this was one way the statement was understood—that the clergy, because of their role as shepherds, were turning themselves into scapegoats for the populace. If they could bear the guilt and accept the responsibility, ordinary people would not have to. This seems to be the position of Hans Asmussen, one of the declaration's authors:

> It is terrible that we find it impossible to escape or suppress the question of guilt. How we wish we knew nothing of all this and could start anew. But the world grants us no rest; she screams at us with the questions of guilt, and whether we want to or not, we must answer. For that reason *it is necessary for the Church to step into the breach. . . . The church is to blame, the Church of both confessions*. Our guilt stretches far into the past.[27]

In this reading, the Stuttgart Declaration acknowledges the guilt of the church and not of the people, and the guilt acknowledged is that of being

25. Barth, *The Only Way*, 38. We can recall here as well Robert Vansittart's response to Eleanor Rathbone mentioned in chapter 3.

26. See also Wolgast, *Die Wahrnehmung des Dritten Reiches in der unmittelbaren Nachkriegszeit*, 242.

27. Spotts, *The Churches and Politics in Germany*, 93 (emphasis added).

human. Additionally, the implications of the alluded-to behavior remain vague and passive: "because of us, infinite suffering has been brought to many peoples and countries," though what exactly that suffering entailed and who were its victims (particularly, though of course not only, Jews) remains unmentioned. Reference to this suffering, again, comes only after first mentioning German suffering, which remains for many the obvious kind; the declaration, in this light, could be seen as a gentle reminder not to forget others in one's own time of need. Or at least that is the exculpatory implication of the grammar.

It may thus be surprising that the declaration met with the extensive resistance it did. There was a veritable storm of indignation. Many local clergy members refused to read the declaration to their congregations, or did so only with qualifications. And the EKD's leadership saw themselves obliged to explain what they had done. There were four broad arguments in response to the declaration. First, some repudiated the declaration on substantive grounds. Among the most prominent spokesmen for this position was the Tübingen theologian Helmut Thielecke, who delivered a series of lectures on "The Spiritual and Religious Crisis of the Present." A lecture he gave on November 8, 1945, was titled "Excursus on Karl Barth's Lecture in Tübingen," and takes on not only the Stuttgart Declaration, but Barth's even more radical vision directly. According to Thielecke, because Barth was Swiss he did not sufficiently appreciate Germany's historical situation; Germany, for Thielecke, was a victim: one must recognize "what it means when industry is idle, when the cultural bolshevism of a foreign spirit makes itself all too apparent, and when a healthy and culturally gifted people must languish in the torturing feeling that it is always the anvil, never the hammer."[28]

Thielecke's argument works in two directions. First, National Socialism is a symptom of the general secularization of society, which is not a specifically German phenomenon. In this, he shared a worldview with the nationalist historians. Second, seeing the Germans as wholly responsible for National Socialism neglects the impact of the Treaty of Versailles; the guilt lies as much on the framers of that document as on the Germans. Thielecke was not averse to an acknowledgment of guilt in this secularized climate, but this would do everyone good, not just the Germans: "Barth is right when he speaks of a necessity for a confession of guilt. Give us the inner freedom to make it. Give it to us in an attitude of readiness to confess that

28. All quotes from Thielecke are translated in Price and Schorske, *The Problem of Germany*, 121–22. See also Thielecke, *In der Stunde Null*.

we all have need, seven times sevenfold, of forgiveness—Frenchmen, Americans, Englishmen, Germans, Japanese—*and Jews*" [emphasis added]. Of course, such a confession is a matter of faith, not of politics; it would do nothing to improve the current situation, since the Allies made the charges "Pharisaically," as a way to legitimate unfair policies. In the last analysis, according to Thielecke, repentance is misaddressed if it is not toward God: "God is the only one in whose sight we do not cast ourselves away when we admit guilt."[29] Anything else would be self-destructive.

In many ways, Thielecke's argument is a classically nationalist defense against political guilt, much in the tradition of Max Weber, who argued in his famous essay "Politics as a Vocation" after World War I that accepting the "war guilt" clause of the Treaty of Versailles was irresponsible to German national interests.[30] Nevertheless, even considering how soon after the end of the war Thielecke's statement came, the ascription of guilt to Jews is striking. It may have been theologically justified—we are all sinners—and it may in some ways have been politically preferable to the emerging culture of philo-Semitism, in which Jews were as praiseworthy as they were once condemnable (though this would not truly get under way for another few years). Even so, it is striking. It is not surprising, however, that Thielecke's lectures were attended by more than one thousand students and were extremely well received. As Hoyt Price and Carl Schorske put it in their 1947 report, "From the point of view of the nationalistic student body, his is the voice of courage among the sycophants."[31]

* * *

The reaction could not have been more different when Martin Niemöller addressed the same issues in a much-cited speech at Erlangen University (he also made similar remarks in numerous locations, but the Erlangen speech is the most famous, in part because its full text was reprinted in the *Neue Zeitung*).[32] Niemöller's position is based on his conviction that the church should play a much more vigorously political role than it had to that point in time. In a much-quoted letter to his brother, he wrote: "The crimes of Hitler and his helpers are now being blamed on our nation as

29. Price and Schorske, *The Problem of Germany*, 122.
30. In chapter 13 I look more closely at Weber's argument as a background to Karl Jaspers's position.
31. Price and Schorske, *The Problem of Germany*, 122.
32. *Neue Zeitung*, February 15, 1946.

a whole, and, in fact, we are all to blame, but not in the sense that we are murderers, robbers or sadists, but in the sense that we let all these things happen, without doing our utmost for the victims and against the crimes, as we should have done."[33] In the Erlangen speech, Niemöller argued that without a confession, spiritual renewal would not be possible. In this he was clearly thinking along the same lines as Catholic intellectuals like Eugen Kogon and Walter Dirks. As we saw earlier, Kogon argued that "Germany will not have to be afraid of the judge anymore, since it will honestly have passed judgment on itself." For Dirks, who along with Kogon was a leading "political" Christian, "Never before in our life did the opportunities for the Christian renewal of society appear as great." Nevertheless, for Dirks, "[o]nly the Allied forces held us back, but that, we assumed, would not last forever."

Niemöller shared this critique of Allied policy, but in this first campaign for confession he was clearly focused on the deficits of German reaction: "There is much crying and lamenting about our hunger and affliction," Niemöller noted, "but I have not yet heard one man in Germany, whether from the pulpit or anywhere else, express regret for the terrible suffering that we, we Germans, have brought upon others." In a rare specific accounting, Neimöller forthrightly stated, "There is no talk about what happened in Poland, about the eradication of millions in Russia, about the 5.6 million dead Jews," though he still employs the passive and non-specific "what happened," and the vague "eradication." Niemöller is clear, though, that this is all "written down on our people's guilt account, and no one can take this away." Nevertheless, expiation can occur only through confession and contemplation: "There is only one power that could expiate this guilt which has poisoned the world and thus purify the air. That is the forgiving love of God, which, were it to become real, would be such an unbelievable miracle, that we could never fathom it with our reason." The implication is that this is not a matter for negotiation, and specifically not for punishment or persecution by the occupation authorities.

Niemöller, it may be surprising to learn, was a vehement critic of denazification and occupation policy generally. All the same, his speech at Erlangen was met with vigorous critique; several times he had to pause in the face of vocal challenges, while his hosts requested that his audience respect the occasion. Interruptions were especially disruptive at exactly those points where Niemöller spoke explicitly of German crimes. Later, scathing commentaries

---

33. Quoted in Bark and Gress, *A History of West Germany*, vol. 1, 151–52.

THE NEW POLITICAL THEOLOGY 219

were posted on the student bulletin board at the university. In reaction, the Bavarian political authorities instructed the rector of the university to punish the offenders, who were seen as indicative of widespread militarist and Nazi sympathies in the student body. In context, it is easy to see why Niemöller's position fell on deaf ears: "We Christians must accept this guilt and confess it.... Because we Christians in Germany have incurred guilt." No doubts or qualifications were allowed. Nevertheless, in retrospect, one notes again that the guilt incurred is only for not having resisted harder, that the crimes for which Germany is burdened with guilt are the crimes of Hitler and his helpers. Niemöller never mentioned early support for the Nazis and the widespread enthusiasm of many ordinary Germans, to say nothing of intellectuals. In this, Niemöller's argument is very much in line with the discourse, in which the problems of National Socialism are its ultimate implications, not its original essence. One recalls here the survey that showed widespread support for the statement that National Socialism was a good idea badly executed. Given Niemöller's own early nationalism, his portrayal is not hard to understand; of course, as a former concentration camp inmate, he spoke with a virtually unparalleled legitimacy in foreign eyes. Many Germans, however, thought he was a dangerous radical, and indeed he may have been.

Despite accusations that he asserted collective guilt, however, through all his speeches Niemöller preached a rather traditional Protestant message about the importance of repentance for sinners. Here, then, is good reason to believe that the real problem was not with an indefinable collective guilt as bugaboo; again, the problem was one of ordinary guilt and of the dividing line between those to whom the charge applied and those to whom it did not. The question is what fears collective guilt stood in for, and what dragons were slain by repudiating this chimera.

* * *

Situated between these two positions—Theilecke's repudiation of, and Niemöller's vigorous campaign for, the relevance of the declaration—were two kinds of depoliticizing readings (one genuinely depoliticizing, one more self-serving). Hans Asmussen argued strenuously for an apolitical interpretation because of his commitment to the religious dimensions of guilt and its contemplation; in other words, he argued that it was wrong to interpret the Stuttgart Declaration as a political statement. Bishop Meiser, for instance, wrote in this vein that the "Stuttgart Declaration of Guilt is a message from Christians to Christians.... The Stuttgart Declaration is a message under God. . . . The Stuttgart Declaration does not take a position on the political war guilt as such. Nor did it want to evaluate the question of guilt before the forum of the world or history, rather, as said, in the presence of God."[34] Perhaps genuine, but also perhaps naïve.

Bishop Wurm too sought to qualify and circumscribe exactly what could be meant by an acknowledgment of guilt, and argued as well that the declaration must be understood purely religiously:

> [T]he the idea of a collectivity of guilt is a biblical one from A to Z. The Bible views sin not simply in isolation but always in connection with something; it affixes responsibility in an overall context, in all directions. The fathers have eaten grapes and the children's teeth are set on edge; I will visit the sins of the fathers upon the children unto the third and fourth generations. That is one of the rules of life, a divine law which we recognize again and again.[35]

In many ways this is ordinary language for a preacher, though it is possible to find the preface here to be an unusual one: "According to today's slogan," Wurm stated, "not everyone in Israel sinned equally: many kept themselves uncorrupted." In what way that was "today's slogan" is unclear. But whether intentional or not, it is yet another example of the analogy between Germans and Jews, what in psychoanalytic language might be labeled a "fantasy projection."

In an argument redolent of Kästner (though, given the order of publication, any possible influence was probably in the other direction), Wurm wrote, "No married couple can escape the fact that they must assume responsibility for the consequences of their children's behavior, even though in an individual case they may be completely innocent."[36] Again, the strange conclusion one might in retrospect draw is that the repudiation of collective guilt is, on the surface, a matter of semantics. Kästner, we saw, was perfectly willing to accept the debts but not the guilt for what his brother had done; Wurm defended a declaration of guilt with the analogy of a married couple. One is thus left wondering what exactly the target of the defense that falls under the rubric of a "repudiation of collective guilt" could mean. It begins to become a bit clearer in the connection between collective guilt on the one hand and Allied occupation policy and denazification on the other.

34. Quoted in Greschat, *Im Zeichen der Schuld*, 23.
35. Quoted in Spotts, *The Churches and Politics in Germany*, 94.
36. Ibid.

The Protestant Repudiation of Occupation Policy

As already mentioned, even Martin Niemöller was a vigorous opponent of denazification and of occupation policy more generally. No one, however, led the charge more vigorously than Bishop Theophil Wurm (with the possible exception of Cardinal Frings, whose position we will examine shortly). In a January 1946 statement, Wurm said, "We know that our German people today stands accused of causing the terrible world holocaust which has caused such infinite suffering and need throughout the world." (Whether this was the first description of the Nazi crimes as a "holocaust" is probably impossible to determine; at very least, it is an interesting early usage.) Wurm proclaimed he was up to the task: "We do not hesitate to carry the burden of guilt which the leading men of state and party heaped upon our people." Here not only did Wurm reinforce the vehement distinction between regime and *Volk*, but he also claimed that even the crimes of these "leading men" must be understood in context: "These circumstances were given in Germany by the conditions which were created after the last war in consequence of the reparations burdens and the mass unemployment connected with them. These conditions finally bred an atmosphere of despair, and only this," Wurm argued, "explains how an extreme and fanatical nationalism could come to power." Wurm then combined the limitation of responsibility to the leadership and the comparative relativization: "Every people has its Jacobins who come to power under certain circumstances."[37]

The real danger for Bishop Wurm and many others who attempted to limit any implication of the Stuttgart Declaration was that it might be used to legitimate harsh treatment of Germany. As a result of the crimes committed by leading individuals, Wurm argued, Germany "is *therefore* threatened with measures of expiation [*Sühnemassnahmen*]" [emphasis added]. Although it may not be theologically clear how one could be threatened with expiation (everywhere else, others are arguing that this must be self-generated), Wurm was well understood; his formulations were wholly consonant with the widespread feeling that Germany was the true victim. In perhaps one of the most egregious statements in all postwar history, especially considering the moral authority of the source, Wurm practically lectures the Archbishop of Canterbury—a city, it is important to point out, whose architectural majesty was destroyed by German firebombs, to say nothing of the human costs: "It is clear to us that our citizens would not be

37. Quoted in Price and Schorske, *The Problem of Germany*, 121.

dying of hunger on the roads, our soldiers would not be withering away in detention camps, if millions had not been forced previously to endure a similar fate." So far so good, but then comes a classic application of the inevitable *Aber*: nevertheless, "[i]t is from a sense of deep concern that we call your attention to one fact: good has not simply triumphed over evil with the Allied victory." The real culprit producing the true paramount suffering, for Wurm, is denazification: "What has been done since then in many occupation zones in the sphere of Denazification was likewise not always designed to awaken the impression of a higher degree of justice and humanity." All this is perhaps run-of-the-mill equivocation, but Wurm exceeds the bounds in the next sentence: "To squeeze the German people together in an ever more crowded space and to reduce its possibilities for life as much as possible cannot, in fundamental terms, be evaluated any differently than the extermination plans of Hitler against the *Jewish race*."[38] Niemöller's statement that Germany must acknowledge the crimes that were committed against Poland produced catcalls. But this statement by Wurm raised no hackles, and the bishop remained one of the most influential religious and political figures in the emerging Federal Republic of Germany.[39]

Wurm, it is important to note, did not represent the ultra-Right wing of the church, but embodied mainstream thinking on denazification. In the spring of 1946, the EKD began a concerted campaign against denazification. The church leaders' declaration (issued on May 2) did recognize some need for cleansing: "The so-called denazification is concerned with freeing the German people from the destructive influences of National Socialism. The necessity of such purification is recognized by the church." Again, however, the symbolic boundary is of the utmost importance. They supported punishment, but only for those "who have committed a crime in connection with National Socialist rule." They found it inappropriate to hold accountable people who "joined National Socialist organizations out of pure motives and in ignorance of their true nature." After all, they only wanted to free Germany from "the destructive influences of National Socialism," which clearly were not co-extensive with National Socialism *per se*.[40] As was the case for the policy debates that we examined earlier, many Germans felt that early enthusiasm was forgivable idealism; only later opportunism was condemnable.

38. Quoted in Greschat, *Im Zeichen der Schuld*, 29 (emphasis added).
39. Wurm, born in 1868, retired in 1949 and died in 1953.
40. Quoted in Price and Schorske, *The Problem of Germany*, 124.

We will soon see this argument again as a defense raised by ultraconservatives, who sought to qualify their early support for the regime as justified while distinguishing themselves from those "truly responsible" for the later criminal policies and aggressive war. Echoing an earlier assertion by Kogon, everyone is entitled to a political mistake (though many failed even to acknowledge that early support for the regime was a true mistake). The important boundary, again, is between National Socialism itself, and the *destructive influences* of National Socialism. As such, widespread popular support for the Nazis before, say, 1943 was not really culpable. This declaration by the EKD also called into question the legal basis for charging those "who have committed a crime," insofar as it raised the legal principle *nulla poena sine lege* (no punishment without law): charging Germans for crimes that were not illegal under the Third Reich offends the natural sense of justice. Most important for many Protestant leaders, however, was the fear that "indiscriminate punishment" and "harsh treatment" would create sympathy for communism. As we already saw in the discussion of denazification in chapter 6, Wurm told the *New York Times* that there was "something Bolshevistic" about the American program. Of course, one could point out that some in the Protestant church—namely, Martin Niemöller—remained strongly nationalist; thus a repudiation of denazification was not always motivated by a fear of communism but sometimes by a fear of damage to national honor. Partly for this reason, Niemöller—who lost many American supporters when he traveled to the United States with his openly communist daughter—himself remained open to neutralist positions and largely closed to strategies of Western integration. In this, as we will see, Niemöller shared much with the SPD leader Kurt Schumacher.

* * *

Throughout 1946 and 1947, Protestant leaders continued to debate the virtually inextricable questions of denazification and the meaning of the Stuttgart Declaration. On the one side, Niemöller and his associates sought a reaffirmation of German guilt and the necessity of repentance as the only road to renewal through God. On the other side, Wurm and even Asmussen argued that this was too much to inflict on the German people at that time, when they were suffering so under occupation and denazification. For Niemöller and others, criticism of Allied occupation policy (namely denazification—which was justified) had led to an "accounting mentality" (*Aufrechnungsmentalität*—which was not) in which continual assessment of damages caused to Germany was distracting from the theologically *sui generis* need for confessing guilt. For their opponents, the role of the church was to provide comfort and alleviate misery where they found it in their people; further accusations would be too much to bear.

That is not to say, of course, that Niemöller was not also highly critical of the occupation. The difference between the two camps is, again, one of symbolic distinctions. For Niemöller and his supporters, the theological import of repentance was a matter for God; this was a matter of conviction, and was not mitigated by circumstance. Following Barth, it did not matter who was making the accusation—one could also learn from a sinner. For Wurm, Meiser, and others, theological and political imperatives were clearly tied together. They were reluctant to attempt to separate out the theological from the political because they believed the world would misunderstand it. This assumes, of course, that they felt there was sufficient warrant for a specific theological confession before God for what Germans had done in the Third Reich. There is good reason to believe that many in the Protestant church did not truly believe such warrant existed, at least not for themselves or for wide segments of the population.

Niemöller continued to push his two-track strategy throughout 1946 and 1947, calling for a boycott of the *Spruchkammern* while pressing for further reinforcement of the Stuttgart Declaration; Wurm and others continued a more one-sided attack on denazification. But Niemöller did achieve something of a victory. The result was two separate statements from late 1947. The first of these—the so-called "Darmstadt Message"— was justified by a *critique* of the traditional Lutheran teaching on the separation of the two kingdoms of heaven and earth, which underlay Niemöller's political strategy. But the argument—summarized in a speech by Karl Barth—was used to *support* the qualification of the critique of denazification through a reinvigorated confession, rather than to mitigate the power of confession by pointing a finger at the sins of others. The final draft of the Darmstadt Message was, again, a compromise; furthermore, only a minority were at the final meeting to approve it, and it was considered at the time a dangerous product of a fringe group. This is partly why it does not have the place in memory that the Stuttgart Declaration does. But, in effect, it was the Darmstadt Message that secured the memory not of itself, but of the Stuttgart Declaration as a recognition of guilt. It did so by hardening the debate: either one accepted the meaning of an acknowledgment as sanctioned by the Darmstadt Message, or one opposed the Stuttgart Declaration; it was no longer possible or necessary to debate its meaning.

The Darmstadt Message begins with a recognition, if not of "collective guilt" (*Kollektivschuld*), then with an acknowledgment of "common guilt" (*Gesamtschuld*)], though it does not offer an explanation of the difference:

> We have been given the message of reconciliation with God through Christ. . . . This message will not be heard, accepted, and followed and realized if we do not allow ourselves to be acquitted of our common [*gesamt*, not *kollektiv*] guilt, of the guilt of the fathers and our own, and if we do not allow ourselves through Jesus Christ, the good shepherd, to be called home also from all false and evil ways that we as Germans in our political will and action have followed into error.

The message then enumerates the errors, including dreaming of a special German destiny, which led to unrestrained use of political power; resisting necessary changes in society with a "Christian Front," thereby collaborating in the conservative defense of entrenched powers ("We denied the right to revolution, but we tolerated and approved the development of an absolute dictatorship"); drawing a self-righteous line between good and evil, light and darkness, just and unjust with political means, thus denying the universal availability of God's grace; and even failing to heed the Marxist concern for material inequality, thus not making the cause of the poor and disenfranchised a matter for Christianity. (This last point—with its socialist overtones—was hotly contested, and partly contributed to the narrow place of the Darmstadt Message in memory). In sum, this statement provided a much more thorough reckoning with the failed *politics* of the church. Nevertheless, critics in later periods have charged that there was still no description of *specific* acts in the context of National Socialism or naming of victims.[41]

Following the Darmstadt Message, moreover, came a decisive repudiation of denazification at the end of 1947 in the form of a proclamation from the Church Leadership of the State of Hesse, which was led by Martin Niemöller.[42] The proclamation was a harsh denunciation. Instead of producing insight and reconciliation, denazification measures were yielding bitterness and resistance, and were being misused as an "instrument of revenge." The fault for this bitterness and resistance was with the measures themselves, which required "a great part of the population to justify themselves and to prove themselves innocent." Such matters as these, the proclamation states, the church had been arguing for a long time, to no effect. It

---

41. The full text of the Darmstadt Message (*Darmstädter Wort*) is reprinted in Greschat, *Im Zeichen der Schuld*, 85–86.

42. "Kanzelabkündigungen der hessischen Kirchenleitung zur Jahreswende 1947/48 betreffend die Entnazifizierung," reprinted in Kleßmann, *Die doppelte Staatsgründung*, 367–87.

isn't that the church has not sought "a real liberation from the evil spirit [*Ungeist*] of National Socialism." But today "a complete catastrophe is apparent." "The attempt to purge National Socialism by means of this law is a total failure." In fact, "this kind of denazification has led to conditions that at every turn remind of the years of terror that lie behind us." The reason is that hundreds of thousands of people now find themselves under relentless pressure to use any means, honest or dishonest, to wash themselves clean. As a result, one can only conclude that "the ancient system of blood revenge [*Sippenrache*] has returned"; too many Germans have been forced into a crisis of conscience. The fault for all of this lies, the proclamation implies, entirely with the nature of the policy. As such, the leaders of the Protestant church in Hesse were calling on all Christians, as a matter of conscience, to refuse to cooperate any further with these measures. Trials against individual criminals should continue, but "the period of schematic evaluation of entire groups of persons because of their membership in organizations or institutions of the National Socialist dictatorship" must end, and it should be hastened by German refusal to participate. The Protestant church, it is clear, had finally come into its own as a political force.

The Catholic Church

The situation of the Catholic Church was much simpler, in part because of the history and institutional structure of Catholicism. Unlike Protestantism, Catholicism was rigidly hierarchical and autonomous from local political institutions. This had two implications. First, there was no possibility of significant internal dissent, for instance in the form of an apostate faction siding with or against the Nazis: obedience to the church was always paramount. Second, because the church was not dependent on local political authorities, it could not be integrated into any political program. Unlike the Protestants, the Catholic Church in Germany was thus able to resist any effort at *Gleichschaltung* (assimilation). Indeed, the desire to avoid any attack on church autonomy seems to have been a primary motivation for Catholic policy (though this characterization might be disputed by church officialdom): on July 20, 1933, the papal nuncio signed a concordat with the Nazi government of Germany, thereby ensuring the inviolability of the church.[43]

---

43. There is an extensive, and often quite polemical, literature on the role of the Catholic Church during National Socialism. Some that I have consulted include Phayer, *The Catholic Church and the Holocaust*; Kertzer, *The Pope against the Jews*; Conway, *The Nazi Persecution of the Churches*; Goldhagen, *A Moral Reckoning*.

The Catholic hierarchy was thus in a paradoxical situation in the aftermath of the war. Through their agreement with the Nazis, they had avoided being infiltrated. This in turn contributed to their reputation as an anti-Nazi organization. Nevertheless, this reputation was not entirely deserved, since official Catholic resistance to the Nazis was at least in part motivated by the desire to maintain autonomy in addition to any possible substantive political disagreement. Indeed, the *Reichstag* deputies of the Catholic Center Party had voted for the Enabling Act (*Ermächtigungsgesetz*), and the church had lifted its ban on Catholic membership in the Nazi Party. The concordat, moreover, served Nazi as well as Catholic interests, enabling the party to claim a legitimacy that had to that point eluded them. That is not to say that the Catholic Church did not have valiant opponents of National Socialism in its ranks and did not offer institutional resistance. But later critics charged that the concordat also signaled to lay Catholics that resistance was not necessary. In the wake of the war, moreover, the March 1937 papal encyclical titled "With Burning Concern" (*Mit brennender Sorge*), in which the Vatican warned of violations of religious freedom and human rights, was held up as evidence of the church's proper conduct. The official church explanation for not having done more is that there was nothing more that could have been done, and symbolic gestures would have hampered its ability to protect its loyal subjects. Whether the church actually retained significant abilities in this regard is disputable. At any rate, that the church deserved the full extent of its anti-Nazi reputation is not quite as clear as was maintained.

Official postwar doctrine for the German Catholic Church was framed by Pope Pius XII's first statement after the surrender of Germany, titled "The Church and National Socialism." This statement began by recognizing the ways in which the church had been oppressed institutionally and the resultant suffering of the clergy and their followers. But the statement explicitly denied any regrets about church policy, maintaining that all the major decisions had been the right ones given the circumstances. The pope defended the concordat as having strengthened the church's position and prevented disruption of ecclesiastical affairs (it was indeed Pius XII—formerly Cardinal Pacelli—who before becoming pope had been the papal nuncio to Germany and subsequently the Vatican secretary of state who signed the concordat). The statement praised the millions of Catholics "who had never ceased, even in the last years of the war, to raise their voices" and who had, despite everything, continued to follow "a Catholic way of life." As further evidence of the church's correct behavior, the statement recalled the above-mentioned 1937 encyclical as having provided "light, leadership, and comfort and strength to all those who took the Christian religion seriously." It was not the church's fault if some had not done so, if some had allowed themselves to be blinded by prejudice. But "no one could accuse the church of failing clearly to point out the true character of the National Socialist movement and the danger it presented to Christian culture."[44] The prediction in this last sentence proved untrue: the church was roundly attacked in the 1960s for covering up its lack of action.[45]

Despite this clear statement by the pope, some German Catholic clergymen were indeed embarrassed by the concordat. Partly as a result of this discomfort, participants in the German bishop's conference at Fulda on August 23, 1945, criticized Catholic individuals who, they believed, were guilty of errors.[46] "We most deeply deplore," the conference statement read, "that many Germans, also from among our ranks, have let themselves be deluded by the false teachings of the National Socialists, remaining indifferent to the crimes against human freedom and human value, that many supported the crimes by their attitude, and others even became criminals themselves."

Nevertheless, any guilt is qualified in at least three ways. First, as the statement just quoted asserted, it was individual Germans who were being condemned, not all Germans and, more important, not the church or clergy as institutions; this is clear through the distancing strategy that resorts to the third person. Second, also according to the statement, any errors seemed to be passive, matters of having "let themselves be deluded." And third, the remainder of the statement offered contextual considerations as mitigating factors. On the one hand, "[a]ll those bear a heavy responsibility who were in a position to know what was going on, who could have used their influence to prevent these crimes, but failed to do so, even made these crimes possible and thereby proclaimed their solidarity with the criminals." On the other hand, an "inevitable *Aber*" follows: "*But* we also know that with those who were in a subordinate position, especially civil servants and teachers, party membership often did not mean an inner agreement with the terrible deeds of the regime. Quite a few joined out of ignorance of the activities and goals of the party, many out of necessity, and many also out of the good intention of preventing evil."[47] Ultimately, guilt had to be decided on a case-by-case basis, "in

44. Quoted in Spotts, *The Churches and Politics in Germany*, 29–30.

45. Rolf Hochhuth's stage play—*Der Stellvertreter*—is the most prominent example of this attack.

46. The text of the Fulda Conference Statement is reprinted in Kleßmann, *Die doppelte Staatsgründung*, 377–78.

47. Ibid., 377 (emphasis added).

order that the innocent do not have to suffer with the guilty. For this we bishops were engaged from the beginning and we will also engage ourselves in the future." The implied conclusion of the Fuldau conference was thus, following the Vatican, that the church had not done anything wrong; all guilt was individual. As a result, the Catholic Church had no reason to question its own doctrines, to examine its relationship to politics (indeed, the conference prohibited clergy from taking an explicitly political role), and as a result to reorganize.

* * *

That the Catholic bishops meant their promise to engage against "collective judgments" was already clear in their early statements on Allied policy, and became increasingly so in their attacks on denazification. In the last months of the war, a number of prominent Catholic clergymen indicated that they would continue to see the invading Western armies as the enemy. The reason was that they did not believe the Western Allies sufficiently grasped the danger from communism. For the church, there was no greater fear than that the Germans, in response to hardships of the occupation, would be driven into the hands of the godless communists. Against the Nazis the church had preserved its autonomy; against the Soviets they had no such hope. Their appeal for leniency for the German people was thus not primarily based on notions of Christian charity; instead, it was a political matter. One indicator of this is that in the early weeks of the occupation, church authorities called for stricter control of the DPs, who were seen as a force of disorder.

As Cardinal Frings of Cologne, perhaps the most important Catholic in postwar Germany, put it, "After the Third Reich we had expected improvement. Instead everything has become worse." At the first postwar assembly of Catholics in Cologne, Frings even managed to shock his congregation by speaking not of the need for spiritual renewal, but of the barbarity of the Russians, who had executed his brother. Frings repeatedly reminded that the central task of the church was to protect its flock from communist atheism. As for National Socialism, Frings simply asserted, "We German Catholics are not National Socialists." As for collective guilt, it was summarily dismissed as an obviously unacceptable proposition. As Bishop von Galen put it in a July 1945 sermon, "If anyone today contends that the entire German population and each of us made himself guilty through atrocities committed by members of our population during the war, that is unjust." And, "If anyone says that the entire German population and each of us is implicated in the crimes committed in foreign countries and especially in the concentration camps that is an untrue and unjust accusation against many of us."[48]

Again, German Catholic reactions to collective guilt were legitimated by the pope himself. In February 1946, at an investiture of German cardinals, the Pope stated that "[i]t is wrong to treat someone as guilty when personal guilt cannot be proved, only because he belonged to a certain community. It is meddling in the prerogatives of God to attribute collective guilt to a whole people and to try to treat them accordingly." It is thus no surprise that the Protestant Stuttgart Declaration aroused various degrees of scorn from the Catholic hierarchy. According to Cardinal Jäger of Paderborn: "I respect the spirit of Bishop Wurm's declaration on the subject of war guilt, but such statements should not be made in the open hearing of youth. In order to influence a man you must acknowledge what was right and straight in him." Cardinal Frings was, characteristically, not so diplomatic. In his New Year's Eve message of 1946, he condemned "those who cannot do enough to proclaim the guilt of their own people to the world and to confess repeatedly before mankind." In this, Frings presaged the tone of German neoconservatives in the 1980s, who charged that the preoccupation with "mastering the past" by the Left in the 1960s was a form of ridiculous national "self-flagellation." Of course, one does not have to wait until the 1980s to find such statements. As we will see shortly, ultraconservative intellectuals who were tainted by their early support for the Nazi regime worked hard to discredit any sense of guilt in the immediate aftermath of the war.

Without a sense of collective guilt to stand in the way, Frings and others led vigorous attacks against denazification and Allied policy more generally, not even stopping short of equating the occupation authorities with the Nazis (Frings claimed conditions worsened with the occupation). In a July 1945 sermon, for instance, Bishop von Galen of Münster charged that occupation policy "can only be explained on the grounds of the hate and thirst for revenge of our former enemies of war." He charged the British with intentionally starving the Germans. Pointing out the hunger among their own people, British authorities angrily demanded a retraction. Von Galen did as he was told, but only to the letter. In an interview he explained his views by arguing that the British had not yet (July 1945 after all!) restored the liberties denied Germans like himself by the Nazis. As a result, he could see no difference between the British Military Government and National Socialism. As evidence, he claimed that political prisoners were being held in "concentration camps," in which they were even (!) denied mail and packages; while the Nazis had merely pensioned off their opponents in the civil service, he charged, the British were dismissing them summarily. Ultimately, the real danger for von Galen was that this would all lead to radicalization of the population, which was an open invitation to the communists. In this vein, an Easter 1946 pastoral letter criticized the expulsion of the Germans from Selesia and Czechoslovakia as evidence of Allied duplicity. The AMG forbade the letter to be read because they feared it would foster "resentment, unrest and possibly riot."[49]

Cardinal Frings was also not hesitant to express his condemnations. He called putative Allied indifference to hunger and cold in the German population "an act against humanity." When faced with British billeting policy, under which British soldiers could commandeer shelter according to their needs, Frings said that forcing Germans out of their homes "seems to me to contradict all rules of humanity." In response to British dismantling of the German arms manufacturer Krupp, Frings argued this would destroy the city of Essen. Most famously, in his New Year's 1946 sermon, Frings instructed his congregation that it would not be immoral to steal what one needed to stay nourished and warm, coal in particular. The widespread practice of creative appropriation thus became known by the verb "to frings" (*fringsen*), to engage in petty theft. Most generally, Cardinal Frings argued that "all guilt is most deeply and ultimately guilt toward the Lord God and . . . it must be expiated before God. . . . [T]he Lord God is the final judge of all mankind." His concern was that "when men judge men—particularly victors, the vanquished—*pharisaeism* very easily results" [emphasis added]. Like many others we have already seen, Frings rejected denazification with the *nulla poene sin lege* principle: denazification thus should be limited to "making judgments upon actions which were previously subject to legal punishment."[50] The not too subtle fear, for Frings, was that if denazification was too widespread, only the Social Democrats and communists would remain unscathed.

Conclusion

While the history of the German churches throughout and following the period of National Socialism is a fascinating story in its own right, it is important to remember the purpose of outlining it here. The main point

49. Ibid., 63, 64.
50. Ibid., 65, 96.

here is to lay the foundation for understanding the afterlives of these early formulations. And indeed they were quite consequential. They reflected and helped to establish a discursive environment for the interpretation of the Nazi past and for confronting charges, as well as one's own feelings, of guilt. This discursive environment lived on not only in the future political statements of the churches, but in the official discourse of the Federal Republic. Future speakers drew language and logics from these formulations, to say nothing of their personal roles in creating them (Gustav Heinemann is but one example). Moreover, these formulations served not just as prisms shaping the interpretation of National Socialism, parts of the history of memory. The Stuttgart Declaration, Frings's charges, and Niemöller's speeches all became part of the "memory of memory" of the Nazi period, objects of commemoration in and of themselves.

While there were important differences between the Protestant and Catholic approaches, it is perhaps even more striking how similar they were. It is in this sense that we can speak of a discursive environment—not as a perfect unity, but as varying degrees of shared perception. It is important to note, however, that these perceptions were in many ways uniquely German; it was not as if others did not see things very differently. In this regard, the 1947 report of Hoyt Price and Carl Schorske[51] (written on behalf of the Council on Foreign Relations) is an important piece of evidence that other understandings were possible, not just from the perspective of a new generation in the 1960s who did not bear the same biographical relation to events, but at the time these positions were being formulated. It is not, that is, as if the German speakers were unaware of alternative assessments to their own.

Two examples from Price and Schorske are most illustrative. First, in reaction to the vehemence of the *nulla poene sin lege* argument, Price and Schorske point out the contradiction between arguing that a lack of a "natural sense of right" during the war could be excused with an appeal to the very same sense of right immediately after the war:

> Thus participation in the lawless Nazi movement is justified by the fact that the Nazi state made no laws against the excesses it encouraged, whilst the natural sense of right is invoked against the denazification law which has a fixed scale of penalties in accordance with the magnitude of the offenses, and which unlike Nazi judicial procedure, allows to the accused full opportunity for defense. It would seem moral confusion of a high order when the sense of right has as its norm the lawless condition which the Nazis legalized.

51. An intellectual exile, Carl Schorske went on to an enormously distinguished career as an intellectual historian in the United States at Wesleyan and then Princeton.

Second, where the churches resisted denazification and collective guilt so vigorously out of a fear of communism, Price and Schorske hint that there are costs to too vigorous a *Realpolitik* defense against communism. Regarding the Protestants, for instance, they argue that "[g]iven the nature and purpose of the law, and the support which the political parties have accorded it, the [governing council of the Protestant church] does not further the democratic cause by making itself the leading spokesman of the opposition." In their summary of the positions of the churches on collective guilt and denazification, they argue:

> The charge of collective guilt is a loose one by either moral or sociological standards. It implies censure of those individuals or groups who gave their lives in the fight against Nazis. The admission of collective guilt, moreover, is no necessary part of a complete repudiation of Nazism. Rejection of collective guilt by spokesmen of the churches, therefore, cannot of itself be regarded as harmful to the democratic cause. These spokesmen, however, have combined, and confounded, the issue of collective guilt with an analysis of the causes of Nazism. The attribution of the rise of Nazism to the Treaty of Versailles and the accusation that the victors in World War I are the guilty parties are mis-readings of a complicated history which might contribute to an aggressive nationalist revival. They serve only to discourage that critical examination of Germany's history which is so sorely needed if the Germans are to break the shackles of the past.

As a semi-official report of the Western Allies, this statement should be recalled in the context of the continually vigorous defenses against putative collective guilt accusations.[52]

52. Price and Schorske, *The Problem of Germany*, 125, 122–23.

CHAPTER 11

The Politics of the Past?

The Potsdam communiqué of August 2, 1945, called for "the eventual reconstruction of German political life on a democratic basis." The rhetoric of all four powers (the United States, Britain, France, and the Soviet Union) had long agreed that "democratization" was the overriding goal for Germany, though such agreement was only possible because the term "democratization" was never specifically defined. The Potsdam agreement implied a gradual reconstruction modeled on the American ideal of grassroots participation, meaning that political responsibility would begin first at the most local levels and then only slowly be allowed to develop at higher levels, never fully attaining the degree of national integration characteristic of the Nazi (or Bismarckian) system. Nevertheless, the Soviets preempted any Western plans (which, in this regard, were still vague) by granting licenses to four "antifascist" parties earlier than the West had anticipated, on June 10, 1945. They were motivated at least in part by the propaganda advantage of appearing to be the first to begin the "democratization" process, though doing so also served to preempt any limitations on the central organization of the Communist Party in their zone that might emerge from Potsdam. Indeed, the "Appeal of the Central Committee of the German Communist Party to the German People" appeared without delay on June 11, 1945. The Western Allies thus followed earlier than they otherwise had wanted, the Americans on August 13 (though revising the licenses on August 27 to restrict organization to the local level only), the British on September 15, and the French not until December.[1]

---

1. Eschenburg, *Jahre der Besatzung*, 171–72; Rogers, *Politics after Hitler*, 21; Naimark, *The Russians in Germany*, especially 257–58, 271–75.

There was no real disagreement over what kinds of parties would be licensed in all four zones. The Allies agreed that the major nonfascist political traditions should be represented, but that there should not be too many parties.[2] For both the Allies and the Germans, memory of how narrow factionalism had made it impossible to build coalitions in the Weimar Republic, and thus contributed to the political chaos that represented National Socialism's opportunity to gain power, stood as a powerful warning against there being too many parties.[3] Moreover, the dislocations of war and the devastation of the German social and economic structure had eroded the classic social bases of the pre–Nazi Party landscape.[4] The goal was thus to establish broad-based parties representing the spectrum of acceptable worldviews (*Weltanschauungen*). As we will see, this created particular challenges for both the Christian Democrats and the liberals, whose postwar organizations tried to bridge deeply entrenched schisms.[5]

The early establishment of political parties created unusual difficulties for both the Allies and the Germans. For their part, the occupation authorities faced administrative challenges and the overriding need to maintain order. The early strategy in the Western zones was thus to appoint German administrators first at the local level, and then at higher levels. Very quickly, the Western Allies reformed the German province (*Land*) system, and appointed minister-presidents to deal with the affairs left to the Germans and to carry out the directives of the occupation authorities. The Western Allies did not want to deal with the inconvenience of conflict,

---

2. See especially Rogers, *Politics after Hitler;* Wolgast, *Die Wahrnehmung des Dritten Reiches in der unmittelbaren Nachkriegszeit.* Different licensing procedures in the different zones resulted in slightly different party spectrums. In the American zone in particular there was a wider array of allowed parties, including some on the far Right.

3. It was not until after the founding of the Federal Republic that a constitutional amendment introduced the so-called "5 percent clause," which served to limit the number of parties in the Parliament by distributing seats proportionally to only those parties that had received at least 5 percent of the votes. This prevented small parties from gaining single or small numbers of seats based on a direct proportion of their election results, thus limiting splintering and the resultant difficulties of building coalitions with many small parties.

4. See especially Linz, *The Social Bases of West German Democracy.*

5. General accounts of the history of the West German party system include Heidenheimer, *The Governments of Germany;* Rogers, *Politics after Hitler;* Gabbe, *Parteien und Nation;* Kleßmann, *Die doppelte Staatsgründung;* Walter, *Neubeginn—Nationalisozialismus—Widerstand;* Wolgast, *Die Wahrnehmung des Dritten Reiches in der unmittelbaren Nachkriegszeit.* Relevant documents can be found in Kleßmann, *Die doppelte Staatsgründung;* especially in Flechtheim, *Dokumente zur parteipolitischen Entwicklung in Deutschland seit 1945.*

negotiation, and consensus-building as they sought to reestablish order. For that matter, neither did many Germans. The minister-presidents operated—within their allowed purviews—autocratically. Opinion polls showed that of all the promised freedoms, moreover, a political party was the one most Germans were willing to give up first in favor of material security.[6]

This low valuation of political parties tapped a deep vein in German political culture, which had always favored the state over society. Society was theorized as a fractured cauldron of competing and changing interests. Only the state could rise above the partial concerns of factions and unite the people. As agents of society, parties were suspect. During the imperial period, political parties were not constitutional elements of the state. While they had a bit more secure status in the Weimar period, this was when the worst fears (or best hopes) of the critics of party politics were fulfilled. Distaste for party politics was one factor contributing to support for the so-called *"Führer-State"* (leader state) of National Socialism. Beyond this history of the German state, however, many ordinary Germans were simply indifferent to political life, feeling they had paid dearly for their recent enthusiasms and preferring instead to let the entire enterprise proceed *ohne mich!* (without me), as a later slogan put it.

To their credit, the two most important political figures of the postwar period—the Catholic conservative Konrad Adenauer and the Social Democrat Kurt Schumacher—tacitly agreed on the importance of a vigorous party system, including a strong opposition. Indeed, both criticized the minister-president system, scorning what they charged was hypocrisy of the Allies: this was no model of democracy. Rightly, however, they saw the potential of a vigorous but disciplined partisanship in organizations that could fulfill the tasks of the transcendent state without at the same time being immune from challenge and change. They were both deeply concerned with the apathy they saw in the population as a reaction to the disappointments and distortions of German passions, and worked hard to overcome it.

The major question for German politicians during the occupation period, however, was who had the right to lead. The claim of an historical right by Kurt Schumacher on behalf of the Social Democratic Party, and the vigorous response to it by Adenauer, was the central agony of immediate postwar politics.

6. Merritt, *Democracy Imposed*, 327–31. See also Edinger, *Kurt Schumacher*, 76.

Schumacher, Social Democracy, and Nazis

Background

Kurt Schumacher was the very embodiment of German political martyr-dom, a condition not unrelated to his claim to be the only legitimate leader for the new Germany.[7] Schumacher was both a Social Democrat and a nationalist, which gave his postwar rhetoric a quality that is perhaps sur-prising: Marxism is, in many versions, an internationalist constellation; and, from our contemporary vantage point, we sometimes wrongly associ-ate nationalism more with the Right than Left. Schumacher was con-cerned, however, that Social Democracy not be associated, particularly by the younger generation, with a politics of national decline.

Unlike many Social Democratic leaders, Schumacher himself did not stem from working-class origins. After losing an arm fighting in World War I, Schumacher studied law and economics in Berlin and wrote a doc-toral dissertation on Marxist state theory, subsequently worked as a news-paper editor, and then served in the Württemberg state legislature. He was elected to the *Reichstag* in 1928. The only speech he ever gave there was a response to Goebbels's 1932 accusation that the Social Democrats were a "party of deserters," in which Schumacher referred to National Socialism as an "appeal to the inner swine in human beings," and labeled the National Socialist movement "the ceaseless mobilization of human stupidity."[8] With the Nazi seizure of power on January 30, 1933, Schumacher backed away from the classic hostility between the Social Democrats and communists and called for a common front against the Nazis, to no avail. In doing so, he thus elevated himself to a high rank on the Nazi's list of internal enemies. Nevertheless, he declined to flee, feel-ing an obligation not to abandon his party comrades. He was arrested in July 1933, sent to Dachau two years later, and remained there for many years. Expecting him to die shortly of his illnesses and injuries, the Nazis released him in 1943, after which he lived quietly with his sister and her family in Hannover. Though he was not involved with the July 20, 1944, conspiracy (indeed, as we will see, he had little positive to say about the conspirators and what he saw as their reactionary motives), he was

7. See especially Edinger, *Kurt Schumacher.*
8. Discussed in ibid., 42; Herf, *Divided Memory,* 240–41; see also Albrecht, *Kurt Schumacher,* 70–71. Similar analyses to the readings I undertake in this chapter—though with somewhat different emphases—can be found in Wolgast, *Die Wahrnehmung des Dritten Reiches in der unmittelbaren Nachkriegszeit;* Herf, *Divided Memory;* Baumgärtner, *Reden Nach Hitler.*

nevertheless arrested again and held until April 1945, when Hannover was "liberated" by the Americans.

First Principles

After his release near war's end, Schumacher set to work immediately to reestablish the SPD, to assume leadership of it, and to have it assume leadership of the new Germany.[9] Already on April 19, 1945, surviving members met to begin reorganizing the party. In this, they had a distinct advantage over the other parties (with the exception of the communists): their identity was intact and, following years of martyrdom, their self-regard was stronger than ever. More than the Christian centrists or the liberals (who eventually would form, respectively, the CDU and FDP), the SPD picked up where it had left off, ready finally to fulfill what they saw as their destiny. (Schumacher himself faced only the briefest challenge to his own role. During an October 1945 meeting with the SPD exile committee from London, that group's leader, Erich Ollenhauer, made a brief and ineffective play for leadership; Ollenhauer eventually succeeded Schumacher after his death in 1952.)[10]

While some points of emphasis changed slightly over time, the main themes of Schumacher's (and by extension the whole party's) position were already clear in a May 6, 1945, speech Schumacher delivered to the Hannover SPD (thus before the unconditional surrender), titled "We Do Not Despair!" There Schumacher laid out an orthodox Marxist explanation of the rise of National Socialism, emphasizing the failed politics of 1848 but, more important, the economic and political imperialism of the 1870s. In particular, he identified the "coalition of heavy and military industry and indeed of the entirety of modern finance capital with the powers of Prussian militarism," which, he declared, worked "against the interests of the workers and their political and social ideas." The result was a culture whose hallmark was "blind faith in the exclusive determining role of violence." This faith, according to Schumacher, was stronger and more destructive in Germany because, lacking a successful liberal tradi-

9. On the SPD in this period, see especially Klotzbach, *Der Weg zur Staatspartei;* Walter, *Neubeginn—Nationalsozialismus—Widerstand;* Wolgast, *Die Wahrnehmung des Dritten Reiches in der unmittelbaren Nachkriegszeit.*

10. Another source of dissent within the party came from Wilhelm Högner, minister-president of Bavaria, who favored a federalistic approach, which contrasted sharply with Schumacher's ideas for a centrally planned economy and national integration.

tion, the Germans were "intellectually and spiritually defenseless": "At the time, when successful struggles for political freedom were playing out [Germany's] inner history was still a purely feudal, military, and authoritarian history. The German middle class had been unable to bring its revolution of 1848 to a clear political result and in its most important regards [thus] made a coalition with the forces of reaction." As a result, Germany's economic elite was "more brutal . . . than that of the propertied fanatics of any other country." Without question, for Schumacher it was thus "big capital and its political agents who set the Third Reich in the saddle and led to war."[11]

Schumacher's description of the Nazis[12] in 1945 continued in the same vein as his 1932 *Reichstag* speech: "Under the Swastika flag assembled all those who, after the First World War, were unable to find their way back to an orderly life, all frauds from the business world, all the defective and unfit, all civil servants with poor grades and professional inadequacies, all failures and justly disadvantaged, the lazy and incompetent at life. They gave the party before 1933 its stamp."[13] (One is reminded of Carl Jung's 1936 description of Hitler as the embodiment of all the worst inadequacies of German society, and of Dorothy Thompson's description of the Nazis as the dregs of German society, quoted in chapter 3). As a result, Schumacher argued, the Nazi party had no original ideas of its own; for him, it was important to distinguish the transformations the Nazis brought about from the genuine revolution predicted by Marxist analysis. As in everything else, the Nazi "revolution" was, in his view, bogus and incomplete.

Schumacher was no less clear about the burden of guilt for National Socialism. For him there was no question that the "German name is defiled by the concentration camps, the persecution of the Jews, the barbaric execution of the war, the plundering and slave hunting in the occupied territories."[14] Schumacher was thus much more specific than virtually any other German speaker we have seen thus far, and certainly more than his rival Adenauer, particularly in that he included the Jews on the list of victims and dramatically enumerated Germany's war crimes. For those who sought exculpation by denying knowledge of what had transpired in the camps, for

11. Albrecht, *Kurt Schumacher*, 204–6.

12. After the war, Schumacher always referred only to the Nazis, never National Socialists, because he did not think them worthy of the name "socialist," and did not want such an association in people's minds. See Herf, *Divided Memory*, 219.

13. Albrecht, *Kurt Schumacher*, 210.

14. Ibid., 252.

example, Schumacher had no patience. As he stated in his August 1945 call for the rebirth of the SPD, "Their perpetual excuse 'I didn't know that!' is without moral and political value. It may be," he charged, "that they did not know everything, but they knew enough. Of the concentration camps they at least knew enough to have a dreadful fear." Indeed, "this fear was one of the main pillars of the system." Again describing in substantially more specific terms than most others, Schumacher sarcastically remarked that ordinary Germans certainly accepted the plunder their fathers, sons, and husbands brought back from the war (as we will see in the next chapter, the Norwegian writer Sigrid Undset made a similar—and consequential— charge in the summer of 1945). Most important, "they saw with their own eyes with what bestial meanness one humiliated, robbed, and hunted the Jews." No more powerful indictment of ordinary Germans is to be found anywhere in the discourse than the following: "They not only remained silent, they would even have preferred it if Germany had left them peace and even guaranteed them a little bit of profit with a victory in the Second World War."[15]

On the one hand, Schumacher thus identified a common guilt across German society, which he condemned with near totality: "They [presumably the majority of Germans] allowed and encouraged that a hoard of adventurers untested in capabilities and character snatched power for themselves, and they allowed this hoard to run things [*wirtschaften lassen*] uncontrolled. The complicity [*Mitschuld*] of large segments of the people for the bloody dominion of the Nazis lies in their belief in dictatorship and violence! This guilt cannot be expunged." He added the uncommon connection that it was this failure that had brought Germany to its current powerlessness, and argued that recognizing this connection was the "prerequisite" for a renewal through "repentance and change."[16]

On the other hand, Schumacher continued to reject the concept of "collective guilt," which he referred to in October 1945 as "a great historical lie with which one cannot undertake the reconstruction of Germany." He welcomed admissions of guilt like the Stuttgart Declaration only if they did not "extend guilt to people and currents which had always been deadly enemies of the Nazis," in other words to himself and his party comrades. Later, he distinguished among "actual Nazis," "hundreds of thousands of politically guilty," and "the great number of those who through their insolence,

15. Ibid., 217.
16. Ibid.

cynical and corrupt behavior supported the atmosphere of Nazism in busi-
nesses, on the street, and at home." While he advocated strict punishment,
most of the latter two categories should not, in his view, be included in
criminal prosecutions, though they should be disadvantaged: "The good
job belongs first to the proven enemy of the Nazis and only last to any old
harmless follower of the Nazis if no one better is available." As for the
"shameless heroes," they should be assigned "the hard and dirty work of
reconstruction." Former Nazis would be allowed to join the SPD only
under the strictest of conditions. A party statute called for their application
to be examined by a special committee appointed by the local party leadership council. None of this, however, applied to young people, whom
Schumacher characterized as having been defenseless against misleading
miseducation.[17]

While Schumacher later objected to what he saw as punitive policies
imposed by the Western Allies (seemingly in a manner not entirely consistent with his insistence that Germans acknowledge that the Nazis are to
blame for their postwar suffering), his major concern early on was with the
communists. As he noted, the communists were "the only party in Germany
which confesses the guilt of the whole German people for Nazism and thus
for the war." In fact, the Communist Party's early "Appeal" of June 11, 1945,
did indeed contain such language. After condemning the "conscienceless
adventurers and criminals . . . the carriers of reactionary militarism . . . the
imperialistic commanders of the Nazi Party, the leaders of the large banks
and concerns," the appeal continued:

> Not only Hitler is guilty of the crimes that were committed against humanity!
> The ten million Germans who voted for Hitler in the free elections of 1932,
> although we Communists warned "Whoever votes for Hitler votes for war!"
> carries its proportion of guilt.
>
> All those German men and women who indecisively and meekly stood by
> while Hitler seized power, while he destroyed all democratic organizations,
> above all the workers' labor movement, and the best Germans were locked up,
> tortured and lost their heads carry their proportion of guilt. All those Germans
> who saw "Greater Germany" in the wild militarism and the rearmament and
> glimpsed in the marching and exercising the uniquely blessed salvation of the
> nation carry guilt. . . .
>
> Hitler never would have been able to seize power, secure it, and lead his
> criminal war against the will of a unified and determined people.

17. Ibid., 215–17, 226–27.

Indeed, the communists even charged themselves:

> We German Communists declare that we also feel guilty because, despite the bloody sacrifices of our best fighters, as a result of a number of errors, we were unable to forge the anti-Fascist unity of the workers, farmers, and intellectuals against all opponents, to assemble among the working people the forces to topple Hitler.[18]

This language of the Communist Party is indeed superficially similar to that of the Stuttgart Declaration, in which church leaders acknowledged their guilt for not having prayed harder and made even greater sacrifices. But for Schumacher, the communist acceptance of collective guilt as expressed in the appeal was nothing but the disingenuous manifestation of reactionary forces: everyone is guilty, so no one is guilty. "This thesis, which declares every Nazi and every capitalist guilty in order to offer them an excuse . . . is a thoroughly reactionary formula which hinders the political emergence of a new, purged German people." The overriding purpose of this "naïve propaganda of contrition," Schumacher argued, was to underwrite Soviet demands for reparations.[19]

Nevertheless, Schumacher's response to the communists also implied a critique of the Western Allies. The Communist statement, he said, "does not contain a genuine admission of guilt, one which would encourage *all of the other enemies of Nazism* to examine their own policies in a self-critical manner," primarily meaning other Germans, but leaving open the possibility of Nazism's external opponents.[20] Indeed, in October 1945, Schumacher quipped, "We were sitting in concentration camps while other peoples were making alliances with the Hitler government." At the SPD's second Party Congress in 1947, he stated that "[w]e opposed the Nazis at great cost when it was still fashionable for the rest of the world to bid for their good will."[21] In this, Schumacher sounded similar to Wilhelm Röpke; by October 1945, Schumacher had already complained about the specter of "Vansittartism."[22]

Schumacher dismissed as well the July 20, 1944, conspiracy, whose efforts, from his perspective, came too late and for the wrong reasons:

18. The text of the "Appeal" is reprinted in Kleßmann, *Die doppelte Staatsgründung*, 411–14.
19. Albrecht, *Kurt Schumacher*, 279–81.
20. Ibid., 281 (emphasis added).
21. Edinger, *Kurt Schumacher*, 147.
22. Albrecht, *Kurt Schumacher*, 315.

"Before then, the officers of July 20, 1944 did not protest against Hitler's policies, against the concentration camps, the Pogrom against the Jews, the demoralization and bestialization of the German nation, or against the barbaric conduct of the war." Rather, he asserted, it "was only the fear of being pushed into the background in their own military sector that mobilized them." Consistent with his economistic analysis, Schumacher argued that "the revolt of July 20 did not emerge among its reactionary participants from any feeling of responsibility toward the German people or the world. It was concern over the fate of their own class and its property and their social position."[23] Only the Social Democratic resistance, it seems, was legitimate and well-motivated (Schumacher also accused the churches of fundamental failures).

All this analysis leads to one preordained conclusion: "Today in Germany," he said in his major address to the first national congress of the SPD in Hannover in May 1946, "democracy is no stronger than the Social Democratic Party. All of the others needed the war potential and supremacy of the Anglo-Saxon powers to discover their love for democracy. We did not need that; we would be democrats today even if the British and Americans were fascists." Because "Social Democracy was the only party in Germany that cleaved steadfastly to the principle of democracy and peace which has proven itself over the course of events," only the SPD had a right to lead. As the August 17, 1945, communiqué following the meeting between the Hannover SPD and the London exiles stated baldly:

> The Social Democrats in the underground did not shrink from the severest sacrifice, in order to be there as the strongest party after the collapse. . . . The Social Democratic Party, aware of being the only party in Germany whose politics of democracy and peace has withstood the test of the judgment of history, stands before its greatest task: to build a new better Reich out of the ruins of Germany.[24]

Leadership was thus his and his party's right.

Schumacher and the Jews

One of the most important differences between Schumacher's early rhetoric and that of other early leaders in postwar Germany was the priority it assigned to reparations, specifically to Jews. In June 1945, the SPD

23. Ibid., 275.
24. Ibid., 394, 231, 251.

declared, "The new state must repair what was transgressed against the victims of fascism, it must repair what the fascist rapacity perpetrated against the peoples of Europe."[25] Nevertheless, despite the admirable appearance (and indeed reality) of this sentiment, even the SPD's rhetoric was not free of the *Aufrechnungsmentalität* (balance-sheet mentality) we have already seen. In the summer of 1945, Schumacher stated that "[w]e want to deliver reparations. . . . But we do not want to commit suicide." Initiating without subtlety what would be a long-term indictment of occupation policy, he warned, "One cannot excuse the injustice today by pointing to past injustice. . . . The Nazi policy of plunder must not be a model for the policy of the United Nations."[26]

At the first national congress of the SPD in 1946, Schumacher stated, "Our first thoughts concern the dead." His list included:

> The victims of fascism among our own people. The dead from the freedom struggles of oppressed peoples. The army of millions of victims of the war and of all nations. The women and children who were swept away by bombs, hunger, and illness. The Jews who fell victim to the bestial racial madness of the Hitler dictatorship. All who, without regard to nation or race, lost their life in struggle against dictatorship, oppression, and the mad illusion of domination.

He vowed not to forget the SPD's own victims, and promised to erect a memorial to these freedom fighters who "gave their blood for the existence of an 'other' and better Germany."[27]

As elsewhere, Schumacher's inclusion of Jews on the list of those to be remembered was important and distinguished him from many of his contemporaries, though for this audience he did not single Jews out exclusively. By 1947, however, he highlighted the degree to which he was "astounded to see that today the part of humanity which was most persecuted by the Third Reich receives so little help and understanding from the world outside." In an implied distinction between himself and Adenauer and others, Schumacher exhorted, "Let's talk for once about that part of humanity which as a result of the frightfulness of the blows which it actually received had to become the symbol of all suffering. Let us talk for once about the Jews in Germany and the world."[28] He reminded his audience,

25. Kleßmann, *Die doppelte Staatsgründung*, 415.
26. Albrecht, *Kurt Schumacher*, 277.
27. Ibid., 386.
28. Ibid., 508.

however, that the SPD had opposed the Nazis while the rest of the world was still accommodating Hitler. He expressed outrage that current German suffering was said to be justified in view of their own culpability, again vitiating his earlier demand that people blame the Nazis for Germany's predicament.

That these remarks were also not solely for a German audience is obvious when one considers that Schumacher was at the time planning a trip, at the invitation of the Jewish Labor Committee of the American Federation of Labor, to the United States for late summer and early fall of 1947. In numerous speeches he would make on the trip, Schumacher vowed that he would pursue harsh punishment for crimes against the Jews and that he wanted to make anti-Semitism illegal; in a speech in San Francisco, he added that punishable individuals included those who "acquired wealth as a result of those persecutions." He made clear, however, that this did not mean collective guilt: "The whole German people, *those who are innocent and those who are guilty*, have an obligation for reparations to the Jews."[29] Nevertheless, these admirable statements once again were not free of a subtly implied political compensation for the Germans:

> Social Democracy opposes racist anti-Semitism with the same determination and relentlessness with which it rejects totalitarianism. With the same seriousness with which *we want to ensure that the Germans should not become a second-class people with fewer rights*, we fight for the Jews with all of the other peoples of the earth. In this sense, the cause of Jews in a new Germany is also a German cause and a cause for *the equal treatment of all people.*[30]

The implication, perhaps not so subtle when one is looking for it, is the classic equation of Germans and Jews.

Schumacher and the Allies

Throughout the following year, Schumacher's critical rhetoric concerning the occupation became more aggressive. At the 1948 party congress in Dusseldorf, he argued that the SPD "must protect Germany against the rapacity of the conquerors." Too much punishment, he warned, would only backfire. While he had always agreed that Germany's warmaking capacity should be eliminated, the extent of the "dismantling" was too much for him: "We have the honest intention to pay reparations, but we warn all

29. Quoted in Herf, *Divided Memory*, 258 (emphasis added).
30. Albrecht, *Kurt Schumacher*, 562 (emphasis added).

victors, big and little, not to rip pieces from the German people, leaving wounds which will fester for many years to come."[31]

It is thus no wonder that American, and particularly British, authorities found Schumacher difficult to deal with, and were greatly concerned with the possibility that he would be West Germany's new leader. Schumacher was arrogant and autocratic, and thus for many embodied discredited Prussian characteristics. As early as May 1945, he had bristled that the "victors are now going to make their peace terms, not ours," seeing no necessary limitation on German national interest with the collapse of National Socialism. He would continue to assert the independence of German interests from either block: "Only the SPD . . . ('Neither Russian nor British, French nor American') . . . spoke solely on behalf of the new Germany." And Schumacher himself did so with confidence: "What [Hitler] did, I probably know a great deal better from personal experience than those gentlemen throughout the world who now waste their ink on articles that will some day stand as monuments of human stupidity and heartlessness."[32] As for the victors, "perhaps they did not have quite so good an understanding of certain crucial issues at stake in contemporary Germany as the responsible leaders of the Social Democratic Party." As a high-ranking British officer put it, "the almost hysterical tone of his speeches was not particularly appealing, and the dislike of many British [officers] of this kind of rhetoric, which they compared to Hitler's speeches, was quite understandable."[33] Then again, they had their reservations about Schumacher's opponent as well.

Adenauer, Christian Democracy, and National Socialism

Fractured Origins

The initial conditions for the formation of the Christian Democratic Union (and its Bavarian sister party the Christian Social Union) was quite different from that for the SPD.[34] Before the Third Reich banned all parties but the NSDAP in 1933, there was a diverse array of parties representing interests across a spectrum, including national conservative, Catholic,

31. See Edinger, *Kurt Schumacher*, 154–55.
32. Ibid., 147–48.
33. Quoted in Bark and Gress, *A History of West Germany*, vol. 1, 118.
34. For background, see especially Becker, *CDU und CSU*; Heitzer, *Die CDU in der britischen Besatzungszone*; Mitchell, "Materialism and Secularism."

Protestant, and liberal, among others. Given the postwar desideratum of limiting the number of parties and the long and destructive history of conflict between confessional orientations (which split what otherwise might have been shared centrist interests), there was good reason—yet scant precedent—for creating a large umbrella party that would represent a united Christian worldview. Nevertheless, in part due to the regional restrictions on German political activity and in part to the diversity of intentions and positions, efforts to form what would become the CDU were highly fractured in the early months.[35]

The three most important circles were those in Berlin, Frankfurt, and Cologne. Though these groups aimed to overcome entrenched Catholic-Protestant suspicion, they were largely Catholic-dominated, though groups in places like Heidelberg and Stuttgart had a more Protestant cast. The Berlin group, which got the earliest start, was chaired by Jakob Kaiser, a leader of the Catholic trade union movement of the Weimer period, Center Party member of the *Reichstag* in the last year before the Nazi seizure of power, and active participant in various opposition activities who was forced into hiding following the July 20, 1944, coup attempt.[36] The Berlin CDU's program was at least in part influenced by that of the Frankfurt circle, the principal figures of which included Eugen Kogon and Walter Dirks, co-editors of the enormously significant journal *Frankfurter Hefte*. Both the Frankfurt and Berlin CDUs saw themselves as bridging the divide between Christian and socialist approaches. As Kogon and Dirks put it, however, they were strongly opposed to any sort of restoration or even mere recombination of old groups: "We do not want today," they wrote, "simply to take up where our predecessors had to stop in 1933 as if nothing has happened since then."[37] (In 1950, Dirks wrote a highly critical essay about what he called the "restorative character of the epoch," which became a standard reference for those on the Left).[38]

In contrast, both Dirks and Kogon and their Frankfurt colleagues sought in 1945 to build a party inspired by what they called "living Christianity." The Frankfurt program thus called for "[j]ustice, tolerance towards the fellow citizen, truthfulness, cooperative economic reason and

35. Kleßmann quotes a French newspaper in this regard: "This party is socialist and radical in Berlin, clerical and conservative in Cologne, capitalist and reactionary in Hamburg and counter-revolutionary and seperatist in Munich." *Die doppelte Staatsgründung*, 143.
36. See Conze, *Jakob Kaiser.*
37. See Eschenburg, *Jahre der Besatzung*, 187–89. For a more thorough analysis of Dirks and Kogon's program as editors of *Frankfurter Hefte*, see Ewald, *Die gescheiterte Republik.*
38. Dirks, "Der restaurative Charakter der Epoche."

respect for other peoples and their ways of life."[39] Given the socialist cast of their Christianity, however, both the Frankfurt and Berlin programs called for much more radical economic measures than were later sustainable within the CDU, and likely beyond what the Western Allies would have accepted. Kaiser proclaimed repeatedly that the bourgeois age had come to an end, and thus concurred in this regard with Schumacher, though Kaiser distinguished between "Christian socialism" and "collective socialism." Kaiser's Berlin program, like the Frankfurt approach, called for socialization of mining and utilities, close control of industry, and restrictions on large estates and the like. Given the tension between the capitalist West and the socialist East, the new Germany, he argued, could serve as a "bridge" or "broker" (*Makler*) between East and West (the same term Bismarck had used in the 1870s). Moreover, the new Germany should pursue a "third way," also a long-standing and not necessarily unburdened trope. Throughout the occupation period, Kaiser and his program remained a strong challenge to the more Western- and market-oriented principles of the Cologne circle. However, the Berlin CDU was unable to maintain its independence from Soviet control and Kaiser fled to the West in 1948, where he nevertheless remained a powerful voice in the CDU of the Federal Republic.

This failure to promote the CDU in Berlin, however, does not entirely explain the triumph of a Western, federalistic, "social market" orientation over Kaiser's neutral, centralized, "Christian socialist" program. (Of course, neither Kaiser's nor Kogon's and Dirks's socialist program for the CDU succeeded, but the CDU's later orientation toward a market economy was not quite like that found in the West, for instance among figures like Henry Stimson and John J. McCloy. "Christian democracy" was more overtly Christian than right of center parties in other countries, and even though Adenauer was decidedly oriented toward the West in foreign policy, the CDU retained an odor of anti-Americanism in its condemnation of "materialism.")

Common to all three leading programs was an emphasis on the importance of the rule of law, though this emphasis proved to be double-edged. On the one hand, it marked a clear boundary against not only National Socialism but against authoritarian traditions on the German Right overall; this was one of the significant transformations of German political culture, an attempt to appeal to the Right with Christianity rather than

---

39. On the *Frankfurter Leitsätze* (Frankfurt guiding principles), see Schmidt, "Hitler ist tot und Ulbircht lebt," 80–82; Eschenburg, *Jahre der Besatzung*, 188–89.

THE POLITICS OF THE PAST? 249

statism. On the other hand, the repeated insistence on legality, as we will see, also implied a rebuke to the occupation authorities, whose various re-education, denazification, and dismantling measures many Germans viewed as nothing short of vengeful plunder. In none of the programs, moreover, was there more than passing mention of the racial component of National Socialist ideology.

While the notion of collective guilt was never acceptable to them, all three programs and at least some of Adenauer's rhetoric in the first months included substantially more discussion of guilt than critiques of their supposed "repression of the past" (both at the time and later) might lead one to expect. According to the Berlin CDU's "Appeal" of June 26, 1945, "Out of the chaos of guilt and disgrace into which the deification of a criminal adventurer plunged us, an order in democratic freedom can only arise if we concentrate on the culture-forming moral and spiritual power of Christianity." Further, the "terrible extent of injustice that the Hitler time brought requires calling the guilty and their helpers unrelentingly to account, in strictest legality though without vengefulness." According to the Cologne group's "Guiding Principles" (*Leitsätze*), "National Socialism covered the German name in all the world with shame and disgrace. This never would have come over us if wide circles of our people had not allowed themselves to be led by a greedy materialism." Again, while no collective guilt, it certainly sounds like an acknowledgment (or accusation) of *majority* guilt (though for what, exactly, is an important question): "All too many succumbed . . . to the National Socialist demagogy, which promised every German paradise on earth. . . . Without their own moral fiber, many succumbed to the racial arrogance and to a nationalistic power frenzy."[40]

Wartime

At this point in the second half of 1945, Konrad Adenauer was not yet actively involved in the formation of the CDU because he was too busy with his work in devastated Cologne. Nevertheless, for reasons to be discussed shortly, Adenauer's distance from party developments did not last long, and it was Adenauer who gave the overriding stamp to the party by early 1946. At the age of seventy, Adenauer became the CDU's and later the Federal Republic's leader, which he remained for almost twenty years.

While Adenauer did not bear the physical signs of martyrdom as did Schumacher, and belonged more to the "inner emigration" than to the

40. Quotations from Kleßmann, *Die doppelte Staatsgründung*, 421–23.

opposition, the Nazis years were indeed difficult for him and his family. Despite the fact that Schumacher guided his party to pick up where it had left off in 1933, Adenauer was for many the key symbol of the restorative character of the Federal Republic. This shows how politicized the concept of "restoration" was. Indeed, Adenauer's political socialization occurred not in the Weimar Republic but in the years before World War I, a period dominated by the Prussian state. As a Rhinelander, Adenauer bore his own version of anti-Prussianism, some features of which were similar to those long held outside of Germany. In the immediate aftermath of World War I, he was even associated with proposals for a separate Rhineland republic.[41]

Elected mayor of Cologne in 1917, however, Adenauer became one of the leading figures in the Catholic Center Party and a significant player at the national level, as well as president of the Prussian State Council (*Staatsrat*). As such, he did accept the participation of the National Socialists in the Prussian government, though largely because he thought they would be such an obvious failure that it would be a good way to discredit them. After the Nazis seized power in 1933, they dismissed him as mayor when he refused to allow their flags to be hung from city government structures. By then in his late fifties, Adenauer retreated from public life entirely. During the Third Reich he was forced into hiding but was arrested several times, and was lucky to have survived the last such occasion, in which only the intercession by his son, a low-ranking officer in the *Wehrmacht*, was able to obtain his release. Adenauer's wife Gussie had been forced to reveal his whereabouts while in hiding, after which she attempted suicide. She died in 1948 because of her resultant poor health.

There are various explanations for Adenauer's nonparticipation in the July 20 and other opposition efforts, ranging from his skepticism of the ability of military officers to pull it off, to distaste for the opposition movement's Prussian cast, to fear of a new stab-in-the-back legend. Having supported Franz von Papen's presidency, he was not a particular target of the Nazis (or at least no more so than many others); but with his record of leadership in Cologne, his name was also at the top of Anglo-American lists of potentially acceptable German leaders in spring 1945. Indeed, the Americans summoned him after they had secured most of Cologne and asked that he accept an appointment as mayor; he declined out of fear that, since the war was not yet over, his three sons (still fighting in the *Wehrmacht*) would be shot should news of his cooperation get

41. Schwarz, *Adenauer*; Prittie, *Adenauer*; Köhler, *Adenauer*.

out. At first, he was therefore an "advisor," and became mayor only after May 8, 1945, after which he faced enormous tasks of rebuilding his city under the most strenuous circumstances with few and changing guidelines.

Mayor

The beginning of the postwar political reconstruction was the appointment of a city council, which had its first meeting on October 1, 1945. The representative of the British Military Government (Cologne was transferred from American to British control on June 21, 1945), Major J. Alan Prior, opened the session with a harsh lecture on the need for re-education. Every German he met, Prior noted, expressed repugnance of the Nazis. "Nevertheless," Prior declared, "the fact remains that for twelve years Germany obviously supported the systematic plundering of Europe and willingly took part in it. In the end, it is the nation itself, which tolerated such a government over time, that is responsible for the governmental leadership of a country." At the end of his statement, Prior emphasized that anyone who cared about the rebirth of Germany had to acknowledge the importance of re-education, and that the evidence of this acknowledgment would be commitment to the denazification of public life. He had, he said, been hearing much too much about rehabilitation of former Nazis.[42]

As would be characteristic for much of his public rhetoric after 1945, Adenauer's response to Prior traced a fine line, providing just enough carefully formulated acknowledgment of Prior's assertions to placate the British officer. Observing the devastation of his city, Adenauer began by identifying the perpetrators: "The cursable ones who came to power in the fatal year 1933 are guilty for this unspeakable misery, for this indescribable suffering." He did refer to the "seduced and crippled people," however, thus seeming to identify at least a passive weakness on the part of some. But he then warned that the real reason Germany was in such ruins was that the Nazis wanted to prepare the ground in which thoughts of revenge might take root. He thought it especially important to state that "[w]e, you and I, are not the guilty for this misery," though they bore the burden of cleaning it up. As Adenauer wrote years later in his memoir, "I learned to experience the cruelties of National Socialism, the consequences of dictatorship. . . . I experienced the fall of the German people into chaos." At the October 1 meeting, he promised that he and his city

---

42. See Adenauer, *Erinnerungen*, 30–31. See also Schwarz, *Konrad Adenauer*, 79–81.

council "will go to work together. Bowed, deeply bowed, but—ladies and gentlemen—not broken." Later, in his memoir, he explained that he "did not champion the concept of a collective guilt of all Germans, but I considered us obliged to compensate the injustices in the past also to our German compatriots, and I felt the urge to let the poor people from the concentration camps be brought back to their hometown as quickly as possible." In order to accomplish the latter, Adenauer dispatched city busses to Buchenwald, Dachau, and Theresienstadt to transport prisoners from Cologne back to the city.

Exactly six days after his October 1 speech, the British authorities summoned Adenauer, where they dressed him down in a humiliating fashion, dismissed him from his post, and forbid him from entering the city. There are numerous explanations for Adenauer's dismissal, ranging from his refusal to have city trees cut down for fire wood (establishment of a green belt was one of his accomplishments as mayor before the Nazi period), to Social Democratic machinations. Whatever the reason, the event was fateful, for after a brief period of retreat Adenauer turned his copious talents to the inchoate CDU in Cologne and throughout the British zone, gave it his personal stamp, built it into a well-functioning party throughout the West, and ultimately brought it to lead the new state for seventeen years, fourteen of them under his own chancellorship.

In March 1946, Adenauer was elected chairman of the CDU in the British zone, and was the principle author of what would become the dominant early statement for the party, the so-called "Neheim-Huesten program." He immediately presented the outlines of the program in a March 6 radio address, which I discuss later, titled "Democracy is for us a Worldview,"[43] but a "Basic Principles Speech" (*Grundsatzrede*) he delivered at the University of Cologne on March 24 is widely recognized as the most comprehensive statement he gave during the first two years of his new career.[44] The latter is indeed an enormously rich window into his personal and political vision, and makes clear how steadfast that vision was from the depths of wartime despair to the challenges of international brinkmanship during the Cold War. This goes to my assertion at the beginning of this book that Adenauer's politics of the past was not merely a matter of the exigencies of state after 1949, but expressed a deeply held worldview. This speech of March 24 provides the clearest evidence.

43. Adenauer, *"Die Democratie ist fuer uns eine Weltanschaaung,"* 1–9.
44. Adenauer's biographer, Hans-Peter Schwarz, who edited the essential collection of Adenauer speeches, singled out the March 24 speech as the most comprehensive from this

Worldview

Adenauer began the "Basic Principles" speech with a special defense of his native city, pointing out that nowhere was the voting percentage for Hitler as low as in Cologne. His point, however, was that "[c]atastrophes, the unleashing of elemental, demonic violence, nevertheless affect the guilty as well as the not guilty." After noting that Germany was successful in climbing out of the misery of the previous postwar catastrophe, he then raised a series of questions signaling his deep dismay: "How was it possible that the revival of the German spirit was so short? . . . How was the National Socialist Reich, at first greeted with rejoicing by many well-meaning people [*Harmlosen*],[45] then despised and cursed, though feared, by many, very many Germans because of its unfathomable vileness and baseness, how was that possible in the German people?" He referred with despair to "crime upon crime of the greatest magnitude," and to his bewilderment that the war both began and was followed through to the necessary defeat. Repeating a formulation he had already offered in his October 1, 1945, speech at the Cologne city council meeting, Adenauer stated that since 1933 he had often been ashamed to be a German; he now qualified this by adding that perhaps he knew "more than many others about the atrocities that were perpetrated by Germans against Germans, of crimes that were planned against humanity." Nevertheless, witnessing how Germans, though suffering, were bravely facing the many postwar emergencies, he was once again proud: "The German people is enduring this most difficult period in its history with heroic strength, perseverance, and patience, with a patient strength that is stronger than any need."[46]

Following these paragraphs of outrage and despair, of question upon question, Adenauer turned to the task of a sober analysis, though not without making clear his position on guilt: "I demand no acknowledgment of guilt from the whole German people [*gesamten deutschen Volkes*], although many Germans have a very heavy guilt, many a guilt which while less heavy nevertheless is still guilt. I also do not believe that the more reasonable and reflective people in the non-German countries require such a public declaration of guilt." His reason for undertaking an analysis of National Socialism was to provide a remedy directed toward the future: "National Socialism was what

period. The text is reprinted in Schwarz, *Konrad Adenauer,* 82–106. See also Herf, *Divided Memory,* 213–20; Wolgast, *Die Wahrnehmung des Dritten Reiches in der umittelbaren Nachkriegszeit,* 131–38; Baumgärtner, *Reden nach Hitler,* 119–27.
45. Here again is the German preference for, or exculpation of, early over later support.
46. Schwarz, *Konrad Adenauer,* 82–84.

directly led us into catastrophe. That is correct. But National Socialism would not have been able to come to power in Germany if it had not found a receptive audience for its poison seed in wide segments of the population." National Socialism, then, is a mere symptom of other trends, trends that he believed were certainly of concern elsewhere as well.[47]

According to Adenauer's analysis, the major source of National Socialism was the "materialism" that resulted from the decline of the Christian world-view. Because he believed that wide segments of the population were receptive to National Socialist ideology, he argued that it was "not correct to now say that the bigwigs, the high military or large industries alone are guilty. Certainly they bear a full amount of guilt, and their personal guilt, for which they must be brought to account before German courts, is ever greater according to their power and influence." Instead, Adenauer argued, "wide segments of the population, the farmers, the middle class, the workers, the intellectuals did not have the right spiritual attitude, otherwise the victorious march of National Socialism through the German people in the year 1933 and after would not have been possible." Indeed, Adenauer believed that large segments of the German population had since even before 1870 been under the destructive sway of a particular idea of state power—largely Prussian in origin—which did not maintain sufficient respect for the individual. As a result of this "deification" of state power, "militarism became the dominant factor in the thought and feeling of the widest segments of the people." This process, however, was only a manifestation of the wider developmental trends of "increasing industrialization, the concentration of large masses of people in the cities and the uprooting of people connected to it," all of which "prepared the way for the devastating spread of the materialistic worldview in the German people." This worldview in turn "led to a further exaggeration of the concept of the state and of power, to the depreciation of ethical values and of the value of the individual person."[48]

National Socialism may have been the eventual outcome of this process in Germany, but not only the National Socialists were responsible. In fact, Marxist socialism seemed to him to have the same basic fault (this is partly why Adenauer always referred to National *Socialism* rather than to Nazis, for indeed for him National Socialism was a combination of two virulent trends—nationalist militarism and collectivist socialism).[49] Thus, the "materialistic worldview of Marxism contributed to this development in very great

47. Ibid., 84–85.
48. Ibid., 85.
49. See note 12.

scope." For Adenauer, "[w]hoever strives for a centralization of political and economic power in the state or in a class and who as a result advocates the principle of class conflict, is an enemy of the freedom of the individual; he necessarily prepares the way for dictatorship in the thoughts and feelings of his supporters, even if it is another who takes the prepared path."[50]

The only antidote, Adenauer believed, was re-Christianization, which is why he insisted—over objections both in Germany and outside—on calling the party the *Christian* Democratic Union: "The fundamental principle of the program of the CDU, the principle from which all the demands of our program stem, is the core idea of Christian ethics: The human being has his own dignity, and the value of each individual person is inalienable." In contrast, the "materialistic worldview makes the person into an object, into a small machine part in an immense machine." Democracy, as a result, must be understood not just as a governmental form but as a "worldview" (*Weltanschauung*).[51]

Most of Adenauer's understanding of Germany—his explanation for its past and its prospect for the future—lay in his belief that the presence and role of Christianity in Germany was especially weak. Germany, he claimed, was one of the least religious and most unchristian countries in all of Europe, something that could be traced back to before 1914. Taking Berlin as an example, and despite the fact that its citizens had "many valuable characteristics," Adenauer said he always had the feeling when in Berlin of being in a "pagan city" (*heidnischen Stadt*). He identified Berlin as the locus of National Socialism, Social Democracy, and communism, "parties which consciously and intentionally fought Christianity." Of course, Berlin was also one of the most Jewish cities in Europe, though he did not say that Berlin's Jewish culture had anything to do with his sense that it was a "pagan city." (Adenauer was never an overt anti-Semite, and indeed vigorously professed to be a philo-Semite, though as we will see his was a peculiar sort of philo-Semitism). Even if his characterization of Berlin as a "pagan city" had nothing, for him, to do with its Jewish culture, it is reasonable to assume that at least some German listeners made that association.[52]

* * *

50. Schwarz, *Konrad Adenauer,* 85–86.
51. See Adenauer's speech on democracy as a worldview mentioned above. Quotes here from ibid., 86.
52. Ibid., 88.

In this major speech of March 24, 1946, Adenauer also presented his formula for the punishment of Nazi criminals, a formula that is echoed in virtually all his subsequent political work on such issues. "Active National Socialists and active militarists, who were responsible for the war and its prolongation, and among these belong especially certain economic elites, must be removed from their positions." They should be judged by German courts, and they should be fined according to their degree of guilt. "The suffering that they brought over Germany and the entire world is a crying shame [*schreit zum Himmel*]." But, again, this must be a very discriminating judgment: "[W]e only want to affect those who are truly guilty; the fellow-travelers, those who did not oppress others, who did not enrich themselves, did not commit any criminal acts, one should *finally* leave in peace" (emphasis added). The most remarkable feature of this statement, of course, is the emphasis on "finally" when it was only March 1946, a few short weeks after the Council of States had passed, under pressure from the American Military Government, the "Law for the Liberation from National Socialism and Militarism," which put denazification in German hands and began its second *Meldebogen* phase (as described in chapter 5); the *Spruchkammern* had hardly begun.

Those "fellow travelers" with National Socialism would certainly be allowed in the CDU, if for the time being they could not perform any party functions. In a formula he had already introduced in prior weeks, Adenauer made clear that his reference to "militarists," who in his account were directly responsible, did not include soldiers: "The soldier, regardless of rank, whether officer or not, who fulfilled his duty in a respectable manner and did not do anything else, is not an active militarist." "If one rejects . . . harmless fellow travelers and soldiers who believed they were doing their duty, one is doing nothing short of cultivating a misguided and extreme nationalism." In the same vein, Adenauer called for spiritual re-education of the country's youth, though he insists this must come from Germans, that it will be ineffectual and resented if it comes from the occupation authorities.[53]

After brief mention of the CDU's intention to pursue an "equalization of burdens" program for the German population, as well as aid for the expellees who had somehow to be provided for and integrated (though at this point as well as later Adenauer was also calling for the return of Eastern territories), Adenauer turned his full attention to his rival at the head of the SPD and his claim to be the legitimate heir to power in the new Germany. This claim Adenauer repudiated on both formal and substantive grounds, along with all of Schumacher's accusations against the CDU.

53. Ibid., 92.

One such accusation was that the CDU was a "party of reaction," one piece of evidence for which was the claim that the CDU was providing a home for former Nazis. Adenauer denied this (though we should keep in mind his above-quoted statement about former "fellow travelers" being welcome). "Certainly," Adenauer replied, "we accept, just as the SPD and KPD [communists], unburdened former National Socialists as members; they may not, however, assume any leading positions for the time being. We absolutely reject being a party of the right, we also reject being a party of the left." As for Schumacher's charge that the CDU was a party representing propertied interests, operating purely on economic motives, Adenauer was purported to be deeply offended. His response was to attack Schumacher's disputational stance altogether: "Dr. Schumacher does not even bother to try to produce a piece of evidence for his claims. The entire method is reminiscent in embarrassing fashion of the propaganda methods from a time that lies behind us."[54]

Adenauer's response to Schumacher's charge that the CDU was a reactionary party was thus to imply that Schumacher employed methods better associated with the Nazis. He added that Schumacher's charges were especially ridiculous because the areas in which support for the CDU was higher had suffered much more in the war than those that were supporting the SPD, though the exact logic of this statement is not particularly clear. A perhaps more problematic part of Adenauer's logic is his defense against Schumacher's claim—perhaps the central point of the SPD's belief that it alone was uncompromised—that the so-called "middle-class" (*Bürgerlich*) parties had been agents of "large capital," which had enabled the rise of National Socialism. "It is not correct," Adenauer answered, "as Dr. Schumacher claims, that large capital [*Grosskapital*] called National Socialism to life in order to keep the middle-class parties under control." Adenauer asserted that he himself was no friend of large capital and likewise of trusts and cartels. He condemned these forces for not using their power and means for social benefit, and asserted that he certainly did not want to see them restored. As for their connection to National Socialism, he dismissed the charge as absurd: "National Socialism was from the first moment on sharply directed against the Jews. But in large capital the Jews were enormously influential. Does anyone believe that these influential Jewish gentlemen helped their archenemy, namely the National Socialists, to political power? No, that would mean vastly underestimating the intelligence and cleverness of these gentlemen." Surely, this is an unfortunate formulation, and perhaps surprising given Adenauer's place in memory as a purposeful philo-Semite: Adenauer excuses large capital with the defense that the Jewish powers controlling it were too "clever" to support the Nazis.[55]

Adenauer continued to indict Schumacher by innuendo: "The inventors of National Socialism were military circles, were high military. They recognized that there were two emblems with fabulous attraction for the great proportion of the German people, the words 'national' and 'socialism.' . . . [T]hese militarists . . . made them into one term and created a new kind of Socialism, National Socialism." As for Schumacher's claim that the SPD had an eighty-year history of commitment to peace and democracy, Adenauer listed mistakes the party made from 1870 to 1914. His point was that "[a]ll people have mistakes, and all parties have mistakes as well, the main thing is that one knows that one has mistakes and that one does not act so superior to all others." The fact that Schumacher failed to acknowledge this, Adenauer argued, was an indication that Schumacher did not truly understand the principle of democracy, the essence of which demands respect for the beliefs of other parties. As for Schumacher's claim to have a right to leadership (*Führung*), Adenauer noted that he had "already heard very similar justification for the claim to leadership of the state from other parties: from the Prussian conservatives, who demanded the leadership of the state for themselves, from the National Liberals, who claimed that they alone possessed the education and property and therefore could lead alone." He continued: "As far as I'm concerned, one should finally make an end with the word leader [*Führer*] and leadership [*Führung*] in Germany." Instead, Adenauer charged, one should speak of "responsibility." He regretted that "from the official statements of the SPD the old Prussian spirit is speaking, the reckless undemocratic pursuit of sole power as only the Prussian *Junkers* possessed."[56]

The last sections of his speech Adenauer reserved for occupation policy, his critique of which at this early point, in comparison to even a year later, was more foreboding than dire. He stated his confidence that the British Military Government had the best intention to help Germany out of the ruin Hitler had brought on it, and acknowledged that occupation is unpleasant for victors as well as for vanquished. But he asserted that Germany had a right not to be judged solely on this epoch of its history,

55. Ibid., 98–99.
56. Ibid., 99–100.

warned that burdens placed on Germany must not exceed its ability to bear them, and that privation is not a good foundation for peace. He asserted as well that a solution to the so-called "German question" must be found because Germany's unity has an "organic nature." Partition, he asserted, would leave a "dead body" in the middle of Europe that would be just as dangerous as a victorious National Socialist Germany would have been (here he was alluding to Churchill's comment on the danger of debilitating the German economy).[57]

Accusing the Allies

Within a year, Adenauer's warnings had developed into full-blown accusations. In an April 13, 1947, campaign speech at the University of Cologne, for instance, he made clear his sense of the continuities of German suffering:

> The disappointments that we have suffered in the two years since the collapse are heavy. The future appears dark and ominous before us; we do not know what will come. It would be only understandable if a general apathy would grip the German people . . . a certain nihilistic mood is appearing, a mood almost of hopelessness: everything is pointless; we cannot help ourselves and the Allies do not want to help us.

National Socialism had destroyed law, the punishment for which followed. But now that the German people stood again on the foundation of law, "[w]e hope and trust that the Allies, who according to their own declarations were pulled into the war for the sake of justice, in order to stand against the National Socialist breach of law—we may hope and trust that nevertheless the idea of law is finally paramount again for the Allies as well, and applies to the German people too." In the course of recent events— primarily a severe winter without sufficient food and shelter—right stood on the German side, according to Adenauer, whose remarks in this context bring us back to the wartime issues we examined at the very beginning of the book:

> We surrendered unconditionally. Unconditional surrender of the leaders of the National Socialist army is a purely military matter. Unconditional surrender has existed in every war; it means nothing other than that those who unconditionally surrender cease hostilities and turn themselves, their troops and their weapons over to the enemy. But the unconditional surrender of the leaders of the German

57. Ibid., 104–5.

army [now German rather than National Socialist army] never had the consequence that Germany ceased to exist. It never meant that for Germany the right
to self-determination [*die Völkerrechtliche Bestimmung*] was suspended. . . . Those
to whom injustice has occurred—and we must recognize that in the National
Socialistic period injustice was done—do not thereby have the right themselves
to do injustice.

Adenauer further lectured the Allies that they were not meeting their legal
and moral responsibilities to the German people, according to the Hague
conventions: "According to these regulations they have the responsibility to
arrange for the subsistence of the regions occupied by them so far as the population is not able to do so for itself. Has that happened? I can only say it has
not happened!" For evidence, he referred to the report by former U.S. president Herbert Hoover in which Hoover said, "You can have vengeance or
peace, but you can't have both." Striking here is the contradiction between
Goebbels's earlier framing of "unconditional surrender," with all the criticism
Roosevelt took for its supposedly "Carthaginian" impulse, and Adenauer's
sense that Roosevelt line's meaning was obvious—that unconditional surrender was ordinary and had nothing to do with vengeance.[58]

Also in the April 13 campaign speech, Adenauer addressed the question
of the as-yet-unreturned prisoners of war. He suggested that it would not
be unreasonable for the Allies to reconsider their general attitude to "fellow travelers" (presumably including the prisoners of war). Adenauer's reasoning here was that the Allies themselves had negotiated with the Nazis,
implying the Soviet nonaggression pact. But, in a statement similar to ones
to be found in the writings of Wilhelm Röpke (with whom Adenauer was
positively impressed), Adenauer reminded the Western Allies as well that
they had participated in the Berlin Olympics "to pay homage to Hitler."
Adenauer thus made the following accusation: "If the Allies had only
worked half as hard on keeping Hitler small, as they currently are doing
with Franco, then it never would have come to war!" As for the discussions
concerning the future territory of Germany, which only rekindled outrage
over the Potsdam agreement, Adenauer charged that these considerations
were in violation of the Atlantic Charter, which in his reading prohibited
territorial changes and population transfers against the wishes of the people who lived there (recall the discussion of Sumner Welles in chapter 4).[59]

58. Adenauer, *"Die Democratie ist fuer uns eine Weltanschaaung,"* 27–30.
59. Ibid., 35.

Similarly, in a speech delivered a year later on July 21, 1948, by which time the Western Allies had already agreed to create a partial West German state, Adenauer recalled wartime Allied agreements while rejecting what he took to be self-righteousness on the part of the Allies:

> It is true, through National Socialism it became clear what depths the people in Germany were capable of, which one never would have believed. But does this apply only for German people? [Strong applause.] Has the world since Hitler's death and the disappearance of National Socialism become just, peaceful and quiet? Did the Germans agree in Quebec that the Russians should occupy half of Germany? Did the Germans participate at Yalta and Potsdam? How do you think a German, English or American historian in twenty or thirty years will judge all of this? I do not believe that he will say Germany is guilty for everything.

Referring to a book by Max Picard recently published in Switzerland titled *Hitler in Ourselves!* [*Hitler in Uns Selbst!*], Adenauer stated, "In foreign people as well there is a piece of Hitler, and indeed no small piece. For this reason, we Germans do not need to go around forever in sackcloth and ashes doing penance because things started in Germany."[60] Indeed, this "sackcloth and ashes" formulation would have many afterlives in the Federal Republic, particularly in the late 1970s and 1980s, when neoconservatives rejected the accusatory stance of the New Left of the 1960s.

In the excerpt of his July 21 speech just quoted, it is not entirely clear what Adenauer meant about Quebec, in what manner Germany could have participated at Yalta or Potsdam, and whether the correct deduction from the mistakes of others is release of Germany from guilt. What he seemed to be implying—and the gist of the larger story—is perhaps somewhat clearer if one connects these statements to those he made the following month at the second party congress of the CDU on August 28, 1948. There Adenauer once again asserted the importance of the Christian worldview. The reason that the CDU sought a Christian foundation for politics is that in most of the world it is absent. It is not just that politics elsewhere (both inside and outside of Germany) is not Christian: "In the greatest parts of the world an *anti*-Christian spirit rules, to which the current situation owes itself." Once again, Adenauer called for taking an historical perspective, but instead of referring to Quebec and Yalta, he had something else in mind:

60. Schwarz, *Konrad Adenauer,* 119.

National Socialism committed terrible crimes, crimes about which historians will write with horror in later times, but the Morgenthau Plan, which thank God was not carried out although it was worked out and prepared in all the details, represents a crime against humanity that worthily stands by the side of the National Socialist crimes. [Lively shouts of "Quite right!"] If one planned right down to the operational details to allow 30 to 40 million Germans to die by choking them economically then the outline and contemplation of such a plan betrays such an abyss of cruelty and inhumanity that by God no one can any longer speak of a Christian spirit. This Morgenthau Plan is finished. But the time will come when those who devised it will be ashamed to talk about it. But I have the feeling that some manifestations of this Morgenthau Plan are still affecting us. It is time for this to stop.

Once again, Morgenthau's plan appears as the embodiment of the anti-Christian spirit, the source of German suffering.[61]

Theodor Heuss and the Dualities of German History

Neither Kurt Schumacher nor Konrad Adenhauer was a hesitant man given to doubts when it came to worldview. With proud—sometimes too proud—bearing, both reserved their dismay for the actions of others. This was not entirely the case with Theodor Heuss, who would become the first—and nearly uniformly honored—president of the Federal Republic of Germany. Very much like Thomas Mann, Heuss saw ambiguities, ambivalences, and dualities in German history. Despite his reputation for moral leadership and his sometimes high-flown rhetoric, Heuss was philosophically the least dogmatic of the three principal founding fathers of the Federal Republic; his worldview was neither the teleological materialism of Schumacher's Marxism nor the conservative antimaterialism of Adenauer's political Christianity. Rather, for Heuss, "fairness"—a term that, he lamented, had no equivalent in German—was the essence of democracy.

As with the CDU, liberals faced many challenges forming a party, including the emergence of distinct positions in different regions.[62] Moreover, there were many liberals who argued that they should throw their support behind a larger middle-class umbrella party and seek a distinct voice within it. Indeed, some did this. But for many liberals, the CDU's insistence on a Christian worldview, to say nothing of the socialist

61. Ibid., 125.
62. On the German liberals after 1945, see Hein, *Zwischen liberaler Milieupartei und nationaler Sammlungsbewegung*.

forces within that emerging party, were unacceptable. Liberalism had always been a smaller—though durable and significant—force in German politics, and many liberals thus embraced the idea of continuing in that tradition as an alternative between the CDU and the SPD, hoping to advance their minority interests as a pivotal partner, which they did more successfully for more years than they could have imagined.[63]

Background

Theodor Heuss was as authentic a liberal as could be found, raised in a family committed to the principles of 1848, later becoming a protégé of Friedrich Naumann, the major figure in the liberal tradition before World War I.[64] Unlike the professional party politicians Adenauer and Schumacher, Heuss was a broader intellectual, steeped in the ideas of German humanistic culture and arts—a writer, journalist, and lecturer— though he also served in the *Reichstag* from 1924 to 1928 and then again from 1930 to 1933, at which time, as we saw in chapter 6, Heuss made the "political mistake" of voting for the Enabling Act that brought Hitler to absolute power. Despite this admitted error (Heuss played down its impact, though later in life he judged it much more harshly), Heuss was thoroughly disgusted with Hitler, whom he nevertheless, like many others, vastly underestimated. In 1932, Heuss published a book titled *Hitler's Way*, in which he repudiated Nazi ideas and what he perceived as the overwhelming vulgarity of the movement and its participants. In Heuss's analysis, moreover, National Socialism had important similarities to Marxism; he described National Socialism's pseudoscientific analysis of race as analogous to that of class. "In place of class and class struggle," he wrote, "Nazis use blood and race. . . . The psychological schema of simplification and the moralizing formation of typological elements is the same."[65] Nevertheless, Heuss also claimed that "the birthplace of the National Socialist movement is Versailles, not Munich."

With the rise of the Nazis, Heuss lost both his political and journalistic positions, though he managed to continue writing under a pseudonym;

---

63. On the history of German liberalism, see Sheehan, *German Liberalism in the 19th Century;* Langewiesche, *Liberalismus in Deutschland.*
64. For background of Heuss, see Burger, *Theodor Heuss als Journalist;* Hamm-Brücher, *Gerechtigkeit erhöht ein Volk;* Winter, *Theodor Heuss.* For a detailed analysis of Heuss's postwar rhetoric, see Baumgärtner, *Reden nach Hitler.*
65. Quoted in Herf, *Divided Memory,* 228.

while not a direct participant in the July 20, 1944, coup, he was in contact with its leaders and was slated for a position in the new government if the coup attempt were to succeed. Indeed, in the aftermath of the war, when many Germans were still highly suspicious of the opposition as somehow unpatriotic, Heuss lectured and wrote repeatedly of opposition members as evidence of a heroic "Other Germany." More than virtually anyone else, Heuss contributed to the rehabilitation of the opposition, and not just of the conservative circles behind the July 20 coup attempt.

Much of Heuss's postwar thinking appeared in the numerous pieces he wrote as an editor for the *Rhein Neckar Zeitung*, one of the first newspapers to be granted a license by the Americans after the war. Most of what he wrote there appeared in numerous speeches as well, most comprehensively in "In Memoriam" (delivered in the Stuttgart State Theater on November 25, 1945, as part of a hastily organized "Memorial Day for the 'Victims of Fascism,'")[66] and "On Germany's Future" (delivered on March 18, 1946, in Berlin at the invitation of the communist-led Cultural Association for the Democratic Renewal of Germany [*Kulturbund zur Demokratischen Erneuerung Deutschlands*]).[67]

"In Memoriam"

Heuss's main point in Stuttgart on November 25, 1945, was the importance of memory, though the degree to which Heuss saw this as an uphill battle so soon after the end of the war, in the midst of destruction and desolation, seems strange. Early on in the speech, Heuss answered imagined critics who might dismiss the need for remembrance, particularly in such a ceremonial context as a "Memorial Day for the 'Victims of Fascism'": "Here one may call out alarmed: Yes, but do you want to do this forever, always these monstrosities, these *KZ*- [concentration camp] and torture-stories, these defamations and removals, these killings [though more literally "this being killed" (*dieses Umgebrachtwerden*)], this injustice upon injustice, do you really want to keep talking about it?" Heuss's answer was that such remembrance is essential for the moral well-being of the nation: "We want to accord such a day its lasting solemnity and dignity because we should and must, not only out of respect for the suffering, for the dead, for the killed, but for the sake of our moral future as a people as well." He continued to list names of friends and important victims, but noted that names

66. Heuss, *Die Große Reden*, vol. 1, 63–71.
67. Heuss, *Aufzeichnungen*, 184–208.

fade from memory; he thus asked, "Will everything then be done—forgotten? Perhaps a pile of material for historians and novelists. But exactly this may not happen." Later, he warned that the German people may not "make it too easy for itself to put these evil things behind them like a vile dream." Heuss's insistence on the importance of memory thus appeared more thorough than that of Adenauer or Schumacher: for Adenauer, it was there at the beginning, but faded quickly; for Schumacher, it seemed somehow instrumentalized.[68]

What, then, did Heuss insist on remembering? In the first place, he charged that the "outside world did not have and does not have a sufficient understanding of the muffled opposition [*dumpfen Widerstand*] that was present and was brewing in this period in Germany." Just because the opposition was not obvious, he implied, does not mean it was not present and important: "It did not participate in the marching parades on the streets, but consumed its anger in the back rooms, and it sought its escape." This too, for Heuss, was an essential part of the story—the passive resistance, "inner emigration," personal distaste, all of which, he said, must eventually become part of the historical image of National Socialism. By the same token, he did charge that the "German people made it too easy on itself, too easy in its masses, to give itself over to the chains of National Socialism." But he believed this was never complete: "It was a situation of civil war in which only one group had the weapons." For Heuss, however, this latency of German freedom was part of a long tradition, the failed tradition of 1848.[69]

Toward the end of this speech, Heuss assessed the damages:

> The inner-German political victims and by their side the hundreds of thousands, even millions of foreigners who were tortured to death, they speak for what became the heaviest and most expensive sacrifice of National Socialism: the honor of the German name,[70] which sank in filth. In declaring this, angry, depressed, ashamed to have been defenseless victims of this darkest period of German history, we feel the duty to once again clear the name of our people.

For Heuss, "[t]he memory of those who innocently suffered, who died bravely, will with its calm and quiet glow be our beacon in the darkest years through which we will pass," though he did not here specify how. With this

68. Heuss, *Die Große Reden*, vol. 1, 63–64.

69. Ibid., 63–64.

70. How the foreign victims spoke for the honor of the German name remained unstated. From later perspectives, moreover, Jewish lives rather than the German reputation was the heaviest sacrifice.

speech, however, Heuss inaugurated a tradition of ritualistic memory, one that acknowledges the past as providing moral lessons, without at the same time sinking into guilt. Similar here to Thomas Mann, for Heuss "the heaviest and most expensive sacrifice"—what Mann called "ignominy" and Heuss called "shame"—was not guilt, but rather was the German reputation.[71]

"On Germany's Future"

Heuss's March 1946 speech in Berlin was even more comprehensive than "In Memoriam," more like the party and campaign speeches of Schumacher and Adenauer. In his thoughts on the future of Germany, Heuss noted as he had in his diaries at the end of the war the coincidence of the unconditional surrender on May 8 and of the 140th anniversary of Schiller's death on May 9.[72] For Heuss, like Mann, this and other dualities defined German history: "On the one side the rapture of thought, of intellectual excesses, which can contemplate and accomplish the greatest things, on the other side the laughable servitude. This indulgence in boundless Romanticism and a petty-bourgeois complacency [*Versorgungsideal*] side by side." Such dualities defined German history, the "disintegration" (*Zerbrochenheit*) of which prevented Germany from developing a clear historical identity. As a result, Germany "stand[s] and will continue to stand under the burden of our history, rich with greatness, because the history of the fight for freedom among us in Germany, which we also knew, was and remains a history of defeat." As a result, Heuss argued—in many ways similarly to the historian Gerhard Ritter—that the "question of the German historical image stands before us as the most difficult task in culture and politics. This is not to be accomplished by establishing a cleansing enterprise and letting the brown color be washed off in order that another color can be smeared on from already prepared buckets; rather, the requirement is that we re-introduce the non-instrumental truth in the area of science and acknowledge that the scientific questioning must be free."[73] The emblem that Heuss gives to this process is an expression from the poet Hölderlin: "sacred sobriety" (*heilige Nüchternheit*).[74]

71. Ibid., 71. We will look at Heuss's "collective shame" formulation of 1949 shortly, though it is important to note that the language was already present in his 1932 book, in which he referred to Nazi anti-Semitism as an "occasion for shame for the rest of us."

72. See Baumgärtner, *Reden nach Hitler*, 97.

73. Heuss, *Aufzeichnungen*, 191–92, 200.

74. Herf, *Divided Memory*, 237.

Heuss's posture toward the past thus appears to be quite different from Adenauer's and Schumacher's: for Adenauer, memory provides a clear lesson in recognition of the dangers and mistakes others imposed on Germany; for Schumacher, memory places the Nazi "antithesis" in an historical dialectic leading to the Marxist "synthesis." For Heuss, however, remembering is more contemplative, less filled with accusations and program. When Adenauer mentioned Picard's *Hitler in Ourselves!* he intended to make the point that other people besides Germans must denounce Nazi-like qualities in themselves. Where "Hitler" could be found in Adenauer himself is not the point, though Adenauer certainly did find him in Schumacher. Perhaps because of his own self-confessed mistake of voting for the Enabling Act, Heuss's rhetoric displayed a bit more inwardness, and did not always exclude Heuss himself from the need at least for self-examination. He may not have believed himself guilty, or even part of a community of "collective guilt," but his belief that "the most terrible and the most horrible that National Socialism did to us is that it forced us to be ashamed to be German" included him in a category into which neither Adenauer nor Schumacher would have placed themselves. (Although Adenauer also said he had been ashamed, he meant during the war; when he saw his compatriots facing defeat and its humiliations without crumbling, he said he was once again proud.)

Nevertheless, even Heuss included in the midst of his acknowledgment all the classic exculpations. On the one hand, he pointed out as clearly as possible—addressing his speakers in a way that neither Schumacher nor Adenauer ever did—that even mundane anti-Semitism was culpable. Referring to the Nazi expression "It's only a Jew" (*Ist ja bloss ein Jude*), Heuss argued that "this 'It's only a Jew' was the beginning. From there on the German soul became sick because it no longer saw in people the human, the dignity of the human being. This laziness of thought, this abdication of self-responsibility, led entirely of necessity to what we later experienced." On the other hand, the end of this sentence does not specify "what we later experienced," and whether it was Germans who experienced it or others. Earlier in the speech on Germany's future, he had acknowledged that "this war was caused by Germany and was desired by its leadership," but after describing the ideology of that leadership concluded, "In this way we were *forced* into this war" (emphasis added). He asserted that "[w]e all became dirty in this period and through this period," though dirty is not exactly guilty, and does not necessarily imply fault. He described a "guilt of passivity" and concluded from it that "[t]here is no escape from the joint German fate [*Gesamtschicksal*]. We are and remain jointly responsible [*gesamthaftbar*] for that which we experienced."[75]

*   *   *

While Heuss had long spoken of shame and discussed the dualities of German history, two written statements from 1949, both of which he repeated frequently in speeches as federal president, distilled his thoughts in this regard. In a May 1949 essay commemorating the fourth anniversary of the end of the war, Heuss distinguished his own thinking from the views of Adenauer and Schumacher. For Adenauer, there was definitely a sense of *defeat* tied to May 8, 1945, an empathy for the destruction of his city and country, and the suffering of the people, though this is not to say Adenauer was not happy to see the National Socialists go; for Schumacher, May 8, 1945, was unequivocally a day of *liberation*. For Heuss, "[i]n its essence this May 8th, 1945 remains the most tragic, most questionable paradox of history for each of us. But why? Because we were simultaneously liberated and destroyed."[76] In December 1949, shortly after assuming the presidency, Heuss made the following statement at a meeting of the Society for Christian-Jewish Cooperation, employing a trope we have come to know well: "One has spoken of a collective guilt [*Kollektivschuld*] of the German people. The word collective guilt and what stands behind it is a crude simplification [*simple Vereinfachung*], it is a reversal namely of the same way the Nazis commonly saw the Jews: that the fact of being a Jew already contained within it the phenomenon of guilt." In contrast, Heuss offered collective shame: "Something like a collective shame [*Kollektivscham*] has grown and remained from this time."[77]

Politics and the Past

There is perhaps something misleading about focusing on these and only these three political voices in the occupation period— Schumacher, Adenauer, and Heuss—selected because of their later importance. The only one of the three who was obviously the singular primary voice in his party was Schumacher. Indeed, Adenauer acknowledged the irony of his October 1945 dismissal by the British from Cologne City Hall. Had this

75. Heuss, *Aufzeichnungen*, 189–90.
76. Quoted in Kirsch, *"Wir haben aus der Geschichte gelernt,"* 47.
77. Heuss, *Die Großen Reden*, vol. 1, 100.

not happened, he likely would not have pursued the career he did. Even more than with Adenauer, it is not obvious that the focus in these early years was on Heuss rather than on a number of other figures in this period, both within and outside the liberal camp. One thinks of Württemberg-Baden minister president Reinhold Maier, Carlo Schmid, future federal president Gustav Heinemann, or perhaps a bit later of Ernst Reuter, to name only a few others who could have been included in a more comprehensive account.

Even given this retrospective distortion, however, Heuss alongside Adenauer and Schumacher make good choices. Their respective positions were complex and multivalent, and thus one should not be too easily tempted into a pat classification. Nevertheless, at a very general level it does seem as if these three particularly represent as clearly as possible three distinct interpretative frames, what literary critics call "metanarratives"—the general forms that shape particular narrative contents. In this regard, it might be useful to see Schumacher as a *revolutionist*, in which National Socialism is the negative moment in a dialectical process moving ineluctably toward the future. Adenauer can then be seen as a *devolutionist*, whose story points to decay in the historical process and thus seeks a return to lost values. For his part, in step with this perspective, Heuss is an *evolutionist*, relatively free from the more dramatic teleologies of his colleagues, marking a more modest sorting out of the valuable and the dangerous, inviting reflection, flexibility, and ambivalence.

Heuss's view is perhaps the most telling, insofar as it sometimes seems to contradict its stated goals, insisting on memory but failing to prescribe it, acknowledging the past but failing to specify it, accepting responsibility and the need for contemplating it but undermining this with the same grammar as his colleagues, identifying ordinary anti-Semitism as the beginning but then replacing the Jewish victims with the German. I will return to the central question of the ways in which this revived political discourse marked a restoration or indicated a caesura. But before doing so, I take up a somewhat distinct discourse on the difference between guilt and shame, so clear here, as alternative paradigms for the future of German political culture.

CHAPTER 12

The Philosophy of Guilt

In 1946, the Columbia University anthropologist Ruth Benedict published a book version of a report she had written during the war for the Foreign Morale Analysis Division of the U.S. Office of War Information. Since then, *The Chrysanthemum and the Sword* has become a classic, most remembered for its contrast between a Japanese culture of "shame" and a Western culture of "guilt." "A society that includes absolute standards of morality and relies on men's developing a conscience," Benedict wrote, "is a guilt culture by definition." "True shame cultures," in contrast, "rely on external sanctions for good behavior, not, as true guilt cultures do, on an internalized conviction of sin. Shame is a reaction to other people's criticism." Perhaps the most important difference for Benedict is in how individuals in guilt cultures and in shame cultures process misdeeds. In a guilt culture, a "man who has sinned can get relief by unburdening himself. This device of confession is used in our secular therapy and by many religious groups which have otherwise little in common. We know it brings relief." On the other hand, "[w]here shame is the major sanction, a man does not experience relief when he makes his fault public even to a confessor. So long as his behavior does not 'get out into the world' he need not be troubled and confession appears to him merely a way of courting trouble. Shame cultures therefore do not provide for confessions, even to gods."[1]

In the book's conclusion, Benedict characterized the Allied occupation policies in Germany and Japan as appropriately different, in the former case aimed at internal renewal through awareness of guilt, in the latter aimed at external transformation sensitive to Japanese shame. In a comparison of German and Japanese collective memories of World War II, the journalist

1. Benedict, *The Chrysanthemum and the Sword*, 222–23.

Ian Buruma followed Benedict's lead when he wrote, "The Germans, riddled with guilt, feel the need to confess their sins, to unburden their guilt and be forgiven." In contrast, "the Japanese wish to remain silent and, above all, wish others to remain silent too, for the point is not guilt in the eyes of God, but public shame, embarrassment, 'face.'" Whether or in what sense Buruma's characterization is accurate that Germans are "riddled with guilt," however, is obviously a complex question.[2]

Certainly, the distinction between guilt cultures and shame cultures is tricky, as is any such broad schema. *The Chrysanthemum and the Sword* has generally come to be regarded as a relic of another age, and has been criticized for its reliance on what is too strong a notion of national character, and especially for what is perceived to be its implication that guilt cultures are both historically more advanced than shame cultures and morally superior to them.[3] Benedict's approval, moreover, of the different occupation strategies—if so much coherence could be attributed to them—is not quite so obvious at a half-century's remove, though the fact is that both Germany and Japan have indeed been peaceful and prosperous members of the community of nations.[4] So Benedict could not have been too far wrong, and the book has remained continuously in print since 1946.

As with most such scholarly classics, the account is at least somewhat more subtle than memory indicates. Benedict pointed out, for example, that even in guilt cultures one may also experience shame, as "when [a person in a guilt culture] accuses himself of gaucheries which are in no way sins." She noted that "[s]hame is an increasingly heavy burden in the United States and guilt is

2. Buruma, *The Wages of Guilt*, 253.

3. For example, "In a culture where shame is a major sanction," Benedict wrote, "people are chagrined about acts which we expect people to feel guilty about" (220). Benedict thus dispassionately describes Japanese culture as a sort of institutionalized hypocrisy: "'Respecting yourself' often implies exactly the opposite behavior from that which it means in the United States. . . . It had no implication, as it would in the United States, that even if thoughts are dangerous a man's self-respect requires that he think according to his own lights and his own conscience" (ibid.). Another such example is Benedict's argument that "*Makoto* does not mean what sincerity does in English usage . . . for calling a man 'sincere' in Japan has no reference to whether he is acting 'genuinely' according to love or hate, determination or amazement which is uppermost in his soul" (215–16). Additionally, "In Japan 'respecting yourself' is always to show yourself the careful player. It does not mean, as it does in English usage, consciously conforming to a worthy standard of conduct—not truckling to another, not lying, not giving false testimony. . . . When a man says 'You must respect yourself,' it means, 'You must be shrewd in estimating all the factors in the situation and do nothing that will arouse criticism or lessen your chances of success'" (219).

4. On Japanese reactions to World War II, see Dower, *Embracing Defeat*.

less extremely felt than in earlier generations." On the one hand, Benedict agreed that this could rightly be interpreted as "a relaxation of morals." Our concern over the rise of shame and the decline of guilt comes from the fact that "we do not expect shame to do the heavy work of morality. We do not harness the acute personal chagrin which accompanies shame to our fundamental system of morality."[5] On the other hand, she also admitted that another interpretation is possible: after all, she noted, "[m]odern novelists . . . who in the early years of this century celebrated the new Western individualism, became dissatisfied with the Occidental formulas and tried to celebrate sincerity . . . as the only true doctrine."[6] As we will see, European conservatives between the World Wars were vigorous advocates of shame over guilt. There is hardly a greater critic of guilt culture from east or west, moreover, than Friedrich Nietzsche, who in many ways embodied fin de siècle Germany.

For all its weaknesses, numerous contemporary analysts of Germany have found this fundamental distinction useful by avoiding the implication that shame and guilt are stages in a developmental process. As Aleida Assmann has put it, "Shame culture and guilt culture stand . . . for two forms of cultural treatment of a disruptive evil. . . . Instead of a historical development in which a higher guilt culture succeeds a lower shame culture, it is more reasonable to assume a dialectic in which two behavioral systems continually reactivate each other."[7] In a study of intellectuals like those Benedict referred to as dissatisfied with Occidental guilt, moreover, literary critic Herman Lethen has shown that World War I discredited the guilt principle for many European thinkers: "The fact that the civilized nations could engage in such horror, that individuals were able to suspend conscience for the sake of military operations, neither informed introspection nor generated confessions." As a result, "[w]e would be much nearer the mark in saying that the collective gaze following World War One was averted from the complex of issues identified by a guilt culture."[8] According to Lethen, shame—which he follows Benedict in seeing as "fixing the genesis of internal authority in social violence"—was a more helpful framework for "the construction of a self more able to bear the immense pressures that rapid modernization placed on the bourgeois individual." It enabled the war's losers "to subvert the fiction of the self-made individual that is part of

5. Benedict, *The Chrysanthemum and the Sword*, 222–24.
6. Ibid., 213.
7. Assmann and Frevert, *Geschichtsvergessenheit/Geschichtsversessenheit*, 90–91.
8. Lethen, *Cool Conduct*, 11.

the concept of a guilt culture."⁹ The culture of Weimar, according to Lethen, thus depended on a manly "conduct of cool." In this light, it is not surprising that the two major philosophical alternatives of the Weimar period were, first, a dominant conservative embrace of Nietzschean nihilism coupled with a radical critique of modernity (supporting a shame culture) and, second, a less-successful, liberal, neo-Kantian existentialism coupled with a defense of humanism (supporting a guilt culture). In Germany, the former was part of the broader cultural universe of which National Socialism was a part, while the latter went underground or into exile.

*   *   *

The historical question I address in this and the next chapter is whether and in what ways this nexus of dominant nihilism verus squelched humanism was reversed after 1945. Indeed, many accounts of post–World War II German intellectual culture either skip over the possibility of a persisting radical conservatism (part of a shame culture) or characterize it as a phenomenon so marginalized as to be nearly totally irrelevant. One manifestation of this is the place that has been ascribed to the philosopher Karl Jaspers, particularly to his 1946 book *Die Schuldfrage* [*The Question of German Guilt*]. According to the German-Israeli historian Dan Diner, for instance, "Jaspers's discussion of the theme [German guilt] in 1945–46 reads like a founding text for the new (West) German collective identity. . . . Jaspers's . . . confessional text," Diner claims, "acquired quasi-normative significance for the old Federal Republic."¹⁰ In the historians' dispute of 1985, the sociologist and philosopher Jürgen Habermas attacked neoconservatives, claiming that their attempt to limit the role of Holocaust memory in the Federal Republic violated basic commitments of West German political culture, namely—if not exactly guilt—then acknowledgment and acceptance of responsibility for Germany's Nazi past. Habermas's main referent for this tradition was Karl Jaspers. For Habermas, Jaspers's approach was the *sine qua non* of a healthy German political culture, and any implication that it was not obvious and untouchable was unacceptable.¹¹

Even those who ascribe more power or even legitimacy to purportedly discredited conservative traditions ascribe Jaspers's argument for guilt to

9. Ibid., 15. See also Assman and Frevert, *Geschichtsvergessenheit/Geschichtsversessenheit*, 88–96.

10. Diner, *Beyond the Conceivable*, 219.

11. Habermas, *The New Conservatism*. See also the chapter on Jaspers in Habermas, *Philosophical-Political Profiles*.

official culture and the conservative shame tradition to the private sphere. In his study of the radical conservative writer Ernst Jünger, for instance, Elliot Neaman argues that "[o]fficial unequivocal antifascism [guilt culture] repressed the legacy of pre-Nazi German culture [shame culture], seen as contaminated and compromised by the Nazi assimilation of the romantic-classicist German pantheon."[12] As the political scientist Jan-Werner Müller puts it in his study of postwar intellectuals in the Federal Republic:

> Two cultures opposed each other in early postwar Germany. On the one side, there was an official public culture of guilt and democratic humanism, sanctioned by the Allies through the licensed journals, and centered on emigrants and liberals such as Jaspers. On the other side stood an obstinate culture of silence, in which honour was preserved through taboos. The culture of guilt and communication, not surprisingly, dominated in public, but the counterculture of silence became more characteristic for the private and semi-private life of the young republic.[13]

Herman Lethen states, on the one hand, that "[i]n the context of the Nuremberg trials, the statement of the Protestant Church, and denazification, a guilt culture is a matter of official prescription."[14] (Of course, there is good reason to doubt that the mere facts of the Nuremberg trials, the statement of the Protestant Church, and denazification indicate anything much at all about the success of a guilt culture, since, as we have seen, they were widely repudiated.) On the other hand, Lethen insightfully demonstrates that the "distinction between shame and guilt cultures is instructive as a myth, the reality of a wish projection that was persuasive to a generation of critical intellectuals."[15]

As we will see, many discredited conservatives self-consciously adhered to a recalcitrant notion of honor and repudiated Jaspers, in the process asserting the existence of what they believed to be an oppressive "official culture of guilt." As we just saw, even Jaspers's proponents in subsequent decades (like Diner and Habermas) argued that Jaspers's vision predominated. Jaspers himself could be said to have been trying to help establish the culture of guilt; *Die Schuldfrage* includes measured responses to the litany of perceived "cool" objections to Allied policy and German introspection. However, the myth of Jaspers's success in doing this, paradoxically, is at least in part the product of his opponents, who took him as the representative of

12. Neaman, *A Dubious Past*, 10.
13. Müller, *Another Country*, 31.
14. Lethen, *Cool Conduct*, 173–74.
15. Ibid., 13–14.

the new public culture (or mistook the public culture as following Jaspers), whether or not he really was; characterizing official culture in this way made it easier for them to scorn it, for it had scorned them. In the process, they intentionally minimized their own continued influence. Jaspers himself viewed his effort to introduce a culture of guilt as a near total failure.

It is thus crucial to ask how this claim that Jaspers's vision achieved the "quasi-normative status" attributed to it came about. Why, that is, do we believe that the dominant culture was in fact "guilty"? Was that culture one of unequivocal antifascism, as the just-quoted claim of Elliot Neaman argues, and indeed as the scholarly literature often assumes? Or is Aleida Assmann more accurate, for example, when she argues that a "deeper confrontation with the question of guilt in the postwar society has been blocked by a still widely functioning, even in part newly elaborated shame culture"? In this chapter and the next, my aim is to see how the claim that the official culture was a guilt culture and the private one a shame culture arose. This is, however, a question distinct from whether that claim was in fact true. (It is possible, for instance, that Diner is right. Jaspers's argument did achieve quasi-normative status, just not until many decades later; and *Die Schuldfrage* may indeed have been conceived as a founding document of the political culture even if no one accepted it at the time; but the previous chapter has also given us reason to at least question the claim that a new guilt culture predominated).

Whether or not Jaspers's *Schuldfrage* achieved "quasi-normative status," it has achieved a quasi-mythological status in collective memory, specifically in "the memory of memory" of National Socialism. The philosophical rigor of the argument as well as the common reification of that which appears on the printed page, however, have both served to distract from the fluid discursive origins of the argument and its dialogical specificity (which, as we will see, were in part highly personal). The book's transposability to completely alien contemporary debates about transitional justice, combined with a hagiographic approach to Jaspers, moreover, have contributed to *Die Schuldfrage*'s iconic status, in the process distracting from other interesting historical statements. Who now, after all, reads Karl Barth? And that is to say nothing of Julius Ebbinghaus or Theodor Litt, whose work we will consider shortly for comparison. Why is this so? There are good reasons; they just are not as obvious as one might assume.

Jaspers and the Idea of the University

In the immediate aftermath of the war, Karl Jaspers was perhaps uniquely placed to speak on behalf of positive German traditions. A former protégé of Max Weber, Jaspers represented the liberal view of German nationalism; a neo-Kantian existentialist philosopher, Jaspers stood for humanistic ideals (yet also appreciated darker readings of Nietzsche like that by his friend Martin Heidegger). Having been stripped of his university position in 1937 and married to a Jew, Jaspers was entirely free of National Socialist taint. In April of 1945, Jaspers joined a "committee of thirteen," approved by the Americans, for the purpose of preparing the reopening of Heidelberg University, where he had been a leading figure.[16] At this early juncture, Jaspers was quite optimistic that he and his colleagues could contribute to a period of renewal through genuine self-examination:

> The mood was exhilarating. The transformation within the spiritual and political world through ourselves, not through directives of the military government, was our shared hope. That this freedom was given to us by the American Military Government so soon, that they helped us to help ourselves . . . and that we were actually granted an unusual freedom to use our own initiative was like a miracle.[17]

For Jaspers, however, as he made clear in an August 15, 1945, speech at the reopening of the Heidelberg medical faculty, the hoped-for transformation could occur only through a genuine confrontation with the past: "We ourselves became different since 1933. . . . Something has happened with us through the twelve years that is like a recasting of our essence. . . . We must distance ourselves from the past around us and in us."[18] This belief, it turns out, was exactly what separated Jaspers from most of his colleagues, who he unhappily came to believe were more interested in a restoration, a return to the *status quo ante* of 1933. This resistance to reform, we will see, was for Jaspers a devastating indicator for the German future.

Jaspers's approach and outlook were indeed unusual among his academic colleagues. In his study of inaugural addresses by rectors at reopening German universities, Eike Wolgast concluded, "In their remarks about the Third Reich, most rectors made do with brief remarks—like the politicians and church figures the view to the future was for them much more important than a serious confrontation with the past."[19] While university

16. On Jaspers's role, and the denazification of Heidelberg University more generally, see Remy, *The Heidelberg Myth*.

17. Jaspers, *Schicksal und Wille*, 167.

18. Jaspers, "Erneuerung der Universität," in *Hoffnung und Sorge*, 32. The speech is described in the book as "a first public statement on the Hitler state, its crimes, and our guilt and on our task."

19. Wolgast, *Die Wahrnehmung des Dritten Reiches in der unmittelbaren Nachkriegszeit*, 287–328; quotation from 299.

rectors highlighted the political catastrophe of the present, they rarely addressed the possible connections between politics and intellectual life; few inquired into the historical origins of National Socialism and the role of the universities. When failures of the universities were mentioned, they were minimized: resistance might have been honorable, but it was considered futile, even foolhardy. Indeed, though in *Die Schuldfrage* he rejected such equivocations, even Jaspers himself took the self-exculpatory position against which Karl Barth had warned:

> Thousands in Germany sought or found death in resistance against the regime, most anonymously. We survivors did not seek death. We did not take to the streets as our Jewish friends were led away, did not scream until one destroyed us as well. We preferred to remain alive with the weak, but also correct, justification that our death would not have been able to help. That we live is our guilt.[20] We acknowledge before God what humbles us.[21]

Jaspers's conventional, and unsubstantiable, defense here that all resistance meant death can be seen as a cultural reflex, given his general repudiation of such equivocations; that even Jaspers is subject to the reflex is telling.

Litt and Ebbinghaus

Two exceptions to the dominant posture that avoided inquiry into the complicity of the universities are worth considering here, if only very briefly. The first is Theodor Litt, professor of pedagogy in Leipzig. In 1932, Litt had proposed a resolution to the university senate condemning the activities of Nazi student groups. In the following year, he was prevented from delivering a lecture attacking basic tenets of the National Socialist approach to science: for Litt, science could not be placed in the service of imposed theories, in particular the so-called "racial" view of history. In 1937, Litt was forced into early retirement. After the war, he was offered the rectorship of Leipzig University, but declined, in part because of his discomfort with the denazification of the Leipzig professoriate.[22]

---

20. As we will see, Martin Heidegger quoted this line in response to his former student Herbert Marcuse, who had written to Heidegger demanding an explanation of Heidegger's failure to publicly repudiate his Nazi past. See Marcuse and Heidegger, "An Exchange of Letters," in Wolin, *The Heidegger Controversy*, 163.

21. Jaspers, *The Question of German Guilt*, 66.

22. The philosopher Hans-Georg Gadamer agreed to assume the rectorship, though he subsequently fled to the West, assuming Jaspers's vacated chair at Heidelberg in 1948.

For Litt, the central problem for the university was not the complicity of individual professors with National Socialism, but the simultaneous denial by some of any role at all combined with the unwillingness of the university and occupation authorities to accept acknowledgments of responsibility from others. On the one hand, for Litt, were those radical conservative figures like Ernst Jünger or Oswald Spengler, who denied any responsibility for their ideas that had contributed to or were adopted by the Nazis. Their late repudiations of National Socialism, for Litt, were at least partly disingenuous: "It was not the first time that an idea that caused no scruples either in its author or in its readers as long as it existed only on paper aroused terror of itself as soon as it took tangible shape in practice."[23] On the other hand, Litt argued strenuously that the mere fact that one had retained an academic post in the Third Reich did not amount to complicity with the regime; in particular, Litt was instrumental in the defense of his colleague, the sociologist Hans Freyer, who not only had retained his post, but whose ideas were part of the "conservative revolution" of which National Socialism, some would argue, was a particular variant (defenders of the conservative position, we will see, argued that National Socialism was a perversion of what they still believed to be defensible positions). In the process, Litt compared the Soviet denazification efforts—and Soviet policy more generally—to National Socialist strategies.

Litt's position, in many respects, was similar to that of Eugen Kogon, who we earlier saw during these same postwar years to be defending the right to a political mistake. But as for Kogon, for Litt this right could only be retrospectively legitimated by a thorough acknowledgment of the mistake. Litt thus rejected what he saw as the predisposition "in certain parties"—and not just those who were culpable—"to regard it as a duty to overlook our recent past entirely."[24] Failure to inquire into the historical sources of National Socialism in Germany, Litt argued, would only serve those who sought to condemn German traditions wholesale. In his lecture and subsequent book *On the Mission of Philosophy* [*Von der Sendung der Philosophie*], Litt was very nearly brutal in his assessment. He charged his contemporaries with taking it too easy on themselves, and catalogued the

23. Quoted in Muller, *The Other God that Failed*, 365. One should recall, in this context, Thomas Mann's condemnation of Ernst Jünger's "saber rattling."

24. As we will see, Jaspers faced the same reaction, particularly when his colleagues warned him that even if his arguments were correct, it was not wise to make them so publicly. We encountered the same argument in the debate over the Stuttgart Declaration in chapter 10, where many believed it was inappropriate to make statements in public that might have given the occupation authorities some kind of moral advantage.

temptations of self-deception. And he demanded more from them than even critical distancing: "There can and will be no resurrection of our people unless it masters every touch of weakness, every attempt at self-deception, looks with determination into the face of the truth, and does not attempt to repress anything from its consciousness that can be robbed of its thorn only through the most honest accounting." For Litt, the experience of National Socialism was "[an] unmasking of man, which in its cruel mercilessness has no equal." Only accepting this lesson would prevent it from happening again:

> It would be a glaring mockery of the summons of this historical moment, if we— ALL of us, for we all contributed to this unmasking—wanted to exempt ourselves from admitting openly to that which came to light, and by doing so do not carry upwards from the abyss of error, suffering, and guilt into which we fell the only thing that it can grant us: the clarity of knowledge about ourselves and the determination to resist the self-endangerment whose horror has become apparent to us. Only the truth makes us free![25]

This and other statements did not endear Litt to the Soviet authorities, and he was forced to flee to the West, where he accepted a chair at the university in Bonn. His personal intercession on behalf of figures such as Freyer, however, seemed to insulate him from much of the scorn Jaspers experienced from his colleagues.

The second exception to the general trend on the part of university leaders not to acknowledge responsibility for the Nazi past was Julius Ebbinghaus, rector of Marburg University, which was the first German university to reopen (Jaspers's August 15 speech at Heidelberg was at the reopening of only the medical faculty, which preceded the reopening of the university at large). Ebbinghaus delivered the opening speech as well as a number of others at Marburg, and reprinted these in a widely read book titled On Germany's Change of Fate [Zu Deutschlands Schicksalswende].[26] Ebbinghaus had worked closely with AMG authorities

25. Litt, Von der Sendung der Philosophie, 23. The last sentence is in response to the Nazi slogan, Arbeit macht frei (work makes free), which was famously inscribed over the gates of Auschwitz.

26. Ebbinghaus, Zu Deutschlands Schicksalswende. For a more general account of the reopening of the universities, see Tent, Mission on the Rhine. Unlike Jaspers's Die Schuldfrage, neither Litt's Von der Sendung der Philosophie nor Ebbinghaus's Zu Deutschlands Schicksalswende were reprinted, except the latter as part of Ebbinghaus's collected works. Anecdotal evidence for the absence of these works in German and other memory is that the Columbia University Library, one of the major research libraries in the world, does not have a copy of Ebbinghaus's

on the reestablishment of the university at Marburg, and shared with Jaspers an appreciation for American goals.[27]

Ebbinghaus was an orthodox neo-Kantian philosopher, and as such emphasized the transcendental status of conceptual universals: truth and right were pure forms, standing above empirical realities rather than at their service. Ebbinghaus thus held the values of "liberty, equality, and fraternity" to be incorruptible principles; no system that opposed them could be considered just. Hitler's victory would therefore have meant robbing Germans of their fatherland, for a fatherland only exists where "people live freely together according to the laws of man." As part of this understanding, despite the fact that his audience was filled with soldiers recently returned from the front, Ebbinghaus categorically rejected the argument that fighting to the end had merely been a matter of doing one's patriotic duty: "Only surrender to the enemy would have been an act of patriotism, and whoever fought on was in an absolute and irrevocable sense fighting against Germany."[28] The true horror for Ebbinghaus, as a Kantian, was the conflict between the ethical imperatives individuals faced as human beings and the demands of the state.

Like Jaspers and Litt, Ebbinghaus was particularly concerned with reestablishing the autonomy of scholarship and of the university. For Ebbinghaus, like the others, the heart of the problem of National Socialism in the universities was its subordination of science to a political agenda. As a Kantian, who like Jaspers was influenced by Max Weber's conception of the value-freedom of scientific inquiry, Ebbinghaus understood the practice of science to be inherently opposed to tyranny because the fundamental principle of science is rationality, and the fundamental principle of tyranny is irrationality; freedom was thus both the precondition and the result of scientific work. Only science can prevent the destruction of law and freedom. Indeed, Ebbinghaus lashed out at the students for not having grasped this fundamental principle—their agitation during the early years of National

original book (it has the collected works). And despite the fact that Columbia has exceptionally strong history and German departments, both Litt's book and Ebbinghaus's collected works have been checked out only once, the former not since 1948.

27. The American officer responsible for the reconstruction of universities in the American zone was Edward Harthshorne, who, as mentioned in chapter 3, was a close associate of Talcott Parsons, with whom he had worked on ideas about German society, culture, university life, and re-education. Hartshorne was shot and killed while traveling on the *Autobahn* between universities. He had worked closely with Ebbinghaus, who delivered a moving eulogy. Parsons wrote an obituary for the *American Sociological Review*.

28. Ebbinghaus, *Zu Deutschlands Schicksalswende*, 17. Compare this to the politicians' denial that soldiers were "militaristic."

Socialism, he charged, had helped the National Socialist penetration (*Gleichschaltung*) of the universities. The professors as well, according to Ebbinghaus, were guilty of a lack of political insight, though usually not of the same kind of activism and misunderstanding of science as the students. Ebbinghaus defended science as a pure enterprise, ideally taking place "as though on an island."[29] Here again we see the common temptation to retreat into culture, even in a politicized context.

From University to Polity

Numerous minor differences among Litt, Ebbinghaus, and Jaspers contributed to the differences in the mnemonic longevity of their statements. Jaspers was a somewhat more prominent figure, and he was a better, more accessible writer than either Litt or Ebbinghaus. He was also more skilled in making a generalized, and generalizable argument, such that *Die Schuldfrage* has been carried over to other contexts, particularly to discussions about how to confront the legacies of authoritarian regimes in Latin America in the 1980s and in Eastern Europe after 1989.[30] Both Ebbinghaus and Litt remained more within the ambit of German academic debates, even when they took their arguments to the public sphere.[31] Jaspers, however, did so more regularly and more ardently, and believed the scholar was responsible to the public in a way not entirely traditional for German academia; this was especially true in later years, when Jaspers's contributions to debates about German rearmament, atomic weapons, and the statute of limitations for National Socialist crimes drew attention to his earlier work.[32] Indeed, at least part of *Die Schuldfrage*'s iconic status is the result of its later rereading and rediscovery in light of Jaspers's political interventions in the more receptive context of the 1960s. From another perspective, as we will see, Jaspers's reputation is also partly due to his proximity to other, more notorious figures, like Martin Heidegger. The elaborate discourse over Heidegger's philosophical

29. Ibid.

30. See Kritz, *Transitional Justice*.

31. One reason for this is that, despite his prominence and centrality to the debates of his time, Jaspers was always something of a philosophical outsider, having begun as a physician with a work on psychopathology, thus coming to academic philosophy from beyond the often orthodox confines of the guild.

32. Before 1933, Jaspers had often avoided political discussions, and admired his mentor Max Weber's political writings only from a distance. With the advent of National Socialism, and particularly with its demise, Jaspers sought a much more substantial political voice than he had theretofore been comfortable with. See Jaspers, *Wohin treibt die Bundesrepublik*.

and political legacies, particularly vigorous in the 1980s, involved ever-greater attention to Jaspers's central personal role, through his relationship not only to Heidegger—which we will examine below—but to Hannah Arendt as well, whose wide-ranging work and intriguing biography have occasioned significant intellectual historical interest in the past few decades.

Both Litt's and Ebbinghaus's primary concern seemed to be the fate of the university and its membership. Jaspers too was directly concerned with the university; he had published a book called *The Idea of the University* in 1923 and pointedly reissued it in 1946; he also delivered numerous lectures on the purposes of scholarship in the immediate postwar period. But for Jaspers, the university was less a special "island" separate from society than it was a model for society. Jaspers did not just speak in the university about the university, but made his arguments about the public to the public, in part through his involvement with the short-lived, though centrally important journal, *Die Wandlung* [*The Transformation*], for which, in 1945, he wrote the opening editorial statement. Like Martin Niemöller and his followers, Jaspers thus saw the deficits of a separation between spirit and politics; spirit was not just to be left alone by politics, it must address and guide the political. The paradox, as we will see, is that while Jaspers believed that intellectuals had a political responsibility, like Ebbinghaus he rejected political understandings of German national identity.

Die Schuldfrage

On October 25, 1945, the *Neue Zeitung* carried a letter from the Norwegian novelist Sigrid Undset, winner of the Nobel Prize. Undset had passed the war in American exile, during which time she was active in discussions of German character and theories of re-education, not least as an attendee at Richard Brickner's Columbia Symposium, discussed in chapter 3. Undset was deeply skeptical about the possibility of a German turnaround. For her, the horror was simply too much to be overcome with institutional restructuring or reexamination of basic values. "The greatest hindrance to German re-education," Undset argued, "is not German thinking, but rather the actual deeds which have been committed as a result of this thinking." Interestingly, Undset's inflection of guilt was more longitudinal than latitudinal (in other words, guilt shared over time rather than guilt of all present at one time): she acknowledged that in a nation of 70 million people there would be a mix of good and bad, intelligent and stupid. The real problem is with "millions of German children," who are burdened with "fathers who took part in the atrocities against civilians, women and children." Moreover, beyond the legacies of actual perpetration of atrocities, "[c]ountless German children have parents who experienced a fleeting prosperity as a result of the plunder of Europe . . . pocketing some of the booty which had been taken from the dead!" And German mothers were as guilty as the fathers, having taken over "homes and properties of people in occupied territories, even keeping family portraits which they occasionally offered to sell back to their owners at a high price!"[33]

At the request of "an American editor,"[34] Jaspers undertook a response to Undset, which contained the seeds of his more elaborate arguments in *Die Schuldfrage*. For Jaspers, there were two fundamental problems with Undset's argument. First, her condemnation appeared total and her assessment of Germany's future hopeless. For the existentialist Jaspers, "[t]here cannot be hopelessness when people live with people." Jaspers believed fervently in the possibility for repentance and conversion: "The freedom, the possibility of a turn-around, remains for everyone, even the guilty." Furthermore, "[w]hoever is condemned without hope, can no longer answer." But the Allies had stated that the German people should not be destroyed, that they will be given a chance; Jaspers thus felt compelled and entitled to answer, and to reject Undset's outlook of hopelessness.[35]

Second, Undset's condemnation appeared to Jaspers to be illegitimately collectivistic: "To condemn summarily a people as a whole or every member of this people seems to me to violate the claim of being human. No verdict on an individual person," Jaspers argued, "even less so on all members of a people is true, that claims 'that is the way they are.'" Insofar as Undset blamed a unitary German world of ideas, Jaspers said, she was employing the same logic as the Nazis, a logic that is "a means of mutual hatred of peoples and groups. It was applied in the most evil way by the National Socialists and was drummed into people's heads by their propaganda." Jaspers agreed with Undset's outrage, but argued that the issue was "in what sense every German must feel complicit."[36] This was the central question Jaspers attempted to work out in *Die Schuldfrage*, which had its origins as a series of lectures in Heidelberg in 1945–46.

*   *   *

33. *"Die Umerziehung der Deutschen," Neue Zeitung,* October 25, 1945. Such an idea was likely behind Henry Morgenthau's thoughts—never pursued—about removing German children to Anglo-American schools.

34. This is the way Jaspers put it at the beginning of his essay to justify why he undertook a response to Undset, even though he said he would have preferred to pass over her accusations.

35. Jaspers, *"Antwort an Sigrid Undset,"* in *Hoffnung und Sorge,* 47.

36. Ibid., 47–49.

Despite its reputation as the definitive statement of postwar German guilt culture, Jaspers's *Die Schuldfrage* had none of the totalistic condemnations of Undset, Jung, or even Barth. Ever the philosopher, Jaspers believed that "to arrive at truth we must differentiate."[37] His distinctions among criminal, political, moral, and metaphysical guilt are well known, even hackneyed. Criminal guilt refers to those acts for which one may be held liable in a court of law; political guilt refers to the responsibility one bears for the political system in which one lives by virtue of being a citizen (political "responsibility," Jaspers argued, is borne even by those who opposed the regime); moral guilt refers to whatever personal failings one demonstrated in attitude, demeanor, or action (for instance, enthusiasm for the regime's successes or turning a blind eye to one's suffering neighbor); and metaphysical guilt is closest to the Christian notion of original sin, guilt stemming from the knowledge that such things are possible in the world. The four types of guilt, one notes, can be divided in two different ways: criminal and political guilt are public, while moral and metaphysical guilt are private; by the same token, criminal and moral guilt are absolutely individual, whereas political and metaphysical guilt can be shared (if it is unclear what exactly it would mean to say collective).

Types of Guilt	*Private*	*Public*
Individual	Moral	Criminal
Collective	Metaphysical	Political

But the importance of Jaspers's argument is not entirely captured by the typology, which is what has nevertheless captured the mnemonic imagination.

Jaspers's rhetorical strategy was to establish from the outset a community of discourse with his compatriots: "We must learn to talk with each other," he pleaded, "and we mutually must understand and accept one another in our extraordinary differences." The obstacle here was "the great diversity in what we believed all these years, what we took to be true, what to us was the meaning of life. . . . What we must painfully renounce is [thus] not alike for all. . . . We are divided along different lines of disappointment." Jaspers therefore rejected what he saw as the false distinction between exiles and "inner emigrants" ("At times we seem to hear a *pharisaical* note in the charges, from those who perilously made their

37. Jaspers, *The Question of German Guilt*, 22.

escape . . . this note we deem ourselves entitled to reject without anger) and between party members and mere bystanders ("We dissociate ourselves from the *pharisaism* of those who think the mere absence of a party badge makes them first-class people"): "The only common denominator may be our nationality which makes us all jointly guilty and liable for having let 1933 come to pass without dying."[38] Jaspers argued from the standpoint of one suffering the same fate as his compatriots and made no effort to excuse himself from the burdens of which he spoke. Nevertheless, it remained for him to work out—both philosophically and personally— what this bond of common nationality could mean.[39]

Jaspers was at this juncture simultaneously more resigned to the situation of *vae victus* (woe to the vanquished) than many of his compatriots as well as more positively inclined toward the Western authorities, whose political culture he believed to be motivated by principles of right, law, and fairness. By the same token, Jaspers rejected—as many of his compatriots did—that anything good could come of accusations or demands for introspection from outside. He mentioned the "placard actions" (discussed in chapter 5) and their slogans accusing the Germans of guilt for the atrocities in the camps. "It is only human," he said, "that the accused, whether justly or unjustly, tries to defend himself." Such accusations—like those of Sigrid Undset—Jaspers considered both crude and, in the case of the placards, born of illegitimate motives: "That condemnation by the victorious powers became a means of politics and impure in its motives—this fact itself is a guilt pervading history. . . . Evil is evil even when inflicted as retribution." But noting this, Jaspers argued, must never lead to superiority or self-exculpation: "If we use the words, 'guilt of the others,' it may mislead us. If they, by their conduct, made events possible, this is political guilt. But in discussing it we must never forget for a moment that this guilt is on another level than the crimes of Hitler."[40] Jaspers's tone was thus significantly different from that of many others who spent great time outlining the

---

38. Important to note in this statement is that the unifying German guilt appeared to have been for allowing the Nazis to come to power, rather than for the Holocaust. On the one hand, one could criticize this for neglecting the specificity of Jewish suffering. On the other hand, Jaspers in the process differentiated his arguments from those who refused to condemn the war's beginning because of its end.

39. Ibid., 5, 12, 78, 97, 98.

40. "In general, it may be correct that 'the others are not better than we.' But at this moment it is misapplied. For in these past twelve years the others, taken for all in all, were indeed better than we. A general truth must not serve to level out the particular, present truth of our own guilt." Ibid., 91.

responsibility of Germany's enemies (though he did nevertheless mention the "guilt of others").[41]

Such accusations from outside, however, while morally irrelevant, were not without practical meaning for Jaspers. He concluded his response to Undset by saying that Germans should well note that one as intelligent as Undset could hold such opinions as she did. "We cannot be indifferent," Jaspers argued, "to what the world thinks of us, for we are part of mankind—are human before we are German."[42] Where Mann and others spoke of German humiliation before the world, however, Jaspers was less morally concerned by the charge—if it was illegitimate, it was the charger's fault. There was a risk, but it was a political one: "The political question," Jaspers seemed to warn, "is whether it is politically sensible, purposeful, safe and just to turn a whole nation into a pariah nation, to degrade it beneath all others, to dishonor further, once it had dishonored itself." What the Allies thought, however, was ultimately irrelevant for Germans: "Those charges from without are no longer our concern. We must clarify the question of German guilt. This is our own business."[43] For Jaspers, this meant filling the idea of pariahdom with content.[44]

The central question for Germans, then, was what they made out of their own condition: "The guilt question is more than a question put to us by others, it is one we put to ourselves. It is a vital question for the German soul." The reality they had to face, Jaspers argued, was that the Germans had in fact become a "pariah people" (Undset's reaction was proof). The concept of pariahdom was for Jaspers and many others a very powerful one, not incidentally because the classical example of a "pariah people," as articulated by Max Weber, was the Jews.[45] Even for Jaspers, who did not see German Jews as in any way less German and who even in 1945 refused to believe that anti-Semitism had ever really been widespread among the population,[46] the appeal of this historically surprising analogy was irresistible. We already saw Jaspers's charge that Undset's collectivistic condemnation drew on the same logics

41. Ibid., 41, 84.

42. This is nearly identical to Erich Kästner's evaluation of the relevance of Carl Jung.

43. Here Jaspers's argument matched that of Eugen Kogon.

44. Ibid., 22, 42, 43.

45. For a seminal discussion of Jaspers's use of the pariah concept in *Die Schuldfrage*, on which my account draws a great deal, see Rabinbach, "The German as Pariah," in *In the Shadow of Catastrophe*, 129–65.

46. Letter from Karl Jaspers to Hannah Arendt, April 19, 1947: "I have never thought 'the people' to be really anti-Semitic. A spontaneous pogrom never took place, however much the Nazis may have wished for one and tried in vain to provoke it." Regarding his wife's status as a

against Germans that the Nazis had used against Jews (and Jaspers repeated the argument in *Die Schuldfrage*). Later in the book, Jaspers continued to make the association: "A world opinion which condemns a people collectively is of a kind with the fact that for thousands of years men have thought and said, 'The Jews are guilty of the Crucifixion.' Who are the 'the Jews'? A certain group of religious and political zealots whose relative power among the Jews of that time, with the Roman occupation authorities, led to the execution of Jesus."[47]

So what should the Germans make of their pariah status? Would it be thoroughly negative or would it yield new insight? "Here we Germans face an alternative. Either acceptance of the guilt not meant by the rest of the world but constantly repeated by our conscience comes to be a fundamental trait of our German self-consciousness—in which case our soul goes the way of transformation—or we subside into the average triviality of indifferent, mere living." For Jaspers, the moral and political imperative was clear: "There is no other way to realize truth for the German than purification out of the depth of consciousness of guilt." Like of the Jews for Christ? Jaspers did not go that far, though as we saw some church leaders did.[48]

Nevertheless, this was Jaspers's vision for the future of Germany, and it is why *Die Schuldfrage* is considered a founding text for a new political culture:

> Full frankness and honesty harbors not only our dignity—possible even in impotence—but our own chance. The question for every German is whether to go this way at the risk of all disappointments, at the risk of additional losses and of convenient abuse by the powerful. The answer is that this is the only way that we can save our souls from a pariah existence. What will result from it we shall have to see. It is a spiritual-political venture along the edge of the precipice. If success is possible, then it will be only at long range. We are going to be distrusted for a long time to come.

But elsewhere, Jaspers put a more positive inflection on the pariahdom experience, suggesting that it might even produce special insights. First of all, he argued, reminiscent of the historians' arguments we examined in chapter 8, it

---

German Jew, Jaspers wrote to Arendt on June 27, 1946: "I am not German in any crucially different way from the way she is German." Kohler and Saner, *Hannah Arendt–Karl Jaspers Correspondence*, 46, 82. In an autobiographical essay of 1967, Jaspers wrote of the time before National Socialism: "In the early period of our marriage we had no occasion to contemplate Jews and Germans. At that time Jewish Germans and German Jews were self-evidently the same. The Germanness of my wife was not increased through me." Jaspers, *Schicksal und Wille*, 164.

47. Jaspers, *The Question of German Guilt*, 35–36.
48. Ibid., 111–12. See chapter 10.

would have been a mistake to isolate Germany from all other nations: "What broke out in Germany was under way in the entire Western world as a crisis of faith, of the spirit. This does not diminish our guilt—for it was here in Germany that the outbreak occurred, not somewhere else—but it does free us from isolation." The point here was that the fact that the catastrophe occurred in Germany "makes us instructive for the others." This is the positive inflection of pariahdom—the possibility of one's own experience of transformation serving as a model to others who have the same long-term needs but are not pressed as much by contemporary circumstances to take up the challenge: "By our feeling of collective guilt we feel the entire task of renewing human existence from its origin—the task that is given to all men on earth but which appears more urgently, more perceptibly, as decisively as all existence, when its own guilt brings a people face to face with nothingness."[49]

"Shall we admit that we alone are guilty?" Jaspers asked: "No—if we as a whole, as a people, as a permanent species, are turned into *the* evil people, the guilty people as such." Instead, Jaspers called for grasping the positive moment in Germany's unique status: "Today we Germans may have only negative basic features in common," Jaspers observed. The question was whether this would be enough: "The answer lies in the draft of the ethos which is left to us—and if it were the ethos of a people deemed a pariah people in the world today." Everything depended, therefore, on recognizing the positive element of pariahdom. "What happens in Nuremberg," Jaspers thus argued, "no matter how many objections it may invite, is a feeble, ambiguous harbinger of a world order, the need of which mankind is beginning to feel." The fact that Germany could do nothing about it does not reflect badly on German honor: "The trial is said to be a national disgrace for all Germans. . . . The national disgrace lies not in the tribunal but in what brought it on. . . . The consciousness of national disgrace is inescapable for every German." But for Jaspers, "[i]t aims in the wrong direction if turning against the trial rather than its cause. . . . Utter lack of power," he argued, "can only cling to the world as a whole." The positive possibility came, however, in recognizing that "it is precisely the German who might become aware of the extraordinary import of this harbinger." The crux, therefore, was what kind of pariah people would the Germans choose to be: humiliated outcasts or possessors of special insight because they have worked through their guilt.[50]

* * *

49. Ibid., 10, 83, 75.
50. Ibid., 90, 12, 19, 54, 48, 54.

The challenge Jaspers set himself was thus a truly monumental one—a plea to his noncriminal compatriots to overcome their defenses and to realize where they too had incurred guilt. The four-part scheme was not merely a differentiation of guilt, but indeed a recognition of other guilts one may not have been willing to consider out of fear that doing so would result in one's being classed with the execrable. The differentiation of types of guilt thus worked in two directions. On the one hand, it made clear that only a rather narrow class of acts were criminally chargeable.[51] Jaspers's schema rejected a concept of guilt that, like Undset's, condemned indiscriminately or, like Jung's, "spreads itself out over a whole neighborhood" (though of course Jung was also at some pains to argue that it is only the *feeling* of guilt that spreads out in this way, not the legal burden).

On the other hand, Jaspers's argument was that just because one rightly felt free from the dangers of a criminal prosecution, the matter was not so easily finished. Jaspers's aim, put simply, was to make his compatriots—even those who had opposed the regime—*feel* guilty. By the same token, he wanted them to *feel* the appropriate *kind* of guilt and for the right reasons, and to do the right thing with these feelings. "True," he said, "among our people many were outraged and many deeply moved by a horror containing a presentiment of coming calamity." But this was not enough to free them from political responsibility: even if one had done almost everything one could to stop it, one still bore the burden of repairing it. This was the condition of collective identity: the only possibility would be to renounce one's Germanness, which was not possible anyway. Jaspers called upon his indifferent compatriots to see the costs of their own weakness: "[E]ven more went right on with their activities, undisturbed in their social life and amusements, as if nothing had happened." For Jaspers, this was moral guilt, and could not be excused. There was for Jaspers, just as for Thomas Mann, no longer such a thing as nonpolitical existence.[52]

Beyond these ordinary people and their ordinary compromises (which are nevertheless important for them to contemplate in private), those "who in utter impotence, outraged and despairing, were unable to prevent the crimes took another step in their metamorphosis by a growing consciousness of metaphysical guilt." Or at least Jaspers hoped that they would grasp the necessity of recognizing this step. Jaspers thus rejected collective guilt: "To pronounce a group criminally, morally, or metaphysically guilty is an error akin to the laziness and arrogance of average, uncritical thinking."

51. Rabinbach, "The German as Pariah," in *In the Shadow of Catastrophe*.
52. Jaspers, *The Question of German Guilt*, 66–67.

On the other hand, to fail to acknowledge the appropriate kind of individual guilt was at least equally uncritical and lazy; and this guilt—which is metaphysical—had indeed spread itself over the whole neighborhood, to put it in Jung's terms.[53]

Shame, Honor, and German National Identity

Jaspers plea was that the ordinary German who was not criminally guilty acknowledge the manifold ways he was bound up with a reality he did not necessarily—or at least in all its implications—support. "To have been a good soldier" he stated bluntly as an example, "does not absolve one from all other guilt."[54] Being German required reparation in the political world, self-examination in the moral realm, and confession in the metaphysical realm (the same applied to other peoples as well, though the circumstances of their political responsibility and moral guilt were different, and perhaps less burdensome). But a closer reading that attends to the dialogical origins of *Die Schuldfrage* calls attention to other passages, which might otherwise go unnoticed. Certain kinds of evasions, and certain kinds of evaders, were more irksome to Jaspers than others.

Jaspers was, of course, disgusted with the Nazi leaders and their equivocations. But what could one expect? More problematic were certain kinds of intellectuals, particularly those who "went along in 1933, sought leading positions and publicly upheld the ideology of the new power, only to become resentful later when they personally were shunted aside." Arguing in a way similar to Litt, Jaspers stated the problem to be that persons such as these "feel that they suffered under the Nazis and are therefore called for what follows. They regard themselves as anti-Nazis." But this was pure hypocrisy for Jaspers: "In all these years, according to their self-proclaimed ideology, these intellectual Nazis were frankly speaking truth in spiritual matters, guarding the tradition of the German spirit, preventing destructions, doing good in individual cases." Jaspers, however, rejected this exculpatory version of events: "Many of these may be guilty of persisting in a mentality which, while not identical with Party tenets and even disguised as metamorphosis and opposition, still clings in fact to the mental attitude of National Socialism and fails to clear itself."[55] Jaspers's not-so-secret target here? Where for Litt it was mainly

53. Ibid., 67, 33.
54. Ibid., 59.
55. Ibid., 62–63.

Ernst Jünger and Oswald Spengler, for Jaspers it was decidedly Martin Heidegger.

* * *

Martin Heidegger is considered by many to have been the most important philosopher of the twentieth century, credited with providing the philosophical groundwork for the postmodern turn toward language and against philosophical anthropology (the idea, which is the core of humanism, that man has an unalterable essence that stands outside of time). For all its emphasis on temporality, Heidegger's masterpiece, *Being and Time*, is conventionally placed in the pantheon of timeless philosophical works, including Plato's *Republic*, Kant's *Critique of Pure Reason*, and Hegel's *Phenomenology of Spirit*. Heidegger's work has inspired whole schools of discipleship, and has been taken up not only by philosophers, but by literary critics, psychoanalysts, theologians, sociologists, and the polymorphous voices of postmodern theory, be it film theory, architecture theory, queer theory, or the like. His thought has been revered unlike virtually any other in European intellectual circles. All this is despite the fact that Heidegger was also a Nazi.[56]

Jaspers and Heidegger began their friendship in 1920, when they were introduced by Heidegger's mentor, the founding father of phenomenology, Edmund Husserl. They were immediately taken with each other. As Jaspers wrote in his philosophical autobiography, "Only Heidegger struck me as different." Regarding Heidegger's work, Jaspers believed at the time that "Heidegger alone addressed himself to complexes of questions that appeared to me the most profound." At this juncture, Heidegger and Jaspers shared a sense of exclusion from the philosophical establishment, which at the time was dominated by a highly formalistic neo-Kantianism; both saw themselves as outsiders to what Jaspers called the "dull, threadbare, authoritarian, neo-Kantian Scholasticism" of the day.[57] In a letter of

56. The major line of dispute over Heidegger's reputation, especially since the 1970s, is between those who attributed Heidegger's National Socialism to political naiveté of no consequence for his philosophical legacy and those who argue that Heidegger's National Socialism was wholly consistent with his philosophy, thus compromising its legacy. While the literature on Heidegger and the controversy over his work is enormous, see especially Altweg, *Die Heidegger Kontroverse*; Farias, *Heidegger and Nazism*; Ferry and Renaut, *Heidegger and Modernity*; Olson, *Heidegger and Jaspers*; Wolin, *The Heidegger Controversy*. For a more general biographical account, see Safranski, *Martin Heidegger*.

57. Schlipp, *The Philosophy of Karl Jaspers*, 75.

June 27, 1922, Heidegger declared to Jaspers that they are joined "by a rare and self-sustaining battle community" (*Kampfgemeinschaft*).[58]

In actuality, Jaspers and Heidegger had very different philosophical sensibilities; what they shared was largely a sense that something new was necessary. For Jaspers, this was to be a philosophical existentialism that read the Kantian notion of freedom as a sort of world-openness, wholly consonant with liberal humanism; for Heidegger, it was not merely the stuffy moralism of orthodox neo-Kantianism, but the entire project of humanism that was misguided. Heidegger called for a return to the question of "Being": the history of humanism was the history of the "forgetfulness of Being," which had occurred in part by the false worship of technology and rationality. Heidegger's philosophical and, indeed, political language was thus much more deeply metaphysical (in his later works, mystical). In Jaspers's view, Heidegger alternated between brilliant clarity and obfuscation. For Heidegger, Jaspers's work ultimately remained wedded to the conventional view. Even so, their correspondence through the 1920s expressed a genuine admiration and, again, a sense of community in a battle against philosophical complacency. During this period, Heidegger achieved greater fame with his *Being and Time* than Jaspers did with his three-volume *Philosophie*.

Despite an essentially nonpolitical life during the 1920s, Heidegger came to see a transformative alternative in National Socialism. In April 1933, following Hitler's January 30, 1933, assumption of power, Heidegger was elected to the rectorship of Freiburg University; at the end of May, he delivered his now notorious address in which he praised the National Socialist agenda and declared it time for an epochal battle (later, Heidegger maintained that this battle was meant to be a philosophical one for "Being," that it was not meant in any literal sense of real war); the speech included the rhetoric of "blood and soil" and preached a rather rousing nationalism.[59] Interestingly, Jaspers praised the rectoral address, though he also criticized some aspects of its style.

Heidegger joined the Nazi Party on May 1, 1933. Scholars have shaded his activities as rector either as moderate political engagement for the National Socialists or as moderate attempts to lessen their more extreme intrusions into university life. Either way, his philosophical language of the period (and, some argue, of his other periods as well) fit easily with

58. Quoted in Harries, "Shame, Guilt, Responsibility," in Olson, *Heidegger and Jaspers*, 52.

59. Heidegger, "The Self Assertion of the German University," in Wolin, *The Heidegger Controversy*, 29–39.

the National Socialist rhetoric of national renewal and cultic fervor. Nevertheless, caught up in faculty disputes and disagreements with supervising party officials, Heidegger resigned a mere ten months into his rectorship, though without a critical statement. During the remaining period of the Third Reich, Heidegger largely avoided political activities, later complaining that his philosophical renown was exploited for political purposes without his involvement. Nevertheless, he never officially resigned from the party. Even more problematic for his reputation, however, is that he never repudiated his early National Socialism nor acknowledged any guilt for his role in legitimating the regime. (It has been plausibly argued that had he offered such a repudiation or apology, his reputation would have fared much better.)[60]

*　*　*

While Jaspers and Heidegger continued to correspond during the early years of National Socialism, their exchanges grew increasingly less frequent, and ceased altogether after 1937. The next critical incident in their relationship was when the botanist Friedrich Oehlkers wrote to Jaspers on behalf of the Freiburg University denazification committee requesting Jaspers's evaluation of Heidegger's fitness to resume his professorial duties. In his letter, Jaspers described Heidegger this way:

> Heidegger is a significant potency, not through the content of a philosophical world-view, but in the manipulation of speculative tools. He has a philosophical aptitude whose perceptions are interesting; although, in my opinion, he is extraordinarily uncritical and stands at a remove from true science. He often proceeds as if he combined the seriousness of nihilism with the mystagogy of a magician.[61]

Nevertheless, Jaspers argued that "it is absolutely necessary that those who helped place National Socialism in the saddle be called to account. Heidegger belongs among the few professors to have so acted."[62] The question was how much was to be excused by brilliance. Jaspers concluded that "[e]xceptional intellectual achievement can serve as a justifiable basis

60. See especially Olson, "Introduction: A Dialectic of Being and Value," in Olson, *Heidegger and Jaspers*, 6.

61. From a historical rather than personal vantage point, Richard Rorty put it this way: Heidegger "was a rather nasty piece of work—a coward and a liar, pretty much from the first to the last." Quoted in Rabinbach, *In the Shadow of Catastrophe*, 101.

62. Compare the last sentence to Litt and Ebbinghaus's assessment of their colleagues' widespread complicity.

for facilitating the continuation of such work; not, however, for the resumption of office and teaching duties." For Jaspers, education was simply too delicate a matter. "Heidegger's manner of thinking, which to me seems in its essence unfree, dictatorial, and incapable of communication, would today in its pedagogical effects be disastrous." Jaspers's solution, accepted by the committee, was that Heidegger be given emeritus status (including a pension) so that he could continue to work as a philosopher, but that he be prohibited from teaching.[63]

Perhaps the most broadly relevant passage from Jaspers's evaluation letter, however, was his statement of what would have been required of Heidegger after his "mistake" of 1933. In his petition to the committee requesting reinstatement, Heidegger had denied all responsibility for the course of National Socialism. He explained his original motivation as stemming from his belief that "an autonomous alliance of intellectuals could deepen and transform a number of essential elements of the 'National Socialist Movement' and thereby contribute in its own way to overcoming Europe's disarray and the crisis of the Western spirit." The mistake he acknowledged was his belief that he could influence the transformation of National Socialism into something closer to what he envisioned. Heidegger thus seemed to believe not only that he was not wrong, but that it was the other way around: it was the *National Socialists* who failed to understand *him!* For Jaspers, however, "[a] change of conviction as a result of directional shifts in the National Socialist camp can be judged according to the motivations that are in part revealed at the specific point in time. 1934, 1938, 1941 signify fundamentally different stages." In Jaspers's opinion, "for purposes of reaching a judgment, a change of conviction is almost meaningless if it resulted only after 1941, and it is of trifling value if it did not occur radically after June 30, 1934."[64]

All this helps us understand what (and whom) Jaspers had in mind when he wrote in *Die Schuldfrage* that "[i]f a mature person in 1933 had the certainty of inner conviction—due not merely to political error but to a sense of existence heightened by National Socialism—he will be purified only by a transmutation which may have to be more thorough than any other."[65] This he and others expected from Heidegger and never received. Heidegger's former student Herbert Marcuse even wrote to Heidegger

63. Jaspers, "Letter to the Freiburg University Denazification Committee (December 22, 1945)," in Wolin, *The Heidegger Controversy*, 148–49.

64. Wolin, *The Heidegger Controversy*, 61, 150.

65. Jaspers, *The Question of German Guilt*, 63.

asking for it in no uncertain terms: "You (and we) can only combat the identification of your person and your work with Nazism (and thereby the dissolution of your philosophy) if you make a public avowal of your changed views." Heidegger's response did not give an inch: "[Y]our letter shows me" he wrote back to Marcuse, "how difficult it is to converse with persons who have not been living in Germany since 1933 and who judge the beginning of National Socialism from its end."[66] One is reminded of Frank Thiess's response to Thomas Mann (see chapter 7).

This would all amount to nothing more than gossip for intellectual historians, the pathetic tale of a broken man (if indeed that is what Heidegger was), if Heidegger's self-defense had not in fact been a highly theorized political position in the immediate postwar public discourse about the question of German guilt. Heidegger's defense certainly had its pathetic aspects, particularly when, in response to Marcuse's concerns that he had been associated with "a regime that murdered millions of Jews, that made terror into an everyday phenomenon, and that turned everything that pertains to the ideas of spirit, freedom, and truth into its bloody opposition," Heidegger equated this to the postwar treatment of Germans in the East. As we have already seen, however, this was not an uncommon equation. Even more relevant was Heidegger's hint of what we will see elsewhere elaborated much more forcefully: "An avowal after 1945," Heidegger wrote to Marcuse, "was for me impossible: the Nazi supporters announced their change of allegiance in the most loathsome way; I, however, had nothing in common with them."[67] Here, then, was the culture of "cool conduct" that the literary critic Herman Lethen, with whose ideas about shame versus guilt cultures we began this chapter, argued was characteristic of post–World War I Germany, and found described an almost atavistic response of certain Weimar intellectuals—like Heidegger, Ernst Jünger, and Carl Schmitt—in the post-1945 era. It is the heart of what the political theorist Dirk van Laak, in his extensive study of so-called "radical conservatives" from the Weimar period, calls a genuine "counter-discourse" to the culture of guilt of which Jaspers was the most important representative.[68]

Before turning to this counterdiscourse, it is illustrative to see what happened when Heidegger and Jaspers took up their correspondence again after 1945. For his part, on the evidence of his notes and reflections, Jaspers

66. Wolin, The Heidegger Controversy, 161–62.
67. Ibid., 161, 163.
68. Van Laak, Gespraeche in der Sicherheit des Schweigens.

was nearly desperate for an explanation from his friend. He drafted a number of never-sent letters asking for it. This explains in part the opening passage in Jaspers's *Die Schuldfrage*, where he pleaded, presumably with his compatriots but also by implication with Heidegger, for an open conversation: "We must learn to talk with each other, and we must understand and accept one another in our extraordinary differences."[69] All he ever got from Heidegger, however, was one line, which nevertheless contains the entire issue: "I did not visit your house since 1933," Heidegger wrote in 1950, "not because a Jewish woman lived there, but because I was simply ashamed."[70]

69. Jaspers, *The Question of German Guilt*, 5.
70. Harries, "Guilt, Shame, Responsibility," in Olson, *Heidegger and Jaspers*, 61.

CHAPTER 13

The Recalcitrance of Shame

Heidegger, Humanism, and Responsibility

It would be easy to dismiss Martin Heidegger's refusal to disavow his association with National Socialism as psychological weakness were it not that Heidegger's predisposition was common to a particular cultural milieu and that he offered a highly theorized version of his refusal. During and following his "denazification," Heidegger found the French authorities to be more accommodating than the Americans; he had enjoyed a significant reputation in French intellectual life, and had earned the admiration of Jean-Paul Sartre, who repeatedly tried but failed to visit Heidegger. Sartre and Heidegger did, however, begin a correspondence, and Sartre was at least implicitly the addressee of Heidegger's now famous essay—considered by many to be as important as his *Being and Time* and by some to be more important—"Letter on Humanism."[1]

The "Letter on Humanism" was occasioned by Heidegger's early postwar correspondence with a young French follower, Jean Beaufret. The letter's philosophical occasion, however, was Heidegger's attempt to distinguish his own position from mainstream existentialism, particularly as expressed in Sartre's lecture, "Existentialism Is a Humanism." For Heidegger, it decidedly was not. Existence—or in Heidegger's language "Being"—was opposed to essence, which is an abstraction—or, again in Heidegger's language, a "forgetfulness of Being." For Heidegger, the core that all the diverse humanisms in the history of philosophy shared was that they privileged the "*humanitas* of *Homo humanus*, [which] is determined with regard to an already established interpretation of nature, history, world, and the ground of the world."[2] This was the fundamental error of Western thought, according to Heidegger,

---

1. See especially Rabinbach, "Heidegger's 'Letter in Humanism' as Text and Event," in *In the Shadow of Catastrophe*. Heidegger's text is reprinted in Heidegger, *Basic Writings*.
2. Heidegger, "Letter on Humanism," in *Basic Writings*, 225.

which mistakenly favors action over Being because it splits subject from object. The result is the "homelessness" of modern man, characterized by the empty valorization of technology, rationality, and the market, and of knowledge over Being. The latter was clear in philosophy, which since Descartes had held epistemology to be the fundamental philosophical problem; this preoccupation with metaphysics led to an overemphasis on action at the expense of Being.

In perhaps the most famous statement in all of his writing, Heidegger declared at the beginning of the letter that "Language is the house of Being."[3] Language—not man, his essence, thought, or action. There is, as Anson Rabinbach and others have pointed out, an odor of self-exculpation about this statement: nothing as misguided as ethics was appropriate, with its judgment of an individual's acts rather than of Being itself.[4] As Theodor Adorno put it in *The Jargon of Authenticity*, "Language as the House of Being" is an "alibi": Heidegger's approach implied that "the language itself—through its generality and objectivity—already negates the whole man, the particular speaking subject: the first price exacted by language is the essence of the individual. . . . Whoever stands behind his words, in the way in which these words pretend, is safe from any suspicion about what he is at that very moment about to do: speak for others in order to palm something off on them."[5] In other words, if language is the house of Being, individual ethics are mere epiphenomena. Indeed, this implication fit well with Heidegger's prewar writings on conscience, in which he distinguished between a conventional understanding of conscience as an agency that judges us (the agency of guilt) and conscience as "a summons to be what we are authentically: to be ourselves." As Paul Tillich described it, "The call of conscience does not judge anything in particular. Conscience, for Heidegger, rather has to do with a fundamental phenomenon, more profound than any specific judgment about which one might have a so-called bad conscience." This conscience does indeed involve guilt, but here again guilt is understood unconventionally, as a sense "over-against the norms and rule by which we are living," rather than as a verdict on the ordinary things one might do. To be guilty is thus to be authentic to oneself. This was why Heidegger described conscience as the "silent call to be ourselves." In this light, ethical judgment seems irrelevant if not debased.[6]

3. Ibid., 217.
4. Rabinbach, *In the Shadow of Catastrophe*, 98. See also Tillich, "Heidegger and Jaspers," in Olson, *Heidegger and Jaspers*.
5. Adorno, *The Jargon of Authenticity*, 14.
6. Tillich "Heidegger and Jaspers," in Olson, *Heidegger and Jaspers*, 23.

(The similarity to Ruth Benedict's description of Japanese sincerity as "respecting oneself" is striking. See chapter 13.)

* * *

These issues are relevant here in two ways. First, one is struck by the way in which Heidegger's discussion fit within the framework of a "shame culture" described in the previous chapter—a culture, that is, which interprets all acknowledgment and confession as a betrayal of self. Ordinary conscience, for Heidegger, is the external, objective, and rational. But his understanding of conscience as authenticity to self is judged only by oneself; it admits to no external judgments. Where guilt calls one to account for oneself in terms of absolute criteria and to devote oneself to a transformation, Heidegger's conscience as authenticity requires instead "resoluteness." And this resoluteness stems entirely from Being. Resoluteness, in Benedict's framework, was a response to the possibility of shame, where guilt called for admission and transformation. Heideggerian conscience was thus resolutely opposed to transformation, which as the act of an individual is nothing anyway in the house of Being—language, which is greater than any mere speaker.

Second, the claim that Western metaphysics has been a history of the "forgetfulness of Being" was tied to Heidegger's diagnosis of the West, his proposed treatment for these ills, and his resoluteness in the face of the failure of his solutions to triumph. Heidegger, like other thinkers of the so-called "conservative revolution" of the 1920s, was entranced by Nietzsche's nihilism, contrasting it with what was seen as a "half-hearted" nihilism of the West.[7] The history of the West is a history of decay; the only solution was thus a "ruthless nihilism" inspired by Nietzsche, which only Germany could offer. In this light, National Socialism provided the only hope for an alternative to the equally debased liberalism of the West and communism of the East. The problem was that National Socialism turned out to be only one more half-hearted nihilism. Heidegger's only mistake, therefore, was temporarily misrecognizing National Socialism as a potential rebirth of Being. All that Heidegger admitted to in the "Letter on Humanism" was to have momentarily been seduced by essence, to have slipped into a weaker nihilism from which he very quickly recovered.[8]

7. See Herf, *Reactionary Modernism*.

8. As Rabinbach points out, during the historians' dispute in the 1980s the conservative historian Ernst Nolte "maintains that Heidegger's Nazism was entirely justified, even admirable, given the political choices available to him as a German in the epoch of European civil war." Rabinbach, *In the Shadow of Catastrophe*, 101.

Heidegger believed himself to be in communion with others who sought to "refine and temper" the movement. (In this, Heidegger ended up sounding like some of the defendants at Nuremberg, who argued that they remained in government service to try to steer National Socialism from its more dangerous tendencies; one thinks especially of Ribbentrop's final statement. See chapter 5.) The bottom line was that the impulse was unassailable. In his petition to the denazification committee, Heidegger thus wrote that by December 1933 he "realized that it was a mistake to believe that, from the basic spiritual position that was the result of my long philosophical work, I could immediately influence the transformation of the bases—spiritual or non-spiritual—of the National Socialist Movement." Because "the National Socialist ideology became increasingly inflexible and increasingly less disposed to a purely philosophical interpretation," the very fact that he continued to work as a philosopher, Heidegger claimed, was all the evidence one needed of his opposition.[9] As for his 1933 rectoral address, he wrote in his reply to Marcuse that he "expected from National Socialism a spiritual renewal of life in its entirety." In 1948, however, he acknowledged only that he regarded "a few of the sentences as misleading."[10] The possibility that the desire for a rebirth of Being might in fact have been a dangerous impulse did not enter consideration.

A Secret Bond

Heidegger did indeed enjoy "a secret bond" with others who saw in National Socialism the hope for renewal after centuries of decadence; although he meant a secret bond of thinkers before and during National Socialism, it appears to have been relevant in the aftermath as well. Over many years, Heidegger exchanged ideas and accolades with perhaps the only two other thinkers who have achieved the same status in the pantheon of German conservative thought—the writer Ernst Jünger and the legal theorist Carl Schmitt.[11] Heidegger, Jünger, and Schmitt shared not just many aspects of their assessment of National Socialism (first enthusiastic, then claiming—some argue disingenuously—a change of heart), but a

9. Heidegger, "Letter to the Rector of Freiburg University, November 4, 1945," in Wolin, *The Heidegger Controversy*, 63–64.

10. Herbert Marcuse and Martin Heidegger, "An Exchange of Letters," in Wolin, *The Heidegger Controversy*, 162.

11. See as well the brief remarks on Gottfried Benn in the discussion of "inner emigration" in chapter 7.

similar stance concerning how to confront (or not) the memory of the catastrophe. Illustratively, despite enormous similarities, Heidegger, Jünger, and Schmitt represent archetypically different reputational trajectories. Jünger was almost immediately rehabilitated, Heidegger's status was always ambiguous, and Schmitt was forced to speak surreptitiously and has been rehabilitated only recently and largely posthumously.

Again, the reason for exploring these three is not just that they are additional interesting figures for the intellectual historian. Rather, it is that together they constituted a counterdiscourse to Jaspers's discourse of guilt—or at least that is my contention. In order to evaluate whether Jaspers's version was indeed the standard one, to appreciate who were the targets of his argument, as well as to determine if possible who or what was responsible for establishing the myth (not necessarily false) of an official guilt culture, it is necessary to articulate the position expressed by and through these powerful figures. Moreover, their ideas remained a powerful thread, without which it would be difficult to understand many of the notorious controversies about the Nazi past in the history of the Federal Republic. They may indeed have been repressed by official memory; in the process, official memory misconstrues its own origins.

Ernst Jünger's Guiltless Peace

Complex as the case of Heidegger might be, that of Ernst Jünger is even more so. As Lewis Coser (writing under the pseudonym of Louis Claire) put it in his 1948 introduction to Jünger's pamphlet *The Peace*, "he has lived through, and even savored, the whole gamut of multifarious experiences that have assailed and tempted the German intellectual during the last three decades."[12] Jünger's career as a writer began in the milieu of other aspiring young writers who had been shaped by the World War I *Fronterlebnis* (experience of the front). Jünger's novels and other writings of the post–World War I period were leading examples of a radical nationalistic response to that experience, emphasizing the "virtues" of manliness, honor, duty, and national pride. His writings from the pre–World War II period, in which he glorified absolute nihilism and coined the terms *Weltbürgerkrieg* (taken up in the postwar discourse as "European Civil War") and, most notoriously, *die totale mobilmachung*, or "total mobilization" (which was adopted by the Nazi propaganda minister Goebbels).[13] Both at the time and later, Jünger was

12. Claire [Coser], "Introduction," in Jünger, *The Peace*, 10–11.
13. See especially Neaman, *A Dubious Past*; Herf, *Reactionary Modernism*.

considered to have provided substantial intellectual and spiritual support to the early development of National Socialism. His books were widely read not just at the high levels, but by young men in both the party and the military. He was an intellectual hero of early National Socialism.

Jünger served in the German army in occupied Paris for much of the war, where he enjoyed contact with leading lights of French culture. During this period, he walked a fine line between enjoying the cultural indulgences of an occupier (being billeted at the best hotels and sharing in the company of rather notorious military figures) and nurturing loose contacts with various opposition circles (mostly military and aristocratic). During the war, he also kept secret diaries. By his own account and that of his supporters, Jünger declared his opposition to the regime subtly through his novel *The Marble Cliffs*, published soon after the start of war in 1939. How clear this declaration was, however, is called into question by Jünger's privileged status throughout the war. More significant for postwar debates, Jünger began drafting an essay to be titled *The Peace* in 1941, completing it, he claimed, in 1943, but not publishing it until after the war.

The publication of *The Peace* was folded in to the discussion of Jünger's other works, which led to a significant public controversy, particularly in 1946–47. *The Peace* included all the hallmarks of Jünger's apocalyptic worldview, outlining, like Heidegger, the horror of the West. Jünger offered a veritable lamentation for the "man of spirit," whose suffering has been great. "It was not wars or dangers that caused him to fear, but the blind urge which drove the masses—at first in wild exultation and then in a passion of hatred and revenge—along unknown paths which soon led to the flames." This man of suffering "saw the machine arise to domination in cold structures which a titanic will forced up over night as palaces of destruction and Babylonian confusion. All too soon they were to be seen rising like spectral skeletons from the scorched earth to herald the triumph of death. In the same way one builds into a bridge the demolition chamber for blowing it up."[14]

Like Heidegger, Jünger saw the German catastrophe as a mere by-product of the demise of civilization. The implicit message, then, was that nothing as mundane as the responsibility of a particular party was at issue. "We have seen the victims of this war. To their somber ranks all nations add their contingent." "Everyone," Jünger argued, "shared in the guilt, and there is no one who did not stand in need of the healing powers which are to be found in the realm of suffering." As a result, "peace must bear fruit for

14. Jünger, *The Peace*, 31–32.

them all. That is, this war must be won by all." Jünger wanted to be clear, however; he was not calling for an early settlement: "On the contrary, it is desirable that there should be a clear decision by arms and that no corner should remain unpurged by fire. . . . Weapons must create an opportunity for a decision to be made. . . . The peace cannot be a peace of compromise."[15] Nevertheless, that settlement by arms, decisive at its moment, must lead to an exchange between equals built "by reason and not by passion." "Admittedly, that seems difficult after years of total war which created enmities of a bitterness unknown before to peoples with old civilizations. And yet these years in many ways made the opponents more alike." One can only imagine the response of the opponents to this last statement! But for Jünger, "[a]s sons of the earth we are involved in the civil war, in the fratricidal strife." His hope, which later in his life led him to science fiction fantasies of a new order, was that the final battle in this civil war, which can produce neither winners nor losers, would be recognized as a moment for rebirth. As for those who were suffering, "it is no mere chance that we live in the heart of the conflagration; we are in the midst of the fusion, the pangs of birth." It almost sounds like a German holocaust, though here the fire is cleansing.[16]

Particularly relevant for postwar discussions, Jünger reproaches the exiles, who he saw as representing liberalism. Like Heidegger, however, Jünger saw no essential difference between liberalism and communism, both of which failed to grasp the possibility of rebirth: "The view is still widely held that to re-establish order it would suffice to return to the liberal state. But that would merely mean returning to our point of departure. In the polemics which the old liberals sustain against the nihilists, they behave like fathers bewailing their misguided children without seeing that the real fault lies in inadequate education."[17] The triangle is thus complete: communists group liberalism and fascism together as outgrowths of capitalism; liberals group communism and fascism together as varieties of totalitarianism; and conservatives group communism and liberalism together as corrupt humanisms.

15. Federal president Theodor Heuss expressed a similar view in his early postwar notebooks, in which he wrote that he was satisfied that the war had been fought to the bitter end, thus preventing the emergence of a new stab-in-the-back legend or other attempts to imply that the defeat had not been total.

16. Jünger, *The Peace*, 37–38, 43, 66.

17. Ibid., 69. This passage only made it even more surprising that one of Jünger's most significant postwar admirers was Federal president Theodor Heuss, who saw himself as the walking embodiment of the liberalism of 1848.

For Jünger, however, even worse than the complacent German liberals was the "useless . . . criticism of those who watched the terrible contest from the safety of the gallery."[18] One is reminded of Frank Thiess's charge (see chapter 7) that Thomas Mann had made his denunciations from the comfort of the "orchestra seats and loges" of exile. Indeed, the debate over the legacies of Ernst Jünger were very much tied up with the debate over exiles and "inner emigrants," at least insofar as that debate raised the question of the responsibility of intellectuals. With Jünger and other radical conservatives, the question was even more difficult than for other "inner emigrants"; Jünger, like Heidegger, had been an early enthusiast. What responsibility did one bear whose early sympathies gave succor to the movement? Could one simply disavow one's earlier role? Jünger's famous solution, nearly identical to Heidegger's, was to deny that he was responsible for the ways in which his ideas were taken up. In fact, Jünger argued that as a writer he was a mere observer. All the talk of his responsibility he thus dismissed as misguided. "After the War one bangs on the seismographers. One cannot, however, let the barometer be punished for the typhoon, unless one wants to be counted among the primitives."[19] This, then, was his assessment of his role and, by implication, that of his fellow radical conservatives—they were mere diagnosticians.

In his introduction to the American edition of *The Peace*, Coser made it even more explicit than did Jünger:

> It is high time that the moral insanity which gripped America during and after the war concerning all things German—that raving frenzy of hatred so assiduously fostered by the Emil Ludwigs, the Morgenthaus and Vansittarts—gives way to a rational attitude toward what is called, somewhat condescendingly, "the German Problem."
>
> Modern man has a fatal propensity for attempting to free himself of his own feelings of guilt, his own anxieties and terrors, by projecting them onto some scapegoat, some incarnation of absolute evil, which he burdens with all the sins, all the shortcomings that he cannot face within himself.[20]

The Nazis, wrote Coser, had used the Jews; now the Americans were using the Germans. Of course, one might also argue that Coser was using

---

18. Ibid.

19. Quoted in Neaman, *A Dubious Past*, 155.

20. Claire [Coser], "Introduction," in *The Peace*, 9. Coser went on to have an enormously influential academic career as a sociologist in the United States, and was founding editor of *Dissent* magazine, a major journal of the Social Democratic left in the United States.

Ludwig, Morgenthau, and Vansittart in the same way. The implication was that that the indiscriminate judgment of such figures as Jünger would be, for want of a better word—Pharisaical (Coser does not use the word).

As for Jünger's own thoughts on the putative collective guilt of Germany, he offered several clear statements, first in his war diaries and then in his *Treatise on the Rebel* of 1951. In the war diaries, Jünger wrote that the "thesis of collective guilt has two strands that run together. For the defeated it means, I have to stand in for my brother and his guilt." On the other hand, "[i]t gives the victor an excuse for undifferentiated plundering. If the bow is pulled too tightly, the dangerous question arises whether the brother was really so unjust." Accusations of collective guilt, Jünger asserted, would lead to "outbursts of vengeance on the part of the oppressed." Later, in *Treatise on the Rebel*, Jünger offered his evaluation of the occupation years. "We live in times," he wrote, "in which we are constantly approached by powers posing questions." The only honorable course, according to Jünger, was resistance through refusal and silence. "The German has to think about it. After his defeat, the idea was tested to deprive him forever of rights, enslave him, destroy him through the division of Germany." For Jünger, who refused to participate in denazification and thus was temporarily prohibited from publishing, "[t]his trial was more difficult than the war, and one can say that he has survived it, in silence, without weapons, without friends, without a forum in this world."[21]

Interestingly, Jünger found support across the political spectrum following the war. Published remarks on the need for Christian renewal as an alternative to the half-hearted nihilism that Jünger believed had led to disaster gave him a significant following in Christian circles (some of that following paled, however, when it turned out that Jünger's idea of Christianity was based merely on his ideas about the importance of mythology generally). I already mentioned Theodor Heuss's admiration; indeed, Heuss went so far as to award Jünger the Cross of Honor in 1959. Many years later, in the 1980s, Jünger was also a favorite of Chancellor Helmut Kohl; he was held up as an alternative to leftist writers like Günter Grass who had so dominated German literature and politics during the 1960s and 1970s. In a poignant enactment of his call to end the perpetual civil war of equals, Jünger accompanied Helmut Kohl and French president Francois Mitterrand when the two leaders all held hands over the graves at Verdun in September 1984. Given this, more surprising is the fact that Jünger found a following of sorts on the Left. The venerable SPD figure Carlo Schmid

21. Quoted in Neaman, *A Dubious Past*, 146, 186–87.

(not to be confused with Carl Schmitt) was known to have appreciated Jünger's work, and corresponded with him; the best explanation offered (though not a very good one, it seems to me) is that Schmid, like Heuss, felt a bond with Jünger because they were all Schwabian.

More significant, however, was the admiration the writer Alfred Andersch had for Jünger. Andersch, as we saw earlier (chapter 9), was best known as the editor of *Der Ruf* [*The Call*], the journal he edited with Hans-Werner Richter. For Andersch, Jünger provided the ideological inspiration for German self-determination along a third path between East and West. Andersch's admiration for Jünger was certainly not widely shared in *Gruppe 47*, the literary salon founded by Richter after *Der Ruf* was prohibited; but through Andersch, Jünger's radical critique of technically dominated bourgeois society did become a common theme for many West German writers of the Left, who excoriated the pathologies of American consumer culture.

Carl Schmitt's "Silence"

The idea of silent resistance as the only honorable avenue for one—or many—accused of supporting National Socialism was also a central organizing theme in the postwar posture of Carl Schmitt, who is often referred to as "the crown jurist of the Third Reich" as well as being considered, at the distance of several decades, to be one of the most brilliant legal thinkers of the twentieth century.[22] Schmitt—arrested by the Americans, repeatedly interrogated, denied his library and all the accoutrements of his former fame—took as his motto "the safety of silence" (*die Sicherheit des Schweigens*). Despite this, however, Schmitt undertook surreptitious and not-so-surreptitious efforts to delegitimate what he saw as an overwhelming and oppressive culture of guilt, and lamented pathetically the demise of his reputation. Here indeed was the archetypal example of shame, one railing rabidly against the injustice of lost face, refusing to give an inch on the possibility that one could be in any way culpable. Schmitt's was also the most aggressive attack against Nuremberg, denazification, and the culture of guilt he saw embodied in both the churches and Jaspers. When Schmitt referred to the "security of silence," therefore, he meant refusing to acknowledge culpability or to accept disgrace, not merely clamming up about what has happened. Of course, "what has happened" was mostly what has happened to Carl Schmitt.

22. There is an extensive biographical and critical literature on Schmitt, whose reception is complex indeed. On Schmitt's reception in German intellectual circles, see Müller, *A Dangerous Mind*. See also Balakrishnan, *The Enemy;* Scheuerman, *Carl Schmitt*.

The vigor of Schmitt's defense was only partly due to the fact that of the three—Heidegger, Jünger, and Schmitt—he was the most burdened, unable to claim convincingly that he had ever truly broken with the National Socialist regime. Schmitt had been, and continued to be, more thoroughly anti-Semitic than either Jünger or Heidegger, both of whom strenuously disavowed ever having been sympathetic to the racial component of Nazi ideology. Schmitt too argued that his theories did not support anti-Semitism, but he was thoroughly unconvincing; his postwar diaries, moreover, are rife with untheorized, crude, and despicable slogans.[23] Schmitt viewed himself as a victim, first of the Nazis (though it was never exactly clear in what way he was their victim, other than that they failed to triumph), and subsequently of the Allies, particularly in the form of his interrogator, Robert Kempner, a Prussian-Jewish émigré who returned to Germany as a prosecutor at Nuremberg. In his diary, Schmitt expressed his disgust not just with the idea of his interrogation, but with the identity of his interrogator:

> I have been imprisoned, my most intimate property, my library, has been confiscated, and I have been locked up in a cell as a criminal; in short, I have fallen into the hands of this mighty American empire. I was curious about my new masters. But I have until this very day, five long years, not yet once spoken with an American, but only with German Jews, with Herr Loewenstein, Flechtheim and the like, who were not at all new to me but, rather, for a long time well known to me. A peculiar master of the world, these poor modern Yankees, with their ancient Jews.[24]

Indeed, Schmitt had been surprised to have been arrested at all. Throughout his repeated interrogations, he denied any and all grounds for suspicion, including any connection between his own theories of *Grossraum* (an expansive territory for the German *Volk*), which had inspired National Socialist rhetoric and was responsible for Schmitt's fame under the regime, and possible ideological culpability. Most interesting for the purposes of understanding Schmitt's role in German memory, however, were not only his diaries—to which I return shortly—but two works from the immediate postwar months. The first was a legal brief Schmitt wrote on behalf of Friedrich Flick, who was prosecuted at the Industrialists' trial at Nuremberg. In the summer of 1945, Schmitt composed "The International Legal Crime of War of Aggression and the Fundamental

23. On Schmitt's anti-Semitism, see Gross, *Carl Schmitt und die Juden.*
24. Schmitt, *Glossarium*, 264. Translation from Balakrishnan, *The Enemy*, 254.

Norm: No Crime, No Punishment without Law."[25] There were two remarkable features of the document. The first was Schmitt's brilliant articulation of the legal principle *nullem crimen, nulla poena sine lege*. While it would not be accurate to attribute to Schmitt the entire body of criticisms of Nuremberg (see chapter 5), his brief was indeed widely circulated and was likely to have been quite influential, though of course one would have hesitated to ascribe the argument to Schmitt at the time, given his compromised status with the Allies.

The second remarkable feature of the brief, however, was Schmitt's distinction between genocide and a war of aggression. Where he had argued on the basis of *nullem crimen* that Flick should not be convicted on the charge of having planned a war of aggression, since there was no clear legal doctrine prohibiting sovereign states from starting wars of aggression at the time that National Socialist Germany did, he also argued that the principle did not apply to [p]lanned killings and inhuman cruelties" that "are not military actions." "Anyone," Schmitt stated, "who would, with respect to these crimes, raise the pretext of '*nullem crimen*' and seek to refer to previous provisions of criminal law puts himself in an objectionable light."[26] Indeed, there is much to be said for Schmitt's position, which is the strategic opposite of the prosecution's approach of linking the planning of a war of aggression to genocidal crimes; we already saw that this prosecution strategy failed in court and mnemonically, since the memory of Nuremberg conflates Nazi Germany's militarism and its racism by linking the war of aggression with the extermination of the Jews.

Nevertheless, there are good reasons to believe Schmitt's argument was disingenuous, or at least opportunistic. In the first place, Schmitt had, in 1934, already published an essay titled "The *Führer* Protects the Law," in which he defended Hitler's response to the *Reichstag* fire by dismissing the *nullem crimen* principle (Schmitt's defenders argue that the earlier essay was an issue of domestic law while the latter addressed international law). The second reason to doubt Schmitt's sincerity in his 1945 brief, however, was revealed both in his correspondence with Ernst Jünger and in his diaries. In his intellectual portrait of Schmitt, Gopal Balakrishnan points up exactly that portion of the correspondence relevant here. In February 1945, Jünger and Schmitt discussed the relevance of the extermination of the Jews—not for the Jews, but *for Germany*. Both expressed disdain for the horrors, but, again, their primary concern was what this would mean for

25. Schmitt, *Das Internationalrechtliche Verbrechen des Angriffskrieges.*
26. Quoted in Balakrishnan, *The Enemy*, 253.

Germany. Schmitt's prewar and wartime writings had already ascribed a fearful role to the Jews in generating a particular kind of political accounting. At the end of the war, in a letter to Schmitt, Jünger referred to Josephus Flavius's report of "the obstinacy of the Jews in the siege of Jerusalem." Such attempts to destroy the Jews, by analogy, only served to wake the beast of Old Testament morality, Jünger wrote, in which the Jews would seek to exact terrible revenge. Schmitt's repulsive response seems to be that the real reason not to exterminate the Jews was that this would wake the beast again. He quoted Bruno Bauer's line that "in the end, God created the Jews, and if we kill them all, we will suffer the same fate." Later, Schmitt wrote, "As God allowed hundreds of thousands of Jews to be killed, he simultaneously saw the revenge that they would take on Germany; and that which he foresees today for the avengers and those demanding restitution, humanity will experience in another unexpected moment." Once again, we see here the reversal of Jews and Germans.[27]

This appraisal of the situation in early postwar Germany connected directly to Schmitt's thorough repudiation of "re-education," "denazification," and the "culture of guilt," all of which utterly disgusted him. His rejection of these programs were given in both a theorized and a mundane version. The theorized version came in Schmitt's second important essay of the immediate postwar years, "Amnesty and the Power of Forgetting," which was published in several slightly different versions, the first time anonymously in *Christ und Welt* [*The Christian and the World*] in October 1949, a few months later in several newspapers with false attribution, and then finally in 1951 under Schmitt's name (Schmitt was prohibited from publishing, hence the subterfuge). In this brief essay, Schmitt argued that the nature of war had changed from "a collision between two organized, well disciplined armies" into a seemingly endless fratricidal civil war (*Bürgerkrieg*), no longer waged only with military weapons but now with any and all means to undermine one's opponent. This produced a new kind of viciousness that availed itself of particularly despicable tactics:

Each European people knows today what this means. Each knows not just one, but many fifth columns. The denazification was a cold civil war. The emblem of this civil war consists of treating the others as criminals, murderers, saboteurs, and gangsters. In a terrible sense civil war is a just war because each of the parties sits unconditionally on its rights as on a prize. Each takes revenge in the name of right.[28]

27. Ibid.
28. Schmitt, "Amnestie," in Schmitt, *Staat, Großraum, Nomos*, 218–19.

For Schmitt, however, it was a sworn duty to engage in "[f]rontal struggle against the idea of the just war; open demonstration of its historical, juristic, and moral falsity; its character as an instrument of civil war etc."[29]

The question Schmitt posed was thus how to break this cycle of mutual recrimination. The only solution, he argued, was amnesty, which at its core involves a willful forgetting.[30] Implicitly denigrating American gestures to the German population, Schmitt argued that "[a]mnesty is more than the cigarette that one offers to the disenfranchised in order to prove one's own humanity. The cold civil war is not to be ended so cheaply." Instead, "[t]his word amnesty means forgetting, and not only forgetting but also the strict prohibition against mucking around [*herumzuwühlen*] in the past and seeking there grounds for further acts of revenge and further demands for redress."[31] Nothing, then, in Schmitt's opinion, could be worse than what the Jews would now extract.

In his postwar diaries, one finds a much less reasoned (for want of a better word) version of the same arguments. Reflecting the theme of the power reversal between Jews and Germans, Schmitt pretended to Tocquevillian insight:

> The platform of democratic equality is only the springboard for new inequalities. That is de Tocqueville's real fear. The consequential equality is never real, and only in a single fleeting second true: in the moment in which the old privileges are removed and the new are not yet openly consolidated—that is, in the barely tangible moment of the transformation from the old discriminations to the new, that fabulous interval in which neither the Nazis persecute the Jews, nor the Jews persecute the Nazis.[32]

The Jews, it seems, would emerge from the Holocaust as the real winners, preparing to extract their revenge on Germany. Again, this bile-filled rhetoric would be irrelevant if it did not express an important cultural position at the time, and if it did not have numerous afterlives in the official discourse of the Federal Republic. Indeed it did, particularly with the argument—presaged by Chancellor Helmut Schmidt's remark on a 1981 trip to Saudi Arabia that West German foreign policy should no longer be held

29. Schmitt, *Glossarium*, 292; Balakrishnan, *The Enemy*, 258.

30. The obvious inspiration here, though distorted, was Nietzsche's second *Untimely Meditation, On the Advantages and Disadvantages of History for Life*, in which, as mentioned in the introduction, Nietzsche argued that too much history can be "the gravedigger of the present."

31. Schmitt, "Amenstie," 218–19.

32. Quoted in Balakrishnan, *The Enemy*, 240.

hostage to Auschwitz—that the Holocaust prevents Germany from assuming its appropriate place on the world stage.

The diaries (*Ex Captivitate Salus* and *Glossarium*) also expressed Schmitt's disdain for what he felt was expected of him, which he said were "tips for memorial inscriptions in the confessional style." But he did not include himself with the "self-torturers": "If you want to make a confession, go find a priest and do it there." His goal was thus to keep his distance from the current public "spectacle of a brawl between preachers of repentance," referring to the debate over the Stuttgart Declaration and other subsequent public debates about the proper attitude toward the past. "A good conscience that is expedited by the judiciary," Schmitt stated as a maxim, "is the worst." His most putrid scorn, however, Schmitt reserved for Karl Jaspers, who earned the following ditty: "How his penitential speech offends me / How disgusting are his rotten fish / Now he's gotten where he ought to be: / In the news and on the German telewish."[33]

It was not that Schmitt was trying to evade responsibility, he claimed. Rather he was "an intellectual adventurer. . . . I take the risk. I have always paid my bills, and have never played the shirker." And he railed against "most people [who] think taking off a beard is a metamorphosis." "Never complain," he wrote, but also, "Injustice is always ever again my lot."[34] The similarity to Heidegger's response to Marcuse that he had nothing in common with those who rushed to repent is striking, though by no means inexplicable, given the on-going correspondence and, to appropriate a term Heidegger used to describe his prewar relationship to Jaspers, the *Kampfgemeinschaft* (community of battle) among Jünger, Schmitt, and Heidegger.

In this light, the assertion of the literary critic Hermann Lethen, discussed at the beginning of the previous chapter, seems entirely on the mark:

> After 1945, Schmitt repeats an attitude that corresponds to the post–World War One Zeitgeist: he does away with elements of the guilt culture—troubled conscience, remorse—and erects once again the artificial realm of a heroic shame culture. . . . The key concepts of the shame culture are honor and disgrace. After World War One the issue was the disgrace of imperial collapse which, according to the rule of male association and bonding, had to be reversed. At issue now for Schmitt is the honor of which he was deprived as a vanquished foe. Everything the Allies undertook with Schmitt . . . he [thus] experienced as a shaming ritual.

33. Translations from Lethen, *Cool Conduct*, 170–74. See also Schmitt, *Ex Captivitate Salus*.

34. Lethen, *Cool Conduct*, 172–73.

As Lethen puts it, "In Carl Schmitt's *Glossarium* [the second volume of the diaries], amid the rubble, we see the cool persona's final stand." Lethen argues, however, that the difference between the situation after World War I and that after World War II is that "the idea of a post–World War Two shame culture is a phantasm, with no corresponding public discursive space in which to unfold."[35] My own evaluation, however, on the evidence presented in the previous chapters, is that this conclusion is not entirely warranted. Is it really possible to say that Jaspers's vision predominated? Jaspers certainly did not think so.

Epilogue: The Departure of the Repressed

Jaspers, Weber, and National Identity

Without the foregoing excursus into the subterranean world of radical conservatism, one might pass over too easily the monumentality of the task Karl Jaspers undertook. Jaspers was being very specific indeed in *Die Schuldfrage* when he wrote:

> A proudly silent bearing may for a short time be a justified mask, to catch one's breath and clear one's head behind it. But it becomes self-deception, and a trap for the other, if it permits us to hide defiantly within ourselves, to bar enlightenment, to elude the grasp of reality. We must guard against evasion. From such a bearing there arises a mood which is discharged in private, safe abuse, a mood of heartless frigidity, rabid indignation and facile distortions, leading to barren self-corrosion. A pride that falsely deems itself masculine, while in fact evading the issue, takes even silence as an act of combat, a final one that remains impotent.[36]

Heidegger was obviously at the top of Jaspers's address list here, but Jünger (particularly with regard to masculine pride) and Schmitt were not far below.

Jaspers is just as frequently characterized as a proponent of collective guilt as he is as one who rejects it. This, in a way, is the beauty of his formulation: in some distinction to Ebbinghaus's and Litt's demands for a German acknowledgment of responsibility (see chapter 12), the multivalence of Jaspers's argument seems to provide something for everyone, be it something to reject or something to accept. On the one hand, his typology generates a much wider understanding of guilt: it is not limited to only those who perpetrated atrocities; even those who opposed the regime shared in the political responsibility that fell on all Germans and their descendants. On the other hand, one could argue that Jaspers drew a sharp line between "real" guilt—that which is punishable or which might understandably evoke revenge—and the need for a more quiet, private contemplation; as such, he delegitimated any punitive approach, and even opposed re-education. He unequivocally rejected the principle of collective guilt, and indeed subtitled the book *Die Schuldfrage* "On the Political Liability [*Haftung*] of Germany," making clear that "to hold liable does not mean to hold morally guilty."[37] Yet his concept of political responsibility, which he confusingly labeled "political guilt," seems to require exactly what those who were railing against collective guilt were trying to avoid. Indeed, in substance it was little different from Carl Jung's assertion of psychological collective guilt. It was just ever so much more subtle, and not in the least aggressive. It is thus interesting to note in this context that there is not a single reference to Jaspers anywhere in Erich Kästner's collected works, despite Kästner's preoccupation with Jung's similar diagnosis.

* * *

Jaspers, as we saw, argued in *Die Schuldfrage* for a concept of national identity that demanded collective responsibility for the past, which is why the book is taken—rightly so—as a manifesto for a new political culture: not just a new political culture for Germany, but an entirely new *kind* of political culture. The problem for Jaspers was thus to found national obligation without invoking collectivistic principles. "There is no such thing as a people as a whole" he argued. "A people cannot perish heroically, cannot be a criminal, cannot act morally or immorally; only its individuals can do so. . . . The categorical judgment of a people is [thus] always unjust." This is the entire point of Jaspers's differentiation of guilt, which he made "to preserve us from the superficiality of talk about guilt that flattens everything out on a single plane, there to assess it with all the crudeness and lack of discrimination of a bad judge." But Jaspers recognized that something had been lost in the process: "For all the crudeness of collective thinking and collective condemnation we feel that we belong together."[38] How can this be so?

In the heart of *Die Schuldfrage*, past the now-famous typology, Jaspers offered a rather sociological theory. Beginning from the same recognition

37. Ibid., 55.
38. Ibid., 27, 35, 69.

of common humanity that led him to articulate a notion of metaphysical guilt, Jaspers noted that "[e]very human being is fated to be enmeshed in the power relations he lives by. This is the inevitable guilt of all, the guilt of human existence." Precisely this enmeshing is what makes us human in the first place: "In the end, of course, the true collective is the solidarity of all men before God." Nevertheless, "historically we remain bound to the closer, narrower communities, and we should lose the ground under our feet without them." This solidarity has both its benefits and its costs: it provides us with language, culture, material resources, and a sense of identity; by the same token, we cannot simply detach ourselves from these when we do not agree with what is happening in their name:

> [T]he . . . German—that is *the German-speaking individual* [emphasis added]— feels concerned by everything growing from German roots. It is not the liability of a national but the concern of one who shares the life of the German spirit and soul—who is of one tongue, one stock, one fate with all the others—which here comes to cause, not a tangible guilt, but something analogous to co-responsibility.
>
> We further feel that we not only share in what is done at present—thus being co-responsible for the deeds of our contemporaries—but in the links of tradition. We have to bear the guilt of our fathers. . . . The individual cannot wholly detach himself from these conditions, for—consciously or unconsciously—he lives as a link in their chain and cannot escape from their influence even if he was in opposition. . . . [P]olitical conditions are inseparable from a people's whole way of life.

In the era of the modern state, no one can remain aloof from politics and the responsibilities it entails.[39]

Politics as a Vocation for Weber and Jaspers

What, then, can it have meant to be German in 1946? In order to understand Jaspers's answer, it is essential to recognize his debts to Max Weber, one of the founding fathers of contemporary sociology and one of the most important public intellectuals of the Wilhelmine era. As a young man, Jaspers was both personally and intellectually devoted to Max Weber, who became his friend, and whom he later pronounced "the greatest German of our era." On numerous occasions Jaspers undertook work on Weber's life and ideas, most importantly in a commemorative address following Weber's death in 1920,

39. Ibid., 28, 69, 73–74.

then in a short book from 1932 (revised and reissued with a new preface in 1958), and then in an essay on Weber's political thought from 1962.[40] Most relevant here is Jaspers's assessment of Weber's nationalism and of his response to the German defeat in 1918. Weber, Jaspers argued, "was never a 'nationalist' in the sense of blind affirmation of this nation as it is, but rather in the claim on itself and on the people to become what they could be. This 'nationalism,'" Jaspers wrote, "in its unconditionality, honesty, and sobriety was opposed to the average German nationalism which was pathetically without courage, unprepared for veracity, satisfied with presumed security and a stupid arrogance of emotions, but risked its life on command, in military obedience, and without its own moral risk." According to Jaspers, "Max Weber abhorred this frivolous game of nationalist ideas."[41]

Yet a patriot Weber was. As Jaspers wrote in 1962, almost with a note of envy, "In the German nation, he self-evidently lived without question."[42] Never was this more apparent than in Weber's reactions to the German defeat in World War I. Perhaps his best-known essay—"Politics as a Vocation" (*Politik als Beruf*)—was based on a speech he gave to students following his participation in the conference negotiating the "War Guilt Clause" of the Versailles Treaty. In it, Weber drew his enduringly significant distinction between an "ethic of responsibility" and an "ethic of conviction." Weber's goal was to counter pacifist sentiments among the students, which were generating support for the war guilt clause. For Weber, accepting war guilt on pacifist grounds was an example of an ethic of conviction—being guided by a non-negotiable commitment to an idea. In contrast, Weber argued strenuously for what he termed an "ethic of responsibility," a principle of political action guided by instrumental considerations: it would be irresponsible to the German nation, Weber argued, to accept war guilt, however compelling pacifist convictions might be. The distinction, indeed, was tied up with Weber's very conception of modernity, in which rationality—the ability to calculate efficient means to given ends—was the organizing idea; an ethic of conviction, for Weber, was a residue of a premodern era, a world in which one could not yet think in abstract, efficient terms. For Weber, the ends of politics are at the limit arbitrary. An ethic of conviction, therefore, denies reality.

Jaspers presented Weber's position as follows: "Following World War One, Weber turned against the political masochism of an undignified

---

40. These texts are reprinted in Jaspers, *On Max Weber.*
41. Ibid., 31, 167–68.
42. Ibid., 164.

pacifism that wallows voluptuously in guilt feelings 'as if military *success* intrinsically might demonstrate something like divine judgment, and as if the god of battles were not 'with the larger battalions' (*we* have shown: not *always!*).'" Never was Weber more of a German patriot, Jaspers argued, than when he defended the interests of the nation against being compromised by unrealistic convictions: "Weber always opposed all summary criticism of what was collectively German, and all irresponsible, hard-hearted censure with his 'nevertheless' and 'yet.'" Jaspers quoted Weber as saying, "For I believe in the indestructability of this Germany and never have felt being a German so much as a gift of fate as in these dark days of its shame."[43]

For Jaspers, it was thus crucial to imagine how Weber would have responded to National Socialism. After World War I, Weber's answer was an unequivocal no to the question of German guilt. In *Die Schuldfrage*, Jaspers wrote that "[t]his time the war-guilt question . . . is very clear. . . . Germany is guilty of the war through its regime, which started the war at its own chosen moment, while none of the rest wanted it." But it wasn't only the nature of the guilt that had changed for Jaspers—the first time unclear, the second time clear. It was the very possibility of maintaining a Weberian faith in the German nation. "What would have taken place in Max Weber," Jaspers asked in 1962, "if he had seen National Socialism? . . . Would Max Weber then have altogether despaired of the German nation?" Jaspers was convinced that even though Weber would recognize reality—"He could not acknowledge a state as German that nowhere held its dignity in feudal tenure by the nation. For this *state*, though it would end inexorably with it, annihilated this *nation* step by step."—the answer would be no:

> Even if its countenance from 1933–45 was incomparably more desecrated than it had even been in 1918, if all that was abysmally vile had seized the efficiency of technical ability, and if what was still German had been killed or lay dormant— was not something left living, after all, that remained German? [I]t certainly seems to me that to despair of what is German, altogether and completely, for always and in every form, would not have been possible for Max Weber.[44]

The critically important question here, however, is what was possible for Karl Jaspers. Jaspers's own compromise formula, the remnant he rescued from his struggle with the nationalism of his hero Weber, was to engage in the classically German separation of the political and cultural

43. Ibid., 50, 169, 52.
44. Ibid., 181–82.

aspects of identity. Since the political experience of Germany was "an unhappy one . . . a history which precedes from one catastrophe to another," Jaspers saw German identity as largely cultural. This is why, in a June 27, 1946, letter to Hannah Arendt, Jaspers wrote, "Now that Germany is destroyed . . . I feel at ease as a German for the first time." Jaspers was accused by his critics of being the "philosopher of national betrayal."[45] Yet for all his doubts about Weber's liberal nationalism, the book on German guilt is suffused with a rhetoric of "we" and "us." While rejecting equivocations, Jaspers repeated the claim that resistance would have meant death. His typology of guilt, moreover, analytically separated political and moral responsibility, fully in line with the German Protestant tradition; this distinction informed his own reformed sense of national identity. But he also argued that "there can be no radical separation of moral and political guilt. . . . The feeling of guilt, which makes us accept liability, is the beginning of the inner upheaval which seeks to realize political liberty."[46] This was the central ambivalence of the pariah status Jaspers attributed to his nation: on the one hand, the scorn of the world, an abyss of guilt out of which Germany can climb only with the hardest self-examination, if only the world will allow it; on the other hand, if Germany can do this, it will have gained insights and confidence that might even provide a sort of moral authority.

The German Language as Jaspers's Personal House of Being?

The only remaining question, then, is why Jaspers chose to leave Germany in 1948 and to accept Swiss citizenship in 1967. Here is where we find the truest articulation of Jaspers's sense of national identity. The answer, moreover, is decisive for our evaluation of the putative reversal of the shame/guilt balance and thus for our understanding of the initial condition of the Federal Republic as a political culture. Was Jaspers the philosopher of national betrayal, as he was accused and as was seemingly evident in his departure? For Jaspers, it was more obviously the other way around—it was his nation that had betrayed him, both personally and politically. As for the personal, he tells of his wartime inability to purchase a cemetery plot for his wife because she was a Jew, as a result of which "something was torn that could not be made whole again." For Jaspers and his wife, "the experience of being excluded from one's own people by a state that was a criminal

45. Kohler and Saner, Hannah Arendt–Karl Jaspers, 46.
46. Jaspers, The Question of German Guilt, 71.

state changed the relation to this people. What the Germans, to whom we belonged, are to us has nothing more to do with state and locality and grave."[47]

So what did it have to do with? "The German world (*Das Deutsche*) in which I live, from which I come, through which I act, has a wider space than this narrowness, than this national bondage, that by now has become politically absurd, deriving from this Bismarck state that is by now nothing more than a specter." For Jaspers, it was the reaction to *Die Schuldfrage*—which ranged from silence to rejection—and his growing realization that neither his colleagues nor his compatriots wanted the kind of transformation he was preaching, that prompted his leaving: "What drove us away was clear: The absence of consequences for the mass murder of Jews—of the radical distancing from the total criminal state—my isolation in goals for the university—the animosity of the government." For Karl and Gertrud Jaspers, "[a] state and a people that did to the Jews what never should have been allowed to happen and did not grasp this after the catastrophe and did not draw the consequences had lost every claim." Was this an act of national betrayal? He did not think so: "For Germany—if one in this case chooses this demanding expression—I would be able to accomplish more, represent it better, show the Germans a better product and purer kind of thinking, if I were to go to Basel. Of emigration there was no question. I remain in the wider German area [*Raum*], which has since the middle ages been not a political but a linguistic and cultural area."[48]

In this light, it is not quite so obvious that Jaspers's vision could represent the official culture of the new state, that the official culture of West Germany would be a guilt culture. The only possibility for redeeming the claim that Jaspers's vision embodied the official culture, then, is to propose that Jaspers's vision triumphed in the long-term—though to say this without attending to the ways Jünger, Heidegger, and Schmitt's visions have also persisted is misleading. Either way, the strict ascription of guilt to the Federal Republic, or of guilt to the public and shame to the private, does not hold up. Or, one can note, as I did above, the way in which Jaspers's scheme provided something for everyone. And this does indeed seem to be the case. This reading is perhaps the best explanation for why and how Konrad Adenauer, for instance, simultaneously demanded amnesty and exoneration for former National Socialists while pursuing almost as vigorously an unpopular program of "reparations" for Israel. Criminal guilt and

47. Jaspers, "Von Heidelberg nach Basel," in Jaspers, *Schicksal und Wille*, 167.
48. Ibid., 177, 180, 164, 178.

political responsibility are different things. Jaspers's argument was that the distinctions are really only analytical, and should have been harder to draw than they in fact were in postwar Germany.

*   *   *

On the basis of the foregoing narrative, Ruth Benedict's implication that guilt is more advanced—and morally superior to—shame in fact seems rather plausible, especially freed of the overreaching association of guilt and shame with entire cultures. Who today wouldn't prefer the perspective of Jaspers over that of Heidegger, Jünger, and Schmitt? But before coming to this conclusion, it is worth considering that not all distaste for Jaspers's understanding came from the Right.

In the immediate postwar period, perhaps the most interesting example of the criticism of Jaspers emanating from the Left came from Heinrich Blücher, who was Hannah Arendt's husband.[49] According to Blücher, "Jaspers's whole ethical purification-babble leads him to solidarity with the German National Community and even with the National Socialists, instead of solidarity with those who have been degraded." For Blücher, moreover, there is something exculpatory about the generalization involved in "metaphysical guilt," which he viewed as a sort of "original sin." This makes all guilty in the eyes of God and thus effaces real moral differences in the world: "guilt serves the purpose of extirpating responsibility." As a result, this "whole inner-German and inner-dealing talk of reconciliation of the 'National Community' can only serve the Nazis." Blücher's position is thus that he does not "give a damn if they'll [the Germans] roast in hell someday or not, as long as they're prepared to do something to dry the tears of the degraded and the humiliated, and to die for freedom." The problem for Blücher was that this framing of the "guilt question" served "for the vanquished as a way to continue occupying themselves exclusively with themselves." He thus characterized Jaspers's "guilt monograph" as a "Christian/pietistic/hypocritical nationalizing piece of twaddle."[50]

Indeed, while Blücher's analysis is in many respects peremptory (the analysis just quoted was set out in a letter to his wife), there may be something to it. Jaspers did in fact say little about the victims, focusing instead on what he could contribute to the transformation of the German

---

49. In many respects, Arendt seconded her husband's assessment, though her own analysis went in other directions as well.

50. Kohler, *Within Four Walls*, 84–86.

soul, an entity in which, despite all, he still believed. One interesting feature of postwar German discourse, as we have seen again and again, was that speakers often denied national identity as a "Nazi" form of argumentation when it was being used against them (e.g., in collective guilt or national character arguments), but were at great pains to reassert it when they saw positive virtues (e.g., the legacies of German humanistic culture or "positive" German values). In this light, Jaspers's argument seems particularly contrived, despite everything, to see national identity only as a positive resource. His mechanism for accomplishing this, once again, was the separation of German culture from German politics.

CHAPTER 14

Conclusion

In 1950–51, members of the reconstituted Frankfurt Institute for Social Research undertook a series of studies to assess the persistence of fascist attitudes in the German population five years after the end of World War II. The methodological premise of the research was that there was a difference between manifest "public opinion" and latent "nonpublic opinion," which Franz Böhm described in his preface to the research report as the difference between "the sum of opinions we wish people believed we had as our real opinion" versus "the sum of opinions that we truly have."[1]

During their U.S. exile, members of the institute had gained experience with the so-called "focused interview" (later to be called the "focus group") developed by Robert K. Merton and Paul Lazarsfeld at Columbia University's Bureau of Applied Social Research. From that starting point, the Frankfurt researchers developed a "provocation" method they believed would help reveal the hidden nonpublic opinion: they composed a putative letter home from a fictional U.S. Army sergeant conveying a negative assessment of German national character, particularly of the unwillingness of Germans to acknowledge the wrong they had done during the Third Reich, and presented this letter to representative groups of ordinary Germans as the starting point for discussions. The researchers understood this to be a superior method to traditional surveys or even to one-on-one interviews because of their belief that the "opinions and attitudes of people to the themes that have a claim to general or public interest and therefore can form the objects of public opinion do not come about and work in isolation, but in the continuous interrelation between the individual and the mediate and immediate society that affects him." This kind of research was necessary, moreover,

1. Böhm, "Geleitwort," in Pollock, *Gruppenexperiment*, xi.

because the image of German society to be gained from the analysis of either survey data or "the so-called public opinion, which expresses itself in elections, referenda, public speeches, groups, parliamentary discussions, [and] political meetings" was, they argued, misleading. These public statements, Böhm wrote, "are only formal expressions we use when we are wearing our Sunday clothes."[2] Not surprisingly, the researchers found a much more widespread tendency toward "fascist" ideology than standard opinion surveys reported, and particularly a deep well of "resistance" and "avoidance" on the issues of collective guilt and responsibility for the treatment of Jews.

Opinion: Dialogical and Public

This historical piece of social scientific research is especially interesting here for a number of reasons, both methodological and substantive. Methodologically, the study's premise that opinion is a fluid discursive process rather than a static, atomistic result fits well with my effort to highlight what I have called the "dialogical" qualities of "official memory" formation through what I approached as a series of "agonies." Indeed, we have seen the extent to which the public statements I reported are parts of ongoing dialogues in which speakers and writers continually address—implicitly or explicitly—opponents, partners, predecessors, and shifting audiences. I would have missed much in these statements had I not approached them in this way, including my attention to statements both before 1945 outside of Germany and after 1945 within it. As I will reiterate shortly, the notion of the "memory of memory" also aims to capture the on-going and reflexive qualities of the discourse. While I thus agree with the Frankfurt researchers that it is important to capture the interactive quality of opinion formation, it seems to me that one can find this interactivity in public as well as in nonpublic opinion.

Moreover, while it may have been reasonable for the researchers to assume they would find a subterranean nonpublic opinion and that this would differ starkly from the manifest public opinion, I am not convinced that their perception in this regard was accurate. The Frankfurters were rightly suspicious of some of the more optimistic claims by opinion leaders that unacceptable residues of fascism had either been eliminated or had never really been that widespread. The institute's researchers were also correct in their observation that "all that goes over from attitudes into actual public opinion has to run through the control of a truly public articulation,"

2. Ibid., 32, xi.

which "enforces a minimum of reason and morality."[3] Nevertheless, that "control" and "minimum of reason or morality" does not, it seems to me, take exactly the form they imply. I am not challenging their description of the discourse they incited—as they themselves noted, what they found is not really surprising. Rather, I am disputing their expectation of the *public* discourse. What I have found most interesting is that even with the controlling effect of public media, there is still so much in the public discourse that surprises. Even the Sunday clothes, we have seen, can be varied and informative.

Opinion: Public and Nonpublic

The methodological lessons for the study of collective memory formation are thus clear. As I wrote at the beginning of the book, the assumption that official memory is somehow sterile and static in comparison to the memory produced at non-elite levels is as much a prejudice as the idea that only official public memory is important. In reality, the relation between elite and popular culture is an empirical rather than presuppositional issue. In this case, the kind of elite discourse I have found differs from other kinds in the consistency with which certain positions were articulated, as well as in the vocabulary, but the data of my study indicate that there were some strong continuities between the kinds of logic the Frankfurters elicited in their focus groups and the kinds that I have found in public discourse.

One important question concerns the connections between the kinds of debates and their participants I presented in the foregoing pages and the culture of "ordinary" people. It is true that the debates between, say, Erich Kästner and Carl Jung, or Karl Jaspers and Martin Heidegger, were not the first topic of conversation around the country, that many people were not at all interested in such matters or did not read about them (though, again, there was an unusual efflorescence of interest in printed matter and at least some of the works discussed above were read, heard, or heard of by very large numbers of ordinary people, to different extents in different fields). But, again, one would be mistaken to answer the question of the relations between elite public discourse and less exalted vernaculars presuppositionally rather than empirically—simply supposing, that is, that intellectual discourse is irrelevant to ordinary people. Equally as dangerous as elitism is anti-intellectualism—the presumption that public intellectuals and writers serve no purpose and that politicians operate according to different rules, neither distilling common sentiments nor leading opinion, that their work may go

3. Ibid., xiii.

on side by side with the memory work of ordinary people, but that these have nothing to do with each other. To me, however, it has been especially interesting to look not at what ordinary people say when pressed, but at the kinds of arguments and issues that are advanced when well-informed and articulate opinion leaders sat down to work out their ideas about the past and their hopes for the future. This implies no denigration of nonpublic opinion. It merely asserts a belief that public discourse is relevant and telling. (Indeed, even intellectuals have a nonpublic opinion, a bit of which we have seen. But, in contrast to some archival historians, I have found publicly available positions at least as interesting as the hidden-behind-the-scenes motives.)

The House of the Hangman

Perhaps the most interesting reason to consider the Frankfurt study, however, is for the controversy it generated and for the substantive issues at stake in that controversy. Following the publication of the research in 1955, the well-regarded psychologist Peter Hofstätter published a critical, and in many respects polemical, review in the Cologne Journal of Sociology and Social Psychology [Kölner Zeitschrift für Soziologie und Sozialpsychologie]. Defending the "positivist-atomistic" method that the Frankfurters' approach criticized (though they also employed quantitative techniques), Hofstätter disputed their interpretation of their own data. He argued, for instance, that by reinterpreting the data to take into account the large numbers of participants who remained largely silent, among other things, one had to conclude that the data did not convincingly demonstrate more than a 15 percent proportion of participants with an undemocratic attitude. Because this proportion did not differ significantly from that to be found in other countries, Hofstätter argued, one also had to conclude that there was no significant "legacy of fascist ideology" in German attitudes.

On that basis, Hofstätter went on to charge that the critical interpretive methods the Frankfurt researchers employed in their analysis were nothing more than self-fulfilling accusations: in contrast to what he called the Frankfurters' presumption that their method was analogous to the old apothegm *in vino veritas* (in wine, truth), he described their premise as an unfair *in ira veritas* (in anger, truth), claiming that the statements elicited through their provocation method indicated nothing other than that people can be goaded into saying just about anything. He thus characterized their analysis as "nothing but an accusation, or a demand for genuine mental remorse." But for him, "[t]here is simply no individual feeling that could satisfactorily correspond to constantly looking at the annihilation of a million people." As a result, he argued, these accusations were "misplaced or pointless" and did nothing but express "the indignation of the sociological analyst." The Frankfurt researchers, with their implied condemnation of postwar German political culture, were simply asking too much.[4]

The response, printed together with the critique, was by the publication series' senior editor, the venerable philosopher and sociologist Theodor Adorno. Adorno responded in thorough and careful detail to each of Hofstätter's methodological charges, arguing that Hofstätter ignored all qualifications and subtlety. At the heart of his critique, however, was that Hofstätter's charges stemmed not from the limits on this kind of scientific inquiry, but from what Adorno argued was a defensive unwillingness to acknowledge the reality of German nonpublic opinion, a reality Adorno believed the study had demonstrated, if not with total scientific irrefutability in all the details, nevertheless overwhelmingly. For example, where Hofstätter interpreted the large proportion of respondents who remained silent while others articulated undemocratic views as evidence of their disagreement, Adorno argued that there was as little reason to assume they disagreed as to assume that they agreed. "The method," Adorno wrote, "is declared to be useless so that the existence of the phenomenon that emerges can be denied."[5]

For Adorno, this and other refusals in Hofstätter's critique manifested precisely the kind of "collective narcissism" the study had uncovered. Adorno thus sarcastically observed, "Hofstätter considers 'it is hardly possible that a single individual could take upon himself the horror of Auschwitz.' It is [however] the victims of Auschwitz who had to take its horrors upon themselves, not those who, to their own disgrace and that of their nation, prefer not to admit it." Quoting Hofstätter's language, Adorno continued, "The 'question of guilt' was 'laden with despair' for the *victims*, not for the *survivors*, and it takes some doing to have blurred this distinction with the existential category of despair, which is not without reason a popular one" (emphasis added). In a characteristic rhetorical move for him, Adorno then took a common expression—"In the house of the hanged, one should not mention the noose"—and made a subtle play on words to illustrate his point: "But in the house of the *hangman* one should not mention the noose; one might be suspected of harboring resentment."[6]

4. Hofstätter, "Zum 'Gruppenexperiment' von F. Pollock," 99. See also the annotations in Rolf Tiedemann's edition of essays by Theodor W. Adorno, *Can One Live after Auschwitz?* 477–80. For a more extensive discussion, see Wiggershaus, *The Frankfurt School,* 472–78.

5. Adorno, *"Replik,"* 116.

6. Ibid., 115–16 (emphasis added).

Later, in 1959, in what is perhaps one of his best-known essays—"What Does It Mean to Master the Past?"—Adorno again resorted to this formulation to indicate his sense of why the discussion of the Nazi past in the 1950s was, in his view, inadequate.[7] Indeed, Adorno's play on words has become a staple of sarcastic memory of memory since the 1960s. Interestingly, the phrase went through another permutation, sometimes being repeated not as "one might be suspected of *harboring* resentment," but as "one might be suspected of *stirring up* resentment."[8] The difference is in who is being resentful, the victims or the Germans. On the one hand, the Auschwitz survivor Jean Améry, for instance, published a famous essay in 1966 on his *ressentiment* (using Nietzsche's francophone version of the term) at the prosperity of Germans in whose midst he lived. On the other hand, some have charged that it is the Germans *themselves* who become resentful when one demands too much in the way of acknowledgment of the past. This German resentment is captured by the bitter joke that the Germans will never forgive the Jews for Auschwitz, or in reactions such as West German chancellor Helmut Schmidt's statement at the end of a 1981 trip to Saudi Arabia, during which he had negotiated the sale of West German tanks to this sworn enemy of Israel, that "German foreign policy may no longer be held hostage to Auschwitz."[9] We saw it as well in the early postwar warnings that one should not burden Germans with too much guilt, else one risked driving them back to National Socialism. Franklin Roosevelt had a similar sentiment when he saw U.S. occupation troops after World War I not flying the American flag for fear of humiliating the Germans.

Germans and Jews

Obviously, it is from this aphorism—"In the house of the hangman . . ."— that I have taken my title for this book. It seems clear enough that the substantive findings of the foregoing pages bear out at least some of its implication, without, I hope, the overly polemical cast. What is it like to live "in the house of the hangman"? Of what is it possible, and of what impossible, to speak? What is the relationship between the hangman and the others living in his house? What responsibility do these others bear for his work? What can they claim for themselves? One should note that this reference to the "house of the hangman" prescribes no specific answers to

7. Adorno, *Can One Live after Auschwitz?* 3–18.
8. See Claussen, "In the House of the Hangman."
9. See Olick, "Collective Memory and Cultural Constraint."

these questions. After all, even Erich Kästner described the problem as debts borne by family members. Describing postwar Germany in this way (as "the house of the hangman") is thus to ask the question about collective guilt, not to answer it. Most important, it is to ask how and why the Germans themselves asked and answered it.

I am convinced there is something insightful about the "house of the hangman" formulation and the reversal it signals. The claim I made at the beginning of the book on behalf of my strategy—in which I read across institutional fields and discursive contexts—was that doing so would produce insights not possible when taking individual authors or debates on their own. That claim to advantage is clearly redeemed in this regard. As we saw in chapter 12, at the heart of Karl Jaspers's argument in *Die Schuldfrage* was a surprising trope: Germans as the new "pariah people." Explicating the importance of Jaspers's pariah trope, as I noted, was the central contribution of a seminal paper by the intellectual historian Anson Rabinbach.[10] Nevertheless, my broad approach shows—and Adorno's aphorism captures poignantly—that this contemplation of the Germans as the new pariahs was by no means an unusual or isolated matter. By the time we got to Jaspers, it was in fact not very surprising at all.

In virtually every context and author we examined, we saw a version of this peculiar projection of Germans into the status of Jews: Germans were being treated no better than Jews; the same logic that had allowed the extermination of the Jews was now being used by the Allies against Germans; there was no difference between occupation policy and Nazi Jewish policy; pointing out German guilt was "Pharisaical" or "illiberal"; the logic behind diagnoses of German national character was the same as the racial insanity the Nazis had used; the Germans were now being placed in "concentration camps" just like the Jews; . . . and, finally, Germany had become a new pariah people. A particularly interesting version of this projection—one example of which was the 1948 speech by Konrad Adenauer discussed in chapter 11—was in the repudiation of "Morgenthau," Goebbels' "Jewish angel of revenge," whose status as such persisted after 1945, if slightly more coded: not only were Germans being treated as badly as Jews, it was a Jew who was causing them to be treated in this way! One might respond that this overstates the case, and perhaps it does. But we should recall in this context not only Carl Schmitt's unusually extreme comments on the revenge of the Jews but the consistency with which the trope equating Jews and Germans in one way or another appeared and reappeared. Given the

10. Rabinbach, *In the Shadow of Catastrophe.*

structure of the dialogue, it is not accidental that the angel of revenge was a Jew or that the new pariah people were the Germans.

Culture and Character Revisited

Another important consistency that this history of early German memory read across the different agonies has shown is the continued commitment to German national identity, what Friedrich Meinecke called the German *"Character indelibis."* Not one of the writers or speakers we read in the foregoing pages ever seemed to doubt for a second the persistence of valuable and unique German traditions and virtues. Their goal, instead, was to contain the toxic portion of German history so that it could be more easily disposed or handled without contaminating the healthy main body of German identity. The conservative historians like Gerhard Ritter acknowledged the need for some revision, but this was a revision of sorting out and preservation. Even Marxist historians like Alexander Abusch or politicians like Kurt Schumacher were strong nationalists. The closest we came to real self-doubt was with Thomas Mann, the living embodiment of German humanism, who nevertheless saw the legacies of German humanism as containing the seeds of its own corruption within itself. Some of the archconservatives wallowed a bit much in a rhetoric of *"Untergang"* (decline) or *"Götterdämerung"* (twilight of the Gods)—one thinks of Richard Strauss's inscription "In Memoriam" on the score for *Metamorphosen*, signaling his musical borrowing from the funeral march in Beethoven's *Eroica* symphony—but they ascribed this to the misunderstandings of the outside world, not to any essential qualities of German identity, and seemed to imply the hope for a revival.

Even Karl Jaspers, who eventually found it unbearable to live in a Germany that he believed was refusing to face up to its guilt, went into what he himself did not consider a real exile when he moved to Switzerland. I might point out at this juncture that another benefit to having read across so many debates is how it allows one to note the interesting role Switzerland appears to have played in German national identity. Anecdotal as it is given the numbers, we can nevertheless wonder at the frequency with which those voices identified with Germany in one way or the other spoke from this critical distance of Switzerland: Emil Ludwig, Hermann Hesse, Carl Jung, Karl Barth, Wilhelm Röpke, and then ultimately Jaspers, whose case seems to reveal the reason: consistent with the long-standing distinction between *Macht* (power) and *Geist* (spirit), Switzerland seemed to supply the perfect resolution: pure German spirit, no German power. From Switzerland, one could live happily in the house of German language without any of the history of German politics.

The theory of German identity thus remained committed to a sense of Germany's special path (*Sonderweg*). In some versions, that special path brought it to National Socialism. But even in those versions, it could also bring Germany out of National Socialism, and perhaps, on the basis of what it learned from that experience, once again to leadership among nations. It is certainly surprising how many times so soon after the war we could see German speakers and writers expressing the hope not only that Germany could be a reliable partner, but that it could assume a position of moral leadership again.

Traumatic Memory

Another major feature of the history of memory in this period, one that is clear by our reading across the different debates, is the overwhelming preoccupation with short-lived accusations of collective guilt and the perceived need to refute them, perhaps more vigorously than they were charged. In chapter 9, I referred to the memory of these accusations as "traumatic." A most interesting illustration of how enduring that trauma has been came as late as 1996 in the controversy surrounding a book by a young Harvard political scientist, Daniel Goldhagen.

In *Hitler's Willing Executioners: Ordinary Germans and the Holocaust*, Goldhagen charged that Holocaust scholarship neglected the role of widespread anti-Semitic ideology. In other words, he argued, the Holocaust was only possible because ordinary Germans adhered to an ideology of "eliminationist anti-Semitism"; the Holocaust happened because Germans wanted it to happen. Whatever the merits and deficits of Goldhagen's argument (and of the way he presented it), more interesting to me is the storm of indignation the book provoked.[11] While many found its argument unjustly dismissive of previous Holocaust scholarship, disliked its evocative tone, or found unconvincing Goldhagen's explanation of why this particularly virulent form of anti-Semitism arose in Germany but not elsewhere, one of the major points of criticism—fifty years after the postwar "guilt debate"!—was the charge that Goldhagen was advocating collective guilt. Whether because they believed he paid too little attention to the opposi-

11. On the Goldhagen controversy and its aftereffects, see Küntzel et al., *Goldhagen*; Shandley, *Unwilling Germans?*; Eley, *The "Goldhagen Effect"*; Kött, *Goldhagen in der Qualitaetspresse*; Schoeps, *Ein Volk von Mördern?*; Heil and Erb, *Geschichtswissenschaft und Öffentlichkeit*; Wipperman, *Wessen Schuld?*

tion or ascribed too great a role to generalized attitudes rather than actions, Goldhagen's critics used the imputation of collective guilt theory to discredit his entire argument. Interestingly—and illustrating the power of the taboo—Goldhagen himself did not dare engage with the peculiarity of the charge of collective guilt except to deny that he intended any such thing. As a result, he reinforced the illegitimacy of collective guilt theory, even though reformulating the notion might have supported his case.

Yet another interesting feature of this debate concerns one of the ways Goldhagen tried to clarify that he was no collective guilt theorist. After denying that his charges against ordinary Germans amounted to a collective guilt accusation, he added that whatever he had to say about Germans during the Nazi period certainly did not extend to Germans in the Federal Republic, the political culture of which he believed had effected a dramatic turn-around. In this, Goldhagen seems to have validated the strategic claim made by the early leaders of the Federal Republic of Germany that there were no potent remains of National Socialism (one thinks here as well of Hofstätter's resistance to the Frankfurter researchers' contrary findings), though interestingly Goldhagen's *deus ex machina* was American re-education. As we have seen, however, the question of whether there was truly a "zero hour" of German history—whether 1945 or 1949—after which Germany began anew or whether postwar Germany involved a problematic "restoration" or even continuities was—and continues to be—a highly political issue. In his defense against accusations of making collective guilt accusations, Goldhagen sought to assuage fears that his harsh assessment of Germans in the Third Reich was meant to impugn Germans of the Federal Republic. He thus too hastily seemed to seize on a "caesura" argument, or at least left open the question of how such a dramatic turn-around was possible so quickly. As we have seen, it wasn't, or at least not in any straightforward manner.

Restoration or Revolution?

To what extent was the occupation period a genuinely revolutionary period? To what extent did it involve a simple restoration of pre-Nazi traditions and personalities (or, worse yet, continuity with Nazi traditions and personalities)? Or was the occupation period a peculiar interlude of openness and reexamination followed by a restoration in 1949? Part of the problem is with the very terms "revolution" or "restoration," to say nothing of "zero hour" or "caesura," on behalf of which one may not claim too much scientific specificity without inviting trouble. Insofar as there is always some change and there is never complete change, all social situations are better evaluated not as "revolutionary" or not, but in terms of the degree and kind of change they underwent. By the same token, any restoration implies selection, the restoration of something but not of something else; there is never any real going back.

One peculiarity of the postwar German public discourse we might note, moreover, was the co-existence of the zero hour trope with that of the "Other Germany," both of which were used as ways to defend against collective condemnations. The zero hour motif was rooted in the desire to begin again, not to be held accountable for the disasters of the past, to distance oneself from an unacceptable—indeed ungraspable—odium; the only way to do so is through a total break in which nothing remains.[12] Now was the time for re-evaluating *everything*. The "Other Germany," in seeming contrast, argued that the most propitious way to move ahead was to reconnect with an identity that had been repressed or to return to an original tradition that had been lost. Whatever debates there were over who constituted the "Other Germany," and thus about who had the right to speak on behalf of German traditions and who had the right to participate in creating new ones, the senses of rupture and continuity played off of each other without uncomfortable contradiction, each providing what the other could not.

For some, the reinvocation of older values was simply a reflex; indeed, since many had never abandoned older perspectives and saw National Socialism as disruptive, there seemed no reason to question those older frames of reference other than to search for the chink that had led to structural failure. For others, the older values seemed to be a positive resource, an alternative to both National Socialism and the foreign occupation; the Allies, in this view, simply did not understand Germany. Beyond proponents of restoration, of course, were many others who seemed ready to sweep away much; but even here they did so from the position of losers of old battles seeking to settle a score. It seems to me that, for instance, there

12. Walter Dirks—who wrote the seminal essay in 1950 on the "restorative character of the epoch," referred to the "grace of the zero point" (*Gnade des Nullpunkts*). Quoted in Eschenburg, *Jahre der Besatzung*, 159. See Dirks, *"Der restaurative Charakter der Epoche."* Dirks's formulation had an interesting afterlife in the 1980s, when Chancellor Helmut Kohl remarked on a trip to Israel that he enjoyed the "grace of late birth" (*Gnade der späten Geburt*) (Kohl's closer source for the expression was Günther Gaus, the first permanent representative from West Germany to East Germany). Another similar term commonly used in the immediate postwar period was *Kahlschlag*, which literally means deforestation or clearing away. *Nullpunkt* and *Kahlschlag*, of course, could also be used more negatively, the former to indicate a nadir, the later to indicate a destruction of a landscape.

was no greater restoration than Kurt Schumacher's belief in the necessity of revolution, to say nothing of Theodor Heuss's turn towards 1848.

Was the path from National Socialism to the Federal Republic of Germany a restoration or a (revolutionary) zero hour? Both of these readings, as we have seen, are powerful political myths. This was the case at the time; and it was also the case later, when speakers claimed alternately that the first years after the war and of the new state were continuous with what went before (thus a restoration of pre-Nazi ideas or even a continuity of fascism within democracy, as Theodor Adorno worried) and that the real break came only later, in the 1960s (this was the reading that Social Democrats put forward in the 1960s), or that alternately 1945, 1949, or 1955 (the return of sovereignty) were the real breaks (this was the reading put forward by conservatives). Debates about restoration versus revolution have also formed an important line of division in the scholarly literature. The analyst's job, however, is to understand these myths without necessarily adopting them.

From the analytical perspective of the sociology of memory, the path from 1945 to 1948 must be understood as a *reconstruction*—sometimes more, sometimes less dramatic. Reconstruction implies the mixing of the old and the new, a process of critical appropriation.[13] Some of these reappropriations turned out to be more propitious, others turned out to be more brittle. In the end, perhaps no one has captured the ironies of such a transformative moment as postwar Germany better than the preeminent theorist of both revolution and restoration, Karl Marx. In his essay on "The Eighteenth Brumaire of Louis Napolean" Marx famously wrote that the "tradition of all dead generations weighs like a nightmare on the brains of the living. And just as they seem to be occupied with revolutionizing themselves and things . . . they anxiously conjure up the spirits of the past to their service."

Because most of the participants in postwar German public discourse saw themselves as representatives of traditions that had lost or that had not achieved their due, they reached in these familiar directions. But they did so in a context that was in important ways radically different. As Marx also wrote, men make their own history, but not in circumstances of their own choosing. As a result, those old traditions were under pressure to change, no matter how orthodox their first reconstitution seemed. One might take a punning lesson from Adorno: the more things stay the same, the more they change!

13. See Alexander, "The Centrality of the Classics."

The Memory of Memory

This idea of the *reconstruction* of Germany fits well with my effort to capture the workings of collective memory as a reflexive process in time, in which people create meaning not only by remembering a particular past, but by remembering and revising previous ways of remembering that past. Within the sociology of collective memory, there have classically been two distinct approaches. The first is a "traditionalist" or "essentialist" approach, in which the central question is how memory of significant pasts shapes contemporary identity and action. Here the past, conceived as heritage, patrimony, tradition, or even as culture more generally, is the bedrock of collective existence, giving contemporary identities their decisive stamp. In contrast, a "presentist" approach begins by noting the apparent malleability of images of the past—how we not only emphasize different pasts at different points in time, but interpret the same pasts differently over time—and concludes that memory is made largely in the present from present perspectives and for present purposes. The choice is thus between a theory that assumes the past shapes the present and a theory that assumes the present shapes the past.

One solution to this sterile dichotomy (which is, thankfully, not usually practiced as rigidly as it is theorized), is to string together consecutive histories of memory. One might, for instance, study how the Nazi past was represented in the 1950s, in the 1960s, and then in the 1970s, and compare and contrast these different relations to the past. On the one hand, because such a history keeps the general object of memory—the Nazi past—constant, it appreciates the different ways that past has shaped different presents. On the other hand, by tracking changes in the way that past is represented at different points in time, it appreciates the ways different presents shaped the past.

Nevertheless, as I argued in the introduction, successive representations of a past do not follow each other willy-nilly merely as one representation after another, but form a dialogue. The act of representing the past at a particular point in the present does not just involve the relationship between a particular past and a particular present, but is, implicitly or explicitly, a comment on all previous such relationships. Remembering, in other words, is like a conversation: neither the speaker nor the analysts can fully understand any particular utterance except by locating it in a chain of utterances. As the literary critic Mikhail Bakhtin put it, every utterance contains "memory traces" of earlier usages, meaning not that any utterance can be decoded to reveal earlier usages, but that the specificity of every term is the product of an historical process, in the same way that any statement in a conversation is the product of the entire preceding conversation (without itself containing the transcript of that conversation). As Bakhtin wrote, "Each individual utterance is [thus] a link in a chain of speech communion. Any utterance, in addition to its own theme, always responds (in the broad sense of the word) in one form or another to other utterances that precede it."[14]

This theoretical vocabulary is of great help in avoiding the rigid theoretical dichotomy between essentialism and presentism in sociological collective memory research because it sensitizes us to the ways in which any particular image of the past is a reaction to and a comment on not only the past, but on earlier such images of the past. This means that collective remembering is a process of constant revision. Bakhtin also made the important point that references to earlier images need not be explicit or conscious for earlier usages to affect later ones. The memory of memory thus includes not only the specific afterlives of certain images (e.g., Adenauer's reference to the Morgenthau Plan), but also the discursive environment to which such an early image contributed without the subsequent speaker necessarily being aware of the earlier statement. In this light, it is especially important to attend to the ways in which early memories are framed and to the political stakes for the future of memory in that framing process (e.g., how framing Morgenthau as a vengeful Jew contributed to the sense many Germans had that Germany was being irrationally punished, with the result that they framed the legacies of the German past differently than they might have otherwise, whether or not they paid particular attention to the Morgenthau Plan).

As indicated both in the early chapters I devoted to it and in using it as an example in the previous paragraph, the rise of what I call the "Morgenthau myth" is one of the most interesting moments in the memory of memory of National Socialism. In her revisionist account of the origins of the Cold War, Carolyn Eisenberg draws one of the most important lessons from this case of contested memory of memory: in contrast to the conventional understanding that the emergence of the Cold War got in the way of punitive Allied policy (here the replacement of JCS [Joint Chiefs of Staff] 1067 with JCS 1779 is the central emblem, though the Marshall Plan, special amnesties and the general pressure to conclude denazification are also key elements of the story), Eisenberg points out that the retreat from punishment was already established even before the end of the war, particularly in the U.S. Departments of State and War. It is thus not accurate to ascribe

14. Bakhtin, *Speech Genres and Other Essays*, 93–94.

the shift in Allied policy to putative negative legacies of the Morgenthau Plan or to its inappropriateness to a newly tense international context. The shift was already part of preventing the Morgenthau Plan's first formulation, not a result of its ultimate formulation and effect.

By the same token, we might also consider whether it is true that "justice" had to be sacrificed on the altar of "legitimacy" and that German resistance to the concept of collective guilt and self-inquiry was a reaction to the arrogance of re-education and the Anglo-American suppression of the so-called *Antifas*, though it is certainly true to an even greater extent than I have highlighted in the foregoing pages that both Western and West German policy was a complex amalgam of justified and unjustified anticipations of and reactions to Soviet efforts. A plausible alternative reading is that German resistance to introspection and more radical revision of their sources of identity had little to do with the short-lived accusations of collective guilt and re-education policy more generally; instead, it is conceivable that many merely used the problems of Allied policy as an opportunity for avoiding such self-inquiry. Indeed, that much of the condemnation of Allied policy came from the Left during the occupation period should in this way destabilize the Left's memory of memory from the 1960s, during which it stood for "memory" while the Right stood for "repression."

Neither the Left nor the Right, as the foregoing pages give reason to believe, was particularly interested in the kind of engagement with the past pursued by the Left in the 1960s, and for the absence of which the Left blamed the Allies and the Right. Indeed, for all his accusations that Konrad Adenauer was the "Chancellor of the Allies," Kurt Schumacher acquiesced in—even supported—a very great deal of Adenauer's *Vergangenheitspolitik* (policy on the past) in the 1950s, most prominently the rehabilitation of the Nazi-era civil servants. For neither Schumacher nor Adenauer, however, is it particularly convincing to explain that policy in terms of the imperatives of state after 1949, the putative strategic need to purchase "legitimacy" at the price of "justice." Rather, the roots of the rejection of collective guilt and all it might entail were part of general cultural frameworks of memory with which so many public figures approached the question of the Nazi past in the immediate aftermath of the war—varied as the emphases of those cultural frameworks may have been in different hands. The idea that the *Vergangenheitspolitik* of the 1950s was a matter of the imperatives of state is thus itself a particular memory of memory, part of seeing the legacies of National Socialism as concrete administrative problems that needed to be solved quickly. As I pointed out in the introduction, both those who approve Adenauer's choices as prescient and those who condemn them as cynical share the view that they were choices. As we have just seen, however, this view is itself a result of a particular memory of memory, one which rests on a strong distinction between the occupation period and the founding of the state, in the process discrediting the occupation by linking it more to the misery of National Socialism than to the rebirth of democracy. It is also interesting to note how this particular memory of memory has been salient not only for German public discourse, but for many historians of memory as well, who often begin their accounts in 1949 because they see the occupation period—with its "fiasco" of denazification and transformation from punishment to rehabilitation—as a distinct mnemonic landscape (to say nothing of the Anglo-American discourse before the end of the war).

*   *   *

In the foregoing pages we have encountered a number of other such interesting and, from a more dispassionate perspective, perhaps surprising moments in the early memory of memory. Just a few pages ago, I characterized the reaction to the so-called "placard actions" and collective guilt accusations of the first weeks as "traumatic," insofar as the defenses seemed so much more vigorous than the accusations. In a similar way, it was interesting to see Erich Kästner's vilification of Carl Jung, an impression that has lasted in subsequent discourse, which usually designates Jung as the originator of the term "collective guilt" (*Kollektivschuld*) and assimilates him to such putative Germanaphobes as Vansittart, without further examination of his argument.

Memory is necessarily selective; so too is the memory of memory. In one sense, the emblematic treatment of Jung is a predictable example of what Maurice Halbwachs—the founding father of the sociology of collective memory—described as the normal process of winnowing complex memories down to "imagos."[15] Another such process, described by Gary Fine in his work on reputations,[16] is the tendency to see bad as worse and good as better—in other words, for memory to intensify images to polar extremes. What is especially interesting with both Morgenthau and to a less significant extent with Jung is that this winnowing, this simplification to imagos, took place right away rather than over the long-term and was the result of political instrumentalization in charged contexts. Imagos are thus not only a matter of the inertial passage of time but of strategic effort early on; reductive imagos are the stuff of political contest.

15. Halbwachs, *On Collective Memory*.
16. Fine, *Difficult Reputations*.

An even more classic winnowing process is evident in the memory of the Stuttgart Declaration. As we saw, it was not obvious that that statement above all others should be remembered, or that it should have entered subsequent memory discourse as such a clear case of admitting guilt. Another such complex case—though involving a slightly different dynamic—was that of Jaspers. In that case, it seemed to be a rather perverse process of his critics ascribing to his arguments more power and success than even he believed they had. If the literature identifies Karl Jaspers as the founding father of a guilty German culture, this was at least in part due to those who characterized him as such in an effort to repudiate him.

*　*　*

Perhaps the most historically significant aspect of the memory of memory—perhaps the most surprising given our present horizon of expectation, though not nearly so surprising if we place ourselves within the postwar culture—is both the peripheral status of the genocide of the Jews—the Holocaust—and the relatively uninhibited way in which early speakers were able to speak of Jews. One finds in the second half of the 1940s, for instance, references to Jews that no politician or public figure could dare hope to get away with today. One thinks, just to mention one example, of theologian Helmut Thielecke's November 8, 1945, speech, in which he stated that "we all have need, seven times sevenfold, of forgiveness—Frenchmen, Americans, Englishmen, Germans, Japanese—*and Jews*" (emphasis added). Here, again, it is important to remember Tony Kushner's observation, quoted in chapter five, that we need to be careful not to "impose later perceptions on contemporary interpretations and provide a deceptively simple chronology on what was, in reality, a prolonged and complex process which is yet to be completed." Another good example of such distortions in the memory of memory is the fact that we remember the Nuremberg Tribunal for its invention of the idea of "crimes against humanity" when, in effect, the court decided these could be covered by "war crimes." Nevertheless, we now are more likely to view "war crimes" as "crimes against humanity," rather than the other way around. We can recall here Carl Schmitt's early insight that this is what was going on, and his pledge to resist the "moralization" of war it implied. (Others, of course, may not find the moralization of war such an odious idea.)

Pointing out that Germans—or for that matter British and Americans—did not recognize the centrality of anti-Semitism in National Socialist ideology or did not see that the Holocaust was a "civilizational rupture" (as

Hannah Arendt was one of the first to theorize), as well as the reversals, elisions, errors, and selectivity of German memory, however, should not to be mistaken for a moral condemnation, though it could serve as the starting point of critique. On the one hand, simply condemning the famous deficits of German public discourse in the immediate postwar period and in the Adenauer years as *individual* moral failures is to miss the processes of cultural structuring powerfully at work in this discourse. And to describe it as a *collective* moral failure is to move from making a collective guilt accusation against Germans for National Socialism to making a collective "second guilt" accusation against Germans for failing to come to terms with it properly, an accusation that is likely too sweeping, not adequate to the complexities of the history of memory.

Instead, the foregoing pages have offered an account that takes these reactions for what they were—attempts to come to terms with an impossible past. The important question was how these attempts were structured in dialogue with each other and with the past, and what resources were at their disposal. Only on that basis can we begin to assess what role they played in structuring future discourse. By the same token, sociological explanation of this dialogical structuring should not be taken as exculpatory; there is a fine line between culturally organized blind spots and moral and political failure, and both of these, as well as more positive elements, formed the postwar discourse. We need not choose, as Heidegger seemed to imply, between analyzing language as the house of being and respecting the value of individual or political ethics.

Model Germany

For many years, the expression "model Germany" (*Modell Deutschland*) referred to West Germany's corporatist political economy, in which a coordinated wage policy and extensive social security benefits underwrote remarkable stability and a level of economic development that, according to the term, could serve as a model for other Western states. In the last decade or so, however, the term "model Germany" has come to indicate an entirely different complex of issues—namely, those concerned with processing a difficult past. Since 1989, Germany has been the obvious reference point in the growing discourse of collective memory, transitional justice, and postconflict reconciliation. For many countries facing questions of how to deal with the residues of past regimes, Germany has served as a sort of canary in the mine of historical consciousness. How much difficult memory can a nation accept without spoiling its identity? What lessons did Germany learn as it struggled with the challenges of commemoration, and how relevant are these lessons elsewhere?

It is certainly true that the kinds of questions the victors posed to Germany and that, to a very great extent Germans posed to themselves (even if they gave different answers than the Allies), are questions many groups and nations must pose when they make the transition from a less to a more open society and seek to settle old scores. In recent years, world culture has developed a ready lexicon of such questions: What responsibility do ordinary people bear for atrocities committed in their names? How widely should we draw the circle of guilt? What compromises should we make for the sake of peace (and when we make too many short-term compromises are we mistaking quiescence for peace)? How should we place episodes within wider historical trajectories? What different kinds of victimhood need we distinguish, and what rights and reparations should we accord to each? Is it better to remember difficult pasts as a warning to the future or let them slip away so as not to stoke the fires of resentment?

Germany serves as a model for others both because they were the first modern state to face these questions in a manner that has become characteristic of our epoch—one in which what I think of as a "politics of regret"[17] prevails in numerous contexts—and the Allies and the Germans developed novel institutional mechanisms for doing so, including the so-called "Nuremberg principles," denazification, amnesties, reparations to victims rather than just to victors, as well as a regular liturgy of commemorative rituals and language.[18] Since then, international lawyers, states, nongovernmental organizations, human rights entrepreneurs, and many others have explored additional institutional mechanisms like truth commissions, mediation, official apology, and other forms of public regret. They have always done so, it is clear, with an eye toward Germany.

But Germany is a central referent in another sense as well, the sense captured by Hannah Arendt's perception that what happened in Germany both from 1933 to 1941 but especially thereafter marks a sort of "civilizational rupture." As the leading figures of the Frankfurt school, Max Horkheimer and Theodor Adorno wrote in 1940 (thus before the Holocaust), "The fully enlightened earth radiates disaster triumphant."[19] How was this possible? Precisely the values that promised to bring us out of barbarism had brought us to a level of barbarism previously unimaginable.

17. See Olick and Coughlin, "The Politics of Regret."
18. It is, of course, possible to overstate the novelty of these mechanisms. See Bass, *Stay the Hand of Vengeance*.
19. Horkheimer and Adorno, *The Dialectic of Enlightenment*, 3.

It is in this way that the Holocaust appears to many as a decisive blow to the self-conception of Western modernity.[20] In this way, the Holocaust has become not just a German and Jewish memory, but has undergone what Daniel Levy and Natan Sznaider have called a process of "cosmopolitanization," in which the genocide of the European Jews has become the central universal referent for our age.[21] As such, it stands as the emblem for the need for a politics of regret, and underwrites an entire international moral culture (not that this has put an end to genocide).

*   *   *

Is the German story a success or a failure, and do the lessons and vocabulary learned there thus serve as a model or a warning? Here debate seems to be polarized between those who expect far too much and those who expect far too little, between overweening triumphalism and execration of moral failure. The former is evident in those who see the triumph of Stimson over Morgenthau and the fact that the West "won" the Cold War as proof that they were right to fight it, and that the West Germans who "chose" "legitimacy" over "justice" were doing what had to be done. The latter is evident in those who see no real differences among Third Reich, occupation, and Adenauer's Federal Republic, or even think the new memory proposed in the 1960s puts Germans in a position of moral superiority. That this overdrawn polemic is politically and morally bankrupt seems clear in the recent transformations in German memory, in which even the Left has become interested in the memory of German suffering (Günther Grass's recent novel *Crabwalk* is only one example), though former centrists at the same time are rejecting what they claim has become an empty cult of commemorative ritual (here the novelist Martin Walser is only the most prominent example). One might even hope as well for some insight into the gray zones of Allied acts in the war. The point, however, is to undertake these reconsiderations of mnemonic orthodoxies, which may indeed have proven sterile, without abandoning moral distinctions, making it seem as if everyone is simultaneously victim and perpetrator. All nations have suffered, and all have engaged in immoral activity. That does not mean that asking who, what, where, and when questions does not matter, and that it does not matter who identifies the crimes and who seeks to excuse them. That we care about such issues in the ways we do today, however, is perhaps the most important legacy of the German experience.

20. See especially Bauman, *Modernity and the Holocaust.*
21. Levy and Sznaider, *Erinnerung im globalen Zeitalter.*

Works Cited

Abusch, Alexander. *Der Irrweg einer Nation: Ein Beitrag zum Verstaendnis deutscher Geschichte.* Berlin: Aufbau Verlag, 1960.

Adams, R. J. Q. *British Politics and Foreign Policy in the Age of Appeasement, 1935–39.* Stanford: Stanford University Press, 1993.

Adenauer, Konrad. *"Die Demokratie ist fuer uns eine Weltanschauung": Reden und Gespraeche, 1946–1967.* Edited by Felix Becker. Cologne: Boehlau, 1998.

———. *Erinnerungen.* 4 vols. Stuttgart: Deutsche Verlags-Anstalt, 1965.

Adorno, Theodor W. *Can One Live after Auschwitz? A Philosophical Reader.* Edited by Rolf Tiedemann. Stanford: Stanford University Press, 2003.

———. *The Jargon of Authenticy.* Translated by Knut Tarnowski and Frederic Will. Evanston: Northwestern University Press, 1973 [1964].

———. "Replik zu Peter R. Hofstaeters Kritik des Gruppenexperiments." *Koelner Zeitschrift fuer Soziologie und Sozialpsychologie* 9 (1957): 105–17.

Adorno, Theodor W., and Thomas Mann. *Briefwechsel 1943–1955.* Frankfurt: Suhrkamp, 2002.

Albrecht, Willy, ed. *Kurt Schumacher: Reden, Schriften, Korrespondenzen, 1945–1952.* Berlin: Dietz, 1985.

Alexander, Jeffrey C. "The Centrality of the Classics." In *Sociological Theory Today,* edited by Anthony Giddens and Jonathan Turner, 11–57. Stanford: Stanford University Press, 1987.

Allemann, Fritz René. *Bonn ist Nicht Weimar.* Cologne: Kiepenheuer and Witsch, 1956.

Altweg, Juerg, ed. *Die Heidegger Kontroverse.* Frankfurt: Athenaeum, 1988.

American Friends of German Freedom. *Germany after Hitler.* New York: Farrar and Rinehardt, 1944.

Ammon, Herbert. "Antifaschismus im Wandel? Historisch-kritische Anmerkungen zur Aktualität eines Begriffs." In *Die Schatten der Vergangenheit: Impulse zur Historisierung des Nationalsozialismus,* edited by Uwe Backes, Eckhard Jesse, and Rainer Zitelmann, 568–94. Frankfurt: Ullstein, 1990.

Anderson, Mark M. *Hitler's Exiles: Personal Stories of the Flight from Nazi Germany to America.* New York: New Press, 2000.

Annan, Noel. *Changing Enemies: The Defeat and Regeneration of Germany.* Ithaca: Cornell University Press, 1995.

Arendt, Hannah. "The Aftermath of Nazi Rule: Report from Germany." *Commentary* 10 (1950): 342–53.

———. *Eichmann in Jerusalem: A Report on the Banality of Evil.* New York: Viking, 1963.

———. *Responsibility and Judgment.* New York: Schocken, 2003.

Armstrong, Anne. *Unconditional Surrender: The Impact of the Casablanca Policy upon World War II.* New Brunswick: Rutgers University Press, 1961.

Aschheim, Steven E. *Culture and Catastrophe: German and Jewish Confrontations with National Socialism and Other Crises.* New York: New York University Press, 1996.

Aschheim, Steven E., ed. *Hannah Arendt in Jerusalem.* Berkeley: Univeristy of California Press, 2001.

Assmann, Aleida, and Ute Frevert. *Geschichtsvergessenheit, Geschichtsversessenheit: Vom Umgang mit deutschen Vergangenheiten nach 1945.* Stuttgart: DVA, 1999.

Ayçoberry, Pierre. *The Nazi Question: An Essay on the Interpretation of National Socialism (1922–1975).* Translated Robert Hurley. New York: Pantheon, 1981.

Backer, John H. *The Decision to Divide Germany: American Foreign Policy in Transition.* Durham: Duke University Press, 1978.

Bair, Deirdre. *Jung: A Biography.* Boston: Little, Brown, 2003.

Bakhtin, Mikhail. *Speech Genres and Other Essays.* Translated by W. McGee. Austin: University of Texas Press, 1986.

Balakrishnan, Gopal. *The Enemy: An Intellectual Protrait of Carl Schmitt.* London: Verso, 2000.

Baldwin, Peter, ed. *Reworking the Past: Hitler, the Holocaust, and the Historians' Debate.* Boston: Beacon Press, 1990.

Balfour, Michael. "Another Look at 'Unconditional Surrender.'" *International Affairs* 46(2) (1970): 719–36.

Bark, Dennis L., and David R. Gress. *A History of West Germany.* Vol. 1: *From Shadow to Substance, 1945–1963.* Cambridge: Basil Blackwell, 1989.

Barnouw, Dagmar. *Germany 1945: Views of War and Violence.* Bloomington: Indiana University Press, 1996.

Barth, Karl. *The Only Way: How Can the Germans be Cured?* New York: Philosophical Library, 1947.

Bass, Gary Jonathan. *Stay the Hand of Vengeance: The Politics of War Crimes Tribunals.* Princeton: Princeton University Press, 2002.

Bauer, Yehuda. *Out of the Ashes: The Impact of American Jews on Post-Holocaust European Jewry.* Oxford: Permagon, 1988.

Bauman, Zygmunt. *Modernity and the Holocaust.* Ithaca: Cornell University Press, 1989.

Baumgärtner, Ulrich. *Reden Nach Hitler: Theodor Heuss—Die Auseinandersetzung mit dem Nationalsozialismus.* Stuttgart: DVA, 2001.

Becker, Winfried. *CDU und CSU, 1945–1950: Vorlaeufer und regionale Entwicklung bis zum Entstehen der CDU-Bundespartei.* Mainz: Von Hase and Koehler, 1987.

Beevor, Antony. *Fall of Berlin 1945.* London: Penguin, 2003.

Benedict, Ruth. *The Chrysanthemum and the Sword: Patterns of Japanese Culture.* New York: Houghton Mifflen, 1989 [1946].

Ben-Israel, Hedva. "Cross Purposes: British Reactions to the German Anti-Nazi Opposition." *Journal of Contemporary History* 20 (1985): 423–38.

Benn, Gottfried. "Letter from Berlin, July 1948." In *Prose, Essays, Poems*, edited by Volkmar Sander. New York: Continuum, 1987.

Benz, Wolfgang. *Von der Besatzungsherrschaft zur Bundesrepublik: Stationen einer Staatsgründung 1945–1949*. Frankfurt: Fischer, 1984.

———. *Die Vertreibung der Deutschen aus dem Osten: Ursachen, Ereignisse, Folgen*. Frankfurt: Fischer, 1985.

———. *Zwischen Hitler und Adenauer: Studien zur deutschen Nachkriegsgesellschaft*. Frankfurt: Fischer, 1991.

Benz, Wolfgang, ed. *Deutschland unter alliierter Besatzung 1945–1949/55: Ein Handbuch*. Berlin: Akademie Verlag, 1999.

Berg, Nicolas. *Der Holocaust und die westdeutschen Historiker: Erforschung und Erinnerung*. Göttingen: Wallstein, 2003.

Berger, Stefan. *The Search for Normality: National Identity and Historical Consciousness in Germany since 1800*. New York: Berghahn, 1997.

Bergmann, Werner. *Antisemitismus in öffentlichen Konflikten: Kollektives Lernen in der politischen Kultur der Bundesrepublik 1949–1989*. Frankfurt: Campus, 1997.

Bergmann, Werner, Rainer Erb, and Albert Lichtblau, eds. *Schwieriges Erbe: Der Umgang mit Nationalsozialismus und Antisemitismus in Österreich, der DDR, und der Bundesrepublik Deutschland*. Frankfurt: Campus, 1995.

Beschloss, Michael. *The Conquerors: Roosevelt, Truman and the Destruction of Hitler's Germany, 1941–45*. New York: Simon and Schuster, 2002.

Bischof, Günther, and Stephen E. Ambrose, eds. *Eisenhower and the German POWs: Facts against Falsehood*. Baton Rouge: Louisiana State University, 1992.

Blackbourn, David, and Geoff Ely. *The Peculiarities of German History: Bourgeois Society and Politics in Nineteenth Century Germany*. New York: Oxford, 1984.

Bleek, Wilhelm, and Hanns Maull. *Ein ganz normaler Staat? Perspektiven nach 40 Jahren Bundesrepublik*. Munich: Piper, 1989.

Bloxham, Donald. *Genocide on Trial: War Crimes Trials and the Formation of Holocaust History and Memory*. Oxford: Oxford University Press, 2001.

Blum, John Morton, ed. *The Price of Vision: The Diary of Henry A. Wallace, 1942–1946*. New York: Houghton Mifflin, 1973.

———. *Roosevelt and Morgenthau: A Revision and Condensation of from the Morgenthau Diaries*. New York: Houghton Mifflin, 1970.

Bodnar, John. *Remaking America: Public Memory, Commemoration and Patriotism in the Twentieth Century*. Princeton: Princeton University Press, 1992.

Boehling, Rebeccca. *A Question of Priorities: Democratic Reform and Economic Recovery in Postwar Germany*. New York: Berghahn, 1998.

Botting, Douglas. *From the Ruins of the Reich: Germany 1945–1949*. New York: Crown, 1985.

Boughton, James M. "The Case against Harry Dexter White: Still Not Proven," Working Paper WP/00/149. Washington, D.C.: International Monetary Fund, 2000.

Bourdieu, Pierre. *The Field of Cultural Production: Essays on Art and Literature*. New York: Columbia University Press, 1994.

Bower, Tom. *Blind Eye to Murder: Britain, America and the Purging of Nazi Germany—A Pledge Betrayed*. Boston: Little, Brown, 1995.

Bracher, Karl Dietrich, et al. *Geschichte der Bundesrepublik*. 5 vols. Stuttgart: Deutsche Verlags-Anstalt; Wiesbaden: Brockhaus, 1981–86.

Brady, John S., Beverly Crawford, and Sarah Elise Williarty, eds. *The Postwar Transformation of Germany: Democracy, Prosperity, and Nationhood*. Ann Arbor: University of Michigan Press, 1999.

Brandt, Willy. *My Life in Politics.* Translated by Anthea Bell. New York: Viking, 1992.

Braunthal, Julius. *Need Germany Survive?* London: Victor Gollancz, 1943.

Braybrook, Charles. *Here Is Your Hun: A Five Thousand Year Saga of Hun Wars, Murder, Rapine, and Savagery.* London: Allan, 1945.

Breisach, Ernst. *Historiography: Ancient, Medieval, and Modern.* Chicago: University of Chicago Press, 1995.

Breitman, Richard. *Official Secrets: What the Nazis Planned, What the British and Americans Knew.* New York: Hill and Wang, 1999.

Brickner, Richard M. "Germany after the War—Round Table 1945." *American Journal of Orthopsychiatry* 11 (1945): 381–441.

———. *Is Germany Incurable?* Philadelphia: Lippincott, 1943.

Brink, Cornelia. *Ikonen der Vernichtung: Öffentlicher Gebrauch von Fotografien aus nationalisozialistischen Konzentrationslagern nach 1945.* Berlin: Akademie Verlag, 1998.

Brochhagen, Ulrich. *Nach Nürnberg: Vergangenheitsbewältigung und Westintegration in der Ära Adenauer.* Hamburg: Junius, 1994.

Brockmeier, Jens. "Remembering and Forgetting: Narrative as Cultural Memory." *Culture and Psychology* 8(1) (2002): 15–43.

Broszat, Martin, ed. *Zäsuren nach 1945: Essays zur Periodisierung der deutschen Nachkriegsgeschichte.* Munich: Oldenbourg, 1990.

Burger, Reiner. *Theodor Heuss als Journalist. Beobachter und Interpret von vier Epochen deutscher Geschichte.* Münster: Hopf, 1999.

Buruma, Ian. *The Wages of Guilt: Memories of War in Germany and Japan.* New York: Farrar, Strauss, and Giroux, 1994.

Chase, John. "Unconditional Surrender Reconsidered." *Political Science Quarterly* 70(22) (1955): 258–79.

Claussen, Detlev. "In the House of the Hangman." In *Germans and Jews since the Holocaust: The Changing Situation in West Germany,* edited by Anson Rubinbach and Jack Zipes, 50–64. New York: Holmes and Meier, 1986.

Clay, Lucius. *Decision in Germany.* New York: Doubleday, 1950.

Connerton, Paul. *How Societies Remember.* Cambridge: Cambridge University Press, 1989.

Conway, John S. *The Nazi Persecution of the Churches, 1933–1945.* London: Weidenfeld and Nicolson, 1968.

Conze, Werner. *Jakob Kaiser: Politiker zwischen West und Ost.* Stuttgart: Kohlhammer, 1969.

Coser, Lewis. *Refugee Scholars in America: Their Impact and their Experiences.* New Haven: Yale University Press, 1984.

Craig, Gordon A. "Foreword." In William L. Shirer, *Berlin Diary: The Journal of a Foreign Correspondent, 1934–1941,* ix–xiii. Baltimore: Johns Hopkins University Press, 2002.

Crew, David. "Remembering German Pasts: Memory in German History, 1871–1989." *Central European History* 33(2) (2000): 217–34.

Dahrendorf, Ralf. *Society and Democracy in Germany.* New York: Doubleday 1967.

Davidson, Eugene. *The Death and Life of Germany: An Account of the American Occupation.* New York: Knopf, 1959.

———. *The Nuremberg Fallacy.* Columbia: University of Missouri Press, 1998.

Dean, Vera Micheles. "What Future for Germany?" *Foreign Policy Reports* 18 (1943): 282–95.

Deighton, Anne. *The Impossible Peace: Britain, the Division of Germany, and the Origins of the Cold War.* Oxford: Clarendon, 1993.

Department of State. *Documents on Germany, 1944–1985*. Department of State Publication No. 9446. Washington, D.C.: Office of the Historian, Bureau of Public Affairs, 1986.

Diefendorf, Jeffrey M. *In the Wake of War: The Reconstruction of German Cities after World War II*. Oxford: Oxford University Press, 1993.

Diehl, James M. *The Thanks of the Fatherland: German Veterans after the Second World War*. Chapel Hill: University of North Carolina Press, 1993.

Dietrich, John. *The Morgenthau Plan: Soviet Influence on American Postwar Policy*. New York: Algora, 2002.

Diner, Dan. *Beyond the Conceivable: Studies on Germany, Nazism, and the Holocaust*. Berkeley: University of California Press, 2000.

Dinnerstein, Leonard. *America and the Survivors of the Holocaust*. New York: Columbia University Press, 1982.

Dirks, Walter. "Der restaurative Charakter der Epoche." *Frankfurter Hefte* 5 (1950): 924–54.

Dorn, Walter L. "The Debate Over American Occupation Policy in Germany in 1944–1945." *Political Science Quarterly* 72(4) (1957): 481–501.

Dorpalen, Andreas. *German History in Marxist Perspective: The East German Approach*. Detroit: Wayne State University Press, 1985.

Douglas, Lawrence. *The Memory of Judgment: Making Law and History in the Trials of the Holocaust*. New Haven: Yale University Press, 2001.

Dower, John W. *Embracing Defeat: Japan in the Wake of World War II*. New York: Norton, 2000.

Dubiel, Helmut. *Niemand ist frei von der Geschichte: Die Nationalsozialistische Herrschaft in den Debatten des Deutschen Bundestages*. Munich: Carl Hanser, 1999.

Dwork, Deborah, and Robert Jan Van Pelt. *Auschwitz: 1270 to the Present*. New York: Norton, 1996.

Ebbinghaus, Julius. *Zu Deutschlands Schicksalswende*. Frankfurt: Klostermann, 1946.

Eberan, Barbro. *Luther? Friedrich "der Grosse?" Wagner? Nietzsche? We war an Hitler Schuld? Die Debatte um dir Schuldfrage, 1945–49*. 2d ed. Munich: Minerva, 1985.

Eder, Angelika. *Flüchtige Heimat: Jüdische Displaced Persons in Landsberg am Lech 1945 bis 1950*. Munich: Kommissionsverlag UNI-Druck, 1998.

Edinger, Lewis J. *Kurt Schumacher: A Study in Personality and Political Behavior*. Stanford: Stanford University Press, 1965.

Eisenberg, Carolyn. *Drawing the Line: The American Decision to Divide Germany, 1944–1949*. Cambridge: Cambridge University Press, 1996.

Eisenhower, Dwight D. *Crusade in Europe*. Garden City: Doubleday, 1948.

Eley, Geoff, ed. *The "Goldhagen Effect": History, Memory, Nazism—Facing the German Past*. Ann Arbor: University of Michigan Press, 2000.

Elias, Norbert. *Studien über die Deutschen: Machtkämpfe und Habitusentwicklung im 19. und 20. Jahrhundert*. Frankfurt: Suhrkamp, 1992.

Eschenburg, Theodor. *Jahre der Besatzung, 1945–1949*. Stuttgart: Deutsche Verlags-Anstalt; Wiesbaden: Brockhaus, 1983.

Evans, Richard J. *In Hitler's Shadow: West German Historians and the Attempt to Escape from the Nazi Past*. New York: Pantheon, 1989.

Ewald, Hans Gerd. *Die gescheiterte Republik: Idee und Programm einer "Zweiten Republik" in den Frankfurter Heften (1946–1950)*. Frankfurt: Peter Lang, 1988.

Farias, Victor. *Heidegger and Nazism*. Philadelphia: Temple University Press, 1989.

Farmer, Sarah. *Martyred Village: Commemorating the 1944 Massacre at Oradour-Sur-Glane.* Berkeley: University of California Press, 2000.

Farquharson, John. "'Emotional but Influential': Victor Gollancz, Richard Stokes and the British Zone of Germany, 1945–9." *Journal of Contemporary History* 22 (1987): 501–19.

Fehrenbach, Heide. *Cinema in Democratizing Germany: Reconstructing National Identity after Hitler.* Chapel Hill: University of North Carolina Press, 1995.

Ferry, Luc, and Alain Renaut. *Heidegger and Modernity.* Translated by Franklin Philip. Chicago: University of Chicago Press, 1990.

Field, Harry H., and Louise M. Van Patten. "If the American People Made the Peace." *Public Opinion Quarterly* 8(4) (1945): 500–512.

Fine, Gary Alan. *Difficult Reputations: Collective Memories of the Evil, Inept, and Controversial.* Chicago: University of Chicago Press, 2001.

Finzsch, Norbert, and Jürgen Martschukat, eds. *Different Restorations: Reconstruction and "Wiederaufbau" in the United States and Germany: 1865–1945–1989.* Providence: Berghahn, 1996.

FitzGibbon, Constantine. *Denazification.* London: Michael Joseph, 1969.

Flanagan, Clare. *A Study of German Political-Cultural Periodicals from the Years of Allied Occupation, 1945–1949.* Lewiston, New York: Edward Mellen Press, 2000.

Flechtheim, Ossip K., ed. *Dokumente zur parteipolitischen Entwicklung in Deutschland seit 1945.* 3 vols. Berlin: Wendler, 1962–63.

Fleming, Thomas J. *The New Dealers' War: F.D.R. and the War Within World War II.* New York: Basic Books, 2002.

Fletcher, George P. *Romantics at War: Glory and Guilt in the Age of Terrorism.* Princeton: Princeton University Press, 2002.

Forever in the Shadow of Hitler. Translated by James Knowlton and Truett Cates. New Jersey: Humanities Press, 1993.

Foschepoth, Josef. *Im Schatten der Vergangenheit: Die Anfänge der Gesellschaften fuer Christlich-Juedische Zusammenarbeit.* Göttingen: Vandenhoeck and Ruprecht, 1993.

Foschepoth, Josef, ed. *Adenauer und die deutsche Frage.* Göttingen: Vandenhoeck and Ruprecht, 1993.

Foucault, Michel. *Language, Counter-Memory, Practice: Selected Essays and Interviews.* Ithaca: Cornell University Press, 1977.

Fraenkel, Heinrich. *Vansittart's Gift for Goebbels: A German Exile's Answer to Black Record.* London: Fabian Society, 1941.

Frei, Norbert. *Adenauer's Germany and the Nazi Past: The Politics of Amnesty and Integration.* Translated by Joel Golb. New York: Columbia University Press, 2002.

Frei, Norbert, and Franziska Friedländer, eds. *Ernst Friedländer: Klärung für Deutschland: Leitartikel in der Zeit 1946–1950.* Vienna: Olzog, 1982.

Friedmann, Jan, and Jörg Später. "Britische und deutsche Kollektivschuld-Debatte." In *Wandlungsprozesse in Westdeutschland: Belastung, Integration, Liberalisierung, 1945–1980,* edited by Ulrich Herbert, 53–90. Göttingen: Wallstein, 2002.

Friedrich, Jörg. *Der Brand: Deutschland im Bombenkrieg, 1940–1945.* Munich: Propyläen, 2002.

———. *Die kalte Amnestie.* Munich: Piper, 1984.

Fritzsche, Peter. *Stranded in the Present: Modern Time and the Melancholy of History.* Cambridge: Harvard University Press, 2004.

Fröhlich, Claudia, and Michael Kohlstruck, eds. *Engagierte Demokraten: Vergangenheitspolitik in kritischer Absicht.* Muenster: Westfaelisches Dampfboot, 1999.

Fulbrook, Mary. *German National Identity after the Holocaust.* Cambridge: Polity, 1999.

Fürstenau, Justus. *Entnazifizierung: Ein Kapitel deutscher Nachkriegspolitik.* Munich: Piper, 1969.

Gabbe, Jörg. *Parteien und Nation: Zur Rolle des Nationalbewusstseins für die politischen Grundorientierungen der Parteien in der Anfangsphase der Bundesrepublik.* Meisenheim am Glan: Anton Hain, 1976.

Gaddis, John Lewis. *The United States and the Origins of the Cold War.* New York: Columbia University Press, 2000 [1972].

Geis, Jael. *Übrig sein—Leben "danach." Juden deutscher Herkunft in der britischen und amerikanischen Zone Deutschlands 1945–1949.* Berlin: Philo Verlagsgesellschaft, 2000.

Gellman, Irwin F. *Secret Affairs: Franklin Roosevelt, Cordell Hull, and Sumner Welles.* Baltimore: Johns Hopkins University Press, 1995.

Gerhardt, Uta. *Talcott Parsons: An Intellectual Biography.* Cambridge: Cambridge University Press, 2002.

Gerhardt, Uta, ed. *Talcott Parsons on National Socialism.* New York: Aldine de Gruyter, 1993.

Gienow-Hecht, Jessica C. E. *Transmission Impossible: American Journalism as Cultural Diplomacy in Postwar Germany, 1945–1955.* Baton Rouge: Louisiana State University Press, 1999.

Gimbel, John. *The American Occupation of Germany: Politics and the Military, 1945–1949.* Stanford: Stanford university Press, 1968.

Giordano, Ralph. *Die zweite Schuld oder Von der Last ein Deutscher zu sein.* Munich: Knaur, 1987.

Glaser, Hermann. *The Rubble Years: The Cultural Roots of Postwar Germany.* Translated by Franz Feige and Patricia Gleason. New York: Paragon House, 1990. Originally published as *Die Kulturgeschichte der Bundesrepublik Deutschland.* Vol. 1: *Zwischen Kapitulation und Währungsreform 1945–1948.* Frankfurt: Fischer, 1985.

———. "Totschweigen, entlasten, umschulden—Bewältigung der Vergangenheit im Nachfolgestaat." In *Tribüne* 103 (1987): 117–24.

Glees, Anthony. *Exile Politics during the Second World War: The German Social Democrats in Britain.* Oxford: Clarendon Press, 1982.

Glennon, John P. " 'This Time Germany is a Defeated Nation': The Doctrine of Unconditional Surrender and Some Unsuccessful Attempts to Alter It, 1943–1944" In *Statesmen and Statecraft of the Modern West: Essays in Honor of Dwight E. Lee and H. Donaldson Jordan,* edited by Gerald N. Grob, 105–51. Barre, Mass., Barre Publishing Co., 1967.

Goedde, Petra. *GIs and Germans: Culture, Gender, and Foreign Relations, 1945–1949.* New Haven: Yale University Press, 2003.

Goldhagen, Daniel. *Hitler's Willing Executioners: Ordinary Germans and the Holocaust.* New York: Knopf, 1996.

———. *A Moral Reckoning: The Role of the Catholic Church in the Holocaust and its Unfulfilled Duty of Repair.* New York: Knopf, 2002.

Goldman, Aaron. "Germans and Nazis: The Controversy over 'Vansittartism' in Britain during the Second World War." *Journal of Contemporary History* 14 (1979): 155–91.

Gollancz, Victor. *Germany Revisited.* London: Victor Gollancz, 1947.

———. *Our Threatened Values.* Hinsdale, Ill.: Henry Regnery, 1948.

———. *Shall Our Children Live or Die? A Reply to Lord Vansittart on the German Problem.* London: Victor Gollancz, 1942.

Greiner, Bernd. *Die Morgenthau-Legende: Zur Geschichte eines umstrittenen Plans.* Hamburg: Hamnurger Edition, 1995.

Greschat, Martin, ed. *Im Zeichen der Schuld: 40 Jahre Stuttgarter Schuldbekenntnis.* Neukirchen-Vluyn: Neukirchner Verlag, 1985.

Gross, Raphael. *Carl Schmitt und die Juden: Eine deutsche Rechtslehre.* Frankfurt: Suhrkamp, 2000.

Grossman, Atina. "A Question of Silence: The Rape of German Women by Occupation Soldiers." In *West Germany under Construction: Politics, Society, and Culture in the Adenauer Era,* edited by Robert G. Moeller, 33–52. Ann Arbor: University of Michigan Press: 1997.

Habe, Hans. *Ich stelle mich.* Vienna: Kurt Desch, 1955.

———. *Our Love Affair with Germany.* New York: Putnam, 1953.

Habermas, Jürgen. *The New Conservatism: Cultural Criticism and the Historians' Dispute.* Cambridge: MIT Press, 1989.

———. *Philosophical-Political Profiles.* Cambridge: MIT Press, 1990.

———. *Toward a Rational Society: Student Protest, Science, and Politics.* Boston: Beacon, 1971.

Halbwachs, Maurice. *On Collective Memory.* Edited with an introduction by Louis Coser. Chicago: University of Chicago Press, 1992.

Hamm-Brücher, Hildegard. *Gerechtigkeit erhöht ein Volk: Theodor Heuss und die deutsche Demokratie.* Munich: Piper, 1984.

Hartman, Geoffrey, ed. *Bitburg in Moral and Political Perspective.* Bloomington: Indiana Unviersity Press, 1986.

Hattenhauer, Hans. *Geschichte der deutschen Nationalsymbole: Zeichen und Bedeutung.* 2d ed. Munich: Olzog Verag, 1990.

Hättich, Manfred. "Geschichtsbild und Demokratieverständnis." In *Die Zweite Republik: 25 Jahre Bundesrepublik—Eine Bilanz,* edited by Richard Löwenthal and Hans-Peter Schwarz. Stuttgart: Seewald Verlag, 1977.

Haug, Wolfgang Fritz. *Vom hilflosen Antifaschismus zur Gnade der späten Geburt.* Berlin: Argument-Verlag, 1987.

Hayman, Ronald. *A Life of Jung.* New York: Norton, 1999.

Heidegger, Martin. *Basic Writings.* Revised and expanded ed. Edited by David Farrell Krell. San Francisco: Harper Collins, 1993.

Heidenheimer, Arnold J. *Adenauer and the CDU: The Rise of the Leader and the Integration of the Party.* The Hague: Martinus Nijhoff, 1960.

———. *The Governments of Germany.* 2d ed. New York: Thomas Y. Crowell, 1966.

Heil, Johannes, and Rainer Erb, eds. *Geschichtswissenschaft und Öffentlichkeit: Der Streit um Daniel J. Goldhagen.* Frankfurt: Fischer, 1998.

Heilbut, Anthony. *Exiled in Paradise: German Refugee Artists and Intellectuals in America from the 1930s to the Present.* New York: Penguin, 1983.

Hein, Dieter. *Zwischen liberaler Milieupartei und nationaler Sammlungsbewegung: Gründung, Entwicklung und Struktur der Freien Demokratischen Partei, 1945–1949.* Duesseldorf: Droste, 1985.

Heineman, Elizabeth D. *What Difference Does a Husband Make? Women and Marital Status in Nazi and Postwar Germany.* Berkeley: University of California Press, 2003.

Heinemann, Manfred, ed. *Umerziehung und Wiederaufbau: Die Bildungspolitik der Besatzungsmächte in Deutschland und Österreich.* Stuttgart: Klett-Cotta, 1981.

Heitzer, Hostwalter. *Die CDU in der britischen Besatzungszone: Gründung, Organisation, Programm und Politik, 1945–1949.* Duesseldrof: Droste, 1988.

Henke, Klaus-Dietmer. *Die amerikanische Besetzung Deutschlands.* 2d ed. Munich: Oldenourg, 1996.

Herbert, Ulrich, ed. *Wandlungsprozesse in Westdeutschland: Belastung, Integration, Liberalisierung, 1945–1980.* Goettingen: Wallstein, 2002.

Herf, Jeffrey. *Divided Memory: The Nazi Past in the Two Germanys.* Cambridge: Harvard University Press, 1997.

———. *Reactionary Modernism: Technology, Culture, and Politics in Weimer and the Third Reich.* Cambridge: Cambridge University Press, 1984.

Hermand, Jost. *Kultur im Wiederaufbau: Die Bundesrepublik Deutschland 1945–1965.* Munich: Nymphenburger, 1986.

Hermand, Jost, and Wigand Lange. *"Wollt ihr Thomas Mann wiederhaben?" Deutschland und die Emigranten.* Hamburg: Europaeische Verlagsanstalt, 1999.

Herz, John H. "The Fiasco of Denazification in Germany." *Political Science Quarterly* 63 (1948): 569–95.

———. *From Dictatorship to Democracy: Coping with the Legacies of Authoritarianism and Totalitarianism.* Westport, Conn.: Greenwood, 1982.

Herz, Thomas, and Michael Schwab-Trapp. *Umkämpfte Vergangenheit: Diskurse über den Nationalsozialismus seit 1945.* Opladen: Westdeutscher Verlag, 1997.

Heuss, Theodor. *Aufzeichnungen 1945–1947.* Tübingen: Wunderlich, 1966.

———. *Die groaßen Reden.* Vol. 1: *Der Staatsmann.* Tübingen: Wunderlich, 1965.

———. *Hitler's Weg: Eine historisch-politische Studie ueber den Nationalsozialismus.* Stuttgart: Union Deutsche Verlagsgeselleschaft, 1932.

Hillgruber, Andreas. *Zweierlei Untergang: Die Zerschlagung des deutschen Reiches und das Ende des europäischen Judentums.* Berlin: Siedler, 1986.

"Historikerstreit": Die Dokumentation der Kontroverse um die Einzigartigkeit der national-sozialistischen Judenvernichtung. Munich: Piper, 1987. Reprinted as *Forever in the Shadow of Hitler.* Translated by James Knowlton and Truett Cates. New Jersey: Humanities Press, 1993.

Hochhuth, Rolf. *Der Stellvertreter.* Hamburg: Rowohlt, 1963.

Hofstätter, Peter R. "Zum 'Gruppenexperiment' von Friedrich Pollock: Eine kritische Wuerdigung." *Kölner Zeitschrift fuer Soziologie und Sozialpsychologie* 9 (1957): 97–104.

Holler, Regina. *20. Juli 1944: Vermächtnis oder Alibi?* Munich: Sauer, 1994.

Horkheimer, Max, and Theodor Adorno. *Dialectic of Enlightenment.* Translated by John Cumming. New York: Continuum, 1944.

Hughes, Michael L. *Shouldering the Burdens of Defeat: West Germany and the Reconstruction of Social Justice.* Chapel Hill: University of North Carolina, 1999.

Hull, Cordell. *The Memoirs of Cordell Hull.* 2 vols. New York: MacMillan, 1948.

Hurwitz, Harold J. *Die Stunde Null der deutschen Presse: Die amerikanishe Pressepolitik in Deutschland, 1945–1949.* Cologne: Verlag Wissenschaft und Politik,1972.

Huster, Ernst-Ulrich. *Die Politik der SPD, 1945–1950.* Frankfurt: Campus, 1978.

Huster, Ernst-Ulrich, et al., eds. *Determinanten der westdeutschen Restauration, 1945–1949.* Frankfurt: Suhrkamp, 1972.

Iggers, George. *The German Conception of History: The National Tradition of Historical Thought from Herder to the Present.* Revised ed. Middletown, Conn.: Wesleyan University Press, 1983.

Irwin-Zaercka, Iwona. *Frames of Remembrance: The Dynamics of Collective Memory*. New Brunswick, N.J.: Transaction, 1994.

James, Harold. *A German Identity: 1770–1990*. New York: Routledge, 1989.

Janowitz, Morris. "German Reactions to Nazi Atrocities." *American Journal of Sociology* 52(2) (Sept. 1946): 141–46.

Jaspers, Karl. *The European Spirit*. Translated by Ronald Gregor Smith. London: SCM Press, 1948.

———. *Hoffnung und Sorge: Schriften zur deutschen Politik 1945–965*. Munich: Piper, 1965.

———. *On Max Weber*. Edited by John Dreijmanis. New York: Paragon, 1989.

———. *Schicksal und Wille: Autobiographische Schriften*. Edited by Hans Saner. Munich: Piper, 1967.

———. *The Question of German Guilt*. Translated by E. B. Ashton. New York: Fordham University Press, 2000. Originally published as *Die Schuldfrage: Von der politischen Haftung Deutschlands*. Munich: Piper, 1965 [1946].

———. *Wohin treibt die Bundesrepublik: Tatsachen—Gefahren—Chancen*. Munich: Piper, 1966.

Jay, Martin. *Permanent Exiles: Essays on the Intellectual Migration from Germany to America*. New York: Columbia University Press, 1990.

Jesse, Eckhard. "Philosemitismus, Antisemitismus und Anti-Antisemitismus: Vergangenheitsbewältigung und Tabus." In *Die Schatten der Vergangenheit: Impulse zur Historisierung des Nationalsozialismus*, edited by Uwe Backes, Eckhard Jesse, and Rainer Zittleman, 543–67. Frankfurt: Ullstein, 1990.

Jünger, Ernst. *The Peace*. Translated by Stuart O. Hood. Introduction by Louis Clair [Lewis Coser]. Hinsdale, Ill.: Henry Regnery, 1948.

———. *Spiegel der Jahre: Erinnerungen*. Munich: Hanser, 58.

Jung, Carl G. *The Psychology of Nazism: Essays on Contemporary Events*. Translated by R. F. C. Hull. Princeton: Princeton University Press, 1989.

Kaack, Heino. *Geschichte und Struktur des deutschen Parteiensystems*. Opladen: Westdeutscher Verlag, 1971.

Kaes, Anton. *From Hitler to Heimat: The Return of History as Film*. Cambridge: Harvard University Press, 1992.

Kansteiner, Wulf. "Finding Meaning in Memory: A Methodological Critique of Collective Memory Studies." *History and Theory* 41 (May 2002): 179–97.

Kästner, Erich. *Gesammelte Schriften*. Vol. 5: *Vermischte Beitraege*. Zurich: Atrium, 1959.

———. *Werke. Splitter und Balken: Publizistik*. Munich: Carl Hanser, 1998.

Kauders, Anthony D. "History as Censure: 'Repression' and 'Philo-Semitism' in Postwar Germany." *History and Memory* 15(1) (spring/summer 2003): 97–122.

Kaufmann, Theodor N. *Germany Must Perish!* Newark: Argyle, 1941.

Kershaw, Ian. *The Hitler Myth: Image and Reality in the Third Reich*. Oxford: Oxford University Press, 1987.

———. *The Nazi Dictatorship: Problems and Perspectives of Interpretation*. 2d ed. London: Edward Arnold, 1989.

Kertzer, David I. *The Pope against the Jews: The Vatican's Role in the Rise of Modern Anti-Semitism*. New York: Knopf, 2001.

Kettenacker, Lothar. *Krieg zur Friedenssicherung: Die Detuschlandplannung der britischen Militaerregierung waehrend des Zweiten Weltkrieges*. Göttingen: Vandenhoeck and Rupprecht, 1989.

Kettenacker, Lothar, ed. *Ein Volk von Opfern? Die neue Debatte um den Bombenkrieg, 1940–45.* Berlin: Rowohlt, 2003.

Kimball, Warren. *Swords or Plouoghshares? The Morgenthau Plan for Defeated Nazi Germany, 1943–46.* Philadelphia: Lipincott, 1976.

Kirsch, Jan-Holger. *"Wir haben aus der Geschichte gelernt": Der 8. Mai als politischer Gedenktag in Deutschland.* Cologne: Böhlau, 1999.

Kittel, Manfred. *Die Legende von der "Zweiten Schuld": Vergangenheitsbewaeltigung in der Aera Adenauer.* Berlin: Ullstein, 1993.

Klein, Kerwin Lee. "On the Emergence of Memory in Historical Discourse." *Representations* 69 (2000): 127–50.

Kleßmann, Christoph. *Die doppelte Staatsgründung: Deutsche Geschichte 1945–1955.* Göttingen: Vandenhoeck and Ruprecht, 1982.

Klotzbach, Kurt. *Der Weg zur Staatspartei: Programmatik, praktische Politik und Organisation der deutschen Sozialdemokratie, 1945 bis 1965.* Berlin: Dietz, 1982.

Köbner, Thomas, Gert Sautermeister, and Sigrid Schneider, eds. *Deutschland Nach Hitler: Zukunftspläne im Exil und aus der Besatzungszeit, 1939–1949.* Opladen: Westdeutscher Verlag, 1987.

Kochavi, Arieh J. *Prelude to Nuremberg: Allied War Crimes Policy and the Question of Punishment.* Chapel Hill: University of North Carolina Press, 1998.

Kogon, Eugen. *Die unvollendete Erneuerung: Deutschland im Kräftefeld 1945–1963.* Frankfurt: Europaeische Verlagsanstalt, 1964.

———. *Der SS-Staat.* Stockholm: Bermann-Fischer, 1947.

Köhler, Henning. *Adenauer: Eine politische Biographie.* Frankfurt: Propyläen, 1994.

Kohler, Lotte, ed. *Within Four Walls: The Correspondence between Hannah Arendt and Heinrich Blücher, 1936–1968.* New York: Harcourt, 2000.

Kohler, Lotte, and Hans Saner, eds. *Hannah Arendt–Karl Jaspers: Correspondence, 1926–1969.* Translated by Robert and Rita Kimber. New York: Harcourt, Brace, and Jovanovich, 1992.

Kommers, Donald P. *The Constitutional Jurisprudence of the Federal Republic of Germany.* Durham: Duke University Press, 1989.Königseder, Angelika, and Juliane Wetzel. *Waiting for Hope: Jewish Displaced Persons in Post-World War II Germany.* Evanston, Ill.: Northwestern University Press, 2001.

Koshar, Rudy. *Germany's Transient Past: Preservation and National Memory in the Twentieth Century.* Chapel Hill: University of North Carolina Press, 1998.

Kött, Martin. *Goldhagen in der Qualitaetspresse: Eine Debatte ueber "Kollektivshuld" und "Nationalcharakter" der Deutschen.* Konstanz: UVK Medien, 1999.

Kracauer, Siegfried. *From Caligari to Hitler: A Psychological History of German Film.* Princeton: Princeton University Press, 1947.

Kritz, Neil J., ed. *Transitional Justice: How Emerging Democracies Reckon with Former Regimes.* Washington, D.C.: United States Institute of Peace, 1995.

Krzeminski, Adam. "Der Kniefall." In *Deutsche Erinnerungsorte,* edited by Etienne Francois and Hagen Schulze, 638–53. Munich: Beck, 2001.

Küntzel, Mattias, et al. *Goldhagen und die deutsche Linke oder die Gegenwart der Vergangenheit.* Berlin: Elefanten, 1997.

Kurzke, Hermann. *Thomas Mann: Life as a Work of Art: A Biography.* Princeton: Princeton University Press, 2002.

Kushner, Tony. *The Holocaust and the Liberal Imagination: A Social and Cultural History.* Oxford: Blackwell, 1994.

Lach, Dondald F. "What They Would Do about Germany." *Journal of Modern History* 17(3) (1945): 227–43.

Lange-Quassowski, Jutta B. *Neuordnung oder Restauration: Das Demokratiekonzept der amerikanischen Besatzungsmächte und die politische Sozilisation der Westdeutschen.* Opladen: Leske, 1979.

Langewiesche, Dieter. *Liberalismus in Deutschland.* Frankfurt: Suhrkamp, 1988.

Large, David Clary. "Uses of the Past: The Anti-Nazi Resistance Legacy in the Federal Republic of Germany." In *Contending with Hitler: Varieties of Resistance in the Third Reich,* edited by David Clay Large. New York: Cambridge University Press, 1991.

Large, David Clay, ed. *Contending with Hitler: Varieties of German Resistance in the Third Reich.* New York: Cambridge University Press, 1991.

Lenk, Kurt. *Deutscher Konservatismus.* Frankfurt: Campus, 1989.

Leonhard, Wofgang. *Die Revolution entläat ihre Kinder.* Cologne: Kiepenheuer and Witsch, 1990 [1955].

Lepenies, Wolf. *The End of "German Culture": The Tanner Lectures on Human Values.* Harvard University, November 3–5, 1999. Available at www.Tannerlectures.utah.edu.

Lethen, Hermann. *Cool Conduct: The Culture of Distance in Weimar Germany.* Translated by Don Reneau. Berkeley: University of California Press, 2002.

Levkov, Ilya. *Bitburg and Beyond: Encounters in American, German and Jewish History.* New York: Shapolsky, 1987.

Levy, Daniel, and Natan Sznaider. *Erinnerung im globalen Zeitalter: Der Holocaust.* Frankfurt: Suhrkamp, 2001.

———. "Memory Unbound: The Holocaust and the Formation of Cosmopolitan Memory." *European Journal of Social Theory* 5(1) (2002): 87–106.

Lewin, Kurt. "Cultural Reconstruction." *Journal of Abnormal and Social Psychology* 38 (1943): 166–73.

Linz, Juan J. The Social Bases of West German Democracy. Ph.D. diss. Columbia University, 1959.

Litt, Theodor. *Von der Sendung der Philosophie.* Wiesbaden: Dieterich'sche Verlagsbuchhandlung, 1946.

Lockenour, Jay. *Soldiers as Citizens: Former Wehrmacht Officers in the Federal Republic of Germany, 1945–1955.* Lincoln: University of Nebraska Press, 2001.

Loth, Wilfried, and Bernd-A. Rusinek, eds. *Verwandlungspolitik: NS-Eliten in der westdeutschen Nachkriegsgesellschaft.* Frankfurt: Campus, 1998.

Lübbe, Hermann. "Der Nationalsozialismus im deutschen Nachkriegsbewusstsein." *Historische Zeitschrift* 236 (1983): 579–99.

Ludwig, Emil. *How to Treat the Germans.* New York: Willard, 1943.

———. *The Moral Conquest of Germany.* Garden City, N.J.: Doubleday, 1945.

Maguire, Peter. *Law and War: An American Story.* New York: Columbia University Press, 2000.

Mahoney, James. "Path Dependence in Historical Sociology." *Theory and Society* 29(4) (2000): 507–48.

Maier, Charles. *The Unmasterable Past: History, Holocaust, and German National Identity.* Cambridge: Harvard University Press, 1988.

Maier, Reinhold. *Ein Grundstein wird gelegt. Die Jahre 1945–1947.* Tübingen: Wunderlich, 1964.

———. *Die Reden: Eine Auswahl.* Vol. 1. Stuttgart: Reinhold-Maier-Stiftung, 1982.

Mankowitz, Zeev W. *Life between Memory and Hope: The Survivors of the Holocaust in Occupied Germany.* New York: Cambridge University Press, 2002.

Mann, Klaus, and Erika Mann. *Escape to Life.* Boston: Houghton Mifflin, 1939.

———. *The Other Germany.* New York: Sternfeld and Tiedemann, 1940.

Mann, Thomas. *Doctor Faustus: The Life of the German Composer Adrian Leverkühn as Told by a Friend.* Translated by John E. Woods. New York: Random House, 1997 [1947].

———. *Fragile Republik: Thomas Mann und Nachkriegsdeutschland.* Edited by Stephan Stachorski. Frankfurt: Fischer, 1999.

———. *Past Masters and Other Papers.* Translated by H. T. Lowe-Poster. New York: Knopf, 1933.

———. "That Man Is My Brother." *Esquire* 11(3) (1939).

———. *Thomas Mann's Addresses Delivered at the Library of Congress, 1942–1949.* Washinton, D.C.: Library of Congress, 1963.

Mannheim, Karl. *Freedom, Power, and Democratic Planning.* New York: Oxford University Press, 1950.

Manuel, Frank E. *Scenes from the End: The Last Days of World War II in Europe.* South Royalton, Vt.: Steerforth Press, 2000.

Marcuse, Harold. *Legacies of Dachau: The Uses and Abuses of a Concentration Camp, 1933–2001.* Cambridge: Cambridge University Press, 2001.

Marshall, Barbara. "German Reactions to Military Defeat, 1945–1947." In *Germany in the Age of Total War,* edited by Volker Berghahn and Martin Kitchen, 218–39. London: Croom Helm, 1981.

Matz, Klaus Jürgen. *Reinhold Maier (1899–1971): Eine politische Biographie.* Duesseldorf: Droste, 1989.

McLynn, Frank. *Carl Gustav Jung: A Biography.* New York: St. Martin's, 1996.

Meinecke, Friedrich. *The German Catastrophe: Reflections and Recollections.* Translated by Sidney B. Fay. Cambridge: Harvard University Press, 1950.

Merritt, Richard L. *Democracy Imposed: U.S. Occupation Policy and the German Public, 1945–1949.* New Haven: Yale University Press, 1995.

Merritt, Anna J., and Richard L. Merritt, eds. *Public Opinion in Occupied Germany: The OMGUS Surveys, 1945–1949.* Urbana: University of Illinois Press, 1970.

———. *Public Opinion in Semisovereign Germany: The HICOG Surveys, 1949–1955.* Urbana: University of Illinois Press, 1980.

Merzyn, Friedrich, ed. *Kundgebungen: Worte und Erklärungen der Evangelischen Kirche in Deutschland, 1945–1959.* Hannover: Verlag des Amtsblattes der Evangelische Kirche, 1959.

Milward, Alan. *The Reconstruction of Western Europe, 1945–1951.* Berkeley: University of California Press, 1984.

Mitchell, Maria. "Materialism and Secularism: CDU Politicians and National Socialism, 1945–1949." *Journal of Modern History* 67 (June 1995): 278–308.

Mitscherlich, Alexander. *Endlose Diktatur?* Zurich: Artemis, 1947.

Mitscherlich, Alexander, and Fred Mielke. *Der Diktat der Menschenverachtung.* Heidelberg: Lambert Schneider, 1947.

Mitscherlich, Alexander, and Margarete Mitscherlich. *The Inability to Mourn: Principles of Collective Behavior*. Translated by Beverley R. Placzek. New York: Grove Press, 1975 (1967).

Moeller, Robert G. *Protecting Motherhood: Women and the Family in the Politics of Postwar Germany*. Berkeley: University of California Press, 1996.

————. *War Stories: The Search for a Usable Past in the Federal Republic of Germany*. Berkeley: University of California Press, 2001.

————. "What Has 'Coming to Terms with the Past' Meant in Post–World War II Germany? From History to Memory to the 'History of Memory." *Central European History* 35(2) (2002): 223–56.

Moeller, Robert G., ed. *West Germany under Construction: Politics, Society, and Culture in the Adenauer Era*. Ann Arbor: University of Michigan Press, 1997.

Mohler, Armin. *Der Nasenring: Die Vergangenheitsbewältigung vor und nach dem Fall der Mauer*. Munich: Langen Müller, 1991.

Morgenthau, Henry, Jr. *Germany Is Our Problem*. New York: Harper and Brothers, 1945.

Morson, Gary Saul, and Carol Emersen. *Mikhail Bakhtin: Creation of A Prosaics*. Stanford: Stanford University Press, 1990.

Mosberg, Helmuth. *Reeducation: Umerzierhung und Lizenzpresse im Nachkriegsdeutschland*. Munich: Universitas, 1991.

Müller, Jan-Werner. *Another Country: German Intellectuals, Unification and National Identity*. New Haven: Yale University Press, 2000.

————. *A Dangerous Mind: Carl Schmitt in Post-War European Thought*. New Haven: Yale University Press, 2003.

Müller, Jan-Werner, ed. *German Ideologies since 1945: Studies in the Political Thought and Culture of the Bonn Republic*. New York: Pallgrave, 2003.

Muller, Jerry Z. *The Other God that Failed: Hans Freyer and the Deradicalization of German Conservatism*. Princeton: Princeton University Press, 1987.

Naimark, Norman M. *The Russians in Germany: A History of the Soviet Zone of Occupation, 1945–1949*. Cambridge: Harvard University Press, Belknap Press, 1995.

Namier, L. B. *Conflicts: Studies in Contemporary History*. New York: Macmillan, 1943.

Naumann, Klaus, ed. *Nachkrieg in Deutschland*. Hamburg: Hamburger Edition, 2001.

Neaman, Elliot Y. *A Dubious Past: Ernst Jünger and the Politics of Literature after Nazism*. Berkeley: University of California Press, 1999.

Neumann, Franz. *Behemoth: The Structure and Practice of National Socialism, 1933–1944*. New York: Oxford University Press, 1944.

Niemöller, Martin. *Of Guilt and Hope*. Translated by Renee Spodheim. New York: Philosophical Library, 1947.

Niethammer, Lutz. *Deutschland Danach: Postfaschistische Gesellschaft und nationales Gedächtnis*. Bonn: Dietz, 1999.

————. *Die Mitläuferfabrik: Die Entnazifizierung am Beispiel Bayerns*. Berlin: Dietz, 1982.

Niethammer, Lutz, ed. *Lebensgeschichte und Sozialkultur im Ruhrgebiet 1930 bis 1960*. 3 vols. Berlin: Dietz, 1985.

Nizer, Louis. *What to Do with Germany*. Chicago: Ziff-Davis, 1944.

Notter, Harley. *Post-War Policy Preparation, 1939–1945*. Washington: U.S. Government Printing Office, 1950.

Olick, Jeffrey K. "Genre Memories and Memory Genres: A Dialogical Analysis of May 8th, 1945 Commemorations in The Federal Republic of Germany." *American Sociological Review* 64 (June 1999): 381–402.

———. "The Guilt of Nations?" *Ethics and International Affairs* 17(2) (2003): 109–17.

———. "Memory and the Nation: Continuities, Conflicts, and Transformations." *Social Science History* 22(4) (December 1998): 377–87.

———. "The Politics of Regret: Analytical Frames." In *Politics and the Past: On Repairing Historical Injustices*, edited by John Torpey, 37–62. Boulder: Rowman and Littlefield, 2003.

———. "What Does It Mean to Normalize The Past? Official Memory in German Politics since 1989." *Social Science History* 22(4) (December 1998): 547–74.

Olick, Jeffrey K., and Brenda Coughlin. "The Politics of Regret: Analytical Frames." In *Politics and the Past: On Reparing Historical Injustices*, edited by John Torpey, 37–62. Lanham, Md.: Rowman and Littlefield, 2003.

Olick, Jeffrey K., and Daniel Levy. "Collective Memory and Cultural Constraint: Holocaust Myth and Rationality in German Politics." *American Sociological Review* 62 (December 1997): 921–36.

Olick, Jeffrey K., and Joyce Robbins. "Social Memory Studies: From 'Collective Memory' to the Historical Sociology of Mnemonic Practices." *Annual Review of Sociology* 24 (1998): 105–40.

Olson, Alan M., ed. *Heidegger and Jaspers*. Philadelphia: Temple University Press, 1994.

Overy, Richard. *Interrogations: The Nazi Elite in Allied Hands, 1945*. New York: Penguin, 2001.

Paetel, Karl O., ed. *Deutsche innere Emigration: Anti-Nationalsozialistische Zeugnisse aus Deutschland*. New York: Friedrich Krause, 1946.

Peterson, Edward N. *The American Occupation of Germany: Retreat to Victory*. Detroit: Wayne State University Press, 1977.

Phayer, Michael. *The Catholic Church and the Holocaust, 1930–1965*. Bloomington: Indiana University Press, 2001.

Picard, Max. *Hitler in uns selbst!* Erlenbach-Zurich: Eugen Rentsch, 1946.

Pike, David. *The Politics of Culture in Soviet-Occupied Germany 1945–1949*. Stanford: Stanford University Press, 1992.

Plessner, Helmuth. *Die Verspätete Nation: Über die Verführbarkeit bürgerlichen Geistes*. 2d ed. Stuttgart: Kohlhammer, 1959.

Pollock, Friedrich, ed. *Gruppenexperiment: Ein Studienbericht. Frankfurter Beitraege zur Soziologie*. Vol. 2. Edited by Theodor W. Adorno and Walter Dirks. Introduction by Franz Boehm. Frankfurt: Europaeische Verlagsanstalt, 1955.

Poppinga, Anneliese. *Konrad Adenauer: Geschichtsverständnis, Weltanschauung und politische Praxis*. Stuttgart: Deutsche Verlags-Anstalt, 1975.

Popular Memory Group. *Making Histories: Studies in History-Writing and Politics*. London: Center for Contemporary Cultural Studies, 1982.

Poster, Mark. *Existential Marxism in Postwar France*. Princeton: Princeton University Press, 1975.

Prager, Jeffrey. "The Psychology of Collective Memory." In *International Encyclopedia of Social and Behavioral Sciences*, 2223–27. Oxford: Pergamon, 2003.

Price, Hoyt, and Carl E. Schorske. *The Problem of Germany*. New York: Council on Foreign Relations, 1947.

Prittie, Terence. *Adenauer: A Study in Fortitude*. Chicago: Cowles, 1971.

Pronay, Nicholas, and Keith Wilson, eds. *The Political Re-Education of Germany and Her Allies after World War II*. London: Croom Helm, 1985.

Rabinbach, Anson. *In the Shadow of Catastrophe: German Intellectuals between Apocalypse and Enlightenment*. Berkeley: University of California Press, 1997.

———. "The Jewish Question in the German Question." *New German Critique* 4 (spring/summer 1988): 159–92.

Rabinback, Anson, and Jack Zipes, eds. *Germans and Jews since the Holocaust: The Changing Situation in West Germany*. New York: Holmes and Meier, 1986.

Radkau, Joachim. *Die deutsche Emigration in den USA: Ihr Einfluss auf die amerikanische Europapolitik, 1933–1945*. Duesseldorf: Bertelsmann, 1971.

Rees, David. *Harry Dexter White: A Study in Paradox*. New York: Coward, McCann, and Geoghegan, 1973.

Reichel, Peter. *Vergangenheitsbewältigung in Deutschland: Die Auseinabdersetzung mit der NS-Diktatur von 1945 bis Heute*. Munich: Beck, 2001.

———. *Politik mit der Erinnerung: Gedächtnisorte im Streit um die nationalsozialistische Vergangenheit*. Munich: Carl Hanser, 1995.

Reichhardt, Hans J. *Ernst Reuter: Artikel, Briefe, Reden*. 3 vols. Berlin: Ullstein, 1974.

Remy, Steven P. *The Heidelberg Myth: The Nazification and Denazification of a German University*. Cambridge: Harvard University Press, 2002.

Rencontres internationales de Geneve. *L'esprit european*. Neuchatel: Editions de la Baconniere, 1947.

Reuther, Thomas. *"Die ambivalente Normalisierung": Deutschlanddiskurs und Deutschlandbilder in den USA, 1941–1955*. Stuttgart: Franz Steiner, 2001.

Richter, Hans-Werner. *Erfahrungen und Utopien: Briefe an einen jungen Sozialisten*. Munich: DTV, 1990.

Richter, Werner. *Re-Educating Germany*. Translated by Paul Lehmann. Chicago: University of Chicago Press, 1945.

Ritter, Gerhard. *The German Problem: Basic Questions of German Political Life, Past and Present*. Translated by Sigurd Burckhardt. Columbus: Ohio State University Press, 1965.

———. *Europa und die deutsche Frage*. Munich: Bruckmann, 1948.

Robin, Ron. *The Barbed-Wire College: Reeducating German POWs in the United States during World War II*. Princeton: Princeton University Press, 1995.

Rogers, Daniel E. *Politics after Hitler: The Western Allies and the German Party System*. New York: New York University Press, 1995.

Roi, Michael L. *Alternative to Appeasement: Sir Robert Vansittart and Alliance Diplomacy, 1934–1937*. Westport: Praeger, 1997.

Röpke, Wilhelm. *The Solution of the German Problem*. New York: Putnam, 1947.

Rosenfeld, Gavriel D. *Munich and Memory: Architecture. Monuments, and the Legacy of the Third Reich*. Berkeley: University of California Press, 2000.

———. "The Reception of William L. Shirer's *The Rise and Fall of the Third Reich* in the United States and West Germany, 1960–62." *Journal of Contemporary History* 29 (1994): 95–128.

Rothfels, Hans. *The German Opposition to Hitler: An Appraisal*. Chicago: Henry Regnery, 1962.

Royal Institute of International Affairs. *The Problem of Germany: An Interim Report by a Chatham House Study Group*. London: Royal Institute of International Affairs, 1943.

Rubenstein, Richard J. *The Cunning of History: The Holocaust and the American Future*. New York: Harper and Row, 1978.

Rubenstein, William D. *The Myth of Rescue: Why the Democracies Could Not Have Saved More Jews from the Nazis*. New York: Routledge, 1999.

Rückerl, Adalbert. *The Investigation of Nazi Crimes 1945–1978: A Documentation*. Translated by Derek Rutter. Hamden, Conn.: Archon Books, 1980.

Safranski, Rüdiger. *Martin Heidegger: Between Good and Evil*. Translated by Ewald Osers. Cambridge: Harvard University Press, 1998.

Salomon, Ernst von. *The Answers of Ernst von Salomon*. Translated by Constantine FitzGibbon. Preface by Goronwy Rees. Garden City, N.J.: Doubleday, 1954 [1951].

Schelsky, Helmut. *Die skeptische Generation: Eine Soziologie der deutschen Jugend*. Düsseldorf: Diederich, 1957.

Scheuerman, William E. *Carl Schmitt: The End of Law*. Boulder: Rowman and Littlefield, 1999.

Schillinger, Reinhold. "Der Lastenausgleich." In *Die Vertreibung der Deutschen aus dem Osten: Ursachen, Ereignisse, Folgen*, edited by Wolfgang Benz, 183–93. Frankfurt: Fischer, 1985.

Schissler, Hanna, ed. *The Miracle Years: A Cultural History of West Germany, 1949–1968*. Princeton: Princeton University Press, 2001.

Schivelbusch, Wolfgang. *In a Cold Crater: Cultural and Intellectual Life in Berlin, 1945–1948*. Translated by Kelly Barry. Berkeley: University of California Press, 1998.

Schlipp, Philip Arthur, ed. *The Philosophy of Karl Jaspers*. New York: Tudor, 1957.

Schmidt, Ute. "Hitler ist tot und Ulbricht lebt: Die CDU, der Nationalsozialismus und der Holocast." In *Schwieriges Erbe: Der Umgang mit Nationalsozialismus und Antisemitismus in Österreich, der DDR und der Bundesrepublik Deutschland*, edited by Werner Bergmann, Rainer Erb, and Albert Lichtblau, 65–102. Frankfurt: Campus, 1995.

Schmitt, Carl. *Antworten in Nuernberg*. Edited by Helmut Quaritsch. Berlin: Duncker and Humblot, 2000.

———. *Ex Captivitate Salus: Erfahrungen der Zeit 1945/47*. Cologne: Greven Verlag, 1950.

———. *Glossarium: Aufzeichnungen der Jahre 1947–1951*. Berlin: Duncker and Humblot, 1991.

———. *Das Internationalrechtliche Verbrechen des Angriffskrieges und der Grundsatz "Nullum crimen, nulla poena sine lege."* Edited by Helmut Quartitsch. Berlin: Duncker and Humblot, 1994.

———. *Staat, Grossraum, Nomos: Arbeiten aus den Jahren 1916–1969*. Berlin: Duncker and Humblot, 1995.

Schoeps, Julius H., ed. *Ein Volk von Mördern? Die Dokumentation zur Goldhagen-Kontroverse um die Rolle der Deutschen im Holocaust*. Hamburg: Campe, 1996.

Schudson, Michael. "The Present in the Past and the Past in the Present." *Communication* 11 (1989): 105–13.

Schultz, Sigrid. *Germany Will Try It Again*. New York: Reynal and Hitchcock, 1944.

Schulze, Winfried. *Deutsche Geschichtswissenschaft nach 1945*. Munich: DTV, 1993.

Schwab-Felisch, Hans, ed. *Der Ruf: Eine deutsche Nachkriegszeitschrift*. Munich: DTV, 1962.

Schwan, Gesine. *Politics and Guilt: The Destructive Power of Silence*. Translated by Thomas Dunlap. Lincoln: University of Nebraska Press, 2001.

Schwartz, Barry. *Abraham Lincoln and the Forge of National Memory*. Chicago: University of Chicago Press, 2000.

Schwartz, Thomas. *America's Germany: John J. McCloy and the Federal Republic of Germany*. Cambridge: Harvard University Press, 1991.

Schwarz, Hans-Peter. *Adenauer: Der Aufstieg, 1876–1952.* Stuttgart: Deutsche Verlags-Anstalt, 1986.

———. *Konrad Adenauer: Reden 1917–1967.* Stuttgart: Deutsche Verlags-Anstalt, 1975.

Schwarzschild, Leopold. *World in Trance: From Versailles to Pearl Harbor.* New York: L. B. Fischer, 1942.

Sebald, W. G. *On the Natural History of Destruction.* Translated by Anthea Bell. New York: Random House, 2003.

Segev, Tom. *The Seventh Million: The Israelis and the Holocaust.* Translated by Haim Watzman. New York: Hill and Wang, 1993.

Seifert, Jürgen. "Die Verfassung." In *Die Geschichte der Bundesrepublik Deutschland.* Vol. 1: *Politik,* edited by Wolfgang Benz. Frankfurt: Fischer, 1989.

Sereny, Gitta. *Albert Speer: His Battle with Truth.* New York: Knopf, 1995.

Shandley, Robert R. *Unwilling Germans? The Goldhagen Debate.* Minneapolis: University of Minnesota Press, 1998.

Shapiro, James J. *Oberammergau: The Troubling Story of the World's Most Famous Passion Play.* New York: Pantheon, 2000.

Sheehan, James J. *German Liberalism in the 19th Century.* Chicago: University of Chicago Press, 1978.

Sherwood. Robert. *Roosevelt and Hopkins: An Intimate History.* Revised ed. New York: Enigma Books, 2001 [1948].

Shirer, William L. *Berlin Diary: The Journal of a Foreign Correspondent, 1934–1941.* Baltimore: Johns Hopkins University Press, 2002.

———. *The Rise and Fall of the Third Reich: A History of Nazi Germany.* New York: Simon and Schuster, 1990.

Simmel, Georg. "The Ruin." In *Georg Simmel, 1858–1918,* edited by Kurt Wolff, 259–66. Columbus: Ohio State University Press, 1959.

Simpson, Christopher. *The Splendid Blond Beast: Money, Law, and Genocide in the Twentieth Century.* New York: Grove Press, 1993.

Smith, Bradley. *The Road to Nuremberg.* New York: Basic Books, 1981.

Sontheimer, Kurt. *Thomas Mann und die Deutschen.* Munich: Langen Mueller, 2002.

Später, Jörg. *Vansittart: Britische Debatten über Deutsche und Nazis, 1902–1945.* Göttingen: Wallstein, 2003.

Speier, Hans. *From the Ashes of Disgrace: A Journal from Germany, 1945–1955.* Amherst: University of Massachusetts Press, 1981.

Spender, Stephen. *European Witness.* London: The Right Book Club, 1946.

———. *Journals 1939–1983.* New York: Random House, 1986.

Spotts, Frederic. *The Churches and Politics in Germany.* Middletown, Conn.: Wesleyan University Press, 1973.

Stahl, Walter, ed. *The Politics of Postwar Germany.* New York: Praeger, 1963.

Steinbach, Peter. *Nationalsozialistische Gewaltverbrechen: Die Diskussion in der deutschen Öffentlichkeit nach 1945.* Berlin: Colloquim-Verlag, 1981.

———. "Nationalsozialistische Gewaltverbrechen in der deutschen Öffentlichkeit nach 1945." In *Vergangenheitsbewältigung durch Strafverfahren? NS-Prozesse in der Bundesrepublik Deutschland,* edited by Jürgen Weber and Peter Steinbach, 13–40. Munich: Olzog Verlag, 1984.

———. *Widerstand in Widerstreit: Der Widerstand gegen den Nationalsozialismus in der Erinnerung der Deutschen.* Paderborn: Schöningh, 2001.

Steinle, Jürgen. *Nationales Selbstverständnis nach dem Nationalsozialismus: Die Kriegsschuld-Debatte in West-Deutschland.* Bochum: Universitaetsverlag Dr. N. Brockmeyer, 1995.

Stern, Frank. *The Whitewashing of the Yellow Badge: Antisemitism and Philosemitism in Postwar Germany.* Oxford: Pergamon, 1992.

Stimson, Henry L., and McGeorge Bundy. *On Active Service in Peace and War.* New York: Harper Brothers, 1947.

Strothmann, Dietrich. " 'Schlesien bleibt unser': Vertriebenenpolitker und das Rad der Geschichte." In *Die Vertreibung der Deutschen aus dem Osten: Ursachen, Ereignisse, Folgen,* edited by Wolfgang Benz, 209–18. Frankfurt: Fischer, 1985.

Tauber, Kurt P. *Beyond Eagle and Swastika: German Nationalism since 1945.* 2 vols. Middletown, Conn.: Wesleyan University Press, 1967.

Tavuchis, Nicholas. *Mea Culpa: A Sociology of Apology and Reconciliation.* Stanford: Stanford University Press, 1993.

Taylor, A. J. P. *The Course of German History: A Survey of the Development of Germany since 1815.* London: Methuen, 1946.

Taylor, Telford. *The Anatomy of the Nuremberg Trials.* Boston: Little, Brown, 1992.

Tent, James F. *Mission on the Rhine: Reeducation and Denazification in American-Occupied Germany.* Chicago: University of Chicago Press, 1982.

Thielecke, Helmut. *In der Stunde Null : die Denkschrift des Freiburger "Bonhöffer-Kreises": Politische Gemeinschaftsordnung : ein Versuch zur Selbstbesinnung des christlichen Gewissens in den politischen Nöten unserer Zeit.* Tübingen: Mohr, 1979.

Thompson, Dorothy. "The Problem Child of Europe." *Foreign Affairs* 18 (1940).

Thornhill, Chris. *Political Theory in Modern Germany: An Introduction.* Cambridge: Polity Press, 2000.

Turkel, Studs. *"The Good War": An Oral History of World War Two.* New York: Ballantine, 1984.

Ueberschaer, Gerd B., ed. *Der 20. Juli: Das andere Deutschland in der Vergangenheitspolitik nach 1945.* Berlin: Elefanten, 1998.

Van Laak, Dirk. *Gespräche in der Sicherheit des Schweigens: Carl Schmitt in der politischen Geistesgeschichte der frühen Bundesrepublik.* 2d ed. Berlin: Akademie, 2002.

Vansittart, Robert. *Black Record: Germans Past and Present.* London: Hamish Hamilton, 1941.

———. *Bones of Contention.* London: Hutchinson, 1945.

———. *Lessons of My Life.* London: Hutchinson, 1943.

———. "The Problem of Germany: A Discussion." In *International Affairs* 21(3) (1945): 313–24.

———. *Roots of the Trouble.* London: Hutchinson, 1942.

Vollnhals, Clemens. *Evangelische Kirche und Entnazifizierung: Die Last der deutschen Vergangenheit.* Munich: Oldenbourg, 1989.

Vonnegut, Kurt. *Slaughterhouse Five.* New York: Dell, 1991.

Walter, Karin. *Neubeginn—Nationalisozialismus—Widerstand: Die politische-theoretische Diskussion der Neuordnung in CDU und SPD 1945–1948.* Bonn: Bouvier, 1987.

Weber, Alfred. *Farewell to European History or The Conquest of Nihilism.* Translated by R. F. C. Hull. London: Kegan Paul, 1947.

Weber, Max. "Politics as a Vocation." In *From Max Weber: Essays in Sociology,* edited by Hans Gerth and C. Wright Mills, 77–128. New York: Oxford University Press, 1946.

Weiss, Hermann. "Die Organisationen der Vertriebenen und ihre Presse." In *Die Vertreibung der Deutschen aus dem Osten: Ursachen, Eriegnisse, Folgen,* edited by Wolfgang Benz, 193–208. Frankfurt: Fischer, 1985.

Welles, Benjamin. *Sumner Welles*. New York: St. Martin's, 1997.

Welles, Sumner. *The Time for Decision*. New York: Harper, 1944.

Welzer, Harald, Sabine Moller, and Karoline Tschuggnall. *"Opa war kein Nazi": Nationalsozialismus und Holocaust im Familiengedächtnis*. Frankfurt: Fischer, 2002.

Wertsch, James. *Voices of Collective Remembering*. New York: Cambridge University Press, 2002.

Wiesen, S. Jonathan. *West German Industry and the Challenge of the Nazi Past*. Chapel Hill: University of North Carolina Press, 2001.

Wiggershaus, Rolf. *The Frankfurt School: Its History, Theories, and Political Significance*. Translated by Michael Robertson. Cambridge: MIT Press, 1998.

Winter, Ingelore M. *Theodor Heuss: Ein Porträt*. Tübingen: Wunderlich, 1983.

Wippermann, Wolfgang. *Wessen Schuld? Vom Historikerstreit zur Goldhagen-Kontroverse*. Berlin: Elefanten, 1997.

Wolffsohn, Michael. *Ewige Schuld? 40 Jahre Deutsch-Jüdisch-Israelische Beziehungen*. Munich: Piper, 1988.

Wolfrum, Edgar. *Geschichtspolitik in der Bundesrepublik Deutschland: Der Weg zur bundesrepublikanischen Erinnerung 1948–1990*. Darmstadt: Wissenschaftliche Buschgesellschaft, 1999.

Wolgast, Eike. *Die Wahrnehmung des Dritten Reiches in der unmittlebaren Nachkriegszeit (1945/46)*. Heidelberg: C. Winter, 2001.

Wolin, Richard. *The Heidegger Controversy: A Critical Reader*. Cambridge: MIT Press, 1993.

———. *The Terms of Cultural Criticism: The Frankfurt School, Existentialism, Poststructuralism*. New York: Columbia University Press, 1992.

Würmeling, Henric L. *Die weisse Liste: Umbruch der politischen Kultur in Deutschland 1945*. Frankfurt: Ullstein, 1981.

Wyman, David. *Abandonment of the Jews: America and the Holocaust, 1941–1945*. New York: Pantheon, 1984.

Wyman, Mark. *DPs: Europe's Displaced Persons, 1945–1951*. Ithaca: Cornell University Press, 1998.

Zelizer, Barbie. "Reading the Past against the Grain: The Shape of Memory Studies." *Critical Studies in Mass Communication* 12 (June 1995): 214–39.

Zerubavel, Yael. *Recovered Roots: Collective Memory and the Making of Israeli National Tradition*. Chicago: University of Chicago Press, 1995.

Zink, Harold. *The United States in Germany, 1944–1945*. Princeton: Van Nostrand, 1957.

Zuckmeyer, Carl. *Als wär's ein Stück von mir: Horen der Freundschaft*. Frankfurt: Fischer, 1966.

———. *Geheimreport*. Edited by Günther Nickel and Johanna Schrön. Göttingen: Wallstein, 2002.

———. *Des Teufels General*. Frankfurt: Fischer, 1996 [1946].

Index

108–10; war of aggression vs., 308.
See also Holocaust
geopolitics, Potsdam Agreement's
implications for, 87–89
German Christians (organization), 205, 206
German Communist Party, 234, 241–42
German Council of States (Länderrat),
104n26, 124–25, 126
German people. See Volk (German people)
German Protestant Church, 46
German province (Land) system, 235–36
Germany: aggression of, 34; devastation of,
26–28, 100–101; economic aid for, 43;
as "house of the hangman," 325–27; as
Kulturnation, 155–56, 164–66; as model,
287–88, 338–40; reconstruction of,
332–36; religious revival in, 203, 209;
self-cleansing of, as dangerous, 211–12;
territory of, 88, 260, 307. See also Federal
Republic of Germany (FRG)
Gesamtschuld (common guilt), 181, 225,
239–40
Giordano, Ralf, 4n11
Gleichschaltung (assimilation), 205, 226, 281
Globke, Hans, 1
Gobineau, Joseph-Arthur de, 174
Goebbels, Josef: Barth on, 208; on
Morgenthau, 29, 31, 33, 327; on SPD,
237; suicide of, 25; terminology of, 301;
on unconditional surrender, 35, 260; on
Vansittart, 46
Goethe, Johann Wolfgang von:
democratic tradition and, 56; on exile,
146; on Germans and Jews, 176;
as ideal of culture, 153–54, 156, 161;
as influence, 172
Goethe communities, 165
Goldhagen, Daniel, 329–30
Gollancz, Victor, 47, 48, 159
Göring, Hermann, 115, 197
Göring, Matthias, 192
grammars of exculpation, concept of,
212–13. See also Aber (but or
nevertheless)
Grant, Gen. Ulysses S., 35–36, 37
Grass, Günter, 305, 340
Great Britain: attitudes toward
denazification, 50; attitudes toward
Germany, 43; economic aid for, 83–84.
See also British Military Government
Greiner, Bernd, 31, 33
Grossraum, 307, 318

Gruppenexperiment: approach of, 321–22;
critique of, 324–25; defense of, 325–26;
implications of, 322–24
Gruppe 47 (writers), 190, 306
guilt (Schuld): Adenauer on, 251–52, 253;
for allowing Nazis power (not for
Holocaust), 285n38; apolitical
interpretation of, 219–20; churches'
confrontation of question of
(Schuldfrage), 203–4; of church not
people, 215–16; common (Gesamtschuld),
181, 225, 239–40; debts and, 199–200,
220, 327; of Germans vs. National
Socialists, 163–64; as individual, 18,
185–86, 187, 192, 193–98, 228–29, 230,
272–73, 290; of Jews, 217, 337; ordinary,
219; of passivity, 267–68; psychological
vs. moral or criminal, 196–98; questions
about, 139–41; Schumacher on, 239–42;
"second," 4; shame vs., 270–72;
subjective, 191–202; typology of, 284,
289, 312–13, 317. See also collective guilt
(Kollektivschuld); culture of guilt;
Schuldfrage, Die (Jaspers)

Haaretz (newspaper), 55n31
Habe, Hans: on collective guilt, 182–83; on
democratic journalism, 143–44, 148,
178; on Salomon, 122
Habermas, Jürgen, 191, 273
Hague Conventions (1899 and 1907), 106
Halbwachs, Maurice, 336
Handbook for Military Government, 72–73,
74, 78, 92–93
Harris, Arthur, 27–28n6
Harrison, Earl G., 104–5
Hartshorne, Edward, 63, 280n27
Hauptschuldig (major offender), 125
Hayek, F. W., 188
Heidegger, Martin: alternative discourse of,
19, 139n1; on conscience, 298–99;
in context of shame culture, 299–300;
on humanism, 292, 297–99; as influence,
276; Jaspers's relationship with, 282,
291–93, 295–96, 312; Jünger compared
with, 304; legacies of, 281–82, 318–19;
like-minded colleagues of, 300–301;
as Nazi, 121n11, 152n22, 291, 292–93,
299n8; refusal to disavow National
Socialism, 294–95, 297
Heidelberg, CDU in, 247
Heidelberg University, 275

heilige Nüchternheit (sacred sobriety), 266
Heinemann, Gustav, 214, 232, 269
Herder, Johann Gottfried von, 171
Herf, Jeffrey, 109–10n38, 117n1
Hermens, Ferdinand A., 55
Herz, John H., 125–26n20
Hess, Rudolf, 115
Hesse, Hermann, 152, 328–29
Heuss, Theodor: on 1848, 332; background of, 263–64; on defeat as total, 303n15; on dualities of German history, 266–68; as evolutionist, 269; on fairness, 262; on Hitler, 175; on Jünger, 305; liberalism of, 303n17; on Maier affair, 132–33, 134; on May 8, 1945, 268; on memory, 264–66, 267; on opposition, 160; postwar speeches of, 264–68; on teachers as Nazis, 120n9; on temporary status of FRG, 8n22
Himmler, Heinrich, 116, 208
Hindenburg, Gen. Paul von, 36, 152
historiography: compartmentalization of, 29–30; periodization in, 7–9, 26–28
history: as dialogical, 21n43, 333–34; Germans as victimized by, 26; of memory, 4–7; reflections on, 268–69
history, German: dualities of, 266–68; as extreme example of European trends, 166–70, 261, 288; myths about, 11–14; National Socialism as catastrophe in, 161–66, 288, 328, 331; opposition movement and, 158–60; racial view of, 277; recovery of, 170–73; reflections on, 178–79; revision of, 157–58; silence about Jews in, 173–77, 216
Hitchcock, Alfred, 99
Hitler, Adolf: act enabling, 131–34, 227, 263; Allied negotiations with, 30, 44, 96–97, 260; Barth on, 207–8; as catastrophe in German history, 161–66; communists' "Appeal" on, 241–42; cruelty of, 51n22; disdain for, 175; family name of, 143; inability of people to mourn, 163; Jung on, 199, 239; Mann on, 146; *Reichstag* fire and, 308; responsibility for supporting, 51; Schumacher compared with, 246; scorched earth policy of, 31; suicide of, 25; Vansittart on, 45; as victim, 102n20; on *Volk* and regime, 55; voting for, 152, 182–83, 253. *See also* assassination attempt (July 20, 1944)

Hofstätter, Peter, 324–25
Högner, Wilhelm, 124–25, 238n10
Hölderlin, Johann Christian Friedrich, 266
Holocaust: absence of consequences for, 318; attempt to limit memory of, 273; as civilizational rupture, 197, 337–38, 339–40; context of, 329–30; FRG as hostage to, 310–11, 326; as hardly worth mentioning in, 173–77; Morgenthau's response to, 75–76; ordinary vs. demonic qualities of, 197; as peripheral in memory, 337–38; recognition and memory of, 105; relevance of, for Germany not Jews, 308–9; revelations and public opinion about, 42–43; use of term, 221. *See also* genocide
homelessness, 100
Hoover, Herbert, 68–69n6, 134, 260
hopelessness, 259, 283
Hopkins, Harry, 78, 80, 81–82
Horkheimer, Max, 181, 339–40
House of Lords (British), 46–47
House Un-American Activities Committee (HUAC), 30
Hull, Cordell: on Morgenthau, 32; on partition, 76, 80; on pastoralization, 84; on peace, 66–68; on punishment, 65–66; on unconditional surrender, 39, 40; Welles's relationship with, 68–69
humanism: core idea of, 291; education in, 165–66; as essence of Germany, 149, 171–72; Heidegger on, 292, 297–99; nihilism's squelching of, 273–75; questions about, 153–54, 328; recovery of, 170; socialist, 189
Husserl, Edmund, 291

imago, concept of, 336
individual: as enmeshed in power relations, 314; guilt accorded to, 18, 185–86, 187, 192, 193–98, 228–29, 230, 272–73, 290; Jung's shadow theory of, 198–200; role of, in supporting Nazi regime, 139–40
industry: disagreements over, 81–83; dismantling heavy, military, 83–84, 87, 92, 231; internationalization proposed for, 78, 79, 83; Morgenthau on, 29; Nazi subsidy of, 76; potential for social transformation via, 62–63; role in economic integration, 66–67, 68; Vansittart on, 48

JEFFREY K. OLICK is associate professor of sociology at the University of Virginia.